Prospection, well-being, and mental health

Andrew MacLeod
Royal Holloway University of London

OXFORD
UNIVERSITY PRESS

OXFORD
UNIVERSITY PRESS

Great Clarendon Street, Oxford, OX2 6DP,
United Kingdom

Oxford University Press is a department of the University of Oxford.
It furthers the University's objective of excellence in research, scholarship,
and education by publishing worldwide. Oxford is a registered trade mark of
Oxford University Press in the UK and in certain other countries

First Edition published in 2017

Impression: 1

Published in the United States of America by Oxford University Press
198 Madison Avenue, New York, NY 10016, United States of America

British Library Cataloguing in Publication Data

Data available

Library of Congress Control Number: 2016952284
ISBN 978–0–19–872504–6

Printed and bound by CPI Group (UK) Ltd, Croydon, CR0 4YY

Oxford University Press makes no representation, express or implied, that the
drug dosages in this book are correct. Readers must therefore always check
the product information and clinical procedures with the most up-to-date
published product information and data sheets provided by the manufacturers
and the most recent codes of conduct and safety regulations. The authors and
the publishers do not accept responsibility or legal liability for any errors in the
text or for the misuse or misapplication of material in this work. Except where
otherwise stated, drug dosages and recommendations are for the non-pregnant
adult who is not breast-feeding

Links to third party websites are provided by Oxford in good faith and
for information only. Oxford disclaims any responsibility for the materials
contained in any third party website referenced in this work.

Prospection, well-being, and mental health

Acknowledgements

I would like to thank Mick Power, Jo Dickson, Barney Dunn, Michael Evangeli, Richard Moore, Dan Schacter, Fiona Tasker and Mark Williams for reading chapters and providing insightful comments. I am especially grateful to Mark, who read the whole manuscript and provided invaluable, wise advice. On a visit to Philadelphia in 2012, Marty Seligman helpfully suggested to me the idea of writing this book, which was the prompt I needed to make it happen. Everyone at Oxford University Press, notably, Martin Baum, Charlotte Green, and Matthias Butler, has been supportive and enabled me to write the book I wanted to. Robert Kelsey kindly provided one of his wonderful paintings for the cover and I hope others will enjoy it as much as I do. Finally, I want to express my appreciation to Fiona, Euan, and Rhiannon for their encouragement, support, and many useful discussions while writing this book, and, more than anything, for their presence.

Contents

1 Thinking about the future *1*

2 Expectancies *14*

3 Optimism and pessimism *48*

4 Predicting feelings *78*

5 Anticipatory feelings *99*

6 Memory *118*

7 Goals *149*

8 Plans *182*

9 Temporal orientation and mindfulness *204*

10 Intervention *234*

11 Prospection, well-being, and mental health *255*

Name Index *275*
Subject Index *281*

Chapter 1

Thinking about the future

Introduction

This book is about how we think about the future. It is about how we think about our own personal futures and how such prospection is connected to our well-being and mental health. My own past has, in fact, been filled with studying the future. I first started investigating future-directed thinking and well-being over 30 years ago, when after a term of studying mood and memory, my PhD evolved into examining how chronically anxious worriers judge the likelihood of future negative events happening to them. I have been engaged ever since in trying to understand future-directed thinking and its relation to well-being and mental health, moving on from studying anxious worry about the future to trying to understand more about suicidal hopelessness for the future and, more recently, how positive aspects of well-being link to prospection. Much of the research that I have conducted over that period appears at various places throughout this book.

Prospection is one of those activities that we are engaged in much of the time without necessarily being consciously aware of doing so. We do become conscious of it, however, when it goes wrong, in the same sort of way that we might only start to become more aware of our breathing when we are breathless. One strand that will run throughout this book is that there are two distinct ways that prospection goes wrong for our emotional well-being. The first is where our minds are unreasonably preoccupied with aversive things that might happen to us in the future, or, as Mark Twain is reported to have said, 'my life has been full of misfortunes, most of which have never happened'. The second problematic way of thinking is where we lack positive thoughts about the future. This is a subtler kind of difficulty and harder to detect, because absence is just usually less obvious than presence. In the Arthur Conan Doyle story, *Silver Blaze*, the mystery was only solved when Sherlock Holmes realized that the dog, which should have barked in the night if a stranger had approached it, had not, and therefore the culprit could only have been someone familiar to the dog. It required the genius of Sherlock Holmes to spot that something that should have been there was missing. The absence of positive thoughts and feelings about the future, although subtler, is nevertheless as serious a problem, perhaps even more so, than the presence of negative thoughts and feelings.

Prospection covers a wide range of psychological phenomenon and psychological literatures. What it describes goes under a variety of broad names, including prospection, mental time travel, episodic future-thinking, or, just generally, future-directed thinking or future-thinking. Projecting oneself into the future is a complex task. It involves a variety of cognitive processes, including, amongst others, a sense of temporal orientation (the future is different from now, which is different from the past), a sense of self, and the ability to construct scenes or pictures along with the closely connected ability to simulate pathways leading to particular outcomes. Szpunar, Spreng, and Schacter (2014) proposed a scheme with four different modes of future-thinking: simulation (constructing a detailed future representation); prediction (estimating the likelihood of a future outcome); intention (essentially, setting goals); and planning (thinking of organized steps that should be taken to achieve a goal). All four modes will be covered in different places throughout this book: simulation (Chapters 2 and 8), prediction (Chapters 2, 3, and 4), intention (Chapters 7 and 8), planning (Chapter 8). A more detailed plan of these and other aspects of future-directed thinking covered in the book is outlined at the end of the present chapter.

The coverage in this book is wide ranging, but always with a focus on the link between future-directed thinking and mental health and well-being. It will become clear that how we think about the future and our mental health are intimately connected, but lots of questions remain. Are there particular ways of thinking about the future that are good for us? Is it good to be optimistic, even if it is not accurate, or should we, as the Roman philosopher Seneca counselled, start the day by thinking of everything that could go wrong in order to make it easier to bear if the day turns out that way? Is it good for us to think about the future very much at all, or should we aim to live more in the present moment? How good are we at predicting what will happen to us and how we are going to feel in the future, and are people who are low in well-being less, or perhaps even more, accurate? What are the different ways that prospection goes wrong in emotional disturbance? If there are ways of thinking about the future that are beneficial, can they be learned? These are some of the questions that I will attempt to address in this book.

Why does prospection matter?

Being able to think about the future is an invaluable asset that enables a huge amount of human activity: 'much of our actions are guided by the events we anticipate, their envisioned consequences, and our goals and plans in attaining or avoiding imagined states of affairs' (Jeunehomme & D'Argembeau, 2016, p. 254). Theorists, such as Klein (2013) and Suddendorf and Corballis (2007) have pointed out that central to human evolution has been the development of an ability to think about the future in a far-reaching, flexible, and complex way. Such thinking allows anticipation, preparation, and planning, both to avoid threat and to gain rewards, conferring adaptive value at a species level by helping us to live longer and have greater reproductive success. Seligman, Railton, Beaumeister, & Stripada (2013) also endorse the idea of the necessary adaptiveness of prospection, but go further in suggesting that humans are constructed in such a way as to be essentially future-oriented. It is increasingly being recognized that human capacities that are not explicitly prospective may also be driven by our inbuilt future-mindedness. For example, memory researchers have acknowledged that memory exists in order to help us to navigate our way in the present and into the future: 'Memory does not primarily exist to think about the past. It primarily exists to help us to know what to do in the present and to plan for the future' (Szpunar & Radvansky, 2016, p. 209).

The general importance of future-directed thinking is further illustrated by the consistent finding that people rate future personal events as more important, personally significant and positive than past events (e.g. Berntsen & Bohn, 2010; D'Argembeau & Van der Linden, 2004), something that is true even in older adults: Addis, Wong, and Schacter (2008) reported that future events were rated as more personally significant than past events in a sample with an average age of 72. Thoughts about the future also produce, on average, stronger affect in the here-and-now than does thinking about past events. For example, Van Boven and Ashworth (2007) asked student participants to spend some time thinking about similar events that had either happened in the past or would happen in the future, and report how they were feeling right now when thinking about those events. Over a range of events, participants reported stronger affective responses to imagining future events compared to remembering past events. A stronger emotional impact of future, imagined events over remembered ones has also been reported for more emotionally significant events (Rubin, 2014), although, of course, this is not to deny that in some cases certain past events will have particularly high impact, as in the case of post-traumatic stress disorder.

Consistent with prospection being important, people spend a lot of time thinking about the future directly. It is difficult to quantify the amount, and, of course, it will depend on what is meant by the future and how the term is interpreted. Wittmann (2011) has suggested from experimental data that after about two to three seconds humans perceive a new segment of time, that is, the present lasts for about two to three seconds. Clearly, this is not the sort of time frame that most people would have in mind when thinking about the present, and the evidence is that when people hear the word 'future', they typically think of a time period quite distant from the present (Tonn, Hemrick, & Conrad, 2006). The ambiguity about what is meant by the future is something that ongoing research will need to address more carefully than it has done to date.

A straightforward, but probably not very precise way, of estimating how much time people do spend thinking about the future is simply to ask them. A community sample of 100 women ranked time spent thinking about the future higher than time spent on the present or past, and on a percentage rating, present- and future-thinking were allocated similar proportions, with time spent thinking about the past being much lower (Jason, Schade, Furo, Reichler, & Brickman, 1989). Using a very different kind of methodology, D'Argembeau, Renaud, and Van der Linden (2011) asked a small sample of young adults, predominantly students, to note each time that they experienced a thought about the future during the course of one day. Initial instructions emphasized that the research was interested in any type of thought at all, as long as it was about the future. Participants marked a line on a notebook each time they noticed themselves thinking such a thought. The mean number of thoughts recorded was 59, with individuals varying between 27 and 102. Of course, these figures will almost certainly be significant underestimates, as participants are unlikely to notice and record every future-directed thought that they experienced. Caution needs to be exercised in making general descriptive statements, because along with the measurement limitations, the data rely on restricted samples, and future work certainly could address possible influences of age, socioeconomic status and culture. It certainly does appear to be the case that eastern cultures value the past more highly than do western cultures (Guo, Ji, Spina, & Zhang, 2012), perhaps linked to different cultural and philosophical beliefs where events are seen as cyclical rather than linear, in which everything that happens is novel (Gao, 2016).

Leaving aside the question of the precise amount of time people spend thinking about the future, it is clear from both the available evidence and from simple personal introspection, that it is a very important part of our mental lives. People spend most time thinking about their immediate future. Tonn et al. (2006) asked survey respondents how often they thought about what their lives would be like in different time periods in the future. One day from now was most frequently reported, with steady decreases, through to very little thinking about 20 years into the future. This gradient was more marked, indicating a greater focus on the short-term future, for participants under the age of 30. Very similar findings were reported by D'Argembeau et al. (2011). As well as recording when they had a thought about the future, participants were also asked to provide a number of different ratings about the future thoughts that they did have, including which future time period the thoughts referred to. Thoughts about later that day were most frequent, with a virtually linear decline through to thoughts relating to more than ten years from the present, which were very rare. Near future thoughts were also, not surprisingly, represented with greater detail than those in the more distant future (D'Argembeau et al., 2011; see also Trope & Liberman, 2010). A final point worth noting, which is important for much of the remaining content of this book, is that the majority of thoughts (62%) were valenced, that is, they were either positive or negative, with almost twice as many positive as negative future thoughts.

Neglect and recent attention

Despite being so fundamental, Seligman and colleagues (Seligman et al., 2013) have argued, convincingly, that prospection has been relatively neglected in academic explanations of psychological phenomena. These authors propose that the success of mechanistic causal explanations, where the occurrence of a phenomenon is explained by what preceded it, in the physical sciences during the enlightenment period, reduced the need for teleological explanations. Teleology, often closely identified with Aristotle, refers to explaining phenomena by what they are about, what their purpose or end (telos) is. Psychological science, modelling itself on the physical sciences, adopted a different kind of framework intent on explaining psychological phenomena by what went before. Normal everyday explanations involving desires or expectations, for example, were given little prominence, demonstrated clearly in behaviourist accounts, such as associative learning, where present and future behaviour is explained by a person's learning history.

There is perhaps another, more practical reason, for prospection's neglect, which is that thinking about the future is more abstract and difficult to pin down than, for example, memory or attention. Because the future is, by definition, uncertain, there is something more elusive about it, making it more difficult to think about and study in a systematic way. People I meet sometimes ask me what particular aspect of psychology I am interested in. When I reply that my interest is in how people think about the future and how that relates to their well-being and mental health, I am often met with a slightly awkward pause, even when I am speaking with other psychologists. It is not that people are uninterested (I think), but there is just something more nebulous about the future that makes it more difficult to get a firm grip on, compared to what has already happened. That said, there is clear evidence that the study of how people think about the future is gaining in popularity. This burgeoning interest is shown by the appearance of journal special issues on the topic, for example, in social (Epstude & Peetz, 2012), cognitive (Szpunar & Radvansky, 2016), developmental (Suddendorf & Moore, 2011), clinical (Henry, Addis, Suddendorf, & Rendell, 2016), and general psychology (Baumeister & Vohs, 2016). In addition to new empirical work, books too are beginning to emerge (Michaelian, Klein, & Szpunar, 2016; Oettingen, Sevincer, & Gollwitzer, in press; Seligman, Railton, Baumeister, & Sripada, 2016). This book will attempt to synthesise the psychological knowledge that exists about prospection, specifically on the relationship of future-directed thinking to mental health and well-being.

Why does prospection matter?—revisited

As pointed out earlier in this chapter, many have argued that the ability to think about the future in such an extended and personal way will have developed because it had great adaptive value. Such arguments are compelling about how prospection was part of the story of human evolutionary success. But there is something of a disconnect between such evolutionary arguments and how we think about our own and others' well-being, that is, what makes a life good for us. To take a relevant example, do we value effective treatment of anxiety and depression because they make people live longer and more likely to have children? Someone might live longer and have children as a result of receiving successful psychological therapy, or they might not, but it would be very unusual indeed to find clients or therapists, or indeed anyone, who thought the value of therapy lay in those outcomes. Our understanding of what constitutes a good life for us and others extends way beyond longevity and fecundity. In fact, the terms 'adaptive' and 'maladaptive' have come to be used quite differently, albeit in a fairly loose and unexamined way, within the psychological literature, typically referring to emotional well-being. For example, Marchetti, Koster, Klinger, and Alloy (2016) label spontaneous thoughts about the future that lead to emotional well-being as being adaptive, in contrast to maladaptive thoughts, which are those that lead to depression. This pairing of adaptiveness with well-being and mental health is commonplace within the psychological literature and simply illustrates the centrality of emotional well-being in defining a life that is good for people. The aim of this book is to review how thinking about the future relates to what constitutes a good life for a person in terms of their psychological and emotional well-being, and their mental health. The main emphasis will be on understanding prospection in relation to states of low well-being and psychological disorder; the literature relating to positive well-being is sparser, but where it exists it will be reviewed.

Well-being and mental health

Well-being in its most widely used sense can sometimes appear to be synonymous with anything—psychological, biological, social—that is seen to be good for people. In the context of this book, the term is restricted to psychological (as opposed to social or biological) well-being, and will largely be about emotional well-being. The material that will be discussed in the following chapters relates either to positive psychological well-being, for example, life satisfaction or positive affect, or to emotional disturbance, such as anxiety and depression, either at a clinical or sub-clinical level. Other outcomes that could be seen as well-being in a broader sense—health outcomes or academic achievement, for example—will not be the focus of attention here, although they will sometimes be referred to in order to illustrate some of the phenomena under discussion.

It is a matter of some debate whether positive psychological well-being lies at one end of a unipolar dimension, with mental health difficulties like anxiety and depression at the other end. The alternative view is that there are two independent dimensions representing positive mental health and negative mental health (see MacLeod, 2012 for a discussion). In some ways, and certainly for the purposes of this book, it does not matter which position is adopted. It is enough to say that someone experiencing ongoing high levels of anxiety or depression is experiencing a life that is low in well-being (in the sense of living a life that is not good for them in important ways), as is someone who, though not severely anxious or depressed, is low in positive affect, lacks a sense of purpose and has few close relationships.

In the more specific use of well-being, referring to positive aspects of experience, there are two broad approaches (see MacLeod, 2015). Hedonic approaches understand well-being in terms of a person's affective[1] experiences, along with how favourably they view their life. Someone who has frequent positive emotional states, rarely experiences negative emotional states, and is highly satisfied with their life, is high in well-being. Someone low in well-being experiences the opposite. What matters for well-being is whether a person is happy, in the normal everyday sense of the word. This emphasis on subjective experience is captured by the term *subjective well-being* (Diener, 1984), operationalized by a composite measure combining positive affect and life satisfaction, and subtracting negative affect. There is a variety of alternative views, which have

---

[1] Affect, emotion and feeling are terms that are sometimes used interchangeably, although there is also an argument for using them to refer to different phenomena (see, for example, Power & Dalgleish, 2015). In the present book I will, like many others, use them almost interchangeably.

come to be called eudaimonic approaches, all of which share the view that well-being consists of more than being happy. Certainly, being happy might be part of well-being, but a eudaimonic approach would propose someone has high well-being to the extent that their life contains a variety of 'good things' in life, usually thought to reflect the expression of human nature. Lists of these goods often include close relationships, knowledge, achievement, a sense of purpose, and so on. For example, Ryff (1989) proposed six qualities that define well-being: autonomy, environmental mastery, positive relationships, personal growth, self-acceptance, and a sense of purpose. Seligman (2011) suggests positive emotions, engagement, relationships, meaning and achievement. It is assumed that these good things can, and do, lead to happiness but their value is thought to be intrinsic, and does not lie solely in their ability to produce happiness (see MacLeod, 2015 for a discussion).

Mental health, in essence, refers to the presence or absence of disorders represented in the major medical classification systems: ICD-10 (World Health Organization, 2012) and DSM-5 (American Psychiatric Association, 2013). These systems obviously rely on cut-off points for the presence of a particular disorder. For example, Major Depressive Disorder in DSM-5 requires the presence of five out of nine possible symptoms to have been present for two weeks or more. There is also a debate about whether distress and disorder are points on a continuum, or whether there is a qualitative difference at the point that people meet diagnostic criteria. This argument has been pursued most closely in relation to depression, and the evidence favours a continuum (e.g. Ayuso-Mateos, Nuevo, Verdes, Naidoo, & Chatterji, 2010). What the diagnostic systems do provide is a structure for locating a range of different kinds of psychological disturbance and providing clear and universal definitions for the presence of a disorder (i.e. at a certain level of severity). Again, this argument is not central to the present book. We can accept that those who are experiencing mild levels of depression have their psychological well-being (in the broad sense) compromised and that those at the severe end, meeting diagnostic criteria, also have their well-being compromised but to a much greater degree. The main concern of the present book will be anxiety and depression, either at the clinical or at the sub-clinical threshold level, but reference will also be made at points to different disorders such as bipolar disorder and schizophrenia.

Plan of the book

The book is organized into chapters that can be read in isolation as stand-alone discussions, although there are also connections running across chapters.

Chapter 2 will deal with perhaps the most obvious aspect of how people think about the future—what they expect to happen. Two different facts of expectancies will be discussed. The first is predictions for future events, usually measured by presenting people with lists of future positive and negative events, and asking them to rate how likely they think those events are to happen to them. The second type of expectancy revolves more around the active anticipation of personal events—things one is looking forward to or not looking forward to. Evidence about how both types of expectancies are related to affect, anxiety, and depression is reviewed, and underling mechanisms that might explain the altered expectancies shown by mood-disturbed individuals are discussed.

Chapter 3 deals with the related issue of optimism and pessimism. Although sometimes methodologically overlapping with expectancies, there is a variety of ways that optimism and pessimism have been operationalized, including global beliefs about the future, differences in expectancies for self versus others, and a way of explaining events that happen to us. Chapter 3 also reviews evidence on how various indices of optimism–pessimism relate to mood disturbance, along with interesting questions related to accuracy—whether there is a widespread optimistic bias, whether those who are mood-disturbed are more accurate in their estimates for future events than those in average mood states, and whether optimism, even if it is inaccurate, is a good thing.

Thinking about particular events that might happen to us in the future involves feeling states in different ways. Chapters 4 and 5 review two aspects of feeling states—*anticipated affect* (thinking about how we think we *will* feel when an event happens) and *anticipatory affect* (how we feel *in the here-and-now* when contemplating a future event). These two aspects are likely to be related to each other, but are also quite distinct: one is a judgement about a likelihood of a future feeling state and the other is a feeling state, something experienced now when thinking about the future. Chapter 4 discusses findings on prediction for future feelings, or, to give it its usual name, *affective forecasting*. The main issues here are similar to those discussed for optimism–pessimism: is there a general inaccuracy, or even systematic bias, in how people think they are going to feel in the future and, if so, do those who are low in well-being or mood-disturbed depart from this usual bias? Chapter 5 reviews evidence for the existence of anticipatory feeling states and discusses how the feeling states that we experience in the here-and-now when thinking about the future function as guides to action. Hope, or its opposite, hopelessness, and anxiety, are identified as the fundamental anticipatory emotional states relating to thoughts about future positive and negative events respectively. One particular response to anticipatory emotions—a desire to avoid the experience of negative emotion itself—is discussed in some detail.

The interesting question of how we are able to think about the future at all is the topic of Chapter 6. There has been a surge of interest in recent years in how memory is involved in future-directed thinking, especially the ability to think about particular future episodes that we might experience. Chapter 6 reviews the literature on the relationship between memory and prospection, starting from the striking similarities in the problems people have in thinking about the future when they have difficulties remembering episodes from the past, a pattern consistently found in those with emotional disturbance. Questions will be addressed about the involvement of different types of memory in future thought, as well as similarities and differences between past- and future-thinking.

Many of the thoughts that we have about the future relate to our ongoing involvement as active agents in life who have a future trajectory that we are invested in. Chapters 7 and 8 review the literature on goals and plans and their relationship to well-being. Important aspects of goals related to well-being and mental health are discussed, including goal progress, perception of the likelihood of attaining goals, the content of the goals (are some goals 'better for us' than others), whether the goals are about attaining something new or avoiding something bad, and the reasons for having the goals in the first place. Goals, at least most of them, require plans about how to reach them as well as intentions to carry out the plans. Chapter 8 reviews the role of plans and intentions in well-being and mental health.

An interesting question is whether some people are just generally more future-focused than others. Because this book is about well-being and mental health, the follow-on question—whether a future-focus, rather than a past- or present-focus is linked to emotional well-being—is of even greater interest here. Chapter 9 addresses this question. In addition, Chapter 9 also discusses the connection between mindfulness and well-being because mindfulness is often talked about as fostering a focus on the present. If mindfulness is related to well-being does that then imply that a greater focus on the present and, by implication, less of a focus on the future is desirable? The second half of Chapter 9 discusses whether the apparent benefits of a future focus presented in Chapters 7 and 8 can be reconciled with valuing a mindful mindset.

With an emphasis on well-being and mental health and how different ways of the future might be linked to them, the obvious question is whether people can learn to think of the future in ways that would benefit their well-being and improve their mental health. Chapter 10 reviews methods to improve problematic prospection and its associated well-being deficits, some of which are embedded within existing clinical practice and some of which are designed specifically as bespoke future-oriented interventions. The range of approaches is discussed, from very brief, simple techniques, to resource-intensive packages that attempt to alter future-thinking, to provide a vehicle for change in well-being.

On a final note, I have tried to cover the relevant literature and it certainly feels to me that I have covered a great deal of it! At the same time, I am aware that I will almost certainly have omitted important studies and relevant theoretical perspectives. Therefore, apologies in advance to those who have conducted important and valuable work in the area whose work is not represented here. The aim of the book is to help go some way towards answering some of the interesting and outstanding current questions on prospection, well-being and mental health, but even more so to stimulate further work in the area that will identify the next set of interesting questions.

References

Addis, D. R., Wong, A. T., & Schacter, D. L. (2008). Age-related changes in the episodic simulation of future events. *Psychological Science*, **19**(1), 33–41.

American Psychiatric Association (2013). *Diagnostic and statistical manual of mental disorders*. (5th edition). Washington, D.C: Author.

Ayuso-Mateos, J. L., Nuevo, R., Verdes, E., Naidoo, N., & Chatterji, S. (2010). From depressive symptoms to depressive disorders: the relevance of thresholds. *The British Journal of Psychiatry*, **196**(5), 365–371. http://doi.org/10.1192/bjp.bp.109.071191

Baumeister, R. F. & Vohs, K. D. (2016). Introduction to the special issue: The science of prospection. *Review of General Psychology*, **20**(1), 1–2. http://doi.org/10.1037/gpr0000072

Berntsen, D. & Bohn, A. (2010). Remembering and forecasting: The relation between autobiographical memory and episodic future thinking. *Memory & Cognition*, **38**(3), 265–278. http://doi.org/10.3758/MC.38.3.265

D'Argembeau, A., Renaud, O., & Van der Linden, M. (2011). Frequency, characteristics and functions of future-oriented thoughts in daily life. *Applied Cognitive Psychology*, **25**(1), 96–103. http://doi.org/10.1002/acp.1647

D'Argembeau, A. & Van der Linden, M. (2004). Phenomenal characteristics associated with projecting oneself back into the past and forward into the future: Influence of valence and temporal distance. *Consciousness and Cognition*, **13**(4), 844–858. http://doi.org/10.1016/j.concog.2004.07.007

Diener, E. (1984). Subjective well-being. *Psychological Bulletin*, **95**(3), 542–575. http://doi.org/10.1037/0033-2909.95.3.542

Epstude, K. & Peetz, J. (2012). Mental time travel: A conceptual overview of social psychological perspectives on a fundamental human capacity. *European Journal of Social Psychology*, **42**(3), 269–275. http://doi.org/10.1002/ejsp.1867

Gao, X. (2016). Cultural differences between East Asian and North American in temporal orientation. *Review of General Psychology*, **20**(1), 118–127. http://doi.org/10.1037/gpr0000070

Guo, T., Ji, L.-J., Spina, R., & Zhang, Z. (2012). Culture, temporal focus, and values of the past and the future. *Personality and Social Psychology Bulletin*, **38**(8), 1030–1040. http://doi.org/10.1177/0146167212443895

Henry, J. D., Addis, D. R., Suddendorf, T., & Rendell, P. G. (2016). Introduction to the Special Issue: Prospection difficulties in clinical populations. *British Journal of Clinical Psychology*, **55**(1), 1–3. http://doi.org/10.1111/bjc.12108

Jason, L. A., Schade, J., Furo, L., Reichler, A., & Brickman, C. (1989). Time orientation: Past, present, and future perceptions. *Psychological Reports*, **64**(3, Pt 2), 1199–1205.

Jeunehomme, O. & D'Argembeau, A. (2016). Prevalence and determinants of direct and generative modes of production of episodic future thoughts in the word cueing paradigm. *The Quarterly Journal of Experimental Psychology*, **69**(2), 254–272. http://doi.org/10.1080/17470218.2014.993663

Klein, S. B. (2013). The complex act of projecting oneself into the future. *Wiley Interdisciplinary Reviews: Cognitive Science*, **4**(1), 63–79. http://doi.org/10.1002/wcs.1210

MacLeod, A. K. (2012). Well-being, positivity and mental health: An introduction to the special issue. *Clinical Psychology & Psychotherapy*, **19**(4), 279–282. http://doi.org/10.1002/cpp.1794

MacLeod, A. K. (2015). Well-being: Objectivism, subjectivism or sobjectivism? *Journal of Happiness Studies*, **16**(4), 1073–1089. http://doi.org/10.1007/s10902-014-9561-0

Marchetti, I., Koster, E. H. W., Klinger, E., & Alloy, L. B. (2016). Spontaneous thought and vulnerability to mood disorders: The dark side of the wandering mind. *Clinical Psychological Science*. http://doi.org/10.1177/2167702615622383

Michaelian, K., Klein, S. B., & Szpunar, K. K. (2016). *Seeing the future: Theoretical perspectives on future-oriented mental time travel*. Oxford: Oxford University Press.

Oettingen, G., Sevincer, A. T., & Gollwitzer, P. M. (in press). *The psychology of thinking about the future*. New York: Guilford Press.

Power, M. & Dalgleish, T. (2015). *Cognition and emotion: From order to disorder* (3rd edition). Chichester: Psychology Press.

Rubin, D. C. (2014). Schema-driven construction of future autobiographical traumatic events: The future is much more troubling than the past. *Journal of Experimental Psychology: General*, **143**(2), 612–630. http://doi.org/10.1037/a0032638

Ryff, C. D. (1989). Happiness is everything, or is it? Explorations on the meaning of psychological well-being. *Journal of Personality and Social Psychology*, **57**(6), 1069–1081. http://doi.org/10.1037/0022-3514.57.6.1069

Seligman, M. E. P. (2011). *Flourish: A new understanding of happiness and well-being––and how to achieve them*. London: Nicholas Brealey Publishing.

Seligman, M. E. P., Railton, P., Baumeister, R. F., & Sripada, C. (2013). Navigating into the future or driven by the past. *Perspectives on Psychological Science*, **8**(2), 119–141. http://doi.org/10.1177/1745691612474317

Seligman, M. E. P., Railton, P., Baumeister, R.F. & Sripada, C. (2016). *Homo Prospectus*. New York: Oxford University Press.

Suddendorf, T. & Corballis, M. C. (2007). The evolution of foresight: What is mental time travel, and is it unique to humans? *Behavioral and Brain Sciences*, **30**(3). http://doi.org/10.1017/S0140525X07001975

Suddendorf, T., & Moore, C. (2011). Introduction to the special issue: The development of episodic foresight. *Cognitive Development*, **26**(4), 295–298. http://doi.org/10.1016/j.cogdev.2011.09.001

Szpunar, K. K. & Radvansky, G. A. (2016). Cognitive approaches to the study of episodic future thinking. *The Quarterly Journal of Experimental Psychology*, **69**(2), 209–216. http://doi.org/10.1080/17470218.2015.1095213

Szpunar, K. K., Spreng, R. N., & Schacter, D. L. (2014). A taxonomy of prospection: Introducing an organizational framework for future-oriented cognition: Fig. 1. *Proceedings of the National Academy of Sciences*, **111**(52), 18414–18421. http://doi.org/10.1073/pnas.1417144111

Tonn, B., Hemrick, A., & Conrad, F. (2006). Cognitive representations of the future: Survey results. *Futures*, **38**(7), 810–829. http://doi.org/10.1016/j.futures.2005.12.005

Trope, Y. & Liberman, N. (2010). Construal-level theory of psychological distance. *Psychological Review*, **117**(2), 440–463. http://doi.org/10.1037/a0018963

Van Boven, L. & Ashworth, L. (2007). Looking forward, looking back: Anticipation is more evocative than retrospection. *Journal of Experimental Psychology: General*, **136**(2), 289–300. http://doi.org/10.1037/0096-3445.136.2.289

Wittmann, M. (2011). Moments in time. *Frontiers in Integrative Neuroscience*, **5**, 66. http://doi.org/10.3389/fnint.2011.00066

World Health Organization. (2012). *The international statistical classification of diseases and health related problems, ICD-10* (2010 edition). Geneva: WHO.

Chapter 2

Expectancies

Introduction

Expectancies refer to psychological states that are about a degree of belief in what is going to happen in the future. As I am writing this book I have a high expectation of it being completed and published, despite being behind on my schedule, but I don't expect it to ever be a best seller. Expectancies have long been recognized as important in the psychological literature, although, like many other forms of future-directed thought, have probably not received the attention that they merit. This is not to say that they have been ignored altogether. For example, expectancy-value models (e.g. Eccles & Wigfield, 2002) place expectancies of success alongside the value placed on an activity or the outcome of the activity at the heart of motivated behaviour. Within traditional expectancy-value models (e.g. Nagengast, Marsh, Scalas, Xu, Hau et al., 2011), motivation to engage in particular behaviour is predicted by an interaction of how likely outcomes are perceived to be and the value of those outcomes to the person: people take steps to bring about outcomes that they value and that they perceive to be reasonably likely. Not only that, but expectancies are hugely important for well-being and mental health, as will become clear in the present chapter and in other parts of the book.

The emphasis in this chapter is on thoughts that people have about specific future outcomes. More global thoughts about the future, such as a general belief that the future will turn out well, are covered in Chapter 3. Chapter 3 will also discuss expectancies for particular events where those expectancies bear on the issue of optimism versus pessimism and accuracy versus bias. The present chapter examines the relationship of expectancies to well-being and emotional distress, and is divided into two main parts. The first part reviews the literature on the subjective probability judgements people give when presented with a list of events and asked to estimate their likelihood. The second main section of the chapter focuses on the more active, anticipatory aspect of expectancy, where people generate idiographic thoughts relating to their own futures. Expectancies of both kinds, have, not surprisingly, been shown to be strongly related to mental health and well-being.

Subjective probability judgements

Probably the most common way that expectancies have been studied is to present individuals with a range of hypothetical future positive and negative future outcomes and ask them to estimate how likely those events are to happen to them. Typically, likelihood is estimated by selecting a number on a scale of probability, which can vary from one to five through to zero to100. The different literatures on such subjective probability judgements each have a different slant. In the risk judgement literature one of the key questions is how people make judgements about environmental risk (e.g. Slovic & Peters, 2006). How people judge the likelihood of various negative health outcomes, such as heart disease or cancer, is the focus of interest in the public health arena, where the main aim is to help people to adopt health-promoting or health-protective behaviours, for example, attending health checks where appropriate (e.g. McDowell, Occhipinti, & Chambers, 2013). In both of these areas, unrealistically optimistic judgements are often the target of change, where the aim is to motivate safe and healthy behaviour through increasing people's perception of the possibility of future negative outcomes. When thinking about psychological well-being and mental health, however, the issue is normally the opposite one, where people hold views of the future that are unrealistically, or at least unhelpfully, negative. People who score highly on hypomania or who meet criteria for bipolar disorder[1] do show elevated subjective likelihood for some particular positive events, notably those connected with fame and wealth (Johnson, Eisner, & Carver, 2009), but this is an unusual case.

Research has addressed issues such as whether in mood disturbance altered judgements about future expectancies are only for the self or whether they also extend to judgements about others, whether judgements about positive events are affected as well as judgements for negative events, and whether those who are anxious show a different pattern than those who are depressed. Studies compare judgements in individuals who show some mood disturbance with control groups of participants who do not, or correlate levels of mood (usually anxiety or depression) with judgements in community, or more often, student, samples.

Group comparison studies

The most consistent finding in group comparison studies is that, relative to control participants, mood-disturbed individuals judge negative future events

---

[1] Characterized by extreme mood swings from lows of depression to highs of elation where the person has feelings of energy, a sense of importance and (unrealistic) ideas for future plans, often accompanied by lack of sleep and neglect of eating.

as more likely to happen to them. For example, in an early study Butler and Mathews (1983) presented anxious patients, depressed patients, and matched controls with hypothetical future events. The events had been constructed to rule out possible performance effects that might differ between groups (i.e. features of anxiety or depression that might influence the actual likelihood of the events), and items were phrased in a hypothetical way that tried to eliminate differences in relevance due to circumstances (e.g. 'if a burglar surprised you in your own home he would attack you'). Anxious patients and depressed patients gave significantly higher likelihood estimates than the control group for negative events happening to them, without differing from each other. MacLeod, Tata, Kentish, Carroll, and Hunter (1997b) also compared depressed, anxious, and control groups using a different list of events and found strikingly similar effects, which are illustrated alongside the Butler and Mathews (1983) results in Figure 2.1.

Elevated judgements for negative events happening to oneself have also been found in other studies with anxious patients (e.g. Raune, MacLeod, & Holmes,

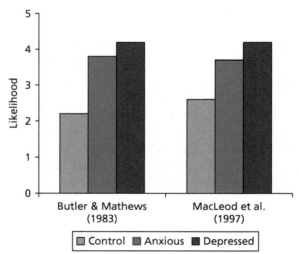

Figure 2.1 Data from Butler and Mathews (1983) and from MacLeod et al. (1997) showing subjective likelihood of negative events happening to oneself, for control, anxious, and depressed participants. In each case, depressed and anxious patients show higher estimates than controls, without differing significantly from each other.

Data from *Advances in Behaviour Research and Therapy*, 5(1), Butler, G, Mathews, A, Cognitive processes in anxiety, 51–62, Copyright 1983, with permission from Elsevier |

From Macleod, A. K., Tata, Philip, Kentish, J., Carroll, F., and Hunter, E., *Clinical Psychology & Psychotherapy* **4**(1), 15–24. Copyright © 1997 by John Wiley Sons, Inc. Reprinted by permission of John Wiley & Sons, Inc.

2005), as well as with chronically anxious worriers (MacLeod, Williams, & Bekerian, 1991), high trait-anxious or high trait-worry students (Bentz, Mahaffey, Adami, Romig, Muenke et al., 2009; Bredemeier, Berenbaum, & Spielberg, 2012; Butler & Mathews, 1987), students high in autonomic arousal (Wenze, Gunthert, & German, 2012), mildly depressed (dysphoric) students (MacLeod & Cropley, 1995), both with and without a history of suicidality (Marroquín, Nolen-Hoeksema, & Miranda, 2013), depressed community participants (Strunk, Lopez, & DeRubeis, 2006; Thimm, Holte, Brennan, & Wang, 2013), and people admitted to hospital with an episode of deliberate self-harm (MacLeod & Tarbuck, 1994).

Addressing an interesting question about the permanence of such effects, Thimm et al. (2013) compared currently-depressed students with matched groups who had either experienced depression in the past but were not currently depressed, or who had never been depressed. Current and previous episodes were assessed with a standardized clinical interview, with those in the recovered group having to have experienced a depressive episode within the last five years. Events were taken from Weinstein's unrealistic optimism scale (Weinstein, 1980), for example 'tripping and breaking a bone' and 'having a drinking problem'. The events did not have a restricted time frame but could relate to any time in the future, as clearly indicated by 'living past 80' being one of the items. Those in the currently depressed group gave higher likelihood estimates than the other two groups, who did not differ from each other, suggesting that at least under these assessment conditions, the elevated likelihood estimates co-occurred with depression rather than representing an ongoing thinking style of those vulnerable to depression. It is, though, worth noting that the fact that those who had recovered from depression were like never-depressed controls, does not exclude the possibility that they remained more vulnerable to such thoughts, should a relevant trigger, for example, a state of low mood, occur (see Teasdale, 1988).

Bredemeier et al. (2012), unlike most other studies, examined different future time frames systematically, asking their participants to judge the likelihood of negative events in the next month, year, and ten years. Self-reported worry correlated with the likelihood estimates of events in the first two time frames but not with the longer, ten-year time frame, except where events were judged to be very high value (i.e. would be very bad if they happened); in this case worry was also correlated with likelihood of those more distant events.

Some studies have also examined likelihood for positive events, although there are fewer of them and the results are not quite as consistent. Lower estimates of the likelihood of future positive events happening to oneself have been found in a range of groups including mildly depressed students (Pyszczynski,

Holt, & Greenberg, 1987), depressed community participants (Strunk et al., 2006; Thimm et al., 2013), depressed patients (MacLeod, Tata, Kentish, & Jacobsen, 1997c), anxious patients (MacLeod et al., 1997c), students scoring high on anhedonic depression (Wenze, et al., 2012), and those high in dysphoria, with or without a history of suicidality (Marroquín et al., 2013). As was the case with negative events, Thimm et al. (2013) found the recovered-depressed participants to be comparable to their never-depressed counterparts, and both showed higher estimates than the currently depressed group. A few studies have not found lower estimates for positive events in mood-disturbed groups. For example, Butler and Mathews (1983) found no difference between their depressed, anxious and control groups for positive events. MacLeod and Cropley (1995) did not find reduced positive expectancies in a group of dysphoric students, although they did find that, whereas depression was correlated with negative expectancies, self-reported hopelessness was correlated with (low) positive expectancies. The specific role of the hopelessness component of depression will be returned to in the second part of the present chapter.

Finally, some studies, rather than examining positive and negative events separately have combined them to give a single index of positive relative to negative expectancies. For example, Cabeleira et al. (2014) had participants rate the likelihood of positive and negative events and combined the scores into an index where they defined scores above zero (higher estimates for positive than negative) as representing a positive bias, and scores below zero (higher estimates for negative than positive events) as a negative bias. Participants generally gave higher estimates for positive events than negative events (i.e. showed a positive bias), but this tendency was less marked for high trait-anxious participants. On some conditions where participants were exposed to previous relevant negative information this priming was enough to lead the high trait-anxious group to actually give higher estimates for negative than positive events. The use of the term 'bias' is something that will be returned to in Chapter 3; there it will be argued that, although tempting to use for a range of situations, its use should be restricted to absolute rather than relative comparisons, where there is an objective baseline against which to compare the judgements. For example, it might just be the case that for most people, life contains more positive than negative events, in which case, judging positive events to be more likely than negative ones would not constitute a bias. Nevertheless, the Cabeleira et al. (2014) study, like the other studies reviewed, does indicate a clear difference in likelihood judgements in those who are mood-disturbed compared to those who are not.

Most studies have examined only self-related judgements (judging the likelihood of events happening to oneself) given the prominence of self-related thoughts in mood disturbance. It is difficult to draw conclusions from the studies that have measured other related judgements because, as well as being few in number, the results are not always consistent. In fact, they are sometimes contradictory. For example, Butler and Mathews (1983) found no difference between depressed, anxious, and control groups on their judged likelihood of positive events happening to others, but the depressed group gave higher estimates than controls of the likelihood of other people experiencing negative events. In contrast, Thimm et al. (2013) found no effects relating to negative events, but their depressed group gave *higher* estimates of positive events happening to others.

Correlational studies

Clearly, there are differences between mood-disturbed and non-mood-disturbed individuals in their expectancies about the likelihood of future positive and, especially, negative events happening to them. Inconsistencies that are there in the findings may relate to the particular samples and the items used in different studies. It is also invariably the case that anxious and depressed groups are not 'pure', given the high correlation between anxiety and depression. For example, in the MacLeod et al. (1997c) study, the depressed patients' anxiety scores were as high as those in the anxiety group. This overlap between depression and anxiety may account for the fact that in the few studies comparing depressed and anxious groups to controls within the one study, there is little evidence of differential mood relationships. Correlational studies afford a better opportunity to examine whether anxiety and depression relate differently to positive and negative expectancies because it is easier to examine their unique and distinctive relationships to judgements.

Two studies by Regina Miranda and her colleagues at Hunter College in New York illustrated differential relationships of positive and negative expectancies with anxiety and depression (Miranda, Fontes, & Marroquín, 2008; Miranda & Mennin, 2007). The way that ratings were made in these studies was somewhat different to most other studies, in that participants decided whether each event would or would not happen and then gave a rating on a five-point scale on how certain they were about their judgements. Negative events rated as 'yes' and then judged as certain, and positive events rated as 'no', and again that judgement subsequently rated as certain, were a particular focus of interest in these studies. In both studies, samples of students rated the likelihood of positive and negative future self-relevant events in this way, as well as completing measures of anxiety and depression. Results were very similar for the number of yes/no judgements and the certainty ratings: judgements of negative events (more yeses and greater certainty) were related to both depression and anxiety whereas positive event judgements (fewer yeses and greater certainty about those) were related only to levels of depression. Similar results—depression and anxiety correlating with elevated negative judgements but only depression correlating with lowered positive expectancies—were reported by Bennet and Corcoran (2010) using the more standard estimates of likelihood on a single scale of probability.

Wenze et al. (2012) also adopted a correlational approach to the specificity question, but utilized measures intended to maximize discrimination between anxiety and depression. The idea that common and distinctive affective qualities might underlie depression and anxiety had initially been suggested by Clark and Watson (1991). These authors suggested that negative affect (e.g. feelings of guilt, tension, or distress) was a common affective substrate of both anxiety and depression, whereas a lack of positive affect (e.g. feeling enthusiastic, proud, or inspired) was specific to depression. The tripartite model of anxiety and depression extended this scheme to three factors (Clark & Watson, 1991), where, alongside a general distress factor common to both disorders, physiological (or autonomic) hyperarousal was proposed as specific to anxiety, with anhedonia uniquely related to depression. Wenze et al. (2012) measured autonomic arousal and anhedonic depression, and correlated each with prediction of negative and positive events. Both measures of affective symptoms correlated with the judged likelihood of negative events but only anhedonic depression correlated (inversely) with judgements of positive events. These findings are broadly consistent with those of Miranda and colleagues (2008), although the greater specificity of symptom measures might have been expected to result in complete rather than partial asymmetry of correlations.

MacLeod et al. (1997b), in their study mentioned earlier in the chapter that included depressed, anxious, and control participants, conducted a post hoc principal components analysis on the self-report measures included in their study. Those measures consisted of two self-report measures, each of anxiety and depression, as well as a measure of positive affect (PA) and of negative affect (NA). Two clear factors emerged, with the first factor being an NA/general distress factor with loadings from all variables except PA. Factor 2 was a high PA/ low depression factor with no loadings from NA or anxiety. What was of particular interest was the way that subjective probability judgements correlated with the two factors. The NA/general distress factor correlated with likelihood judgements for negative but not positive events, whereas the opposite was the case for the PA/low depression factor.

This two-system view was further reinforced by MacLeod, Byrne, and Valentine, 1996. Two different studies with samples of around 250 students in each study completed measures of depression, anxiety, PA, NA, and judged the likelihood of future negative and positive self-relevant events. Additionally, in these studies participants also completed self-report measures of worry and hopelessness. In terms of the sort of two-system view outlined earlier the results were clear. Principal components analysis in both studies produced two very similar factors, which are summarized in Table 2.1. The first factor was clearly a general distress/NA factor, upon which negative expectancies also loaded. In contrast, positive expectancies loaded with PA along with low levels of hopelessness and depression. Confirmatory factor analysis with two factors produced a significantly better fit than with a solution with one factor. There are several notes of caution. First, the two factors were themselves correlated, suggesting that these cognitive-affective systems are not entirely independent. Second, it is possible that a two-factor solution may be influenced by item wording, with predominantly negatively worded items in variables in the first factor and mainly positively worded items in the variables that loaded onto the second factor. It is difficult to un-confound valence of item wording when the factors reflect positivity and negativity, but it nevertheless is a possible contributor to the structure. Finally, the measure of NA and PA only includes high-activation words (e.g. 'excited' and 'interested' or 'tense' and 'irritable') and does not represent low-activation states such as lethargic or calm.

The evidence points to positive expectancies and negative expectancies being distinct, rather than simple polar opposites, and being differentially related to different facets of emotional distress. Finally, as noted earlier, not all studies find these sorts of relationships with anxiety and depression, and the same is true for affect. Peters, Flink, Boersma, and Linton (2010), also in a student sample, did not find any correlations of PA and NA with positive or negative expectancies. However, in this study negative expectancies did not correlate even with neuroticism, which is a highly surprising finding, and does perhaps suggest something unusual about the sample or the items in this particular study.

Table 2.1 Variables loading onto the two factors in MacLeod et al. (1996). Negative expectancies load onto a general distress/NA factor whereas positive expectancies cluster with PA and low depression and hopelessness

Factor 1	Factor 2
Negative Affect (NA)	Positive Affect (PA)
Anxiety	Positive expectancies
Worry	Hopelessness (low)
Depression	Depression (low)
Negative expectancies	

Affect, Emotional Disorder, and Future-directed Thinking, MacLeod, A. K., *Cognition and Emotion*, 1996, Routledge, reprinted by permission of the publisher (Taylor & Francis Ltd, http://www.tandfonline.com).

Summary of the findings

To summarize, mood-disturbed individuals differ from those who are not mood-disturbed by judging positive events as comparatively less likely and negative events as comparatively more likely. Predictions for positive and negative events are overlapping but distinct judgements and relate differentially to cognitive-affective systems. Predictions for negative events relate both to anxiety and depression as well as to NA and worry. In contrast, low predictions for positive events are more strongly related to depression than they are to anxiety and co-occur with hopelessness and low levels of PA.

This, at least partial, separation of positive and negative expectancies in the way that they relate to anxiety and depression is also consistent with theoretical models that distinguish between underlying systems of approach and avoidance (Depue & Iacono, 1989; Fowles, 1994; Gray, 1990) The behavioural inhibition system is a cognitive-motivational system that is sensitive to signals of future aversive outcomes and mediates behaviour—usually avoidance—in response to those signals. A second system, called the behavioural approach, behavioural facilitation or behavioural activation system, is responsible for processing signals of desirable outcomes (see MacLeod et al., 1996 for a fuller discussion).

Processes and mechanisms

The clear connection between mood disturbance and predictions about the likelihood of future events raises the interesting question of what underlies these differences. Understanding the mechanisms that produce such judgements could potentially lead to useful ways of helping people to change their perceptions. How do people go about making judgements about the likelihood of future events happening to them? Such judgements are complex, involving a lot of difficult-to-forecast elements, resulting in high levels of uncertainty. Sometimes objective information is available. For example, figures about the rarity of fatalities from air travel are often quoted to reassure people about the safety of flying, or health risk information is widely disseminated to try to discourage smoking. It may be that people are able to utilize such objective probabilities of events occurring, but for many events objective probabilities either do not exist or will not be widely known, and even where they are known, will not necessarily be seen as relevant (Slovic & Peters, 2006).

Under conditions of uncertainty about future outcomes, people more often use mental shortcuts where they recall or construct information in a way that provides some guide to the answer to the question of likelihood of future events. A key insight from research on judgement processes is that often what is used as a basis for the judgement is not necessarily the *content* of what is brought to mind but the *process* by which it is brought to mind. The metacognitive experience that accompanies any sort of reasoning can be used as the source of information in the judgement, depending on the sort of theory that the person holds about that metacognitive experience. For example, asking people to think of 12 examples of them being assertive should, if content is being used as the basis for judgement, lead them to rate their assertiveness as higher than where they are asked to think of six examples, but the opposite has been reported (Schwarz et al., 1991). Thinking of six examples is relatively easy, whereas thinking of 12 examples is difficult, and this feeling of ease is utilized by an implicit theory that if something is easily processed it is more likely to be the case (Schwarz, 2004). The fluency with which information is processed has been found to be influential in a wide range of judgements (see Alter & Oppenheimer, 2009, for a review).

The *availability heuristic* (Tversky & Kahneman, 1973) is an example of a fluency account of how people make judgements about future likelihood. In their early work, Tversky and Kahneman (1973) argued that when asked to assess the likelihood of a particular future outcome, people often use how easily they are able to bring relevant instances to mind. Tversky and Kahneman (1973) suggested two classes of mental operations that bring things to mind—retrieval of past instances, where similar events are recalled from long-term memory, and the construction of imagined scenarios. The more easily that past examples are recalled, or the easier it is to construct a scenario leading to the outcome happening, the more likely the event is judged to be. The second mechanism—scenario construction—will be used when the event in question is unique or even uncommon, in which case there will not be a database of past experiences upon which to base the judgement. This second aspect of the availability heuristic was renamed the *simulation heuristic* in recognition that as a mechanism it was sufficiently distinct from recall of past instances to warrant separate consideration (Kahneman & Tversky, 1982). The simulation heuristic describes the process of constructing a mental model of reality in which the hypothetical event takes place, with an important component of the model being a set of causal explanations leading to the event's occurrence. The ease with which causal theories producing the outcome can be generated determines the judged likelihood of the outcome.

Those who are low in well-being and overestimate negative future outcomes and/or underestimate positive outcomes should also find it easier to recall negative and more difficult to recall positive memories, and should show comparable effects for constructing positive and negative scenarios. Such effects could arise through, for example, spending more time ruminating on past negative outcomes (Smith & Alloy, 2009) or catastrophizing about future negative ones

(Vasey & Borkovec, 1992). Mood congruence effects could mean that positive information is thought about less, and therefore processed less fluently when it is thought about, leading to lower estimates.

It is also possible that mood states themselves, if they are highly salient, might be used as a direct source of information themselves. For example, someone feels anxious about the ferry crossing they are about to take and the feeling of anxiety gives rise to a judgement that the crossing must be dangerous. This kind of emotional reasoning was identified by Beck (1976) as one of the cognitive biases characteristic of emotional disorders. Therapeutically, what is challenging is that there is often a disconnection between the rational and emotional aspects of judgement, where someone can say that they *know* something is not dangerous but it doesn't *feel* safe. Most studies simply ask people to rate likelihood, but the emotional element of judgements about the future might be accessed to an even greater degree if people are questioned in a different way. Janssen, van Osch, Lechner, Candel, and de Vries (2012) tried to separate out these different aspects of judgement by asking about vulnerability and likelihood, each measured on the same five-point scale (e.g. 'If I keep smoking I feel vulnerable to getting lung cancer at some point in my life.' versus 'If I keep smoking my chances of getting lung cancer at some point in my life are big.'). Both correlated with worry, but the correlations with the vulnerability questions, thought to tap more into feeling states, were significantly higher than those asking about likelihood. In the judgement literature the use of current mood state as a source of information about judgements is known as the *affect heuristic*, and has mainly been studied in relation to risk judgements about environmental and health risks (Slovic & Peters, 2006), where the aim is to be able to foster a reasonably accurate understanding of a range of these risks.

Simulation

The future events that people make judgements about are rarely simple repetitions of a previous event. Tversky and Kahneman (1973, p. 228) note that 'each occurrence of an economic recession, a successful medical operation, or a divorce, is essentially unique, and its probability cannot be evaluated by a simple tally of instances'. For this reason, they suggest that simulation rather than retrieval of a past episode is the basis of most likelihood judgements.

In a fairly simple attempt to operationalize the causal thinking element of the simulation heuristic, Debra Bekerian, Mark Williams, and I (MacLeod et al., 1991) asked participants to generate reasons why an event would come about and reasons why it would not. In a number of studies, chronic worriers (MacLeod et al., 1991), anxious patients (MacLeod et al., 1997c; Raune et al., 2005), anxious adolescents (Kagan, MacLeod, & Pote, 2004), depressed patients

(MacLeod et al., 1997b), and those who were suicidal (MacLeod & Tarbuck, 1994) gave higher subjective probability judgements for future negative events and also were more able to think of reasons why the events would happen as against why they would not. Ease of thinking of reasons was measured by the number of reasons generated, time to first reason, and subjective ratings of difficulty. Where positive events were included, they have also shown group effects of simulation consistent with differences between the groups on likelihood judgements (Kagan et al., 2004; MacLeod et al., 1997b). Measuring causal reasoning in this way gets at an important aspect of simulation but does not cover other aspects.

Gary Brown and colleagues (Brown, MacLeod, Tata, & Goddard, 2002) developed a more comprehensive measure of simulation. Women who were pregnant for the first time were asked to describe a scenario that began with them going into labour at home, and ended with them getting to the hospital with time to spare, a scenario that was unique and highly relevant to all participants. Descriptions provided by participants were then independently rated for dimensions representing *goodness of simulation*, including the flow of the scenario, the logical sequencing of the different elements, and fullness of coverage. Example scenarios from two participants, one scoring more highly than the other on goodness of simulation, are shown in Table 2.2. As predicted, goodness of simulation was related to higher perceived likelihood of the outcome (getting to the hospital in good time), alongside lower levels of worry about it.

The correlational data suggest a link between simulation and perceived likelihood. There is also evidence that asking people to simulate outcomes increases the perceived likelihood of those outcomes. For example, Szpunar and Schacter (2013) created novel events by asking participants to produce lists of familiar people, familiar objects, and familiar locations. The items were then combined randomly, one from each list, to create triads, and participants were asked to imagine a future scenario for each triad. In this study, the procedure was intended to create novel events that participants would not have had direct past experience of. In addition, each description was paired with an instruction to think of an event related to the triad that would provoke a positive, neutral, or negative emotion. The key manipulation occurred the day after the initial generation of the simulations, when half of the items were simulated a further three times before all of the items were simulated once more. Items simulated four times on the second day were judged to be more plausible[2] than items

----

[2] Plausibility, rather than likelihood, was the key variable in order to avoid potential floor effects on likelihood arising from the novelty of the scenarios but, arguably, is a weaker form of likelihood.

Table 2.2 Two example simulations of first-time pregnant women, describing going into labour at home and reaching the hospital in time. P represents a prompt

Participant A

Depending on what stage—I'm taking it from that stage–I'll try to ride out the pain. I'll make a few phone calls—especially to my boyfriend and then my mum. Take a bath, eat something. Next stage—depending on the pain, I'll still be riding it out. By that time my boyfriend will have arrived and we will make our way to the hospital (by car). Then when I arrive they'll tell me what to do. I only live down the road so I would like to stay at home as long as possible.

Participant B

It's your first child—don't know what to expect. You're a bit frightened. No one around you—just to calm really. (P) Scream. (P) Call for help—nearest person is the next door neighbour—whoever I could get in touch with quickly. (P) If it's not all that bad you could get there in a car—say a neighbour's car. But if there's pain you call an ambulance. It would all happen so quickly you wouldn't think—just the first thing that comes to mind. Maybe when you get there you'll think I should have done this, I should have done that.

Brown, G. P., MacLeod, A. K., Tata, P., & Goddard, L. (2002). Worry and the simulation of future outcomes. *Anxiety, Stress & Coping: An International Journal*, 15(1), 1–17 Routledge, reprinted by permission of the publisher (Taylor & Francis Ltd, http://www.tandfonline.com).

simulated just once that day, and this effect was more marked for emotional items, both positive and negative, compared to neutral items. Finally, there is some promising evidence from some of the studies that counter simulation can reduce elevated likelihood judgements about negative events. In chronic worriers (MacLeod et al., 1991) and those who were suicidal (MacLeod & Tarbuck, 1994), counter simulation—thinking of reasons why negative events would not happen—significantly reduced their perceived likelihood. Bentz et al. (2009) also found that generating alternatives to negative scenarios lowered likelihood estimates of those scenarios. Overall, these findings provide support for the causal role of mental simulation, and at the same time offer useful pointers for intervention, which will be discussed more fully in Chapter 10.

Memory

Kahneman and Tversky (1982) suggest that the ease of recall of similar incidents plays a lesser role in judged probability of future, personally relevant events. This is not to say that memory per se does not play an important role, and the involvement of memory in future-thinking will be discussed much more fully in Chapter 6. Studies that do argue for the importance of retrieval of similar instances in judging future likelihood usually have not directly measured retrieval of those instances. For example, Corcoran et al. (2006) asked participants to judge the likelihood of a range of future events and measured availability by asking participants to provide an estimate on a scale of how much the events in question had happened to them in the past. Scores on these two judgements, averaged across all items, correlated, showing that people who judge a set of events as having happened to them frequently in the past also estimate that this set of events is likely to happen to them in the future. However, to be consistent with operation of the availability heuristic it would need to be shown that recall of actual memories (rather than just beliefs about memories measured on a very similar type of scale) correlated at the level of individual items with judged future likelihood. C. MacLeod and Campbell (1992) did ask participants to recall specific memories to short descriptions of common pleasant (e.g. 'a welcome invitation') and unpleasant (e.g. 'a painful injury') events, and measured how quickly they responded. Speed of retrieval and judged likelihood of those events correlated at the individual item level. These results appear to be supportive of the availability heuristic (although of course do not speak to the causal aspect), but the study did not check whether memories were actually being recalled, raising the possibility that, again, some sort of judgement, rather than actual memories, was being elicited. The very fast average latency of 2.5 seconds also casts doubt on whether actual specific memories were being retrieved. Along with colleagues, Mark Cropley and Philip Tata (Cropley, MacLeod, & Tata, 2000), we separated memory into specific memories (recalling a memory that happened on a particular day) and what we called general impression memories (a judgement of whether or not something has happened to you in the past), using similar cues to C. MacLeod and Campbell (1992). Speed of retrieval of the more judgement-like general impression memories did correlate with perceived likelihood of the events happening in the future, but speed to recall specific memories did not correlate with likelihood judgements.

Overall, there is little support for the influence of retrieval of actual memories on likelihood judgements for future events, consistent with Tversky and Kahneman's later emphasis on the simulation heuristic (Kahneman & Tversky, 1982). That is not to say that in individual instances ease of retrieval of a highly salient specific past instance will not be an important influence on future likelihood judgements. De Vito, Neroni, Gamboz, Della Salla, and Brandimonte (2015) found that when asked to think about specific positive and negative future episodes, participants were more likely to report that their negative future episodes were connected to a specific memory, indicating that negative memories may play a stronger role than positive memories in future-thinking. It has been argued that individual negative experiences have consistently greater impact than positive experiences (Baumeister, Bratslavsky, Finkenauer, & Vohs, 2001), supporting the idea that individual negative memories may have greater influence than positive memories on future-thinking, an intriguing idea but one in need of further investigation.

Chapter 6 will discuss the *constructive episodic simulation hypothesis* (Schacter & Addis, 2007), the central point of which is that thoughts about future personal episodes are usually assembled from the episodic elements of different past experiences. Consistent with Schacter and Addis's proposal, the simulation heuristic emphasizes the construction of novel future scenarios, and suggests that in the majority of instances where future events are being predicted, this constructive process will be active. Therefore, in thinking about future events memory does have an important role to play, but that role lies in facilitating the construction of future simulations through the retrieval of episodic information from a range of past experiences, not simply through recalling similar instances and using that retrieval as a guide to the future.

Imagery

Imagery is where someone experiences a mental representation of the same type that arises when an object or stimulus is actually present and perceived (Moulton & Kosslyn, 2011). Visual imagery is the most obvious type, but imagery can represent any sensory percepts. Thus, imagery contrasts with simulation, which emphasizes a verbally-based process of constructing scenarios, including causal thinking about connections between elements in the scenarios. It is worth noting that simulation and imagery are not mutually exclusive processes—simulations, as well as being built of sequential, causal thinking, can be imbued with images. As Moulton and Kosslyn (2011, p. 103) argue 'imagery and simulation are joined at the hip and should be studied together'. It is a challenge to study imagery, where often there is reliance on verbal description to understand a largely nonverbal phenomenon. In many studies, people are asked to form images and then rate those images on a range of variables, for example, vividness or how easy it was to think of the image. Images of past events that someone has directly experienced are perhaps more obvious sources of useful study and have received most attention (e.g. Holmes & Mathews, 2010), but it is also highly plausible that people are able to construct images of the future using perceptual representations garnered from past events and stored in long-term memory.

How do images of future events relate to anxiety and depression? Stöber (2000) asked student volunteer participants to form mental images of a range of positive and negative future events and asked them to rate how vivid and detailed the images were, as well as how quickly they formed them, all of which were highly correlated and combined to form, and ease of imagery score. Depression, and surprisingly, anxiety were both associated with low ease of positive imagery and only anxiety with ease of producing negative images. After controlling for the very high overlap of anxiety and depression (r > .70), however, anxiety correlated only with ease of negative imagery. Much of the experimental work on imagery emotional disorders has been conducted by Emily Holmes and her colleagues. Holmes, Lang, Moulds, and Steele (2008) found depression levels correlated with both high negative and low positive imagery vividness. Morina, Deeprose, Puswski, Schmid, and Holmes (2011), comparing depressed, anxious, and control groups, reported their depressed group to differ from controls only in lower vividness ratings for positive future images. The anxious group gave both higher vividness ratings for negative future event images and lower ratings for positive future events images, although it should be noted that the anxious sample was unusually low in positive affect, strangely, scoring even lower than the depressed patients. Clearly, mood is associated with self-reported image qualities for future positive and negative hypothetical events, but evidence on specificity of relationships is somewhat mixed. Depression does appear to be related reliably to low self-reported image quality (usually vividness) for positive events, whereas anxiety appears to be clearly linked to negative events, but beyond that the picture is less clear. Images about the future are also likely to be important in suicidality. Holmes, Crane, Fennell, and Williams (2007) interviewed depressed and formerly suicidal patients in remission and described frequently reported images directly related to future suicidal behaviour (e.g. images of jumping off a cliff or of their own funeral), a phenomenon that they labelled 'flash forward'.

One possibility is that images are used as a basis for subjective probability judgement. When someone thinks about the possibility of something happening to them, they form a mental image of it and the phenomenal quality of the image gives a guide to likelihood. So, for example, the agoraphobic person considering whether to make the trip to the shops in the face of mounting anxiety might experience a strong anticipatory image of becoming frozen with panic in the middle of the shopping centre and all the other shoppers staring at them. If such an image is vivid and comes to mind quickly that might be used as an indicator of likelihood, thereby increasing the person's reluctance to go out of the house. In contrast, for someone who is depressed, there may be an inability to form images of positive future events happening to them, in the way that other people are able to, which maintains or deepens their low mood and lack of motivation. In fact, a number of the studies that have manipulated subjective probability asked participants to imagine a scenario. However, as Levi and Pryor (1987) point out, such studies usually provide participants with detailed scenarios for them to image, which also contain reasons or explanations for the outcome. To try to separate effects of explanation-based thinking and simple imagery, Levi and Pryor (1987) asked participants to imagine an outcome, explain why an outcome would happen, or both explain and imagine the outcome. The latter two conditions showed an increase in perceived probability of the outcome, whereas simple imagining showed no effect. Such findings are consistent with the narrative simulation-type thinking emphasized by Kahneman and Tversky (1982). However, two caveats need to be inserted here. The first is that imagery may play an important role in expectancy of particular outcomes, especially where the outcome is highly personal, salient, and imageable. Given the greater power of negative events (Baumeister et al., 2001) and what is known about the impact of traumatic memories (McNally, 1997), it is possible that the role of imagery may be more marked for negative events. The second point to note is that it is unlikely, as alluded to earlier in this section, that verbally-based processes focused on future outcomes, proceed without imagery, and therefore imagery will have an important role to play in simulation, combined with explanation-based reasoning.

Summary of processes and mechanisms

Estimating the likelihood of future personal events is a complex task and typically full of uncertainty. Under these conditions, people tend to rely on heuristics, which often utilize how easily the outcome is simulated mentally. The simulation heuristic outlined by Kahneman and Tversky (1982) captures these processes of active scenario construction, where the ease of construction leads to judged likelihood. Imagery is likely to be an important part of these mental simulations, but a scenario does not simply consist of images; it contains narrative coherence and explanation-based thinking about how the event will occur. Memory retrieval is obviously crucial in simulation but probably plays its part through providing a source of episodic (and also semantic) information from a variety of past experiences, which is then combined to construct a new scenario. Mood-disturbed individuals show facilitated simulation of negative self-relevant future outcomes, and also show poorer counter simulation ability—being able to think of alternatives to the events occurring. More evidence needs to be accumulated on simulation of positive future outcomes and its relation to mood disturbance, as well as new methodologies developed to capture the complexities of the simulation process.

Anticipation

So far in this chapter, expectancies have been operationalized through subjective probability judgements—judgements of how likely an outcome is perceived to be, where participants are given lists of possible future outcomes and asked to rate their likelihood. Giving everyone the same items has the benefit of allowing easy comparison across participants and groups, but has its limitations. Some items will be relevant or salient to one person but not to another, even when efforts are made to pick a pool of items that are generally relevant to a particular participant group, such as students. Of course, people will make judgements when asked, but those judgements do not necessarily say anything about how salient or important these items are to the individuals involved. It is perfectly possible for someone to give a high or a low rating to an item but never to have given any real thought to that item happening. Obtaining likelihood judgements from someone on a range of supplied events does not necessarily provide a very clear insight into what day-to-day future-oriented thinking is like for that person. Intuitively, what would seem to matter is how likely people *actively* think things are going to happen to them and the linked issue of how important those things are to them personally.

Some empirical findings also support this divergence between supplied lists of future events and the kinds of thoughts for the future that people have naturally. Hepburn, Barnhofer, and Williams (2006) found that inducing positive or negative moods in participants affected subjective probability judgements but only for lists of provided events; there was no effect of mood induction on likelihood judgements for idiographic events in the future that people had previously volunteered themselves. Judgements of likelihood and value have been found to interact to predict worry for self-generated items (Berenbaum, Thompson, & Pomerantz, 2007) but similar effects were not found for a list of provided items (Bredemeier et al., 2012). In fact, the term 'expectancies' itself has a more active sense entailed in part of its definition: 'to regard as probable or imminent; to envisage; to anticipate'.[3] Subjective probability judgements assessing prediction of standard events on a list would not necessarily be sensitive to this more active anticipatory aspect of future-thinking. It is to this more active element of thinking about the future that the remainder of this chapter now turns.

Looking forward to and not looking forward to

While working for the UK Medical Research Council around 1990, Mark Williams and I were interested in trying to understand more about hopelessness, a way of thinking about the future that is characteristic of those who

---

[3] Oxford English Dictionary (3rd ed.). Retrieved from http://www.oed.com/view/Entry/66449#eid5044106.

are suicidal, and shown to be the particular element of depression that connects with suicidal thoughts and behaviour. Tim Beck's pioneering work in the 1970s and 1980s had led to a greater focus on hopelessness about the future as the active ingredient of depression that led to suicidality (e.g. Beck, Brown, Berchick, Stewart, & Steer, 1990). Measurement of hopelessness had relied largely on a self-report measure—the Beck Hopelessness Scale (BHS) (Beck, Weissman, Lester, & Trexler, 1974)—as a measure of hopelessness about the future. The BHS is a 20-item true/false self-report measure that assesses global outlook for the future (e.g. 'the future seems dark to me' or 'I look forward to the future with hope and enthusiasm', reversed scored). As such, hopelessness operationalized in this way is a very broad construct where someone reports on their general attitudes or orientation towards the future. We were interested in trying to develop ways of getting at the more specific thoughts people have about their own futures.

We developed two measures of future-thinking, one of which was based on the standard autobiographical memory task, where people are given word cues and asked to retrieve memories prompted by those words. This measure is described more fully in Chapter 6. The second measure—the Future-thinking Task (MacLeod, Rose, & Williams, 1993), also sometimes called the Future Fluency Task, emerged from pilot studies. Piloting had shown us that when people were invited to talk openly about the future in an unstructured way they often referred to things they were looking forward to or not looking forward to. D'Argembeau and colleagues have also reported that around 60% of naturally occurring thoughts about the future were valenced, rather than neutral, with about two-thirds of those being positive and one-third negative (D'Argembeau, Renaud, & Van der Linden, 2011).

In the Future-thinking Task people are asked to think separately of things in the future that they are looking forward to and not looking forward to, in various future time frames, for example, the next week or the next five to ten years. Like a standard verbal fluency measure, people are given a time limit, usually one minute for each condition (e.g. things they are not looking forward to in the next week) and have to say aloud as many examples as they can within the time limit. The role of the time limit is to ensure that people continue with the task rather than deciding very quickly that they cannot think of anything, which is especially important in those with low mood. The standard measure is the number of responses people are able to think of in each category, but additionally people can be re-presented with their responses and asked to make ratings of how likely they think they are to come about and how positive or negative they think they would feel if those outcomes happened. These likelihood and value ratings can be treated as separate variables or can be combined with number into a composite score. Table 2.3 shows verbatim responses of one general community participant from MacLeod and Conway (2005) and gives an idea of the sorts of responses that participants provide to the task.

A number of interesting findings have emerged from studies using the Future-thinking Task in a range of clinical and non-clinical participants. First, it is clear that positive thoughts about the future and negative thoughts about the future on this task are independent: the correlations between them are small to medium and are, in fact, positive, probably reflecting a general performance element to the task. Second, they each relate to well-being, which in itself is not surprising, but of more interest is how they relate uniquely to different aspects of well-being and mental health. These findings are reviewed in the remainder of this chapter. Unsurprisingly, participants also generate fewer responses the further the projected time period is into the future, and it is usually the case that any differences observed between groups are found consistently across the different time periods, from immediate future to long-term future. Participants are usually also administered the standard verbal fluency task (e.g. Lezak, Howieson, Bigler, & Tranel, 2012), generating words beginning with letters of the alphabet within a time limit, as a control for general fluency, but it rarely differs between clinical groups or correlates with mood, and shows little correlation with performance on the Future-thinking Task.

Table 2.3 Verbatim responses from one participant from a general community sample on the Future-thinking Task

Looking forward to	Not looking forward to
Next week	Next week
Going out on Friday and Saturday	Board meeting tonight
The weekend	New training course that I am leading
Mother-in-law coming out of hospital	
Half-term—spending time with the children	
Seeing a friend	
Time off work	
Next year	Next year
Daughter starting new school	40 in November
A party in November	Husband has big court case in new year
Christmas	Aggravation with son's homework/exams
Holiday	
Next 5–10 years	Next 5–10 years
Having more free time	Concerns related to children's education
Job developing—career	Parents' possible bereavement
Parents' golden wedding anniversary	

Suicidality and hopelessness

A number of studies have used the task with suicidal participants. Suicidal participants are usually recruited from those presenting to hospital following an episode of deliberate self-harm, normally an overdose. They are seen and tested following the episode, often within 24 hours, in an attempt to capture their thinking as closely as possible to the suicidal state that they experienced. Controls are recruited either from people presenting to the hospital with minor conditions, for example, sports injuries, in order to control for the setting, or are recruited from the general population. When starting the work, we were unsure of exactly what to expect. We thought that suicidal individuals would differ from non-suicidal controls, but didn't know whether to expect more negative, fewer positive, or a mix of more negative and fewer positive responses. The most striking finding is that those who are suicidal show a reduced ability to generate positive future events but show no increase in the number of negative future events they anticipate. For example, MacLeod et al. (1993) found that whereas the groups did not differ on the negative condition, the suicidal participants averaged around only two-thirds of the number of positive future thoughts given by the control participants. Five studies comparing suicidal and non-suicidal participants have found the pattern of reduced positivity in the absence of increased negativity (Conaghan & Davidson, 2002; Hunter & O'Connor, 2003; MacLeod, Pankhania, Lee, & Mitchell, 1997a; MacLeod, Tata, Evans, Tyrer, Schmidt et al., 1998; MacLeod et al., 1993); the one study that has found no difference between groups on either positive or negative future-thinking had low statistical power and reported that their control group included intravenous drug users, who may not have constituted a very clear comparison group (O'Connor, Connery, & Cheyne, 2000). Additionally, those meeting criteria for a Cluster B personality disorder, which is associated with higher levels of suicidal behaviour (e.g. Isometsä, Henriksson, Heikkinen, Aro, Marttunen et al., 1996), show reduced positive future-thinking and equivalent levels of negative future-thinking when compared with other personality disorder types (MacLeod, Tata, Tyrer, Schmidt, Davidson et al., 2004).

Further support for the particular importance of positive future-thinking in suicidality comes from studies that have correlated self-reported hopelessness about the future with positive and negative future-thinking. At least nine studies have reported correlations of self-reported hopelessness with responses on the Future-thinking Task. The results are remarkably consistent, and are summarized in Table 2.4. In eight of the studies, high BHS scores were significantly correlated with having fewer positive thoughts. The one study that did not find an effect was the only study using a student sample (O'Connor &

Table 2.4 Correlations of Beck Hopelessness Scale (BHS) scores with positive and negative future-thinking on the Future-thinking Task in studies identified as reporting the relevant correlations. Positive future-thinking correlates consistently with BHS scores whereas negative future-thinking does not

Study	Sample	Positive	Negative
Conaghan & Davidson (2002)	Older adults (*N* = 66)	−.31*	−.15
Hunter & O'Connor (2003)	DSH (*N* = 22)	−.45*	.07
MacLeod et al. (1997a)	DSH (*N* = 44)	−.37**	.01
MacLeod et al. (1993)	DSH (*N* = 24)	−.48**	.06
MacLeod et al. (2005)	DSH (*N* = 441)	−.35***	.17**
O'Connor & Cassidy (2007)	Students (*N* = 121)	.09	.21*
O'Connor et al. (2000)	DSH (*N* = 20)	−.43*	−.02
O'Connor et al. (2008)	DSH (*N* = 144)	−.34***	−.01
Sidley et al. (1999)	DSH (*N* = 66)	−.49***	.11

Note: DSH = deliberate self-harm.

Beck, A. (1988). Beck hopelessness scale (BHS) San Antonio, TX: Pearson.

Cassidy, 2007). In contrast, only two of the nine studies reported significant correlations between BHS scores and negative future-thinking, one of which was the student study by O'Connor and Cassidy (2007). The other study showing a relationship between negative future-thinking and BHS scores (MacLeod, Tata, Tyrer, Schmidt, Davidson et al., 2005) had a very large sample size, the correlation was relatively small and was significantly smaller than the correlation of BHS with positive future-thinking.

Rory O'Connor and his colleagues have also carried out several longitudinal studies looking at the power of future-thinking to predict outcomes known to be related to suicidality—levels of suicidal intent, levels of self-reported hopelessness, and repetition of attempts. O'Connor, Fraser, Whyte, McHale, and Masterton (2008) followed up 144 attempters for up to two and a half months after discharge. All participants had at least one previous episode prior to the episode that resulted in them being recruited into the study. The Future-thinking Task, along with a number of other measures, was administered when the participants were first seen, normally within 24 hours of the episode. Positive future-thinking predicted suicide ideation at follow-up, controlling not only for initial levels of ideation but also for self-reported hopelessness. This latter finding is consistent with Hunter and O'Connor (2003) who reported that positive future-thinking added significantly to BHS scores in being able to discriminate between suicidal and control participants. However, it should be noted that Sidley, Calam, Wells, Hughes, and Whitaker (1999) also followed up a sample of high-risk attempters, over a period of 12 months and found that positive future-thinking did not predict further suicidal behaviour, albeit in a smaller sample ($N = 36$).

There is some indication that the particular content of positive future thoughts might matter. O'Connor, Smyth, and Williams (2015), using a coding scheme from Godley, Tchanturia, MacLeod, and Schmidt (2001) examined the content of the positive thoughts about the future in a large sample of deliberate self-harm (DSH) patients, using the positive condition of the Future-thinking Task. Those who later went on to repeat DSH over the next 15 months reported a relatively higher number of intrapersonal, positive future thoughts, compared to non-repeaters, and fewer financial- and achievement-related thoughts. Intrapersonal thoughts refer to responses that are about an internal state of the self (e.g. 'being more relaxed'). This effect held even when controlling for a history of previous attempts and suicidal ideation, both known predictors of future suicidal behaviour.

To summarize, the evidence strongly points to suicidal patients as having a deficit in being able to think of things they are looking forward to, in the absence of any increase in things that they are not looking forward to. The importance of positive future-thinking to suicidality is further reinforced by its consistent correlations with self-reported hopelessness, which appears to be unrelated to negative future-thinking.

Depression and anxiety

As indicated throughout this chapter, there has been considerable interest in understanding how future-directed thinking is implicated in anxiety and depression and whether there is specificity between the type of future-thinking difficulty and the type of emotional disturbance. Taking anxiety first, the outcomes from studies using the Future-thinking Task are clear. Anxious patients (MacLeod et al., 1997c), sub-clinically anxious students (MacLeod & Byrne, 1996), and high-scoring anxious adolescents (Miles, MacLeod, & Pote, 2004) all show increased negative anticipation at the same time as having comparable levels of positive anticipation to controls. The picture for depression is also fairly clear. Depressed participants, compared to non-depressed controls, have consistently shown reduced positive anticipation, whether they are students scoring highly on self-reported depression (Kosnes, Whelan, O'Donovan, & McHugh, 2013) or are clinically depressed patients (Bjärehed, Sarkohi, & Andersson, 2010; Lavender & Watkins, 2004; MacLeod & Salaminiou, 2001; MacLeod et al., 1997b), including clinically depressed older adults (Conaghan & Davidson, 2002). Moore, MacLeod, Barnes, and Langdon (2006) also reported that depressed multiple sclerosis patients scored lower on positive anticipation than non-depressed multiple sclerosis patients. Critically, in all of these cases, the reduced positive anticipation was observed in the presence of no increased negative anticipation. Figure 2.2 illustrates the typical finding.

Not every study has shown this neat depressive pattern. MacLeod and Byrne (1996) reported that a student sample meeting diagnostic criteria for both anxiety and depression showed increased negative and reduced positive expectancies, although that might be expected given their elevation in both anxiety and depression. Miles et al. (2004) in their non-clinical adolescent sample found that depression levels were related to increased negative anticipation but not to reduced positive anticipation. Nevertheless, the results, overall, point strongly to reduced positive anticipation being linked to depression and increased negative anticipation to anxiety. This conclusion is further reinforced by findings of depression correlating with positive but not negative future-thinking, and anxiety showing the opposite pattern (Godley et al., 2001; MacLeod et al., 1997c).

Both those who are suicidal and those who are depressed show a similar pattern of reduced positivity without increased negativity. Clearly, depression and suicidality overlap, although the majority of those who are depressed are not

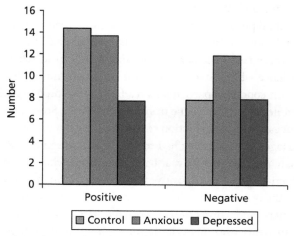

Figure 2.2 Anxious, depressed, and control participant scores for positive and negative future-thinking on the Future-thinking Task. Relative to controls, anxious patients show only increased negative future-thinking, whereas depressed patients show only reduced positive future-thinking.

Retrospective and prospective cognitions in anxiety and depression, MacLeod, A. K., Tata, P., Kentish, J., & Jacobsen, H., *Cognition and Emotion*, 1997, Routledge, reprinted by permission of the publisher (Taylor & Francis Ltd, http://www.tandfonline.com).

suicidal, and many who are suicidal would not meet criteria for a depressive disorder (MacLeod, 2013). Two studies addressed the separation. Conaghan and Davidson (2002) tested two groups of depressed older adults, who were either suicidal or not, as well as a community non-depressed group. Both depressed groups showed reduced positive future-thinking in comparison to the community controls and did not differ from each other. Coming at the question from the other direction, MacLeod et al. (1997a) found that both depressed and non-depressed suicidal individuals generated fewer positive future events than controls but, again, did not differ from each other. It would appear that being depressed and being in a suicidal state of mind show both are sufficient for reduced positive future-thinking.

Finally, further evidence of divergence comes from three studies (MacLeod & Conway, 2005; MacLeod et al., 1997c; Miles et al., 2004) showing that positive future-thinking assessed by the Future-thinking Task correlates significantly with PA and negative future-thinking with NA, whereas the cross-correlations are weak or non-significant. These correlations mirror the sort of two-system view that was outlined earlier in this chapter (See Table 2.1).

Changes in anticipation

Anticipation of future positive and negative events is not necessarily fixed. Two ways that the mutability of such cognitions have been examined is through experimental manipulations and treatment studies. Treatment studies will be discussed in Chapter 10. Hepburn et al. (2006) manipulated mood in a sample of university volunteer participants by getting them to read self-statements of increasing valence while listening to mood congruent music. In the positive mood induction condition participants read a series of progressively uplifting statements while listening to Gigue from Corelli's Violin Sonata no. 5 op. 9; for those in the negative mood induction condition, their statements were progressively depressogenic, which they had to read while listening to Russia Under the Mongolian Yoke by Prokofiev, at half speed! Somewhat unexpectedly, the negative induction led to fewer positive future thoughts on the Future-thinking Task whereas the positive induction produced fewer negative responses. Jong-Meyer, Kuczmera, and Tripp (2007) reported different results with a group of adolescent inpatients who met criteria for a variety of diagnoses but mainly anxiety and depression. After a negative mood induction, participants reported significantly more negative than positive events, and after a positive mood induction there was a trend to produce more positive than negative events.

Thus, it would appear that the ability to think of things looked forward to or not looked forward to, is sensitive to mood, or at least to immediate, experimentally-induced changes in mood. Williams, Van der Does, Barnhofer,

Crane, and Segal (2008) went further in attempting to identify particular individuals who would be most vulnerable to such changes, especially to reductions in positive future-thinking. Before receiving a negative mood induction, participants rated to what extent they usually experienced feelings of hopelessness when in a negative mood, using the Leiden Index of Depression Sensitivity (LEIDS; Van der Does, 2002). The idea here is that it is not simply being in a negative mood that is problematic; rather, that the level of psychological distress will depend on the sorts of thoughts that become activated while in that mood state. Such thoughts might only be activated in that mood state. Following a negative mood induction, high scorers on the LEIDS hopelessness measure showed the greatest loss of positive future-thinking, an effect that was independent of depression.

Similar sorts of effects were reported by O'Connor and Williams (2014), where those who reported generally high levels of brooding showed the greatest reductions in positive future-thinking following a negative mood induction. In a second study, participants were given a negative mood induction and some (particularly unfortunate) participants were also then given a defeat/failure task (e.g. asked to complete anagrams that were, in fact, unsolvable, whilst others completed solvable anagrams). Following the 'double dip' of negative mood induction and task failure, those who had earlier reported feelings of entrapment (often feeling trapped) showed the effect—greater reduction in positive future-thinking compared to those in the other conditions. Again, this effect was independent of depressive symptoms. These results suggest that certain self-reported general characteristics—brooding, feeling trapped, feeling hopeless when in a low mood—indicate vulnerability to loss of positive thoughts under challenges such as low mood or task failure (which is also likely to lower mood). It is not clear whether these labels represent different vulnerabilities or, as seems more likely, are all zeroing in on the same underlying vulnerability.

The propensity to have positive thoughts that are about the self, reported by O'Connor et al. (2015), was mentioned earlier in the chapter as a risk factor for repetition of suicidal behaviour. The tendency to produce self-focused positive thoughts may be an indicator of an internally-focused style that, at least in some people, is associated with poorer well-being and mental health. This interpretation would also explain the fact that Lavender and Watkins (2004) found depressed participants given a rumination task, compared to those given a distraction task, subsequently showed higher Future-thinking Task scores in both negative and positive conditions of the task. These authors did not assess the content of the thoughts produced, but the unexpected increase in positive future-thoughts following rumination may have been accounted for by a preponderance of thoughts related to internal aspects of the self, especially those connected with feeling states.

Mechanisms

Along with colleagues, I have explored a number of mechanisms that might underlie lack of positive future-thinking. The first idea we explored was whether there might be a general cognitive block in being able to think of the sorts of things that people enjoy in the future, meaning that some people are unable to think of possibilities that they themselves might enjoy—a sort of semantic blankness about possible future positive events. To address this question, Clare Conway and I (MacLeod & Conway, 2007) asked suicidal and non-suicidal participants to complete the usual task of thinking of things they were looking forward to, but also asked them to complete the task for what they thought other people would say when participating in the study. The groups differed in the usual way in self-ratings but did not differ in ratings for others—the suicidal group in that situation was as able as controls to think of future positive responses. Clearly, there is no overall semantic type difficulty in generating positive future thoughts, but there is a deficit when those thoughts have to be applied to themselves. A second possibility is that those who are depressed or suicidal have lost their ability to derive enjoyment from the sorts of things that people normally enjoy. Therefore, when asked what they are looking forward to they do not give potential future positive events because, although they can think of them, they don't think they will enjoy them, so they just don't qualify as things they are looking forward to. In a study with depressed inpatients, Eva Salaminiou and I (MacLeod & Salaminiou, 2001) assessed how much enjoyment depressed and non-depressed participants said they would derive from future positive events (both their own and those from a standard list). Although the groups differed on anticipated enjoyment levels, the difference between them on the number of looked-forward-to experiences people generated was still highly significant when anticipated enjoyment was controlled for. A third possibility is that people who are low on things they are looking forward to can think of the sorts of events that they might enjoy in the future, and think they would enjoy them, albeit at a reduced level, but just don't think those things are going to happen to them. They do not give those responses as things they are looking forward to because to look forward to something means that you think it is going to happen, or at least has a reasonable chance of happening. Suicidal individuals, not surprisingly, rate the likelihood as lower even for things they say they are looking forward to, compared to the ratings that non-suicidal participants give for their looked-forward-to items. Those in the general population who are low in well-being (MacLeod & Conway, 2005), as well as those who are suicidal (Vincent, Boddana, & MacLeod, 2004), show poorer planning ability to achieve their goals or what it is that they are looking forward to. These findings are discussed in more detail in Chapter 8, but planning appears to be one way of providing a sense that desired future outcomes will be achieved. A planning deficit would lead to low sense of likelihood of future positive outcomes, hence less to look forward to. Finally, two other enabling factors—having a more restricted social network and having a lower household income—are also related to having less to look forward to (MacLeod & Conway, 2005), indicating that a range of variables, including social and economic factors, are implicated in the sort of deficit in positive anticipation shown by those who are low in well-being, depressed, or suicidal.

Summary of anticipation

Evidence about what people are actively anticipating in the future comes from asking them about what they are looking forward to or not looking forward to. Consistent with theory and evidence from other measures (see Chapter 1) more of these thoughts are about the near than distant future and there are more positive than negative thoughts. In fact, the ratio of about two-thirds positive to negative thoughts is the same as found in naturally occurring future-thoughts (D'Argembeau et al., 2011). A lack of positive thoughts about the future is related to depression, suicidality, hopelessness, and low PA, and some individuals appear to be particularly prone to loss of positive future thoughts when in a low mood. In contrast, increased negative future-thinking appears to be specific to anxiety and elevated NA. Many factors will contribute to loss of positive future-thinking, including cognitive, affective, social and economic factors. Low belief in the likelihood of future positive experiences combined with lack of being able to see how to achieve those outcomes is one key factor, and will be returned to in Chapter 8.

References

Alter, A. L. & Oppenheimer, D. M. (2009). Uniting the tribes of fluency to form a metacognitive nation. *Personality and Social Psychology Review*, 13(3), 219–235. http://doi.org/10.1177/1088868309341564

Baumeister, R. F., Bratslavsky, E., Finkenauer, C., & Vohs, K. D. (2001). Bad is stronger than good. *Review of General Psychology*, 5(4), 323–370. http://doi.org/10.1037/1089-2680.5.4.323

Beck, A. T. (1976). *Cognitive therapy and the emotional disorders*. Madison, CT: International Universities Press.

Beck, A. T., Brown, G., Berchick, R. J., Stewart, B. L., & Steer, R. A. (1990). Relationship between hopelessness and ultimate suicide: A replication with psychiatric outpatients. *The American Journal of Psychiatry*, 147(2), 190–195.

Beck, A. T., Weissman, A., Lester, D., & Trexler, L. (1974). The measurement of pessimism: The Hopelessness Scale. *Journal of Consulting and Clinical Psychology*, **42**(6), 861–865. http://doi.org/doi.org/10.1037/h0037562

Bennett, K. & Corcoran, R. (2010). Biases in everyday reasoning: Associations with subclinical anxiety, depression and paranoia. *Psychosis*, **2**(3), 227–237. http://doi.org/10.1080/17522431003592649

Bentz, B. G., Mahaffey, S. L., Adami, A. M., Romig, D. M., Muenke, R. C., Barfield, S. G., ... DeOrnellas, K. (2009). Debiasing of pessimistic judgments associated with anxiety: A test of the availability heuristic. *Journal of Psychopathology and Behavioral Assessment*, **31**(1), 20–26. http://doi.org/10.1007/s10862-008-9090-4

Berenbaum, H., Thompson, R. J., & Pomerantz, E. M. (2007). The relation between worrying and concerns: The importance of perceived probability and cost. *Behaviour Research and Therapy*, **45**(2), 301–311. http://doi.org/10.1016/j.brat.2006.03.009

Bjärehed, J., Sarkohi, A., & Andersson, G. (2010). Less positive or more negative? Future-directed thinking in mild to moderate depression. *Cognitive Behaviour Therapy*, **39**(1), 37–45. http://doi.org/10.1080/16506070902966926

Bredemeier, K., Berenbaum, H., & Spielberg, J. M. (2012). Worry and perceived threat of proximal and distal undesirable outcomes. *Journal of Anxiety Disorders*, **26**(3), 425–429. http://doi.org/10.1016/j.janxdis.2012.01.001

Brown, G. P., MacLeod, A. K., Tata, P., & Goddard, L. (2002). Worry and the simulation of future outcomes. *Anxiety, Stress & Coping: An International Journal*, **15**(1), 1–17. http://doi.org/doi.org/10.1080/10615800290007254

Butler, G. & Mathews, A. (1983). Cognitive processes in anxiety. *Advances in Behaviour Research & Therapy*, **5**(1), 51–62. http://doi.org/doi.org/10.1016/0146-6402(83)90015-2

Butler, G. & Mathews, A. (1987). Anticipatory anxiety and risk perception. *Cognitive Therapy and Research*, **11**(5), 551–565. http://doi.org/doi.org/10.1007/BF01183858

Cabeleira, C. M., Steinman, S. A., Burgess, M. M., Bucks, R. S., MacLeod, C., Melo, W., & Teachman, B. A. (2014). Expectancy bias in anxious samples. *Emotion*, **14**(3), 588–601. http://doi.org/10.1037/a0035899

Clark, L. A. & Watson, D. (1991). Tripartite model of anxiety and depression: Psychometric evidence and taxonomic implications. *Journal of Abnormal Psychology*, **100**(3), 316–336. http://doi.org/10.1037/0021-843X.100.3.316

Conaghan, S. & Davidson, K. M. (2002). Hopelessness and the anticipation of positive and negative future experiences in older parasuicidal adults. *British Journal of Clinical Psychology*, **41**(3), 233–242. http://doi.org/doi.org/10.1348/014466502760379208

Corcoran, R., Cummins, S., Rowse, G., Moore, R., Blackwood, N., Howard, R., & Bentall, R. P. (2006). Reasoning under uncertainty: heuristic judgments in patients with persecutory delusions or depression. *Psychological Medicine*, **36**(8), 1109. http://doi.org/10.1017/S003329170600794X

Cropley, M., MacLeod, A. K., & Tata, P. (2000). Memory retrieval and subjective probability judgements in control and depressed participants. *Clinical Psychology & Psychotherapy*, **7**(5), 367–378. http://doi.org/10.1002/1099-0879(200011)7:5<367::AID-CPP249>3.0.CO;2-H

D'Argembeau, A., Renaud, O., & Van der Linden, M. (2011). Frequency, characteristics and functions of future-oriented thoughts in daily life. *Applied Cognitive Psychology*, **25**(1), 96–103. http://doi.org/10.1002/acp.1647

de Vito, S., Neroni, M. A., Gamboz, N., Della Sala, S., & Brandimonte, M. A. (2015). Desirable and undesirable future thoughts call for different scene construction processes. *The Quarterly Journal of Experimental Psychology*, **68**(1), 75–82. http://doi.org/10.1080/ 17470218.2014.937448

Depue, R. A. & Iacono, W. G. (1989). Neurobehavioral aspects of affective disorders. *Annual Review of Psychology*, **40**, 457–492. http://doi.org/10.1146/annurev.ps.40.020189.002325

Eccles, J. S. & Wigfield, A. (2002). Motivational beliefs, values, and goals. *Annual Review of Psychology*, **53**(1), 109–132. http://doi.org/http://dx.doi.org/10.1146/annurev. psych.53.100901.135153

Fowles, D. C. (1994). A motivational theory of psychopathology. In W. D. Spaulding (Ed.), *Integrative views of motivation, cognition, and emotion.* (pp. 181–238). Lincoln, NE, US: University of Nebraska Press.

Godley, J., Tchanturia, K., MacLeod, A. K., & Schmidt, U. (2001). Future-directed thinking in eating disorders. *British Journal of Clinical Psychology*, **40**(3), 281–295. http://doi.org/ http://dx.doi.org/10.1348/014466501163698

Gray, J. A. (1990). Brain systems that mediate both emotion and cognition. *Cognition and Emotion*, **4**(3), 269–288. http://doi.org/10.1080/02699939008410799

Hepburn, S. R., Barnhofer, T., & Williams, J. M. G. (2006). Effects of mood on how future events are generated and perceived. *Personality and Individual Differences*, **41**(5), 801–811. http://doi.org/10.1016/j.paid.2006.03.022

Holmes, E. A., Crane, C., Fennell, M. J. V., & Williams, J. M. G. (2007). Imagery about suicide in depression—'Flash-forwards'? *Journal of Behavior Therapy and Experimental Psychiatry*, **38**(4), 423–434. http://doi.org/10.1016/j.jbtep.2007.10.004

Holmes, E. A., Lang, T. J., Moulds, M. L., & Steele, A. M. (2008). Prospective and positive mental imagery deficits in dysphoria. *Behaviour Research and Therapy*, **46**(8), 976–981. http://doi.org/10.1016/j.brat.2008.04.009

Holmes, E. A. & Mathews, A. (2010). Mental imagery in emotion and emotional disorders. *Clinical Psychology Review*, **30**(3), 349–362. http://doi.org/10.1016/j.cpr.2010.01.001

Hunter, E. C. & O'Connor, R. C. (2003). Hopelessness and future thinking in parasuicide: The role of perfectionism. *British Journal of Clinical Psychology*, **42**(4), 355–365. http://doi.org/http://doi.org/10.1348/014466503322528900

Isometsä, E. T., Henriksson, M. M., Heikkinen, M. E., Aro, H. M., Marttunen, M. J., Kuoppasalmi, K. I., & Lönnqvist, J. K. (1996). Suicide among subjects with personality disorders. *The American Journal of Psychiatry*, **153**(5), 667–673.

Janssen, E., van Osch, L., Lechner, L., Candel, M., & de Vries, H. (2012). Thinking versus feeling: Differentiating between cognitive and affective components of perceived cancer risk. *Psychology & Health*, **27**(7), 767–783. http://doi.org/10.1080/08870446.2011.580846

Johnson, S. L., Eisner, L. R., & Carver, C. S. (2009). Elevated expectancies among persons diagnosed with bipolar disorder. *British Journal of Clinical Psychology*, **48**(2), 217–222. http://doi.org/10.1348/014466509X414655

Jong-Meyer, R., Kuczmera, A., & Tripp, J. (2007). The impact of mood induction on the accessibility of positive and negative future events in a group of dysphoric adolescent in-patients. *British Journal of Clinical Psychology*, **46**(3), 371–376. http://doi.org/10.1348/ 014466507X182277

Kagan, L. J., MacLeod, A. K., & Pote, H. L. (2004). Accessibility of causal explanations for future positive and negative events in adolescents with anxiety and depression. *Clinical Psychology & Psychotherapy*, **11**(3), 177–186. http://doi.org/10.1002/cpp.407

Kahneman, D. & Tversky, A. (1982). The simulation heuristic. In D. Kahneman, P. Slovic, & A. Tversky (Eds.), *Judgement under uncertainty: Heuristics and biases.* (pp. 201–208). New York, NY, US: Cambridge University Press.

Kosnes, L., Whelan, R., O'Donovan, A., & McHugh, L. A. (2013). Implicit measurement of positive and negative future thinking as a predictor of depressive symptoms and hopelessness. *Consciousness and Cognition*, **22**(3), 898–912. http://doi.org/10.1016/j.concog.2013.06.001

Lavender, A. & Watkins, E. (2004). Rumination and future thinking in depression. *British Journal of Clinical Psychology*, **43**(2), 129–142. http://doi.org/10.1348/014466504323088015

Levi, A. S. & Pryor, J. B. (1987). Use of the availability heuristic in probability estimates of future events: The effects of imagining outcomes versus imagining reasons. *Organizational Behavior and Human Decision Processes*, **40**(2), 219–234. http://doi.org/10.1016/0749-5978(87)90013-6

Lezak, M. D., Howieson, D. B., Bigler, E. D., & Tranel, D. (2012). *Neuropsychological assessment* (5th edition). Oxford; New York: Oxford University Press, USA.

MacLeod, A. K. (2013). Suicide and attempted suicide. In M. Power & M. (Ed) Power (Eds.), *The Wiley-Blackwell handbook of mood disorders (2nd ed.).* (pp. 413–431). Chichester: Wiley-Blackwell.

MacLeod, A. K. & Byrne, A. (1996). Anxiety, depression, and the anticipation of future positive and negative experiences. *Journal of Abnormal Psychology*, **105**(2), 286–289. http://doi.org/10.1037/0021-843X.105.2.286

MacLeod, A. K., Byrne, A., & Valentine, J. D. (1996). Affect, emotional disorder, and future-directed thinking. *Cognition and Emotion*, **10**(1), 69–85. http://doi.org/10.1080/026999396380394

MacLeod, A. K. & Conway, C. (2005). Well-being and the anticipation of future positive experiences: The role of income, social networks, and planning ability. *Cognition & Emotion*, **19**(3), 357–374. http://doi.org/10.1080/02699930441000247

MacLeod, A. K & Conway, C. (2007). Well-being and positive future thinking for the self versus others. *Cognition & Emotion*, **21**(5), 1114–1124. http://doi.org/10.1080/02699930601109507

MacLeod, A. K. & Cropley, M. L. (1995). Depressive future-thinking: The role of valence and specificity. *Cognitive Therapy and Research*, **19**(1), 35–50. http://doi.org/10.1007/BF02229675

MacLeod, A. K., Pankhania, B., Lee, M., & Mitchell, D. (1997a). Parasuicide, depression and the anticipation of positive and negative future experiences. *Psychological Medicine*, **27**(4), 973–977. http://doi.org/10.1017/S003329179600459X

MacLeod, A. K., Rose, G. S., & Williams, J. M. G. (1993). Components of hopelessness about the future in parasuicide. *Cognitive Therapy and Research*, **17**(5), 441–455. http://doi.org/10.1007/BF01173056

MacLeod, A. K. & Salaminiou, E. (2001). Reduced positive future-thinking in depression: Cognitive and affective factors. *Cognition and Emotion*, **15**(1), 99–107. http://doi.org/10.1080/0269993004200006

MacLeod, A. K. & Tarbuck, A. F. (1994). Explaining why negative events will happen to oneself: Parasuicides are pessimistic because they can't see any reason not to be. *British Journal of Clinical Psychology*, **33**(3), 317–326. http://doi.org/10.1111/j.2044-8260.1994.tb01127.x

MacLeod, A. K., Tata, P., Evans, K., Tyrer, P., Schmidt, U., Davidson, K., ... Catalan, J. (1998). Recovery of positive future thinking within a high-risk parasuicide group: Results from a pilot randomized controlled trial. *British Journal of Clinical Psychology*, 37(4), 371–379. http://doi.org/10.1111/j.2044-8260.1998.tb01394.x

MacLeod, A. K., Tata, P., Kentish, J., Carroll, F., & Hunter, E. (1997b). Anxiety, depression, and explanation-based pessimism for future positive and negative events. *Clinical Psychology & Psychotherapy*, 4(1), 15–24. http://doi.org/10.1002/(SICI)1099-0879(199703)4:1<15:AID-CPP112>3.0.CO;2-#

MacLeod, A. K., Tata, P., Kentish, J., & Jacobsen, H. (1997c). Retrospective and prospective cognitions in anxiety and depression. *Cognition and Emotion*, 11(4), 467–479. http://doi.org/10.1080/026999397379881

MacLeod, A. K., Tata, P., Tyrer, P., Schmidt, U., Davidson, K., & Thompson, S. (2004). Personality disorder and future-directed thinking in parasuicide. *Journal of Personality Disorders*, 18(5), 459–466. http://doi.org/10.1521/pedi.18.5.459.51329

MacLeod, A. K., Tata, P., Tyrer, P., Schmidt, U., Davidson, K., & Thompson, S. (2005). Hopelessness and positive and negative future thinking in parasuicide. *British Journal of Clinical Psychology*, 44(4), 495–504. http://doi.org/10.1348/014466505X35704

MacLeod, A. K., Williams, J. M., & Bekerian, D. A. (1991). Worry is reasonable: The role of explanations in pessimism about future personal events. *Journal of Abnormal Psychology*, 100(4), 478–486. http://doi.org/10.1037/0021-843X.100.4.478

MacLeod, C. & Campbell, L. (1992). Memory accessibility and probability judgments: An experimental evaluation of the availability heuristic. *Journal of Personality and Social Psychology*, 63(6), 890–902. http://doi.org/10.1037/0022-3514.63.6.890

Marroquín, B., Nolen-Hoeksema, S., & Miranda, R. (2013). Escaping the future: Affective forecasting in escapist fantasy and attempted suicide. *Journal of Social and Clinical Psychology*, 32(4), 446–463. http://doi.org/10.1521/jscp.2013.32.4.446

McDowell, M. E., Occhipinti, S., & Chambers, S. K. (2013). The influence of family history on cognitive heuristics, risk perceptions, and prostate cancer screening behavior. *Health Psychology*, 32(11), 1158–1169. http://doi.org/10.1037/a0031622

McNally, R. J. (1997). Implicit and explicit memory for trauma-related information in PTSD. *Annals of the New York Academy of Sciences*, 821(1), 219–224. http://doi.org/DOI: 10.1111/j.1749-6632.1997.tb48281.x

Miles, H., MacLeod, A. K., & Pote, H. (2004). Retrospective and prospective cognitions in adolescents: anxiety, depression, and positive and negative affect. *Journal of Adolescence*, 27(6), 691–701. http://doi.org/10.1016/j.adolescence.2004.04.001

Miranda, R., Fontes, M., & Marroquín, B. (2008). Cognitive content-specificity in future expectancies: Role of hopelessness and intolerance of uncertainty in depression and GAD symptoms. *Behaviour Research and Therapy*, 46(10), 1151–1159. http://doi.org/10.1016/j.brat.2008.05.009

Miranda, R. & Mennin, D. S. (2007). Depression, generalized anxiety disorder, and certainty in pessimistic predictions about the future. *Cognitive Therapy and Research*, 31(1), 71–82. http://doi.org/10.1007/s10608-006-9063-4

Moore, A. C., MacLeod, A. K., Barnes, D., & Langdon, D. W. (2006). Future-directed thinking and depression in relapsing-remitting multiple sclerosis. *British Journal of Health Psychology*, 11(4), 663–675. http://doi.org/10.1348/135910705X85781

Morina, N., Deeprose, C., Pusowski, C., Schmid, M., & Holmes, E. A. (2011). Prospective mental imagery in patients with major depressive disorder or anxiety disorders. *Journal of Anxiety Disorders*, 25(8), 1032–1037. http://doi.org/10.1016/j.janxdis.2011.06.012

Moulton, S. T. & Kosslyn, S. M. (2011). Imagining predictions: Mental imagery as mental emulation. In M. Bar (Ed.), *Predictions in the brain: Using our past to generate a future.* (pp. 95–106). New York: Oxford University Press.

Nagengast, B., Marsh, H. W., Scalas, L. F., Xu, M. K., Hau, K.-T., & Trautwein, U. (2011). Who took the 'x' out of expectancy-value theory?: A psychological mystery, a substantive-methodological synergy, and a cross-national generalization. *Psychological Science*, 22(8), 1058–1066. http://doi.org/10.1177/0956797611415540

O'Connor, R. C. & Cassidy, C. (2007). Predicting hopelessness: The interaction between optimism/pessimism and specific future expectancies. *Cognition & Emotion*, 21(3), 596–613. http://doi.org/10.1080/02699930600813422

O'Connor, R. C., Connery, H., & Cheyne, W. M. (2000). Hopelessness: The role of depression, future directed thinking and cognitive vulnerability. *Psychology, Health & Medicine*, 5(2), 155–161. http://doi.org/10.1080/713690188

O'Connor, R. C., Fraser, L., Whyte, M.-C., MacHale, S., & Masterton, G. (2008). A comparison of specific positive future expectancies and global hopelessness as predictors of suicidal ideation in a prospective study of repeat self-harmers. *Journal of Affective Disorders*, 110(3), 207–214. http://doi.org/10.1016/j.jad.2008.01.008

O'Connor, R. C., Smyth, R., & Williams, J. M. G. (2015). Intrapersonal positive future thinking predicts repeat suicide attempts in hospital-treated suicide attempters. *Journal of Consulting and Clinical Psychology*, 83(1), 169–176. http://doi.org/10.1037/a0037846

O'Connor, R. C. & Williams, J. M. G. (2014). The relationship between positive future thinking, brooding, defeat and entrapment. *Personality and Individual Differences*, 70, 29–34. http://doi.org/10.1016/j.paid.2014.06.016

Peters, M. L., Flink, I. K., Boersma, K., & Linton, S. J. (2010). Manipulating optimism: Can imagining a best possible self be used to increase positive future expectancies? *The Journal of Positive Psychology*, 5(3), 204–211. http://doi.org/10.1080/17439761003790963

Pyszczynski, T., Holt, K., & Greenberg, J. (1987). Depression, self-focused attention, and expectancies for positive and negative future life events for self and others. *Journal of Personality and Social Psychology*, 52(5), 994–1001. http://doi.org/10.1037/0022-3514.52.5.994

Raune, D., MacLeod, A., & Holmes, E. A. (2005). The simulation heuristic and visual imagery in pessimism for future negative events in anxiety. *Clinical Psychology & Psychotherapy*, 12(4), 313–325. http://doi.org/10.1002/cpp.455

Schacter, D. L. & Addis, D. R. (2007). The cognitive neuroscience of constructive memory: Remembering the past and imagining the future. *Philosophical Transactions of the Royal Society of London (B)*, 362, 773–786. http://doi.org/10.1098/rstb.2007.2087

Schwarz, N. (2004). Metacognitive experiences in consumer judgment and decision making. *Journal of Consumer Psychology*, 14(4), 332–348. http://doi.org/doi:10.1207/s15327663jcp1404_2

Schwarz, N., Bless, H., Strack, F., Klumpp, G., Rittenauer-Schatka, H., & Simons, A. (1991). Ease of retrieval as information: Another look at the availability heuristic. *Journal of Personality and Social Psychology*, 61(2), 195–202. http://doi.org/doi:10.1037/0022-3514.61.2.195

Sidley, G. L., Calam, R., Wells, A., Hughes, T., & Whitaker, K. (1999). The prediction of parasuicide repetition in a high-risk group. *British Journal of Clinical Psychology*, 38(4), 375–386.

Slovic, P., & Peters, E. (2006). Risk perception and affect. *Current Directions in Psychological Science*, 15(6), 322–325. http://doi.org/10.1111/j.1467-8721.2006.00461.x

Smith, J. M., & Alloy, L. B. (2009). A roadmap to rumination: A review of the definition, assessment, and conceptualization of this multifaceted construct. *Clinical Psychology Review*, 29(2), 116–128. http://doi.org/10.1016/j.cpr.2008.10.003

Stöber, J. (2000). Prospective cognitions in anxiety and depression: Replication and methodological extension. *Cognition & Emotion*, 14(5), 725–729. http://doi.org/10.1080/02699930050117693

Strunk, D. R., Lopez, H., & DeRubeis, R. J. (2006). Depressive symptoms are associated with unrealistic negative predictions of future life events. *Behaviour Research and Therapy*, 44(6), 861–882. http://doi.org/10.1016/j.brat.2005.07.001

Szpunar, K. K. & Schacter, D. L. (2013). Get real: Effects of repeated simulation and emotion on the perceived plausibility of future experiences. *Journal of Experimental Psychology: General*, 142(2), 323–327. http://doi.org/10.1037/a0028877

Teasdale, J. D. (1988). Cognitive vulnerability to persistent depression. *Cognition and Emotion*, 2(3), 247–274. http://doi.org/10.1080/02699938808410927

Thimm, J. C., Holte, A., Brennen, T., & Wang, C. E. A. (2013). Hope and expectancies for future events in depression. *Frontiers in Psychology*, 4. http://doi.org/10.3389/fpsyg.2013.00470

Tversky, A., & Kahneman, D. (1973). Availability: A heuristic for judging frequency and probability. *Cognitive Psychology*, 5(2), 207–232. http://doi.org/10.1016/0010-0285(73)90033-9

Van der Does, W. (2002). Cognitive reactivity to sad mood: Structure and validity of a new measure. *Behaviour Research and Therapy*, 40(1), 105–120. http://doi.org/10.1016/S0005-7967(00)00111-X

Vasey, M. W. & Borkovec, T. D. (1992). A catastrophizing assessment of worrisome thoughts. *Cognitive Therapy and Research*, 16(5), 505–520. http://doi.org/10.1007/BF01175138

Vincent, P. J., Boddana, P., & MacLeod, A. K. (2004). Positive life goals and plans in parasuicide. *Clinical Psychology & Psychotherapy*, 11(2), 90–99. http://doi.org/DOI: 10.1002/cpp.394

Weinstein, N. D. (1980). Unrealistic optimism about future life events. *Journal of Personality and Social Psychology*, 39(5), 806–820. http://doi.org/http://dx.doi.org/10.1037/0022-3514.39.5.806

Wenze, S. J., Gunthert, K. C., & German, R. E. (2012). Biases in affective forecasting and recall in individuals with depression and anxiety symptoms. *Personality and Social Psychology Bulletin*, 38(7), 895–906. http://doi.org/10.1177/0146167212447242

Williams, J. M. G., Van der Does, A. J. W., Barnhofer, T., Crane, C., & Segal, Z. S. (2008). Cognitive reactivity, suicidal ideation and future fluency: Preliminary investigation of a differential activation theory of hopelessness/suicidality. *Cognitive Therapy and Research*, 32(1), 83–104. http://doi.org/10.1007/s10608-006-9105-y

Chapter 3

Optimism and pessimism

Introduction

'Optimist' and 'pessimist' are terms commonly used in everyday speech. For example, my family sometimes accuses me of being a pessimist. At this point I usually reply that I am not a pessimist, simply a realist, although judging by their groans, they are not always persuaded. The question of realism will be returned to later in this chapter, but first, discussion will focus on the concept of optimism–pessimism, how it has been operationalized in the psychological literature and how it relates to well-being. The title of this chapter contains both 'optimism' and 'pessimism', and this reflects the possibility that they are not simply two ends of a continuum but are, at least partially, independent. Certainly, the data reviewed in Chapter 2 would suggest that positive and negative thoughts about the future are distinct. However, for simplicity, the terms will be used in the current chapter as antonyms but the issue of their independence will be touched upon in some places and will be returned to more fully in Chapter 11.

'Optimists are people who expect good things to happen to them; pessimists are people who expect bad things to happen to them' (Carver, Scheier, & Segerstrom, 2010, p. 879). This sort of orientation to the future is manifest as both a general outlook on life and as expectancies for specific future events. Someone may go through life with an underlying, even unspoken, attitude that the future will be good, and at certain times they will also show high expectancies for specific positive events, both large (e.g. that they will be successful in a job application they have submitted) and small (e.g. that they will find a parking place as they drive down a busy street). Others will see the future in a darker way and be preoccupied with how particular possibilities will turn out badly. The present chapter will review literature on both global and specific manifestations of optimism. Expectancies for specific future events were discussed at length in Chapter 2, but a separate body of work using likelihood judgements to examine optimism will be reviewed in the present chapter. In particular, discussion will focus on two areas of likelihood judgements: how people compare themselves to others on the likelihood of future events and how they utilize new information to alter their beliefs about their future risks.

There is also an important literature on optimism that understands it as an explanatory style. Arising out of the learned helplessness literature, Seligman (2006) developed the idea that optimism can be thought of as a tendency to explain positive events as being due to internal, stable causes, at the same time as seeing negative events as arising from external, transient causes, specific to those events (Forgeard & Seligman, 2012). If someone consistently explains events in a particular way this will determine how they view the future. For the optimist, seeing positive events that happen as being due to their own enduring qualities as a person will mean that positive future events are seen as likely to happen to them again in the future; negative future events will be seen as less likely because the transient, situational causes that are seen as bringing them about are not likely to be repeated. One way of relating the explanatory style view of optimism to the global attitude or specific future judgement literatures is to think of an optimistic explanatory style for experienced events as a mechanism underlying the development of future-oriented optimism. Consistent with this view, Seligman has argued that optimism can be learned by developing an optimistic explanatory style (Seligman, 2006), and a school-based programme to teach young people to explain their experiences in an optimistic way has been implemented and evaluated in a number of settings (Seligman, Ernst, Gillham, Reivich, & Linkins, 2009).

Before turning in detail to some of the literature, it is worth saying a brief word about the concept of *defensive pessimism*, which has become fairly widely known since it was first introduced by Norem and Cantor, 1986. The suggestion is that some people, who are typically anxious, have a way of approaching important situations where they think about what might go wrong and try to take preventive steps. Defensive pessimism has been examined mainly in relation to task performance, where high scorers perform comparably to optimists, although the fact that defensive pessimists are high in anxiety obviously means that it is related to lower emotional well-being. More pertinently for the current chapter, it is not clear that defensive pessimism is really pessimism as defined here. The self-report measure used to measure the concept (Norem & Illingworth, 1993) is a mix of items about simulating things that could go wrong ('I spend lots of time imagining what could go wrong') and planning for how to deal with them ('I try to picture how I could fix things if something went wrong'), and the concept is probably best captured by the item: 'Considering what can go wrong helps me to prepare'. No questions assess an actual belief in the outcomes happening or not happening, which is the definition of pessimism that is being adopted here. Although responses to these questions could be seen as a particular form of pessimism, they can also be seen as a motivational planning strategy. In either case, and given its emphasis on task performance rather than well-being, it is only tangentially related to the discussion in the present chapter.

Global optimism

A global optimistic attitude or orientation to the future is measured by attitudinal self-report questions. The Life Orientation Test (LOT) and its revised version (LOT-R; Scheier, Carver, & Bridges, 1994) are the most widely used self-report measures of optimism, although there is a variety of other measures, some of which are broader in scope than the LOT-R. The LOT-R removed two items from the LOT that were less specific to a valenced view of the future, leaving six items, each measured on a five-point scale, ranging from 'strongly disagree' to 'strongly agree'. The LOT and LOT-R are very highly correlated ($r = .95$; Carver et al., 2010) indicating that results from both scales can be discussed conjointly. The items from the LOT-R items are shown in Table 3.1.

The issue of whether optimism and pessimism are two ends of a single continuum or, at least to some extent, separate dimensions, has already been raised. Some studies have found that the optimism items and pessimism items (first three and last three items in Table 8.1, respectively) correlate differently with other variables, suggesting that they are at least partially independent constructs. Marshall, Wortman, Kusulas, Hervig, & Vickers, (1992) report only a medium sized negative correlation between the two sets of items. Moreover, and consistent with the sort of two-system view outlined in Chapter 2, the pessimism items correlated with neuroticism and negative affect, whereas the optimism items correlated with extraversion and positive affect (Marshall et al., 1992). However, in other studies both subscales behave in comparable ways in how they relate to other variables. Carver et al. (2010) noted that it is not easy to disentangle effects that might be due to method variance from more

Table 3.1 Items from the Life Orientation Test—Revised (LOT-R; Scheier, Carver, & Bridges, 1994). Each item is scored on a five-point scale of agreement, with the last three items reverse scored. High scores indicate optimism and low scores indicate pessimism

- In uncertain times, I usually expect the best.
- I'm always optimistic about my future.
- Overall, I expect more good things to happen to me than bad.
- I hardly ever expect things to go my way.
- I rarely count on good things happening to me.
- If something can go wrong for me, it will.

Scheier, M. F., Carver, C. S., & Bridges, M. W. (1994). Distinguishing optimism from neuroticism (and trait anxiety, self-mastery, and self-esteem): A re-evaluation of the Life Orientation Test. *Journal of Personality and Social Psychology*, 67, 1063-1078. Copyright © 1994 by the American Psychological Association.

substantive effects. Inevitably, optimistic items are worded positively, with the 'good' response being agreement, whereas pessimistic items have the reverse structure—a 'good' response is indicated by lack of agreement. Partly because of this issue, Carver et al. (2010) suggest that the jury is still out on the single continuum versus independent dimensions debate. Given the seemingly inevitable confounding of the construct with the way it is measured, it is not easy to see how the jury could ever reach a verdict. In the present chapter, for the sake of simplicity, optimism and pessimism will be talked about as opposites in how findings are described, although discussion at some points will clarify that they may well not simply be opposites. On a slightly different note, Blackwell et al. (2013) found that LOT-R scores as a whole correlated highly with vividness of imagery to positive future scenarios but not at all with vividness of imagery to negative future scenarios, indicating an asymmetry between positive and negative future event imagery and optimism.

Optimism measured in this global self-report way has been found to correlate with a wide range of desirable outcomes, especially health outcomes (Carver et al., 2010; Forgeard & Seligman, 2012). In relation to mental health and well-being, optimism is, by definition, inversely related to depressive, and especially, hopelessness symptoms. For example, an item from the Beck Hopelessness Scale (BHS; Beck, Weissman, Lester, & Trexler, 1974), discussed in Chapter 2, is 'I can look forward to more good times than bad' (reverse scored). This item would be very at home in an optimism measure, and, in fact, is almost identical to the third item shown in Table 3.1. A negative view of the future is one of the elements of Beck's cognitive triad in depression (Beck, 1976) and it comes as no surprise that, empirically, the relationship is strong. Chang, Yu, and Hirsch (2013) reported in a community sample a correlation of $r = -.67$ between LOT-R scores and self-reported depression levels, as well as a correlation of $r = .73$ between LOT-R and a self-report measure of hope. Hopelessness measured by the BHS correlates highly with LOT-R scores (e.g. Marshall et al., 1992). LOT-R scores also, not surprisingly, correlate highly with measures of subjective well-being—life satisfaction, positive affect, and negative affect (Chang et al., 2013).

Because of (a) strong conceptual similarities between the constructs of optimism, depression, hopelessness, hope, and so on, (b) item overlap of their measures, and (c) the tendency of any affectively-loaded questions to correlate with each other whatever their specific content (Clark & Watson, 1995), such correlations are of limited interest. Of more interest are longitudinal studies assessing whether optimism can predict later fluctuations in well-being, especially following a psychological challenge. The results of such studies are somewhat mixed and claims for the predictive power of optimism do not always pass strict methodological tests. For example, Giltay, Zitman, and Kromhout (2006) followed up a sample of elderly men over a period of 15 years from when they were around 70 until their mid 80s. Participants in this study completed a measure of optimism containing four items—'I still expect much from life', 'I am still full of plans', 'I do not look forward to what lies ahead for me in the years to come' and 'My days seem to be passing slowly', with the latter two items reverse scored. This is a somewhat wider construct of optimism than that contained in the LOT-R, which is more tightly focused on the belief that things will go well or badly, but is still clearly recognizable as an optimistic/pessimistic outlook and does seem especially relevant for older participants. Optimism scores at the first occasion of measurement predicted later depression scores, but unfortunately initial depression scores were not controlled for (or, in fact, measured), making it difficult to draw conclusions about a potential role for optimism in later depression. In other words, optimism and depression scores might simply have tracked each other over time.

Controlling for initial levels of well-being in a longitudinal study allows a test of the ability of optimism to predict changes in well-being. In a study that did just that, Shnek, Irvine, Stewart, and Abbey (2001) measured optimism, along with other psychological variables, in patients who had recently been discharged following hospitalization for ischemic heart disease (myocardial infarction or unstable angina). Depressive symptoms at follow-up one year later were predicted by post-discharge levels of optimism even after controlling for post-discharge depressive symptoms. Those who had higher levels of optimism following discharge also had lower levels of depression at that time, but even accounting for those lower initial levels they still showed lower levels of depression one year later. It is sometimes even possible to measure optimism in advance of a stressor. For example, among those undergoing in vitro fertilization, optimism measured eight weeks before the procedure predicted lower distress two weeks after receipt of a negative pregnancy test, again after controlling for variations in initial levels of distress (Litt, Tennen, Affleck, & Klock, 1992), although the numbers in this study were very small. Such findings have led to a view of optimism as a buffer against distress following negative events (Carver et al., 2010), although not all findings support this specific, as opposed to general, role for optimism. For example, Van der Velden, Kleber, Fournier, Grievink, Drogendijk et al. (2007) followed up victims of a major fire disaster in the Netherlands, where, on the afternoon of 13 May, 2000 a fireworks storage facility exploded in the town of Enshede, killing 23 people and injuring almost 1,000 more. LOT scores of survivors, measured shortly after the event did predict a range of mental health symptoms up to four years later. Unfortunately, results are again reported without controlling for initial levels of distress, making it difficult to argue for an influence of optimism on later symptoms. More pertinent to the buffering hypothesis, a comparison group of residents in a town unaffected by a stressful event also showed the same pattern over time as the Enshede sample.

It would appear that optimism, despite its close conceptual overlap with well-being and mental health measures, can be distinguished from those outcomes, and an argument can be made for it playing a role in how people's well-being unfolds over time, especially following a psychological stressor. Unfortunately, this argument is weakened, as is the case with any longitudinal predictor, when initial levels of the outcome measure are not controlled for. A final note of caution is that even if studies are appropriately conducted and well analysed, a causal role can only be argued for, rather than be being taken as demonstrated. Self-reported optimism, like most psychological constructs, especially those that are on a 'good–bad' dimension, are connected, often intimately, with a wide range of other psychological constructs. Sometimes studies carefully try to control for a range of other known overlapping variables. For example, Giltay, Geleinjnse, Zitman, Hockstra, and Schouten (2004) reported an impressive finding, showing that in a cohort of over 900 elderly community participants in the Netherlands, dispositional optimism predicted mortality over a nine-year follow-up period, during which 42% of the sample died: 57% of participants in the lowest quartile on the optimism measure died, compared to just 30% in the quartile of highest scorers. Much of the mortality was due to cardiovascular causes and relationship to optimism was even stronger when just considering cardiovascular-related mortality. This study controlled for many known risk factors, including age and a range of cardiovascular risk factors. It is worth bearing in mind that no study can control even for the many variables known to overlap with optimism, never mind all of those that are as yet unknown. Therefore, studies showing that optimism is linked to certain positive outcomes are valuable, but it is difficult to say conclusively whether it is optimism per se that is the key variable, or whether optimism is a marker either for another construct or for a broader constellation of psychosocial advantage of which it is a part. This argument will be returned to and discussed more fully in Chapter 11. What we can conclude is that the evidence points to optimism as being a strong candidate for influencing a range of positive outcomes.

Likelihood judgements for self compared to others

Every June in the run up to Father's Day a shelf in my local supermarket is filled with mugs saying things like 'World's Best Dad' or 'Number 1 Dad'. I would not like to hazard a guess at how many such mugs are made—Father's Day is widely celebrated around the world, although not always in June (Bulgaria, for example, celebrates it on December 26th)—but really there should be only one. If thousands of children are giving their own fathers that mug, or one like it, then they must be biased, because there can only be one World's Greatest Dad. Of course, children are allowed to be biased about their own dads, and we would hope that they are. A second line of research on optimism adopts a variant of this kind of logic to understand a bias towards optimism, where people are asked to make judgements about the likelihood of experiencing particular future events for themselves and others. If a large majority of people rate their own chances of experiencing negative events as less than those of others, then they must be biased because they cannot all be lower than average. These kinds of future-directed likelihood judgements in relation to mood disturbance were discussed at length in Chapter 2. What is different where optimism is the focus of interest is the direct comparison of self and other judgements. Studies typically focus on negative events but sometimes positive events are also examined, where the bias would be demonstrated by most people saying that their chances of experiencing such events were above average. Where positive events have been the subject of judgements, the effect is less strong than it is for negative events (Gold & de Sousa, 2012; Weinstein, 1980).

The standard methodology for demonstrating 'unrealistic' optimism is where people are asked to make a single judgement about how likely they are to experience an event relative to the average person, often specified as being of the same age and gender, and sometimes of the same university (studies are frequently conducted with student samples). Each event is presented in this way and judged on a scale, for example, ranging from −3, *much less likely* to +3 *much more likely*. An optimistic bias is where most people's scores are above zero for positive events and below zero for negative events. In an influential study, Weinstein (1980) asked college students to complete this type of judgement for a range of positive and negative events using a scale that ranged from 100% less likely at one end, to five times the average chance at the other end. Almost all of the negative events were rated across the group as below zero (i.e. less than average) and almost all the positive events above zero. The sample scores averaged across items showed that people on average rated their chances of experiencing the negative events as 20% lower than average; conversely positive events were judged to be 15% more likely to happen to oneself than to the average person. This type of finding has been replicated many times (see Helweg-Larsen & Shepperd, 2001). As is the case with global judgements of optimism, there is some evidence of a link to health outcomes. For example, Hevey, McGee, and Horgan (2014) asked patients in a coronary care rehabilitation group to compare their risk of a future cardiac event to a typical other person who has not had a cardiac event, a typical other person with the same type of cardiac event as them, and a typical member of the rehabilitation group. Patients showed the unrealistic optimism effect for all three comparisons. Furthermore, those displaying the greatest unrealistic optimism were less likely to experience a cardiac event in the next six months, even when depression and sociodemographic factors were controlled for.

An interesting variation to the method is to try to calculate a risk score for each individual participant and to then compare their actuarial risk score relative to the population with the risk they estimated. For example, Waters, Klein, Moser, Yu, Waldron et al. (2011), in a large US community sample of over 14,000 women, asked participants, 'Compared to the average woman your age, would you say that you are more likely to get breast cancer, less likely or about as likely.' (Waters et al., 2011, p. 227). A risk calculator using other information about participants, for example, their age, number of first degree relatives having breast cancer, and history of smoking, was then used to allocate women to above, below, or average risk. Subjective judgements were then compared against the actuarial risk. Of those who provided responses to this question, 38% showed a risk estimate consistent with the actuarial risk, whereas 47% were overoptimistic, that is, gave relative risk estimates that were lower than their actual risk as indicated by the objective risk factors. Only 15% were overly pessimistic. This approach of comparison to 'objective' risk is only possible for specified events where risk can be calculated. However, the actual accuracy of risk assessment tools is known to be modest at the individual level because there are many risk factors, as well as interactions of risk factors, that are not known. The use of an objective benchmark against which to compare judgements will be discussed more fully in the next section in this chapter (Accuracy and bias).

In addition to this direct, single judgement method, a second, indirect approach to unrealistic optimism is to ask participants to make two judgements—how likely the event is to happen to them and how likely it is to happen to the average other person. The difference between the two estimates then provides the measure of relative optimism/pessimism. Results using this methodology also provide support for optimism, in that people typically give lower estimates of their own likelihood of experiencing negative events than they give for other people experiencing those same events (Shepperd, Klein, Waters, & Weinstein, 2013). However, the effects are notably smaller using this indirect method, compared to where people make a single judgement. Klein and Helweg-Larsen (2002) conducted a meta-analysis of unrealistic optimism studies. Of the 29 studies examined, 13 used the direct (single comparative rating) method and 16 used the indirect method where two separate judgements were made. Both sets of studies showed the unrealistic optimism effect but the effect was significantly larger in studies using the direct ($r = .43$) compared to the indirect ($r = .18$) method.

There is some evidence that mood affects self–other discrepancies. Salovey and Birnbaum (1989) and Abele-Brehm and Hermer (1993) reported studies that induced positive or negative moods in participants and observed effects on judgements of future negative health-related events for self versus an average other person. In both cases, positive mood enhanced the self-other discrepancy and negative mood showed a tendency to reduce or even reverse it. Consistent with the weaker effects on positive events found in other studies, Salovey and Birnbaum (1989) also reported that judgements of positive future health events showed no effect of mood induction. Helweg-Larsen and Shepperd (2001) further analysed these data to look at effects of self and other judgements separately, something which was not reported in the original papers. The strongest effect appeared to arise from happy mood increasing risk judgements for others, a finding that defies an obvious theoretical explanation. Some of the studies reviewed in Chapter 2, addressing differences between mood- and non-mood disturbed groups, also included judgements for others and can therefore inform this issue of the relationship between self–other differences and mood. A fairly consistent pattern is that both dysphoria and anxiety are associated with lower discrepancies between self and other judgements for future negative events, largely because of the increase in self-related risk judgements found in disturbed mood, which functions to close the gap between self and other judgements (see Helweg-Larsen & Shepperd, 2001).

On a methodological note, it is possible that some of the self–other optimism effect might arise from the use of the word 'average'. Statistically speaking, average is a neutral category but in everyday usage it does not quite have that meaning. For example, when I started in my first academic job, the department had a scale used for marking student research projects. The five categories of the scale were 'excellent', 'good', 'average', 'weak' and 'very weak'. Now, that scale was obviously not a good scale because it mixed together absolute and relative categories; who is to say, for example, that the average was not good? More pertinently, it is also revealing about how people perceive the word 'average'—it is something below good, something to be avoided. It is not a descriptor that anyone wants to have applied to them—who wants to be thought of as average? Sports pundits use 'pretty average' as a diplomatic form of words for a team performance that was really quite poor. So, thinking about one's future in relation to an 'average' person is perhaps not the neutral comparison it is intended to be. On the other hand, it might be argued that the very fact that average has a slightly negative tone and people do not want to think of themselves as average is simply yet another manifestation of the optimistic bias.

What can be concluded from the literature comparing self to an average other? It appears that: (a) most people judge that they are less likely than the average person to experience negative events in the future; (b) this tendency is more marked when they are asked to engage in a single direct comparison between themselves and an average person (single judgement, direct measure); (c) sad mood, dysphoria, and anxiety all appear to reduce over-optimism, and they do so by closing the self-other gap through increasing risk perceptions about the self rather than reducing risk judgements for others; and (d) a lack of pessimism about negative events is more pronounced than an excess of optimism about positive events.

Accuracy and bias

Rather than comparing oneself to the average person, a different approach to bias is to compare judgements of likelihood to an objective benchmark. As argued in Chapter 2, this type of methodology represents the only really convincing use of the word 'bias'. Ever since the well-known study by Alloy and Abramson published in 1979, concluding that depressed people were more accurately able to judge the contingency between their behaviour and outcome on an experimental task, the notion of 'sadder but wiser' (Alloy & Abramson, 1979, p. 441) in depression has become widely known. In the Abramson and Alloy study, participants were asked to judge the degree of correspondence between their pressing of a button and a light coming on. The actual degree of connectedness was not under participants' control but was determined by the experimenter. Participants who were low in depression symptoms overestimated the extent of their control over the outcome, whereas those scoring above a (relatively low) threshold for depression symptoms did not display this bias. The concept has been expanded to a variety of other tasks and judgements (see Moore & Fresco, 2012). Depressive realism presents something of a challenge to proponents of cognitive therapy, contradictory as it is to a fundamental Beckian principle of distorted, inaccurate cognitions being at the heart of emotional disorders (Beck, 1976). However, like many good stories, including some eye-catching psychological ones (see Pashler & Harris, 2012, for a discussion of the replicability crisis in psychology), it is not quite as simple as it would appear to be.

Most tellingly, attempts to replicate the phenomenon with participants who meet clinical criteria for depression, rather than just having some elevated mild depressive symptoms, as was the case in the original study, have generally failed to find the same effects (e.g. Carson, Hollon, & Shelton, 2010; Dobson & Pusch, 1995). Alongside weak measurement of depression, the other main criticism has been that many studies purporting to measure bias have not had a truly objective benchmark with which to compare judgements. However, before even considering the issue of accuracy there is an important distinction to be borne in mind between accuracy and reasonableness. In performing a simple task, like many of the tasks in this accuracy-bias literature, it might be quite reasonable for participants to assume that they can do the task well—they are usually highly educated participants who are used to succeeding at things that they do and familiar with getting better at tasks through practice. The fact that the experimenter is controlling the outcome such that the person is actually not doing the task very well or not improving with practice then opens up a gap between the participant's judgement and the outcome, making their judgement inaccurate. But, at one level, their judgement, despite being inaccurate, might still be quite reasonable. Leaving that issue aside, many studies talk about accuracy and bias when in actual fact there is no objective standard against which to compare judgements. Reference to a 'bias', as suggested earlier, can only validly be made when there is a clear absolute norm to act as a reference point, against which judgements can be compared. In their meta-analytic review of 75 studies, Moore and Fresco (2012) found that there was a small overall effect of depressive realism (Cohen's $d = -.07$), in that, although both depressed/dysphoric participants and non-depressed participants showed a substantial degree of positivity in their judgements, this tendency was less marked in the depressed/dysphoric participants. However, the difference between depressed and non-depressed participants was substantially weaker in studies that used a diagnostic interview rather than self-report to classify participants as depressed, and also significantly weaker in studies that had a clear objective benchmark against which to compare judgements.

Returning specifically to likelihood judgements for the future, the question is whether those who are mood disturbed show a bias when their judgements are measured against an objective benchmark. At this point, it is important to make clear the distinction between accuracy and bias, which are two distinct elements of judgement. Bias refers to the tendency for judgements to be on one side of the benchmark rather than the other, for example, depressed people might consistently tend to estimate their likelihood of positive events to be lower than they actually are. Accuracy, on the other hand, refers to how close to the benchmark the judgements are, irrespective of whether they are above or below the line (i.e. the direction of the deviation is ignored). Figure 3.1 illustrates the distinction. Group A and Group B have equal levels of bias (in this case zero), but accuracy levels are higher in Group B (their scores are closer to zero, which indicates less deviation from the benchmark). Group C shows more bias than either Group A or Group B, but accuracy is equivalent to Group B and better than Group A.

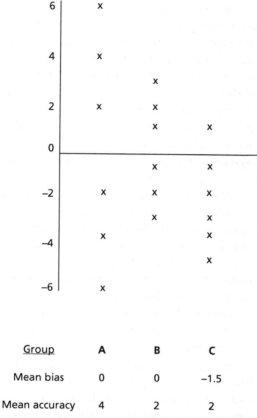

Group	A	B	C
Mean bias	0	0	−1.5
Mean accuracy	4	2	2

Figure 3.1 Accuracy versus bias. Groups A and B show the same overall bias score (zero) but Group B is more accurate, as indicated by scores being close to the line (direction of deviation is ignored and a score of zero indicates accuracy). Group C shows more bias than both the other groups but greater accuracy than Group A and the same level of accuracy as Group B.

Garrett et al. (2014) compared depressed and non-depressed participants' likelihood judgements for negative events, and also compared those judgements against actuarial data on the statistical likelihood of the participants experiencing the events. Consistent with findings reported in Chapter 2, depressed patients gave higher estimates of the likelihood of the negative events happening to them than did controls. Of more interest was that the depressed group's judgements were around 10% higher than base rates, a difference that was statistically significant, whereas the control participants' judgements did not differ significantly from the base rates. It appears, therefore, that the depressed group displayed a pessimistic bias for judgements of future negative events, whereas those in the control group did not. The study did not report accuracy data. One very large caveat to concluding that the depressed participants were biased, though, is that it assumes base rates were the same for the two groups. In fact, studies of depressed patients (e.g. Osby, Brandt, Correia, Ekbom, & Sparén, 2001) consistently show elevated morbidity and mortality compared to population base rates for a wide range of physical disorders, many of which are closely related to the predominantly health-related items presented to participants in the Garrett et al. (2014) study.

The difficulty of getting a precise benchmark against which to compare likelihood judgements is minimized by a different kind of approach where people are asked to make predictions and followed up to see what actually did happen to them. Clearly, this limits the type of predictions that can be examined but does have the benefit of individualized benchmarks. Only a few studies have adopted this longitudinal method, perhaps because of the practical difficulties involved in this kind of study. Dunning and Story (1991) asked psychology students to predict (yes/no) whether a series of events would happen to them during a semester. At the end of the semester, the same participants were asked whether the events had actually happened or not. Note, that the benchmark against which to compare prediction were themselves retrospective judgements of occurrence, which introduces the possibility of bias in the benchmark itself. Leaving this issue aside, students who were higher in depression were *less* accurate, largely because, relative to controls, they over-predicted positive events and under-predicted negative events. That is, given what did actually happen to them (fewer positive and more negative events) during the semester they were actually too optimistic at the outset! The findings themselves are difficult to interpret, but made more so by the fact that the 'depressed' group was formed by taking people scoring nine or above on the Beck Depression Inventory (BDI; Beck, Steer, & Brown, 1996), which is a very low threshold even for mild depressive symptoms.

A second attempt to look at depressive accuracy in subjective probability judgements was conducted by Strunk, Lopez, and DeRubeis (2006), who recruited a community sample of participants and divided them into low, medium, or high depression groups based on their BDI scores. Notably different from Dunning and Story (1991), the low group consisted of those who scored 12 or under on the BDI and a score of 20 or above was required to be in the high depression group. Subjective likelihood judgements of a range of positive and negative events were obtained on a scale of 0–100%, and participants

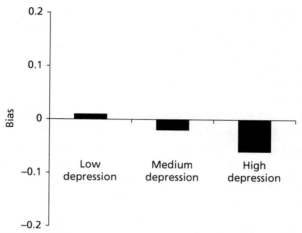

Figure 3.2 Bias scores (difference between predicted and actual) for the three groups in Strunk, Lopez, and DeRubeis (2006). Scores above the line represent a positive bias (over-predicting positive and under-predicting negative), whereas below the line represents a negative bias (under-predicting positive and over-predicting negative). Only the high depression group deviated significantly from zero.

Data from *Behaviour Research and Therapy*, **44**, Strunk, D. R. Lopez, H, DeRubeis, R. J., Depressive symptoms are associated with unrealistic negative predictions of future life events, 875–896, Copyright 2006, with permission from Elsevier.

were followed up 30 days later and asked whether the events had happened or not. Participants generally predicted more positive than negative events. Interestingly, at the end of the 30 days they also reported experiencing more positive than negative events, reinforcing the earlier point that simply predicting more positive than negative events should not itself be considered a bias. Of key interest were the group differences in the relationship between what was predicted and what occurred, which were expressed in bias scores based on over-predicting negative and under-predicting positive events. The scores are shown in Figure 3.2. Unlike the Dunning and Story (1991) results, the high depressed group over-predicted negative events and under-predicted positive events, displaying a pessimistic bias. Neither the low depressed nor the mildly depressed groups showed this pattern and did not deviate significantly from zero[1]. The participants of the high depressed group were *less* accurate (more

---

[1] Strangely, in the Strunk et al. (2006) paper, the low depression group are talked about as showing a positive bias, albeit a non-significant one, whereas the medium depression group are described as showing no bias. That message is sometimes picked up by others citing the study, although both effects are clearly non-significant and therefore both groups are more accurately described as showing no bias.

error) in their predictions, but interestingly, even after partialling out their systematic bias, they were still less accurate: their lower accuracy was not all due to their systematic bias, indicating that they were also just poorer at prediction, with more random error. Wenze, Gunthert, and German (2012) adopted a similar methodology, including how bias was calculated, but with a shorter time frame. Participants predicted the occurrence of positive and negative events over the upcoming week and returned a week later to say which of the events had happened. There was no evidence of bias: both anxiety and depression were unrelated to bias scores. Importantly, the participants in this study were unselected students, few of whom would have been expected to show symptom levels comparable to the high depression group in Strunk et al. (2006).

Such follow-up studies, especially the study by Strunk et al. (2006), represent a laudable attempt to match up prediction with what actually happens to people. The 30-day follow-up made it practically feasible to calculate accuracy, but even allowing this length of time meant that the study was limited in assessing the kinds of things that people might think about for their own lives. The events tended to be either fairly likely to occur in the 30-day period but trivial (e.g. receiving a call from a telemarketer) or serious but highly improbable (e.g. being arrested). This is certainly a problem that was inevitable due to the length of the follow-up period that it was feasible to employ, but also touches upon the problem of any list-based approach to judgements discussed in Chapter 2, where many of the events will not be particularly relevant or salient to individual participants

To summarize, the accuracy of likelihood judgements concerning future self-relevant events is hard to assess, making it difficult to talk of bias or accuracy. In terms of prediction of future positive and negative personal events, there is no evidence of greater accuracy in those who are depressed. The one study that utilized the most stringent cut-off for depression levels (Strunk et al., 2006) found, to the contrary, that those who scored high in depression were less accurate, including a systematic under-prediction of positive events and over-prediction of negative events. There is, in fact, some evidence that those who are depressed make such judgements in a different way than those who are not depressed. Andersen, Spielman, and Bargh (1992) asked participants to make yes/no judgements about whether a range of positive and negative future events would happen to them. Judgements were made either in the normal way or under a cognitive load of trying to remember a six-digit number. Speed of making the judgement was unaffected by the secondary task in those who were depressed but was slowed in the non-depressed group. It appears that those who are depressed make such judgements more automatically as well as more pessimistically, potentially accounting for their greater error.

Changing beliefs

Can a tendency towards over-optimism be changed? Why would you want to? The main issue for emotional well-being is usually about how to increase optimism. However, reducing unwarranted optimism, particularly about health concerns, is also an important practical issue because such optimism might ultimately be maladaptive, for example, through people not paying attention to appropriate health behaviours. On the other hand, the evidence linking global optimism and even unrealistic optimism to positive health outcomes (although much of this evidence does not indicate causality) would argue against trying to reduce optimism.

Increasing optimism will be covered in Chapter 10, but, accepting that reducing over-optimism might in some cases be beneficial, can such a tendency be reduced. The propensity to see oneself as less at risk than the average is quite resistant to change (Shepperd, Waters, Weinstein, & Klein, 2015). Simply providing people with risk information does not change it (Weinstein & Klein, 1996). Janssen, van Os, de Vries, and Lechner (2012) also found that presenting users of tanning beds with information about the associated risk of cancer did little to alter their feelings of risk. However, presenting the same information in the context of a detailed story about a tanning bed user developing skin cancer did increase participants rated feelings of future risk, perhaps because it enabled greater simulation of a similar scenario involving themselves (see Chapter 2) in a way that other ways of presenting information does not.

There have been a number of attempts to look at debiasing methods in other types of optimistic future judgements. For example, Simmons and Massey (2012) offered participants $5 or $50 if they made correct predictions about the likely future results of the team they supported. Neutral fans' (fans who did not support either of the teams involved) judgements were used as a benchmark. Not surprisingly, people were more optimistic about their own team than neutrals were. Giving them $5 did little to sway their judgements but $50 moved them more towards the neutral fans' judged likelihood, although they still did not become as pessimistic as they should have, even when their team was playing a much superior team. Debiasing has also been looked at in relation to the planning fallacy (Kahneman & Tversky, 1979)—where people underestimate how long a task is going to take or how much it is going to cost. Real world examples of the planning fallacy are plentiful. Perhaps the best known of all is the Sydney Opera House with its four-year estimated completion time and $7 million budget being wiped out by a final cost of $102 million, finally opening ten years later than scheduled. Debiasing strategies have been examined in relation to simple laboratory tasks. Asking people to generate best and worst case scenarios for how long a task would take made no difference to estimated completion times for the task (Newby-Clark, Ross, Buehler, Koehler, & Griffin 2000), and getting people to discuss an upcoming task in groups had the effect of making them even more optimistic through engendering an orientation towards factors that would promote successful completion (Buehler, Messervey, & Griffin, 2005). However, asking people to break down the components of the task and estimate time involved in each component of a task helped to produce more realistic overall estimates of completion (Kruger & Evans, 2004).

Finally, there is evidence that there can be natural fluctuations in likelihood estimates. As illustrated in Figure 3.3, Shepperd, Ouellette, and Fernandez (1996) found that students' predictions for upcoming grades moved from overestimation of what they eventually did receive to underestimation as the time to receive the grade approached. The findings were interpreted as evidence of *bracing* against receiving a disappointing outcome, and other studies have found similar effects in areas other than anticipating exam grades (see Carroll, Sweeny, & Shepperd, 2006). Bracing reduces the impact of negative events when they happen through lowering the gap between expectancies and outcomes. The idea of reducing expectations as a way of eliminating disappointment has a long history, as indicated in Chapter 1 with the example of Seneca's injunction to start the day by thinking of how everything could go wrong. The psychological mechanisms of how this process might occur are not entirely clear but it seems to be a kind of anticipatory coping. Given the fundamental anticipatory quality of human nature, it makes complete sense that people do not need to wait until an undesired event actually happens before they engage in self-directed coping thoughts ('it won't be so bad', 'I don't really want it that much', 'It's all a learning experience', 'I've still got my family and friends', and so on). There is little need for bracing if the outcome is distant, and so someone can luxuriate in optimism, but as the moment approaches, dropping expectancies acts to protect oneself against the possibility of a bad outcome. It is also worth noting that anxiety appears to play an important signalling role in bracing. Shepperd, Grace, Cole, and Klein (2005) found that when students contemplating an imminent test result were encouraged to attribute their feelings of anxiety to coffee that they had drunk, they remained optimistic about their test results, whereas students not encouraged to adopt this attribution showed the decrease in optimism illustrated in Figure 3.3. The idea of bracing will be returned to in Chapter 11 in the light of the question posed in Chapter 1 about whether it is better to expect good outcomes (and fail to expect bad outcomes) even if those good outcomes do not come about (or the bad outcomes do).

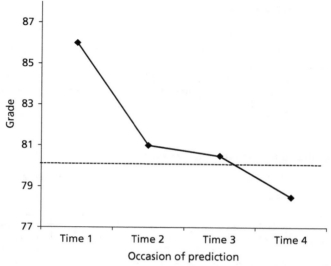

Figure 3.3 Students' predictions of a grade on a piece of work one month before the exam (T1), and five days (T2), 50 minutes (T3) and three seconds (T4) before feedback on the actual grade. The dotted line shows, for comparison, the average grade that was given immediately after T4. Initial over-optimism gives way to no bias, and eventually, seconds before receiving the grade, to an average estimate that is below the average grade.

Optimism as biased correction

Sharot and colleagues have taken a different approach to understanding an optimistic bias, focusing on how people utilize subsequent information to alter their initial predictions of risk. Using an experimental task (Sharot, Korn, & Dolan, 2011), participants are initially asked to make likelihood estimates of a range of future negative events happening to them. The events are chosen to have population base rate probabilities between 10% and 70%, although participants are told that the probabilities of all the events they will see lie between 3% and 77% to allow for underestimation or overestimation of even those events at the extremes. To avoid any effects due to different ends of the scale being used, each event is presented in the form of the judgement being about the likelihood

(a) Initial overestimation corrected strongly:

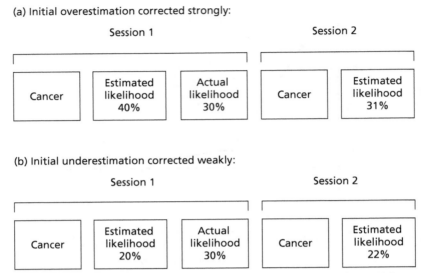

Figure 3.4 The optimistic updating bias (a) illustrates strong adjustment to initial estimates (40% to 31%) when the subsequent baseline information (30%) is lower than the initial estimate (40%); (b) illustrates a lack of corresponding updating (20% to 22%) when the initial estimate (20%) is lower than the subsequent baseline information (30%).

of it happening and also in the form of a judgement about the likelihood of it not happening. Results are generally comparable across the two types of judgement, and for simplicity, the effect is discussed here with likelihood of occurrence, rather than non-occurrence.

In the task (illustrated in Figure 3.4), participants are presented with a description of a negative event and then asked to rate the likelihood of the event happening to them. They are then shown the actual probability of the event, which has been extracted from actuarial statistics. In a second session, participants are shown all the events again and asked to rate probability for a second time. The key measure is how much participants' likelihood judgements change as a result of them having been given the base rate probabilities after their initial estimate, and, critically, whether the degree of change varies depending on whether they initially overestimated or underestimated the risk. If people are being even-handed they should correct their initial underestimates as much as they correct their initial overestimates. The optimistic bias arises when initial overestimations are corrected downwards more than initial underestimations are corrected upwards. Figure 3.4 illustrates the optimistic bias. In (a) an initial estimate of 40% is subsequently corrected downwards to 31% after the person is given the actual base rate of 30%. In contrast, (b) illustrates that an initial underestimation of 20% is corrected upwards to a lesser degree. Sharot et al. (2011) found exactly this effect: participants' estimates moved significantly more when they initially overestimated than when they initially underestimated the negative events, with 79% of participants showing this asymmetry. It appears that in the face of information suggesting that they should alter their risk judgements, people, on the whole, need little encouragement to lower their overestimates of their own future risks but are loathe to increase their underestimates. The effect is not simply the result of people being more likely to remember positive information (i.e. where the base rate was lower than their initial estimate) because memory for the base rates that they were presented with after their initial judgement was equally good when the initial estimates were low compared to where they were high. Participants were also scanned when doing the task and Sharot et al. (2011) reported distinct neural correlates of the cognitive measures. For example, less updating of overoptimistic predictions was associated with weaker neural activity in the right inferior prefrontal gyrus. Moreover, this effect was particularly marked for those who were high in trait optimism.

The basic effect has been replicated a number of times and, consistent with the preferential orientation to positive material found in older adults, the asymmetric updating effect is particularly marked in older age participants (Chowdhury, Sharot, Wolfe, Düzel, & Dolan, 2014), incidentally further providing further validation of the method. Interestingly, younger age participants appear to behave in a similar manner to older age participants. In a study where participants' ages ranged from nine to 26 years, Moutsiana et al. (2013) found that adjustment following good news (i.e. baseline lower than initial prediction) was unrelated to age, whereas age was correlated significantly with a failure to adjust predictions upwards following bad news (i.e. baseline higher than initial prediction). The effect can also be enhanced artificially by administering a drug (L-DOPA) that facilitates dopamine functioning (Sharot, Guitart-Masip, Korn, Chowdhury, & Dolan, 2012) in comparison to a serotonin agonist, implicating the involvement of dopaminergic pathways in the asymmetric updating effect.

Robust as the effect is, there are a number of interesting questions arising from it. The items are all negative. In fact, the phenomenon would really more accurately be described as a failure of appropriate pessimism—people take the opportunity to become less pessimistic but fail to become more pessimistic when really they should. It would be illuminating to see how people respond to positive events. This question is particularly interesting because of the asymmetries between positive and negative aspects of future-directed thinking that have been highlighted throughout this book, as well as the fact that other methods have shown stronger relative biases for negative events than for positive events. It would also be interesting to know the extent to which participants were aware that they were making asymmetric adjustments and their reasons for doing so. Perhaps getting people to think aloud while doing the task might illuminate some of the underlying psychological processes involved. The items used are very largely health-related, where people feel, indeed are being told all the time through public health messages, that they can have control over the outcomes, so perhaps effects are mediated by a sense of control. Control is a strong moderator of the self–other optimism effect (Helweg-Larsen & Shepperd, 2001). This explanation is not necessarily a challenge to the effect shown by Sharot and colleagues; rather it might help to explain some of the psychological mechanisms implicated in how the effect arises.

Do those who are mood-disturbed show the same asymmetry in updating? In two separate studies, Korn, Sharot, Walter, Heekeren, and Dolan (2014) and Garrett et al. (2014) compared depressed patients and matched controls on the updating task. The control participants showed asymmetric updating: they changed their judgements more when their initial judgements were higher than the base rates, compared to where they were lower. They key finding was that the depressed group showed no difference between the two conditions: in contrast to the controls, they were as prepared to increase their underestimates as they were to reduce their overestimates. Some questions of detail remain. In the Korn et al. (2014) study the depressed group's general level of updating was low, showing low responsiveness to subsequent information in general, and the effect was largely dependent on the control group's readiness to change their estimates downwards upon receiving good news (baseline lower than their initial estimate). In contrast, updating in the depressed group was generally high in the Garrett et al. (2014) study, at levels similar to the updating following good news of the control group. Nevertheless, the data do appear to indicate a greater even-handedness in updating in the depressed group, which contrasts with the clear tendency of non-depressed individuals to more readily alter judgements in a favourable direction.

To summarize, there are a number of interesting questions arising from the work of Sharot and colleagues on updating of likelihood judgements, but there is clear evidence of an optimism (lack of pessimism) effect. Moreover, the results are consistent with the broad picture that, given the opportunity, most people have a tendency to think the best for themselves in the future. The studies by Sharot and colleagues showing that this tendency persists, even in the face of information indicating that it is not warranted, is consistent with the other evidence on the resistance of optimistic judgements to debiasing reviewed earlier in this chapter. Given information that they have been too pessimistic, participants appear only too ready to abandon their pessimism, whereas it appears that they show a greater reluctance to change judgements that initially were not pessimistic enough. Moreover, this optimistic bias is stronger in both younger age groups and older adults, and can be enhanced by increasing dopaminergic activity and, most interestingly for the discussion here, appears to be absent in those who are depressed.

Optimism for well-being

Evidence for optimism has largely focused on judgements about future event likelihood. But, as will become clearer in Chapter 4, people also think about how they are going to feel in the future, as well as what they think is going to happen. A small number of studies have examined predictions of future well-being in relation to optimism. There is clear evidence that, at least in younger adults, people judge their future well-being as likely to be higher than their current well-being, a finding that is true for ratings of happiness (Robinson & Ryff, 1999), life satisfaction (Lachman, Röcke, Rosnick, & Ryff, 2008) and positive and negative feeling states (Stolarski, Matthews, Postek, Zimbardo, & Bitner, 2014). A similar effect has also been found (Robinson & Ryff, 1999) for the six dimensions of psychological well-being (PWB) proposed by Ryff (1989), for example, a sense of mastery, personal growth, and positive relationships. Robinson and Ryff (1999) also compared different age groups, to see if this tendency varied by age. A group of young adults (mean age 19 years) was compared with a group of middle-aged adults (mean age 46 years) and a group of older adults (mean age 73) on current levels of PWB and predicted levels in the future (as 40–50-year-olds for the young adults, 65–70-year-olds for the middle-aged group, and 10–15 years into the future for the older adults). There was some variability across the six dimensions of PWB, but the main findings were fairly consistent. On a measure of the difference between predicted and current levels of well-being, the young adults (.57) scored significantly higher than the older adults (−.31), with the middle-aged group (−.18) falling between.

Significance of differences between current and predicted scores (i.e. deviation from zero) were not reported, but, as argued earlier in this chapter, these relative differences are, in any case, not informative about bias. The fact that well-being indicators generally remain relatively stable over the life course (Lachman et al., 2008) could be used as a basis for inferring evidence of bias, but a more convincing test would be to measure predicted well-being for a future time point, follow people up to measure well-being at that point, and compare the two scores. Lachman et al. (2008) conducted exactly such a study with a large US national sample. Participants predicted their levels of life sat-isfaction ten years into the future, and were followed up close to that time, at which point they were asked to rate their current life satisfaction. As shown in Figure 3.5, younger age groups showed over-prediction. This over-prediction showed a steady decline until eventual under-prediction by those participants in the oldest age band, who, when in their 60s and 70s had under-predicted how satisfied they would be with their lives a decade later. Actual life satisfac-tion, in fact, remained largely stable across the age bands, with some small decline in the oldest age group at follow-up (although not as much as they had predicted), so the differences between the age bands were largely the result of changes in prediction. Busseri and Peck (2015) used the same data set as Lachman et al. (2008) to compare current and predicted (as well as past) life satisfaction as a function of depression status, although only in the younger adults (i.e. the age bands known to show higher predictions for future than current life satisfaction). Depressed participants, not surprisingly, reported lower current life satisfaction than non-depressed participants, but showed comparable sized increases in their expected future life satisfaction, leaving them with a similar deficit on expected, as on current levels. Unfortunately,

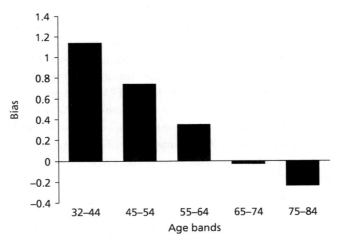

Figure 3.5 Difference between predicted life satisfaction in ten years' time and actual life satisfaction at that time, broken down by different age bands. Bands refer to age at the follow-up time (i.e. at the time actual life satisfaction was measured which was ten years after it was predicted). The over-prediction of future life satisfaction that is evident in younger age declines in a linear way with increasing age.

Data from Lachman, M. E., Röcke, C., Rosnick, C., & Ryff, C. D. (2008). Realism and illusion in Americans' temporal views of their life satisfaction: Age differences in reconstructing the past and anticipating the future. Psychological Science, 19(9), 889–897.

accuracy data on how expectations matched actual life satisfaction ten years later were not reported.

In a German panel study using a five-year follow-up, Lang, Weiss, Gerstorf, and Wagner (2013) found very similar results: younger adults overestimated, middle-aged adults were accurate about, and older adults underestimated, future life satisfaction. Prediction/actual difference was also related to well-being, even after controlling for age and gender. Not surprisingly, those who were relative under-predictors of their future well-being showed highest levels of depressive symptoms and lowest levels of positive affect at the time of prediction, relative to accurate predictors and over-predictors, who had similarly (low) levels of depressive symptoms. Thus, these findings, like others described earlier, provide no support for the sadder but wiser hypothesis. An additional, intriguing finding from the Lang et al. (2013) study was that the older adults who underestimate the most (i.e. were least optimistic) had the best health outcomes (lower mortality and disability) at a later follow-up. Similarly, Cheng, Fung, and Chan (2009) found in a sample of older adults in Hong Kong that those who rated their future selves in one year's time more negatively than their current selves, had lower well-being at that point, but actually had higher well-being one year later. One interpretation of these findings is of lower expectations for the future being helpful in the face of probable life challenges (functional decline in older age)—an example of useful bracing in action.

Chapter summary and concluding comments

Optimism and pessimism are concepts widely used in everyday life. In the research literature they are used as labels for different kinds of phenomena, including a global attitude towards the future, discrepancies between expectancies for self versus an average other person, differences between predictions of what will happen to oneself, and what actually does happen, a preference for using information to lower rather than increase estimates of future risk, and a way of explaining events that happen to oneself. It is not clear to what extent these different measures of the same putative concept actually are measuring the same thing or are identifying separate or partially overlapping constructs. For example, Peterson and Vaidya (2001) reported a low correlation between global optimism and explanatory style and it is rare to find studies using more than one type of optimism measure. Further work on conceptual clarification is needed. Indeed, it is not clear that optimism and pessimism represent a single dimension. For simplicity and consistency with the literature reviewed, the terms were treated as antonyms in the present chapter but it is likely that from some of the findings reviewed here and from the findings described in Chapter 2 that they are at least partially independent. Overall, the evidence does suggest that in general, people are mostly optimistic, or to be more precise, not pessimistic. This outlook might arise because it maintains and enhances positive mood. An important caveat is that in eastern cultures (Japanese and Chinese) the self–other discrepancy has been found to be reduced, eliminated, or even reversed (Chang & Asakawa, 2003; Heine & Lehman, 1995). Furthermore, studies are often conducted in young, middle-class, western university students. A study of middle-aged administrative staff at a UK university showed a significant but relatively small self–other difference (3%) for negative events and no difference at all for positive events, raising a question about the ubiquity of the effect across age groups (Joshi & Carter, 2013). Such sociodemographic factors may also interact: You, Fung, and Isaacowitz (2009) found that older Hong Kong Chinese adults showed lower global self-reported optimism than their younger counterparts, whereas compared with younger US adults, older US adults showed greater optimism. Clearly there is further work to be done in looking at different cultures and in using samples varying in socioeconomic status and age.

A pessimistic outlook correlates, indeed can be thought as an important part of, mood disturbance. However, a lack of pessimism is also of some concern for long-term well-being because of the possible neglect of safety, for example, in relation to prevention of health threats (using sunscreen, attending check-ups, eating healthily, and so on). Efforts have focused on how to reduce this kind of potential over-optimism, especially in relation to health risks. High levels of optimism have turned out not to be easy to shift, for example, through simply giving people relevant information, but various different approaches have shown reductions. There is also evidence to suggest that people do spontaneously shift their perceptions to brace for the possibility of negative outcomes, showing a flexible sort of optimism. Forgeard and Seligman (2012) suggest that flexible optimism, where someone is generally optimistic but can reduce this optimism at certain times, is the most desirable orientation to the future.

The question of realism is never very far away in discussions of optimism and pessimism. A majority indicating that they are below average for likelihood of negative events and above average for likelihood of positive events happening to them is taken as indicating unrealistic optimism. The selective updating results are also indicative of bias because people do not respond the same way to information suggesting that they are not pessimistic enough as they do to information suggesting they are too pessimistic. People who are mood-disturbed are less likely to show these effects, which arguably shows that normal mood is associated with an optimistic bias and depressed mood with greater realism. These arguments have a certain logical appeal to them but without clear objective benchmarks against which to compare judgements it is difficult to talk of accuracy or bias: 'In the absence of objective indicators, and because participants themselves often have little sense of what objectively represents an optimistic versus pessimistic prediction, it may be meaningless to define one point as objectively optimistic, realistic or pessimistic' (Carroll et al., 2006, p. 57). The only truly convincing way to test for accuracy or bias is by comparing predicted with actual outcomes. Practical issues mean that this kind of approach can only be conducted in a limited way. Nevertheless, some studies have tried to look at the issue this way and the best available data suggest that depressed participants are both less accurate and more negatively biased, although further work needs to be carried out before strong conclusions can be drawn. Overall, it is difficult to see optimism as anything other than a good thing, given its connection with emotional well-being and many positive outcomes. It remains for future research to try to identify and understand more about the conditions where this might not be the case.

References

Abele-Brehm, A. & Hermer, P. (1993). Mood influences on health-related judgments: Appraisal of own health versus appraisal of unhealthy behaviours. *European Journal of Social Psychology*, 23(6), 613–625. http://doi.org/10.1002/ejsp.2420230606

Alloy, L. B. & Abramson, L. Y. (1979). Judgment of contingency in depressed and nondepressed students: Sadder but wiser? *Journal of Experimental Psychology: General*, 108(4), 441–485. http://doi.org/10.1037/0096-3445.108.4.441

Andersen, S. M., Spielman, L. A., & Bargh, J. A. (1992). Future-event schemas and certainty about the future: Automaticity in depressives' future-event predictions. *Journal of Personality and Social Psychology*, 63(5), 711–723. http://doi.org/10.1037/0022-3514.63.5.711

Beck, A. T. (1976). *Cognitive therapy and the emotional disorders*. Madison, CT: International Universities Press.

Beck, A. T., Steer, R. A., & Brown, G. K. (1996). *Manual for the Beck Depression Inventory-I*. San Antonio, TX: Psychological Corporation.

Beck, A. T., Weissman, A., Lester, D., & Trexler, L. (1974). The measurement of pessimism: The Hopelessness Scale. *Journal of Consulting and Clinical Psychology*, 42(6), 861–865. http://doi.org/doi.org/10.1037/h0037562

Blackwell, S. E., Rius-Ottenheim, N., Schulte-van Maaren, Y. W. M., Carlier, I. V. E., Middelkoop, V. D., ... Giltay, E. J. (2013). Optimism and mental imagery: A possible cognitive marker to promote well-being? *Psychiatry Research*, 206(1), 56–61. http://doi.org/10.1016/j.psychres.2012.09.047

Buehler, R., Messervey, D., & Griffin, D. (2005). Collaborative planning and prediction: Does group discussion affect optimistic biases in time estimation? *Organizational Behavior and Human Decision Processes*, 97(1), 47–63. http://doi.org/10.1016/j.obhdp.2005.02.004

Busseri, M. A. & Peck, E. (2015). Do (even) depressed individuals believe that life gets better and better? The link between depression and subjective trajectories for life. *Clinical Psychological Science*, 3(3), 715–725. http://doi.org/10.1177/2167702614547265

Carroll, P., Sweeny, K., & Shepperd, J. A. (2006). Forsaking optimism. *Review of General Psychology*, **10**(1), 56–73. http://doi.org/10.1037/1089-2680.10.1.56

Carson, R. C., Hollon, S. D., & Shelton, R. C. (2010). Depressive realism and clinical depression. *Behaviour Research and Therapy*, **48**(4), 257–265. http://doi.org/10.1016/j.brat.2009.11.011

Carver, C. S., Scheier, M. F., & Segerstrom, S. C. (2010). Optimism. *Clinical Psychology Review*, **30**(7), 879–889. http://doi.org/10.1016/j.cpr.2010.01.006

Chang, E. C. & Asakawa, K. (2003). Cultural variations on optimistic and pessimistic bias for self versus a sibling: Is there evidence for self-enhancement in the West and for self-criticism in the East when the referent group is specified? *Journal of Personality and Social Psychology*, **84**(3), 569–581. http://doi.org/10.1037/0022-3514.84.3.569

Chang, E. C., Yu, E. A., & Hirsch, J. K. (2013). On the confluence of optimism and hope on depressive symptoms in primary care patients: Does doubling up on *bonum futurun* proffer any added benefits? *The Journal of Positive Psychology*, **8**(5), 404–411. http://doi.org/10.1080/17439760.2013.818163

Cheng, S.-T., Fung, H. H., & Chan, A. C. M. (2009). Self-perception and psychological well-being: The benefits of foreseeing a worse future. *Psychology and Aging*, **24**(3), 623–633. http://doi.org/10.1037/a0016410

Chowdhury, R., Sharot, T., Wolfe, T., Düzel, E., & Dolan, R. J. (2014). Optimistic update bias increases in older age. *Psychological Medicine*, **44**(9), 2003–2012. http://doi.org/10.1017/S0033291713002602

Clark, L. A. & Watson, D. (1995). Constructing validity: Basic issues in objective scale development. *Psychological Assessment*, **7**(3), 309–319. http://doi.org/10.1037/1040-3590.7.3.309

Dobson, K. S. & Pusch, D. (1995). A test of the depressive realism hypothesis in clinically depressed subjects. *Cognitive Therapy and Research*, **19**(2), 179–194. http://doi.org/10.1007/BF02229693

Dunning, D. & Story, A. L. (1991). Depression, realism, and the overconfidence effect: Are the sadder wiser when predicting future actions and events? *Journal of Personality and Social Psychology*, **61**(4), 521–532. http://doi.org/10.1037/0022-3514.61.4.521

Forgeard, M. J. C. & Seligman, M. E. P. (2012). Seeing the glass half full: A review of the causes and consequences of optimism. *Pratiques Psychologiques*, **18**(2), 107–120. http://doi.org/10.1016/j.prps.2012.02.002

Garrett, N., Sharot, T., Faulkner, P., Korn, C. W., Roiser, J. P., & Dolan, R. J. (2014). Losing the rose tinted glasses: neural substrates of unbiased belief updating in depression. *Frontiers in Human Neuroscience*, **8**. http://doi.org/10.3389/fnhum.2014.00639

Giltay, E. J., Geleijnse, J. M., Zitman, F. G., Hoekstra, T., & Schouten, E. G. (2004). Dispositional Optimism and All-Cause and Cardiovascular Mortality in a Prospective Cohort of Elderly Dutch Men and Women. *Archives of General Psychiatry*, **61**(11), 1126–1135. http://doi.org/10.1001/archpsyc.61.11.1126

Giltay, E., Zitman, F., & Kromhout, D. (2006). Dispositional optimism and the risk of depressive symptoms during 15 years of follow-up: The Zutphen Elderly Study. *Journal of Affective Disorders*, **91**(1), 45–52. http://doi.org/10.1016/j.jad.2005.12.027

Gold, R. S. & de Sousa, P. N. (2012). When does event valence affect unrealistic optimism? *Psychology, Health & Medicine*, **17**(1), 105–115. http://doi.org/10.1080/13548506.2011.582503

Heine, S. J. & Lehman, D. R. (1995). Cultural variation in unrealistic optimism: Does the West feel more vulnerable than the East? *Journal of Personality and Social Psychology*, 68(4), 595–607. http://doi.org/10.1037/0022-314.68.4.595

Helweg-Larsen, M. & Shepperd, J. A. (2001). Do moderators of the optimistic bias affect personal or target risk estimates? A review of the literature. *Personality and Social Psychology Review*, 5(1), 74–95. http://doi.org/10.1207/S15327957PSPR0501_5

Hevey, D., McGee, H. M., & Horgan, J. H. (2014). Comparative optimism among patients with coronary heart disease (CHD) is associated with fewer adverse clinical events 12 months later. *Journal of Behavioral Medicine*, 37(2), 300–307. http://doi.org/10.1007/s10865-012-9487-0

Janssen, E., van Osch, L., Lechner, L., Candel, M., & de Vries, H. (2012). Thinking versus feeling: Differentiating between cognitive and affective components of perceived cancer risk. *Psychology & Health*, 27(7), 767–783. http://doi.org/10.1080/08870446.2011.580846

Joshi, M. S. & Carter, W. (2013). Unrealistic optimism: East and West? *Frontiers in Psychology*, 4. http://doi.org/10.3389/fpsyg.2013.00006

Kahneman, D. & Tversky, A. (1979). Intuitive prediction: Biases and corrective errors. *TIMS Studies in Management Science*, 12, 313–327.

Klein, C. T. F. & Helweg-Larsen, M. (2002). Perceived control and the optimistic bias: A meta-Analytic review. *Psychology & Health*, 17(4), 437–446. http://doi.org/10.1080/0887044022000004920

Korn, C. W., Sharot, T., Walter, H., Heekeren, H. R., & Dolan, R. J. (2014). Depression is related to an absence of optimistically biased belief updating about future life events. *Psychological Medicine*, 44(3), 579–592. http://doi.org/10.1017/S0033291713001074

Kruger, J. & Evans, M. (2004). If you don't want to be late, enumerate: Unpacking reduces the planning fallacy. *Journal of Experimental Social Psychology*, 40(5), 586–598. http://doi.org/10.1016/j.jesp.2003.11.001

Lachman, M. E., Röcke, C., Rosnick, C., & Ryff, C. D. (2008). Realism and illusion in Americans' temporal views of their life satisfaction: Age differences in reconstructing the past and anticipating the future. *Psychological Science*, 19(9), 889–897. http://doi.org/10.1111/j.1467-9280.2008.02173.x

Lang, F. R., Weiss, D., Gerstorf, D., & Wagner, G. G. (2013). Forecasting life satisfaction across adulthood: Benefits of seeing a dark future? *Psychology and Aging*, 28(1), 249–261. http://doi.org/10.1037/a0030797

Litt, M. D., Tennen, H., Affleck, G., & Klock, S. (1992). Coping and cognitive factors in adaptation to in vitro fertilization failure. *Journal of Behavioral Medicine*, 15(2), 171–187. http://doi.org/10.1007/BF00848324

Marshall, G. N., Wortman, C. B., Kusulas, J. W., Hervig, L. K., & Vickers, R. R. J. (1992). Distinguishing optimism from pessimism: Relations to fundamental dimensions of mood and personality. *Journal of Personality and Social Psychology*, 62(6), 1067–1074. http://doi.org/10.1037/0022-3514.62.6.1067

Moore, M. T. & Fresco, D. M. (2012). Depressive realism: A meta-analytic review. *Clinical Psychology Review*, 32(6), 496–509. http://doi.org/10.1016/j.cpr.2012.05.004

Moutsiana, C., Garrett, N., Clarke, R. C., Lotto, R. B., Blakemore, S.-J., & Sharot, T. (2013). Human development of the ability to learn from bad news. *Proceedings of the National Academy of Sciences*, **110**(41), 16396–16401. http://doi.org/10.1073/pnas.1305631110

Newby-Clark, I. R., Ross, M., Buehler, R., Koehler, D. J., & Griffin, D. (2000). People focus on optimistic scenarios and disregard pessimistic scenarios while predicting task completion times. *Journal of Experimental Psychology: Applied*, **6**(3), 171–182. http://doi.org/10.1037//1076-898X.6.3.171

Norem, J. K. & Cantor, N. (1986). Defensive pessimism: Harnessing anxiety as motivation. *Journal of Personality and Social Psychology*, **51**(6), 1208–1217. http://doi.org/10.1037/0022-3514.51.6.1208

Norem, J. K. & Illingworth, K. S. S. (1993). Strategy-dependent effects of reflecting on self and tasks: Some implications of optimism and defensive pessimism. *Journal of Personality and Social Psychology*, **65**(4), 822–835. http://doi.org/10.1037/0022-3514.65.4.822

Osby, U., Brandt, L., Correia, N., Ekbom, A., & Sparén, P. (2001). Excess mortality in bipolar and unipolar disorder in Sweden. *Archives of General Psychiatry*, **58**(9), 844–850. http://doi.org/10.1001/archpsyc.58.9.844

Pashler, H. & Harris, C. R. (2012). Is the replicability crisis overblown? Three arguments examined. *Perspectives on Psychological Science*, **7**(6), 531–536. http://doi.org/10.1177/1745691612463401

Peterson, C. & Vaidya, R. S. (2001). Explanatory style, expectations, and depressive symptoms. *Personality and Individual Differences*, **31**(7), 1217–1223. http://doi.org/10.1016/S0191-8869(00)00221-X

Robinson, M. D. & Ryff, C. D. (1999). The role of self-deception in perceptions of past, present, and future happiness. *Personality and Social Psychology Bulletin*, **25**(5), 596–608. http://doi.org/10.1177/0146167299025005005

Ryff, C. D. (1989). Happiness is everything, or is it? Explorations on the meaning of psychological well- being. *Journal of Personality and Social Psychology*, **57**(6), 1069 - 1081. http:// doi.org/ 10.1037/0022- 3514.57.6.1069

Salovey, P. & Birnbaum, D. (1989). Influence of mood on health-relevant cognitions. *Journal of Personality and Social Psychology*, **57**(3), 539–551. http://doi.org/10.1037/0022-3514.57.3.539

Scheier, M. F., Carver, C. S., & Bridges, M. W. (1994). Distinguishing optimism from neuroticism (and trait anxiety, self-mastery, and self-esteem): A re-evaluation of the Life Orientation Test. *Journal of Personality and Social Psychology*, **67**(6), 1063–1078. http://doi.org/10.1037/0022-3514.67.6.1063

Seligman, M. E. P. (2006). *Learned optimism: How to change your mind and your life* (Reprint edition). New York: Vintage Books USA.

Seligman, M. E. P., Ernst, R. M., Gillham, J., Reivich, K., & Linkins, M. (2009). Positive education: positive psychology and classroom interventions. *Oxford Review of Education*, **35**(3), 293–311. http://doi.org/10.1080/03054980902934563

Sharot, T., Guitart-Masip, M., Korn, C. W., Chowdhury, R., & Dolan, R. J. (2012). How dopamine enhances an optimism bias in humans. *Current Biology*, **22**(16), 1477–1481. http://doi.org/10.1016/j.cub.2012.05.053

Sharot, T., Korn, C. W., & Dolan, R. J. (2011). How unrealistic optimism is maintained in the face of reality. *Nature Neuroscience*, **14**(11), 1475–1479. http://doi.org/10.1038/nn.2949

Shepperd, J. A., Grace, J., Cole, L. J., & Klein, C. (2005). Anxiety and outcome predictions. *Personality and Social Psychology Bulletin*, 31(2), 267–275.

Shepperd, J. A., Klein, W. M. P., Waters, E. A., & Weinstein, N. D. (2013). Taking stock of unrealistic optimism. *Perspectives on Psychological Science*, 8(4), 395–411. http://doi.org/10.1177/1745691613485247

Shepperd, J. A., Ouellette, J. A., & Fernandez, J. K. (1996). Abandoning unrealistic optimism: Performance estimates and the temporal proximity of self-relevant feedback. *Journal of Personality and Social Psychology*, 70(4), 844.

Shepperd, J. A., Waters, E. A., Weinstein, N. D., & Klein, W. M. (2015). A primer on unrealistic optimism. *Current Directions in Psychological Science*, 24(3), 232–237.

Shnek, Z. M., Irvine, J., Stewart, D., & Abbey, S. (2001). Psychological factors and depressive symptoms in ischemic heart disease. *Health Psychology*, 20(2), 141–145. http://doi.org/10.1037//0278-6133.20.2.141

Simmons, J. P. & Massey, C. (2012). Is optimism real? *Journal of Experimental Psychology: General*, 141(4), 630–634. http://doi.org/10.1037/a0027405

Stolarski, M., Matthews, G., Postek, S., Zimbardo, P. G., & Bitner, J. (2014). How we feel is a matter of time: Relationships between time perspectives and mood. *Journal of Happiness Studies*, 15(4), 809–827. http://doi.org/10.1007/s10902-013-9450-y

Strunk, D. R., Lopez, H., & DeRubeis, R. J. (2006). Depressive symptoms are associated with unrealistic negative predictions of future life events. *Behaviour Research and Therapy*, 44(6), 861–882. http://doi.org/10.1016/j.brat.2005.07.001

van der Velden, P. G., Kleber, R. J., Fournier, M., Grievink, L., Drogendijk, A., & Gersons, B. P. R. (2007). The association between dispositional optimism and mental health problems among disaster victims and a comparison group: A prospective study. *Journal of Affective Disorders*, 102(1–3), 35–45. http://doi.org/10.1016/j.jad.2006.12.004

Waters, E. A., Klein, W. M. P., Moser, R. P., Yu, M., Waldron, W. R., McNeel, T. S., & Freedman, A. N. (2011). Correlates of unrealistic risk beliefs in a nationally representative sample. *Journal of Behavioral Medicine*, 34(3), 225–235. http://doi.org/10.1007/s10865-010-9303-7

Weinstein, N. D. (1980). Unrealistic optimism about future life events. *Journal of Personality and Social Psychology*, 39(5), 806–820. http://doi.org/http://dx.doi.org/10.1037/0022-3514.39.5.806

Weinstein, N. D. & Klein, W. M. (1996). Unrealistic optimism: Present and future. *Journal of Social and Clinical Psychology*, 15(1), 1–8. http://doi.org/10.1521/jscp.1996.15.1.1

Wenze, S. J., Gunthert, K. C., & German, R. E. (2012). Biases in affective forecasting and recall in individuals with depression and anxiety symptoms. *Personality and Social Psychology Bulletin*, 38(7), 895–906. http://doi.org/10.1177/0146167212447242

You, J., Fung, H. H. L., & Isaacowitz, D. M. (2009). Age differences in dispositional optimism: a cross-cultural study. *European Journal of Ageing*, 6(4), 247–252. http://doi.org/10.1007/s10433-009-0130-z

Chapter 4

Predicting feelings

Introduction

In anticipating the future, we do not simply predict events, we predict how we are going to feel in relation to the occurrence, or sometimes the non-occurrence, of those events. In fact, the anticipated feeling states associated with future events are likely to be a major factor in what gives those events their significance or value. Some theories of decision making place anticipation of feelings associated with future events at the heart of the decision process. For example, within Decision Affect Theory, Mellers (2000) proposes that when considering a course of action, people anticipate the pleasure and pain that the different options will produce, estimate the probabilities of those experiences occurring, and then choose the option that maximizes pleasure. Note that pleasure and pain can be substituted with the broader concepts of enjoyment and suffering, which reduces any misunderstanding about focusing simply on sensory aspects (Crisp, 2008). Mellers (2000) points out, for example, that pleasure can be obtained from an act of virtue and pain from an injustice. Of course, this general idea is not new. As a description of what motivates people to take particular courses of action, psychological hedonism has been around for a long time[1]. It is, of course, possible to accept that anticipated pleasure and pain do guide actions but may not be the only forces that do so (e.g. Higgins, 2013). Someone may, for example, set out on a course of action that will reveal truth, irrespective of the enjoyment or suffering produced. Whatever degree of weight is given to them, it would be difficult to avoid the conclusion that anticipated enjoyment and suffering are important influences on our actions.

This emotion-related aspect of future-directed thinking—anticipating how we are *going to* feel in the future—is usually referred to as anticipated affect. There is a second emotional aspect of future-directed thinking, which is how we feel in the *here-and-now* when thinking about the future. Thoughts about the

....

[1] Psychological hedonism should be distinguished from evaluative hedonism, which is a value theory that pleasure and absence of pain (our own or others') constitute the only ultimate values, and therefore anticipating pleasure and pain *ought* to be what guides our actions.

future have the power to elicit emotional reactions while they are being entertained. For example, I might predict that I will feel nervous giving an important talk to a large audience (anticipated emotion), without feeling anxious there and then (no anticipatory emotion), especially if the talk is scheduled to take place in six months' time. Half an hour before the talk I can still predict that I will feel nervous during the talk, but might well also now be feeling nervous at the thought of it (anticipatory emotion). It is not only the thought of feeling a negative emotion in the future that gives such a thought emotional potency; additionally, the imagined consequences arising from the future negative emotion will fuel feelings when thinking about the event. I might feel anxious in advance when thinking about the lecture not only because I predict I will feel anxious during it but also because I imagine that feeling anxious during it will make me forget my words or rush too much and deliver a poor performance. In the same way, those prone to panic disorder fear the experience of panic, but also fear what will happen if they do have a panic attack, for example, losing control and making a fool of themselves publicly.

It is likely that anticipated and anticipatory feelings are closely connected. It has been suggested that we use the feelings we experience when thinking about a future event as a guide to how we will feel when the event happens: 'we know which future events will feel good and which will feel bad because we feel good or bad when we simulate them' (Gilbert & Wilson, 2011, p.160). The fact that I can calmly predict feeling anxious in six months' time shows that this is not the whole story, but it might nevertheless be an important part of it. Using how you feel when thinking about something as a guide to how you will feel when it happens is similar in some ways to the affect heuristic described in Chapter 2. It is different in that what is being predicted is specifically the likelihood of particular feeling states (feeling anxious giving the lecture) rather than the likelihood of an event (the audience being bored, forgetting to mention something important), and the affect is specifically tied to imagining the event rather than arising for any other reason.

The rest of this chapter will review anticipated affect and Chapter 5 will deal with anticipatory affect. However, alongside anticipatory and anticipated affect there is one other aspect of emotional experience that needs to be considered, which is the feeling state that someone actually experiences when the anticipated event happens. I might predict that I am going to feel anxious during the lecture, and even feel anxious in the moment when I think about it, but as it turns out, when I give the lecture I don't feel anxious at all. In this case, not only has my anticipated anxiety been inaccurate, but my anticipatory anxiety has been completely unnecessary!

The basis for many behavioural experiments in cognitive behavioural therapy (e.g. Bennett-Levy, Butler, Fennell, Hackmann, Mueller et al., 2004) is that the sorts of events, including emotional states, that people anticipate are not as bad as predicted when they actually happen. The first section of this chapter will cover the actual emotional experience of those low in well-being before going on to discuss anticipated affect in more detail. If, as Mellers (2000) suggests, people base decisions and actions on predicting how they will feel about outcomes, it would seem to be important that people are capable of predicting the enjoyment and suffering associated with different outcomes. Indeed, as already mentioned, it is a main pillar of the cognitive model of emotional disorders that people experiencing emotional difficulties do not accurately predict their feelings. For example, a depressed person, on contemplating whether to meet up with his friends for a drink might think that there is no point because he is not going to enjoy it. If this prediction is accurate then that indicates a problem with being able to respond emotionally in the presence of a potential source of enjoyment; but if it is inaccurate it indicates a quite different type of problem stemming from prediction. Therefore, before discussing affective predictions and their accuracy in well-being, literature relating to actual affective responsiveness to events as they occur will be reviewed.

Actual affect

Depressed mood and loss of interest are the two fundamental criteria for the diagnosis of depression (see Chapter 1), so simply by definition, people who are depressed will experience more negative and less positive affect than those who are not. Similarly, a state of anxious apprehension is fundamental to the anxiety disorders (Barlow, 2014). Nevertheless, there is a reasonably extensive body of naturalistic and experimental research on experienced affect, especially in relation to depression, which paints quite a complex picture.

Experimental studies have presented depressed and non-depressed people with pleasant and unpleasant material, and assessed any differences in mood in response to that material. For example, Sloan, Strauss, and Wisner (2001) presented depressed and non-depressed women with pictures representing positive (happiness, excitement, contentment) and negative (disgust, fear, sadness) facial expressions. Participants rated how they felt upon viewing each picture, and their own facial expressions were also recorded and later coded by independent, blind raters. There was no difference between the groups while viewing negative pictures, but the depressed group reported lower pleasantness and emotional arousal to positive pictures, as well as showing less facial responsiveness. Bylsma, Morris, and Rottenberg (2008), in a systematic review of 19 laboratory studies examining responsiveness in those with major depressive disorder, compared to controls, found evidence of reduced responsiveness to *both* positive and negative stimuli, with the reduction being greatest for positive stimuli. This was true of self-reported mood and behavioural (mainly facial expression) measures, but was not reflected in physiological measures (e.g. heart rate, skin conductance). In other words, both negative and, especially, positive events have less emotional impact on those who are depressed. It is important to note that there is evidence of cultural variation in responsiveness. Chentsova-Dutton and colleagues (Chentsova-Dutton et al., 2007; Chentsova-Dutton, Tsai, & Gotlib, 2010) report evidence that whereas depressed European American women showed dampened positive and negative emotional responsiveness compared to matched non-depressed controls, depressed Asian American women did not show this pattern, even showing a tendency towards the opposite.

The picture is made even less clear, however, because more naturalistic studies find a quite different pattern of results. Experience sampling studies where depressed and non-depressed participants record their moods at random points during the day, as well as events that are happening to them, have consistently found that depressed participants, compared to those who are not depressed, show *enhanced* reactivity to positive events—their mood shows a greater brightening effect following the occurrence of positive events—at the same time as showing no greater negative mood response to unpleasant events (Bylsma, Taylor-Clift, & Rottenberg, 2011; Dunn, 2012; Peeters, Nicolson, Berkhof, Delespaul, & de Vries, 2003; Thompson et al., 2012). Moreover, in terms of specific types of moods, the effect seems to be stronger for negative affect (NA)—depressed individuals show a particularly marked reduction in negative affect following positive events. Positive affect (PA) does improve with positive events but equally so for depressed and non-depressed participants. Unpleasant events are also mood influencing: they produce increases in NA and decreases in PA, but to similar degrees for depressed and non-depressed participants. Of course, the NA starting point of the depressed group is always significantly higher than that of the controls, so the greater reduction in NA following positive events does not completely normalize it, but it does close the gap (Bylsma et al., 2011). This greater reactivity to positive events in those who are depressed is still compatible with an overall lower level of mood because of the low starting point and the fact that most of life does not consist of positive events.

It is outside the scope of this book to reconcile the differences between the experimental and naturalistic studies, but there are some implications for prospection. If there is clear evidence of differences in anticipated affect between controls and clinical or sub-clinical groups, and equivocal evidence of actual affective differences when events occur, then it places even more weight on the importance of prospection. For example, someone who is depressed might anticipate that they will feel especially bad if they have an argument with their boss, and that meeting up with friends will not lift their mood. If the reality is not like that, or at least not as much like that as anticipated, prospective cognitions take on a real significance, consistent with the cognitive model (Beck, 1976), which places emphasis on interpretation of events, rather than the reality of them. The person is likely to end up avoiding a difficult discussion with their boss and not bothering to meet up with friends, both of which might have improved things for them. It should be borne in mind that there are other, subtler ways in which actual, experienced mood might be affected. One example was reported by McMakin, Santiago, and Shirk (2009). Dysphoric and non-dysphoric students watched sad and humorous film clips while their mood was continuously measured through use of a slide lever that they could move from left to right to reflect any momentary mood changes. Against hypothesis, both groups showed similar mood responsiveness to the clips. This comparable responsiveness to the humorous film clip is shown in Figure 4.1, where the increase in mood can be seen for both groups. Mood

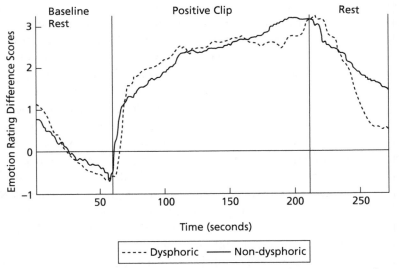

Figure 4.1 Dysphoric and non-dysphoric individuals' moment-by-moment mood responses to a humorous film clip, at baseline, during the clip and in a resting period after the clip. The comparable resting and rise can be seen, followed by the faster decay in the dysphoric group.

The time course of positive and negative emotion in dysphoria, McMakin, D. L., Santiago, C. D., Shirk, S. R., The Journal of Positive Psychology, 2009, Routledge, reprinted by permission of the publisher (Taylor & Francis Ltd, http://www.tandfonline.com).

was also measured for a resting period after the end of the clip. Figure 4.1 also shows that the decay from the peak at the end of the clip to the end of the rest period was faster for the dysphoric group. McMakin and colleagues suggest that initial reactivity might be spared in dysphoria but that there are problems maintaining improvements in mood. This is only one finding and needs to be replicated, but it is worth noting the similarity to well-being therapy (Fava & Ruini, 2003), which is based around the idea that a major problem in depression lies in the premature termination of naturally occurring elevations in mood. For example, someone may begin to feel enjoyment but that feeling triggers thoughts such as 'I don't deserve this' or 'this won't last' that then diminish the enjoyment of the moment.

Emotional disturbance and predicted affect

Anyone who has spent time listening to anxious or depressed people talk, or who has experienced anxiety and depression themselves to a reasonable degree, which must be most of the population, knows that it involves anticipating feeling bad in future situations. My colleagues and I conducted two studies that examined anticipated affect in patient samples. The Future-thinking Task (See Chapter 2), which elicits numbers of things people are looking forward to or not looking forward to also has an extended version in which after generating items, people are re-presented with their items and asked to rate how likely they think they are to happen and how they think they would feel if they did happen. In a study with depressed patients, MacLeod and Salaminiou (2001) administered the long version of the positive condition only. They also constructed a list of 75 items that had been generated by previous completers of the task, all of which had been generated by at least two people and were judged to be general enough to have broad relevance (e.g. see my family, travel abroad, have some more free time). The groups differed on all three variables: number of items they generated, ratings of anticipated affect on those items, and ratings of anticipated affect on the provided items. Therefore, as well as being able to think of fewer things they are looking forward to in the future, those who were depressed anticipated less pleasure from them, an effect that was not simply restricted to items they had generated themselves but was true for the generic list of the things people typically say they look forward to. Using the same task, MacLeod et al. (2005) found that within a large sample of suicidal patients, anticipated affect for positive items correlated significantly with levels of self-reported hopelessness, whereas the similar measure for negative items did not. Thus, it appears that, at least in the case of suicidality, anticipating lower positive feeling from future positive events may be particularly important. Gard, King, Gard, Horan, and Green (2007) elicited thoughts about what people were looking forward to using an experience sampling method. Participants were bleeped at various points in the day and asked, amongst other things, what they were looking forward to and how much pleasure they anticipated from it. Participants meeting criteria for schizophrenia or schizoaffective disorder anticipated less pleasure than controls, especially for goal-directed activities, which were activities focused on an end, such as making dinner, travelling somewhere, or working.

Picking up on the two themes of specificity and vulnerability, discussed in relation to expectancies for events in Chapter 2, there are data touching upon those themes in affective prediction too. Wenze, Gunthert, and German (2012) measured recent levels of anxious arousal (e.g. 'I was trembling or shaking') and anhedonic depression (e.g. 'I felt nothing was enjoyable') from the Mood and Anxiety Symptom Questionnaire (Watson & Clark, 1991) in a student sample, and asked them to predict how much of a range of positive and negative emotions they expected to feel over the next seven days. Both autonomic arousal and anhedonic depression correlated with how much participants expected to feel negative emotions, but only anhedonic depression correlated (inversely) with positive emotion prediction, mirroring the findings discussed in Chapter 2 on likelihood judgements for positive and negative events. Finally, on the theme of vulnerability, Marroquín, Nolen-Hoeksema, and Miranda (2013) screened a university sample to create three groups, a non-dysphoric group (BDI < 6), and two dysphoric groups (BDI > 15), who either reported or did not report a past suicide attempt. Importantly, the two dysphoric groups were comparable on BDI scores, so any differences between them could not be accountable by differing depression levels, although they were not matched on more specific levels of anhedonia. Participants were presented with a set of hypothetical positive and negative events that might happen, asked to immerse themselves in imagining the events happening and rate how happy or unhappy they thought they would feel in those circumstances. Consistent with the MacLeod et al. (2005) findings, there were no differences between the groups on predicted happiness for negative events, but all three groups differed from each other for positive events, with the control group giving the highest ratings and the dysphoric attempters the lowest ratings. A further analysis controlling for likelihood estimates of events showed that affective forecasting for positive events still differentiated the two dysphoric groups from each other, although no longer the controls from the dysphoric non-attempters. Therefore, in this study, lower anticipated happiness from future positive events appeared to be a marker of suicidal history, which is one of the main predictors of future suicidal behaviour (MacLeod, 2013).

Accuracy

The studies just described suggest that reduced anticipated affect arising from future positive events is important in emotional distress. These studies did not set out to address the issue of accuracy of such reporting. As outlined at the beginning of this chapter, those who are depressed, for example, may well derive less enjoyment from what happens to them, and therefore predicting less happiness might be calibrated with the reality of their experience, although the data on actual experience are not entirely clear on this issue. Accuracy of predicting how we will feel—affective forecasting, as it is often called—is in fact, an area that has gained a lot of attention in the past ten years. Not much of this work has been specifically in relation to well-being, and the most highly publicized finding has been that people generally overestimate how strongly they are going to feel in response to future events. This has led many to conclude that we are very poor at predicting our future affect. For example, Kashdan and Biswas-Diener (2015, p. 7), in a book aimed at the general public, state that 'we humans are horrible at guessing how happy we will feel in the future'. The evidence relating to this general area is reviewed in the following two sections (I will argue that we are not as bad as all that), and the few studies that have examined the issue in relation to disturbed mood will be reviewed in detail.

The impact bias

The 'impact bias', which describes the tendency to overestimate the emotional impact of future events, has captured a great deal of attention in the area of future-thinking about affect, and has been given wide coverage in the media, as well as in academic circles. The bias is demonstrated in its simplest form by asking people to estimate how they will feel about some future event and then recording how they do actually feel when the event occurs. A standard finding is that people overestimate how good they will feel following positive events and also how badly they will feel following negative events. In other words, people exaggerate in their minds the impact that those events will have on them. The effect has been demonstrated in a range of laboratory and real life situations (see Gilbert & Wilson, 2011). As an example, Hoerger, Quirk, Chapman, and Duberstein (2012) asked a university sample to predict how they would feel if they did or did not have a date on the upcoming Valentine's Day, which was one month away. Participants were followed up and they recorded how they actually felt on the evening of Valentine's Day, as well as the following two evenings. Analysis focused on congruent predictions and occurrence, that is, those who predicted they would have a date and did, and those who correctly predicted that they would not have a date. Daters significantly overestimated how good they would feel; in contrast, the non-daters actually felt better than they predicted they would. In other words, the daters' and non-daters' reported actual experiences were significantly closer to each other than their predicted experiences.

Whether the same phenomenon is found for bigger questions in life is harder to answer because the practicalities are more challenging. In an early study, Sieff, Dawes, and Loewenstein (1999) set out to answer the question of whether people show this bias when anticipating and then receiving the results of an HIV test. The intention was to get predicted and actual emotions from the same group of participants who had an upcoming test, but this proved to be difficult, with only a small subsample ($N = 25$) being followed up, all of whom received negative results (i.e. not HIV+). Instead, a separate sample, all of whom had received their results, was used as a comparison group for the sample who predicted how they would feel. This less-than-ideal practice of having different groups predicting the emotion, and experiencing the emotion is common in many of the studies examining the impact bias, and is often the best that can be done. There were more extreme scores in the group who were predicting their responses to the two possible test outcomes (predictors) compared to the group who had received their test results (experiencers). Figure 4.2 illustrates

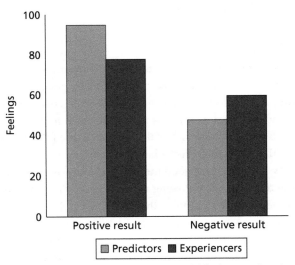

Figure 4.2 Predictors, who estimated how they would feel on getting the result of an HIV test compared to a different group of experiencers who actually had received the result of such a test. Low scores represent feeling worse. Predictors estimated the impact of the result to be more significant than the experiencers actually experienced.
Sieff, Elaine M., Dawes Robyn M., and Loewenstein George. "Anticipated versus Actual Reaction to HIV Test Results." *The American Journal of Psychology* **112**, no. 2 (1999): 297–311.

this impact bias: the predictors thought they would feel better about a negative result and worse about a positive result than the experiencers actually did feel when they got the results. However, within the sample of predictors that the researchers were able to follow up, there was no difference between the predicted and actual scores, perhaps due to small numbers ($N = 25$).

How does a phenomenon like the impact bias arise? Gilbert and Wilson (2011) suggest a number of mechanisms. To the extent that people rely on their memories of how they felt as a source of information for predicting their future feelings in similar situations, their forecasts will be biased if they do not remember typical instances. Commuters standing on a platform asked simply to recall an example of a time they had missed their train, produced instances where they felt just as bad as a different group asked to recall their worst example of missing a train (Morewedge, Gilbert, & Wilson, 2005). The interpretation here is that people spontaneously recall atypical instances (worst examples) because they stand out more, although it is also possible that participants were interpreting those kinds of examples as being what the researcher was interested in. A second source of the bias is through focusing only on particular aspects of a future event, for example, the early part. Such a focus does not take into account adaptation and the fact that other things are also taking place beside the event in question that will moderate its effect. Riis et al. (2005), using an experience sampling method to record mood, found no difference between end-stage renal dialysis patients and healthy controls, but on a simple question asking participants how they thought they would fare if they were in the other group, the controls predicted that they would feel worse if they were in the patients' situation and the patients predicted they would feel better if they were healthy. Kahneman, Krueger, Schkade, Schwarz, and Stone (2006) suggest that people are likely to focus on the initial stages--so *becoming* ill or *becoming* healthy—and ignore the adaptation that takes place as other things in life exert their usual influence on mood. Drawing attention to these other aspects of life can reduce the bias. For example, students asked to predict how they would feel if their football team won or lost were less prone to give biased (i.e. more extreme) forecasts if they were also asked to give a detailed description of what would be happening on the day that they were predicting (Wilson, Wheatley, Meyers, Gilbert, & Axsom, 2000), thus drawing attention to other aspects of experience.

Why would such a bias exist? Could it be adaptive? It is quite plausible that giving excessively high estimations of good feelings arising from future events motivates action aimed at bringing about the events, as predicated by psychological hedonism theories such as Decision Affect Theory (Mellers, 2000). Without the anticipation of feeling good, perhaps there would be no stimulus to action. Suggesting that anticipated feeling motivates behaviour is uncontroversial, although not everyone would agree that it is all there is to motivation. However, the implication of there being a ubiquitous bias to overestimate future feeling is that anticipating the amount of actual pleasure or pain from future events is not sufficient to motivate behaviour—it has to be exaggerated. Of course, such post hoc adaptational accounts are all too easy to think of. Imagine a situation where people were completely accurate in their forecasts—what they predicted was what they got. The adaptational account in that case would presumably be along the lines that it is adaptive to have accurate forecasts because it motivates behaviour at the same time as giving appropriate reinforcement for the behaviour in line with anticipation; otherwise, people would be disappointed in receiving less reward than they anticipated, and would not repeat goal-directed behaviour. This is not to say that an adaptative account is wrong, just that it is very easy to think of post hoc adaptive explanations. Of course it is true that humans have survived through adaptation but that does not mean to say that every common aspect of human experience and behaviour is adaptive.

In attempting to support a motivational aspect to affective forecasting, Morewedge and Beuchel (2013) first manipulated forecasts of how happy people thought they would feel with winning $5 on a memory test by priming participants' thoughts about winning other lower or higher amounts on a lottery. The manipulation produced the desired contrast effect, in that those primed with thoughts of a bigger lottery win anticipated less pleasure from succeeding in the task and gaining the $5 than did those primed with thoughts of a small lottery win. The low prime group (i.e. the group that anticipated more pleasure from winning $5) then spent longer when participants were allowed to spend as long as they wanted preparing for the memory task. It is interesting to show such priming effects on actual reward-directed behaviour alongside influences on anticipated feeling, but of course it is possible that the low prime group could value the $5 more when they actually do get it, and as a result would feel better in the experience of obtaining it, not just in the anticipation of getting it. What this study shows is that people are motivated by thoughts of outcomes that make them feel good, but it does not itself show that their forecasts have to be biased in order to act.

If we do consistently overestimate our future affect, why do we not learn that we do this and reduce our overestimations? For negative events this is not such a puzzle because predicting negative feelings is likely to lead to avoidance behaviour and therefore there is often no opportunity for people to realize that their negative predictions are not as bad as they thought. This is the very basis of avoidance in clinical problems, notably in various forms of anxiety where someone will avoid the situation that they think will make them anxious, for example, the socially anxious person who avoids parties. Behavioural experiments, where people are encouraged to test out their predictions, are designed to overcome just this sort of avoidance. In behavioural experiments, people are given the opportunity to experience a feared situation in order to, hopefully, see that the situation, including how they feel, is not as bad as they thought. However, for positive events, assuming people do experience them and the experience is not as great as they thought it would be, why does this not lead to disappointment and become demotivating for pursuing future positive experiences? Nothing is as great as you think it is going to be therefore why bother? One possibility is that, unless there is a stark contrast between what we expected to feel and what we do feel, we do not remember that our forecasts were overestimations. People seem to misremember their forecasts as being more accurate than they actually were (Meyvis, Ratner, & Levav, 2010). Wenze et al. (2012) also found that people's subsequent recall of the extent of emotions they experienced during one week was higher than their reported experience of the emotions measured by daily experience sampling during the week, although still not as high as predicted.

Critique of the impact bias

Despite strong claims, along with an apparent array of evidence, for the existence of an impact bias, there is some doubt about whether it is quite as compelling a phenomenon as it appears. Two telling points have been made that, whilst not debunking it, certainly tone down the claims that can be made about the impact bias.

First, when looked at closely, the evidence does not always support the existence of an impact bias. Levine, Lench, Kaplan, and Safer (2012, 2013) have drawn attention to a number of factors qualifying the conclusions that can be drawn from the evidence. The first issue is misinterpreting the prediction question. They argue that the conversational pragmatics of asking people to predict how they will feel, for example during the week after they get a worse grade than expected, means that it really equates to asking them how they will feel about the event, or how they will feel when they think about the event, rather than literally how they will feel during the rest of that week. The strong presence of the event in the prediction question necessarily leads people to interpret the question that way. In support of this argument, Levine et al. (2012) found that people did report interpreting the question in this way when prompted and that the impact bias could be reduced or eliminated when the prediction question was clarified. Also, there is a distinction between predicting intensity and predicting duration. People seem to be more accurate at predicting the intensity of their feelings than they are their duration. For example, there is greater accuracy when people are asked to predict and then report on how they feel immediately after the target event (Levine et al., 2013). Even a very small delay to the actual ratings makes a difference. What we are clearly less good at is anticipating the sort of adaptation that takes place, although, in fairness, that is also an important part of the impact bias phenomenon.

Second, the impact bias addresses only the issue of absolute accuracy: it assesses whether people's predictions deviate at all from their (or more commonly, other people's) reported experience of the same event. But, people could still be *relatively* accurate, that is, those who give high estimates of feeling good do actually feel good and those who give low estimates do feel less good, even if not to the degree that they thought they would. People can be inaccurate in an absolute sense but their forecasts can still be relatively calibrated to what actually happens. Absolute and relative accuracy are independent phenomena and it seems reasonable to consider both when thinking about accuracy. Clearly, if people were systematically overestimating their affect (absolute bias) and at the same time there was no correlation between forecasts and actual experience then that would paint a clear picture of inaccuracy. However, if despite overestimating affect, their forecasts were correlated with what they actually experience, that would add an important qualification to any statements about accuracy. One of the reasons that such data have not been presented might be because in many studies the forecasters and the experiencers have not been the same people—forecasts of one group of people for a discrete event have been compared with the experience of a different but comparable group for the same event. Even in those studies there are indications that people have some calibration. For example, the data from Sieff et al. (1999) presented earlier in Figure 4.2 show that, consistent with predictions, those who received a positive test result did show greater distress than those who received a negative result, albeit not to the same degree as predicted. In other words, people's predictions were excessive but were along the right lines.

There are a number of studies where people have actually been followed up, enabling correlation between their predictions and actual experiences, as well as examining differences between them. Mathieu and Gosling (2012) obtained the data from 11 such published articles, amounting to 16 different studies and over 1,000 participants. Effect sizes for absolute inaccuracy—the extent to which people overestimated their affect was .49 whereas effect sizes for relative accuracy—the relationship between their two scores—was .56. Taken together the results suggest that, although there is evidence for an impact bias, people are also reasonably good at predicting how they would feel. There is clear evidence for both inaccuracy (absolute) and accuracy (relative).

In summary, the evidence suggests that predicting how we will feel is quite imprecise, as might be expected, and that the tendency is to overestimate our future affective states resulting from positive and negative events. However, at least some of the evidence might have come about because of the conversational pragmatics of how the question is asked, and is less strong in any case for predicting intensity of emotion when measured immediately following the event. Alongside these debates about the extent of absolute accuracy or inaccuracy, the evidence is clear that people are reasonably accurate in a relative sense: those who predict they will feel strong affect do so and those who predict they will experience less do experience less.

Dysphoria and accuracy

There are a number of interesting individual variations in how people forecast the future, including how accurate they are. For example, Zelenski, Whelan, Nealis, Besner, Santoro et al. (2013) found that introverts over-predicted the amount of negative affect and feelings of self-consciousness that they would experience when behaving in an extraverted way. Hoerger, Chapman, Epstein and Duberstein (2012), in a laboratory task where people had to predict how they would feel upon seeing positive and negative pictures after being given descriptions of what was in the pictures, found that people were generally accurate even eight to ten weeks later (no general impact bias). In the Hoerger et al. (2012a) study measures were also taken of emotional intelligence, and these scores predicted level of accuracy, even after controlling for general intelligence, which was also measured. What is of interest for the topic we are concerned with here, is what the effects are in relation to mental health and well-being. A small number of studies have simultaneously examined accuracy in relation to dysphoria, although not depressive disorder, and those studies will now be reviewed in detail.

Yuan and Kring (2009) had dysphoric (BDI > 17) and non-dysphoric (BDI < 10) participants predict how they would feel on winning or losing a gambling task. The task was adapted from Mellers, Schwartz, and Ritov (1999) and was presented as a circle with varying percentages of winning and losing indicated by different colours (see Figure 4.3). As well as varying chances of winning or losing, there were also different amounts that could be won or lost ($8 versus $32). Participants provided ratings on four different moods—happy, contented, disappointed, irritated—upon being asked how they thought they would feel following various outcomes, for example, how happy they would feel if they won $32, where there was a 20% chance of winning. In the actual game, which took place two to four weeks later, the same circle was presented

☐ Win $8 ■ Lose $8

Figure 4.3 Pie chart of a type presented to participants. The colour and proportion of slices indicated the probability associated with winning or losing a particular amount of money. In this condition the participant is presented with a large (80%) chance of winning $8 and a small (20%) chance of losing $8.

Dysphoria and the prediction and experience of emotion, Yuan, J. W., Kring, A. M. Cognition and Emotion, 2009, Routledge, reprinted by permission of the publisher (Taylor & Francis Ltd, http://www.tandfonline.com).

and a spinner, which participants were (fictitiously) told was random, landed on either a win or loss. The various amounts and prior probabilities were the same as on the forecasting task, and participants immediately rated their mood on the four dimensions. So, participants were now rating their actual mood on the same outcomes for which they had predicted their moods. The ratings on happiness and contentment were analysed for situations where participants had won money, and disappointment and irritation were examined in relation to loss conditions.

Consistent with Mellers et al. (1999), and as would be expected, there were straightforward main effects on the mood ratings of amount of money and prior probabilities. For example, predicted and experienced positive affect was greatest on conditions of winning a high amount of money ($32) when it was unlikely (20%) and was lowest with an unexpected loss. The effects comparing predicted with actual experience and particularly involving dysphoric versus non-dysphoric participants were what was of interest. Contentment, irritation, or disappointment, showed no effects, not even a straightforward impact bias of predicted affect being higher than experienced affect. The means for happiness for the two groups, averaged across the different probability and monetary value conditions (for which there were no effects), are shown in Figure 4.4. There was a trend for the dysphoric group to predict less happiness than the non-dysphoric group, and they were significantly lower on experienced happiness

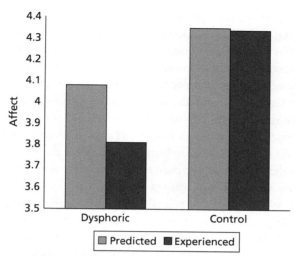

Figure 4.4 Dysphoric and control (non-dysphoric) participants' predicted and experienced happiness on various results from a gambling task. Compared to controls, dysphoric participants tended to predict less happiness but experienced even less.

Dysphoria and the prediction and experience of emotion, Yuan, J. W., Kring, A. M. *Cognition and Emotion*, 2009, Routledge, reprinted by permission of the publisher (Taylor & Francis Ltd, http://www.tandfonline.com).

after winning, compared both to their own initial predicted ratings and to the experienced happiness ratings of the control group. The control group showed no difference between conditions. So, compared to controls the dysphoric group predicted less happiness but they ended up experiencing even less!

The results support the idea of low anticipated positive affect in depression, possibly having a deleterious motivational impact, but the fact that the dysphoric group experienced even less happiness than their already low predictions is certainly not consistent with an account that emphasizes dysfunctionally inaccurate affective forecasts in those who are depressed. Obviously, the task was very artificial and was explicitly chance-driven, or so people were led to believe. Clearly, most of the activities that people might pursue in real life are related to their ability and effort so it is difficult to draw wider conclusions from this study.

In something closer to real life, Hoerger et al. (2012b), in their Valentine's Day study described earlier in the chapter, also looked at the relationship of dysphoria levels (in an unselected student sample) to the predicted and actual experience of having a Valentine's date or not. As indicated earlier, analyses focused on cases where predictions matched actual outcomes. Dysphoria was correlated (inversely) with both predicted and experienced scores on a composite measure of high positive/low negative affect, but, in contrast to Yuan and Kring (2009), the relationship was significantly stronger for prediction than it was for actual experience: those high in dysphoria both experienced and, especially, predicted more negative/less positive feeling. Dysphoria was also associated with greater overall inaccuracy (measured as average deviation from actual scores), and also with what the authors called bias, which indicates the direction of the relative difference between anticipated and actual experience. Based on a combination of overall inaccuracy being related to dysphoria and the relative bias score being in a negative direction the authors inferred that dysphoria was associated with a negative forecasting error. An actual measure of absolute bias was not reported.

Finally, the Wenze et al. (2012) study referred to earlier in the context of predicting feelings, also followed up participants to measure their actual experience of affect. As well as predicting a range of positive and negative mood states over the next seven days, participants carried a handheld device that that alerted them four times per day to record their actual mood on these days, rating the same emotion adjectives that they had used to make predictions at the initial session These ratings were used as an indicator of how much participants actually experienced emotions during the week. Consistent with an impact bias participants predicted higher levels of emotions, positive and negative, than they actually reported experiencing during the week. Interpreting analyses with dysphoria (both autonomic activation and anhedonic depression showed similar patterns) was more complex. Dysphoria was associated with even more extreme overestimation for negative moods but less overestimation for positive moods. Given that people generally overestimated negative moods, the fact that dysphoria, was associated with even more of that overestimation was interpreted as evidence of an exaggerated impact bias for negative events related to dysphoria. On the other hand, given that people generally overestimated positive experiences too, the fact that dysphoria was associated with lower scores on this overestimation was interpreted as showing that dysphoria was linked with a reduced forecasting bias for positive experiences. In other words, against a backdrop of generally excessive prediction, the tendency of dysphoric individuals to be more negative and less positive leads them to be both more biased (for negative experience predictions) and less biased (for positive experience predictions). A similar procedure to Wenze et al. (2012) has been utilized with a sample meeting criteria for schizophrenia or schizoaffective disorder (Brenner & Ben-Zeev, 2014). The findings showed that these participants estimated higher affect than they subsequently reported during the week, but the study did not address issues of accuracy and was also limited in not having a control group against which to compare the patients' scores.

Summary

Predicting future feeling states is a key aspect of thinking about the future and is likely to be particularly important in making choices about which future courses of action to pursue. Studies have examined predictions about future mood states in clinical and sub-clinical groups, and there is also a substantial literature on whether those who are depressed or dysphoric differ on the actual experience of situations when they happen. The answer to this latter question is equivocal, with conflicting results from experimental and naturalistic studies, as well as from different outcome measures. In contrast, it is clear that those who are low in mood do predict much less enjoyment from what would normally be thought of as positive events and activities, reinforcing the role of prospective thinking in mood disturbance. The overall context is that strong claims have been made about the tendency of people generally to overestimate the impact of future events on mood states, and there is evidence that this is indeed the case. However, the conclusion that we are very poor at predicting our future emotional states has been overstated. A small number of studies have measured both predicted and actual affect with the aim of assessing bias in dysphoric participants, against the background of the general tendency to overestimate emotional impact. The results have been conflicting, with different studies suggesting that, relative to non-dysphoric controls, dysphoric individuals are positively biased, negatively biased, and both positively and negatively biased in their predictions! The definitive study, which has yet to be conducted, would involve dysphoric, preferably clinically depressed, participants, predicting affect and recording actual experienced affect on both an experimentally controlled task and in a naturalistic setting. The two groups could then be compared on their predicted and actual affect across the two different tasks, using different measures of affect. Such a design would also allow conclusions about absolute bias, rather than simply relative bias, to be drawn.

An important caveat needs to be inserted at this point. Implicit in the discussion of anticipated affect and explicit in some theoretical accounts, is the idea that it is the potential affect present in future events that gives them their significance. As indicated at the beginning of this chapter, this sort of psychological hedonism can be held to varying degrees and there are other values that might be present in future events. But even within a well-being framework there are more value possibilities than simply affect. For example, Edmondson and MacLeod (2015) asked participants to generate things they were looking forward to in the future and, in an attempt to get at the underlying value of those positively anticipated events, asked participants to list things that were good about each of the things they were looking forward to. Those value responses were then coded for the presence of the six different aspects of well-being proposed by Ryff (see Chapter 1). Positive relationships, environmental mastery, and personal growth were the most common themes in the value responses of individuals, including those who were depressed. For example, someone might be looking forward to going on holiday because he can spend more time with his wife (positive relationships), or looking forward to finishing university because she will be able to start up her own business (environmental mastery). With the increased understanding of the multi-faceted nature of well-being there is a need for these more sophisticated concepts to be adopted when attempting to understand what is valuable, and motivating, about future events. Of course, it may all boil down to affect in the end (someone values spending more time with his wife because it makes him feel good) but it might not. These are important empirical questions about fundamental values inherent in how people see and move forward in the future.

References

Barlow, D. H. (Ed.) (2014). *Clinical handbook of psychological disorders: A step-by-step treatment manual* (5th edition). New York: Guilford Press.

Beck, A. T. (1976). *Cognitive therapy and the emotional disorders*. Madison, CT: International Universities Press.

Bennett-Levy, J., Butler, G., Fennell, M., Hackmann, A., Mueller, M., Westbrook, D., & Rouf, K. (2004). *Oxford guide to behavioural experiments in cognitive therapy*. Oxford: Oxford University Press.

Brenner, C. J. & Ben-Zeev, D. (2014). Affective forecasting in schizophrenia: Comparing predictions to real-time Ecological Momentary Assessment (EMA) ratings. *Psychiatric Rehabilitation Journal*, **37**(4), 316–320. http://doi.org/10.1037/prj0000105

Bylsma, L. M., Morris, B. H., & Rottenberg, J. (2008). A meta-analysis of emotional reactivity in major depressive disorder. *Clinical Psychology Review*, **28**(4), 676–691. http://doi.org/10.1016/j.cpr.2007.10.001

Bylsma, L. M., Taylor-Clift, A., & Rottenberg, J. (2011). Emotional reactivity to daily events in major and minor depression. *Journal of Abnormal Psychology*, **120**(1), 155–167. http://doi.org/10.1037/a0021662

Chentsova-Dutton, Y. E., Chu, J. P., Tsai, J. L., Rottenberg, J., Gross, J. J., & Gotlib, I. H. (2007). Depression and emotional reactivity: Variation among Asian Americans of East Asian descent and European Americans. *Journal of Abnormal Psychology*, **116**(4), 776–785. http://doi.org/10.1037/0021-843X.116.4.776

Chentsova-Dutton, Y. E., Tsai, J. L., & Gotlib, I. H. (2010). Further evidence for the cultural norm hypothesis: Positive emotion in depressed and control European American and Asian American women. *Cultural Diversity and Ethnic Minority Psychology*, **16**(2), 284–295. http://doi.org/10.1037/a0017562

Crisp, R. (2008). *Reasons and the good*. Oxford: Oxford University Press.

Dunn, B. D. (2012). Helping depressed clients reconnect to positive emotion experience: Current insights and future directions. *Clinical Psychology & Psychotherapy*, **19**(4), 326–340. http://doi.org/10.1002/cpp.1799

Edmondson, O. J. H. & MacLeod, A. K. (2015). Psychological well-being and anticipated positive personal events: their relationship to depression. *Clinical Psychology & Psychotherapy*, 22(5), 418–425. http://doi.org/10.1002/cpp.1911

Fava, G. A. & Ruini, C. (2003). Development and characteristics of a well-being enhancing psychotherapeutic strategy: Well-being therapy. *Journal of Behavior Therapy and Experimental Psychiatry*, 34(1), 45–63. http://doi.org/10.1016/S0005-7916(03)00019-3

Gard, D. E., Kring, A. M., Gard, M. G., Horan, W. P., & Green, M. F. (2007). Anhedonia in schizophrenia: Distinctions between anticipatory and consummatory pleasure. *Schizophrenia Research*, 93(1–3), 253–260. http://doi.org/10.1016/j.schres.2007.03.008

Gilbert, D. T. & Wilson, T. D. (2011). Previews, premotions and predictions. In M. Bar (Ed.), *Predictions in the brain* (pp. 159–169). Oxford: Oxford University Press.

Higgins, E. T. (2013). *Beyond pleasure and pain: How motivation works.* New York: Oxford University Press, USA.

Hoerger, M., Chapman, B. P., Epstein, R. M., & Duberstein, P. R. (2012a). Emotional intelligence: A theoretical framework for individual differences in affective forecasting. *Emotion*, 12(4), 716–725. http://doi.org/10.1037/a0026724

Hoerger, M., Quirk, S. W., Chapman, B. P., & Duberstein, P. R. (2012b). Affective forecasting and self-rated symptoms of depression, anxiety, and hypomania: Evidence for a dysphoric forecasting bias. *Cognition & Emotion*, 26(6), 1098–1106. http://doi.org/10.1080/02699931.2011.631985

Kahneman, D., Krueger, A. B., Schkade, D., Schwarz, N., & Stone, A. A. (2006). Would you be happier if you were richer? A focusing illusion. *Science*, 312(5782), 1908–1910. http://doi.org/10.1126/science.1129688

Kashdan, T. & Biswas-Diener, R. (2015). *The power of negative emotion: How anger, guilt and self-doubt are essential to success and fulfillment.* London: Oneworld Publications.

Levine, L. J., Lench, H. C., Kaplan, R. L., & Safer, M. A. (2012). Accuracy and artifact: Reexamining the intensity bias in affective forecasting. *Journal of Personality and Social Psychology*, 103(4), 584–605. http://doi.org/10.1037/a0029544

Levine, L. J., Lench, H. C., Kaplan, R. L., & Safer, M. A. (2013). Like Schrödinger's cat, the impact bias is both dead and alive: Reply to Wilson and Gilbert (2013). *Journal of Personality and Social Psychology*, 105(5), 749–756. http://doi.org/10.1037/a0034340

MacLeod, A. K. (2013). Suicide and attempted suicide. In M. J. Power (Ed.), *The Wiley-Blackwell handbook of mood disorders* (2nd ed.). (pp. 413–431). Chichester: Wiley-Blackwell.

MacLeod, A. K. & Salaminiou, E. (2001). Reduced positive future-thinking in depression: Cognitive and affective factors. *Cognition and Emotion*, 15(1), 99–107. http://doi.org/10.1080/0269993004200006

MacLeod, A. K., Tata, P., Tyrer, P., Schmidt, U., Davidson, K., & Thompson, S. (2005). Hopelessness and positive and negative future thinking in parasuicide. *British Journal of Clinical Psychology*, 44(4), 495–504. http://doi.org/10.1348/014466505X35704

Marroquín, B., Nolen-Hoeksema, S., & Miranda, R. (2013). Escaping the future: Affective forecasting in escapist fantasy and attempted suicide. *Journal of Social and Clinical Psychology*, 32(4), 446–463. http://doi.org/10.1521/jscp.2013.32.4.446

Mathieu, M. T. & Gosling, S. D. (2012). The accuracy or inaccuracy of affective forecasts depends on how accuracy is indexed: A meta-analysis of past studies. *Psychological Science*, 23(2), 161–162. http://doi.org/10.1177/0956797611427044

McMakin, D. L., Santiago, C. D., & Shirk, S. R. (2009). The time course of positive and negative emotion in dysphoria. *The Journal of Positive Psychology*, 4(2), 182–192. http://doi.org/10.1080/17439760802650600

Mellers, B. (2000). Choice and the relative pleasure of consequences. *Psychological Bulletin*, 126(6), 910–924. http://doi.org/10.1037//0033-2909.126.6.910

Mellers, B., Schwartz, A., & Ritov, I. (1999). Emotion-based choice. *Journal of Experimental Psychology: General*, 128(3), 332–345. http://doi.org/10.1037/0096-3445.128.3.332

Meyvis, T., Ratner, R. K., & Levav, J. (2010). Why don't we learn to accurately forecast feelings? How misremembering our predictions blinds us to past forecasting errors. *Journal of Experimental Psychology: General*, 139(4), 579–589. http://doi.org/10.1037/a0020285

Morewedge, C. K. & Buechel, E. C. (2013). Motivated underpinnings of the impact bias in affective forecasts. *Emotion*, 13(6), 1023–1029. http://doi.org/10.1037/a0033797

Morewedge, C. K., Gilbert, D. T., & Wilson, T. D. (2005). The least likely of times how remembering the past biases forecasts of the future. *Psychological Science*, 16(8), 626–630.

Peeters, F., Nicolson, N. A., Berkhof, J., Delespaul, P., & deVries, M. (2003). Effects of daily events on mood states in major depressive disorder. *Journal of Abnormal Psychology*, 112(2), 203–211. http://doi.org/10.1037/0021-843X.112.2.203

Riis, J., Loewenstein, G., Baron, J., Jepson, C., Fagerlin, A., & Ubel, P. A. (2005). Ignorance of hedonic adaptation to hemodialysis: A study using ecological momentary assessment. *Journal of Experimental Psychology: General*, 134(1), 3–9. http://doi.org/10.1037/0096-3445.134.1.3

Sieff, E. M., Dawes, R. M., & Loewenstein, G. (1999). Anticipated versus actual reaction to HIV test results. *The American Journal of Psychology*, 112(2), 297. http://doi.org/10.2307/1423355

Sloan, D. M., Strauss, M. E., & Wisner, K. L. (2001). Diminished response to pleasant stimuli by depressed women. *Journal of Abnormal Psychology*, 110(3), 488. http://doi.org/10.1037/0021-843X.110.3.488

Thompson, R. J., Mata, J., Jaeggi, S. M., Buschkuehl, M., Jonides, J., & Gotlib, I. H. (2012). The everyday emotional experience of adults with major depressive disorder: Examining emotional instability, inertia, and reactivity. *Journal of Abnormal Psychology*, 121(4), 819–829. http://doi.org/10.1037/a0027978

Watson, D. & Clark, L. A. (1991). The mood and anxiety symptom questionnaire. Unpublished manuscript, University of Iowa, Department of Psychology, Iowa City.

Wenze, S. J., Gunthert, K. C., & German, R. E. (2012). Biases in affective forecasting and recall in individuals with depression and anxiety symptoms. *Personality and Social Psychology Bulletin*, 38(7), 895–906. http://doi.org/10.1177/0146167212447242

Wilson, T. D., Wheatley, T., Meyers, J. M., Gilbert, D. T., & Axsom, D. (2000). Focalism: A source of durability bias in affective forecasting. *Journal of Personality and Social Psychology*, 78(5), 821–836. http://doi.org/10.1037/0022-3514.78.5.821

Yuan, J. W. & Kring, A. M. (2009). Dysphoria and the prediction and experience of emotion. *Cognition and Emotion*, 23(6), 1221–1232. http://doi.org/10.1080/02699930802416453

Zelenski, J. M., Whelan, D. C., Nealis, L. J., Besner, C. M., Santoro, M. S., & Wynn, J. E. (2013). Personality and affective forecasting: Trait introverts underpredict the hedonic benefits of acting extraverted. *Journal of Personality and Social Psychology*, 104(6), 1092–1108. http://doi.org/10.1037/a0032281

Chapter 5

Anticipatory feelings

Introduction

The feelings that are evoked when thinking about upcoming events are sometimes called *immediate emotions* or *anticipatory emotions* in an attempt to distinguish them clearly from anticipated emotions (discussed in Chapter 4) that someone predicts that they *will* feel *when* an event happens. Because the term immediate emotions might be confused with feelings experienced at the actual time the event occurs, I will use the term anticipatory emotions to describe those feelings that someone experiences in the here-and-now when thinking about something that is in the future. The present chapter will deal with these emotional states that arise when anticipating the future.

Somatic markers

One of the most striking and well-known claims for the importance of anticipatory emotions is the Somatic Marker Hypothesis (Damasio, 2005). The idea behind the hypothesis is that choices about what action to take are influenced by memories of emotional states that have previously arisen from certain situations. If a similar situation arises it activates the emotional state again, which is then used as a guide to interpreting the situation and making behavioural choices. Importantly, this process is not dependent on reasoning, although reasoning can then be applied to the feeling state that arises. But if the judgement and choice to be made is complex then the feeling state itself will be used as a guide to what to do. Moreover, this can occur in a fairly automatic way, even, it has been claimed, at a level below conscious awareness. At a neurological level, this anticipatory process depends on activity in the ventromedial prefrontal cortex and the amygdala (Bechara, Damasio, Tranel, & Damasio, 1997). When the system is not functioning properly, that is, when these anticipatory feelings are absent or weakened, it has been characterized as a sort of 'myopia for the future' (Bechara, Dolan, & Hindes, 2002, p. 1690), although of course that would only apply to future situations that were dependent on effective functioning of the system (i.e. presumably there would also be situations where people could rely on retrieved memories of previous situations to choose appropriately, or think through options in a purely cognitive way, rather than to have to tap into an affective state to make an effective choice).

Much of the evidence for the somatic marker hypothesis comes from experimental studies using the Iowa Gambling Task (Bechara, Damasio, Damasio, and Anderson, 1994). In the task, players, who are unaware of the rules, are presented with four decks of cards and have to choose a deck from which to turn over a card. The experimenter controls the rate at which they turn the cards by saying 'go' before each turn. The game is structured so that participants receive large rewards when they choose a card from decks A or B and small rewards from decks C and D. However, they also sometimes get a penalty, which they cannot predict. The penalty is large when cards from decks A and B are involved and small in those cards from decks C and D. The game is stopped after 100 turns and is structured in such a way that players end up winning more money if they consistently choose cards from decks C and D. Various measures can be derived from the task: effectiveness (number of cards chosen from the good decks); skin conductance responses while they are pondering a choice (before the experimenter tells them to go on each turn); and participants' understanding of the game, which is probed periodically. Not surprisingly, gamblers perform poorly on the task, being overly attracted to the rewards of cards from decks A and B, while being insensitive to the punishments associated with those cards (see Brevers, Bechara, Cleeremans, & Noël, 2013 for a review).

Those who have suffered brain injury, particularly frontal injury, also perform less well on the task. Bechara et al. (1997) compared a control sample with patients who had bilateral, prefrontal damage. Patients performed poorly, compared to controls, and most were not able to give an account of what was happening in the game, even by the end. Interestingly, Bechara et al. (1997) point out that even the patients who were able to work out the rules still continued to choose cards from A and B, whereas control participants who were not able to say what the rules were, did, nevertheless, play more effectively by choosing from decks C and D. Of particular interest are the skin conductance responses (SCRs) shown by participants while they were contemplating which deck to choose. After a number of penalties had occurred, control participants showed elevated SCRs in the contemplation period. Patients, on the other hand, did not show elevated SCRs, even by the end of the game. Bechara et al. (1997) argue that the patients had lost the ability to experience anticipatory emotions, which are shown by SCR elevations, and that this resulted in poorer choice performance. There are critiques of these findings (e.g. Fernie & Tunney, 2013), which focus largely on whether, as claimed by Bechara et al. (1997), the anticipatory signals precede conscious knowledge. This particular debate is not crucial to the point being made here, which is that there is clear evidence of an anticipatory affective response that functions as a guide to action.

Liking versus wanting

A second line of work, which shares with the Somatic Marker Hypothesis a neurological level of explanation, is the work of Berridge and colleagues on the distinction between *liking* and *wanting* (Berridge & Kringelbach, 2013; Berridge, Robinson, & Aldridge, 2009; Kringelbach & Berridge, 2012). Liking, also sometimes referred to as gustatory pleasure, refers to the positive response that occurs to a pleasant stimulus as it is experienced (see Chapter 4). Wanting is the emotional response someone experiences to a future pleasant stimulus that is anticipated but has not yet occurred. The ventral tegmental area, nucleus accumbens and orbitofrontal and cingulate cortex, along with associated dopamine pathways have long been thought to be the neural circuitry of pleasure. Kringelbach and Berridge (2012) argue that, in fact, these are the systems that support desire or wanting. There are various sources of evidence for this position. Mice genetically engineered to have an excess of dopamine move more quickly towards a reward (food) but do not show any elevated pleasure response (licking their lips) on gaining the reward. That is, they seem to have a strong desire to gain a reward but show little additional enjoyment from it once gained. Conversely, dopamine-free rats show no interest in moving towards a food reward but do show normal lip-licking when the reward is placed in their mouths, suggesting unimpaired ability to enjoy a reward when it happens. Berridge and Kringelbach (2013) argue that in contrast to this quite neurologically diffuse traditional pleasure system, which turns out to be associated with anticipation, there are highly specific 'hedonic hot spots' that, if stimulated, produce greater liking responses. What these data show, as well as localizing the different systems, is that the two systems can be distinguished meaningfully and appear to be separable. Obviously, in a well-functioning system the two aspects are integrated so that we desire things that will make us feel good and we feel good when we get the things that we desire. It has been argued that a key problem in addiction is where, over time, people actually come to desire things that they do not want, that is the desire, or craving, increases while the enjoyment or pleasure derived from the substances declines (Berridge et al. 2009).

Knutson and Greer (2008) have outlined an anticipatory affect model in which all future outcomes that are uncertain produce feelings of arousal, and the valence of this arousal depends on whether cues indicate that there are potential gains or potential losses in these future outcomes. Neuroimaging studies suggest two, at least partially, dissociated systems. In a meta-analysis of fMRI studies that involved participants completing a task where cues indicated that they might gain or lose money (Knutson & Greer, 2008), anticipating a gain was associated with increased activity in the nucleus accumbens, whereas both gain and loss anticipation were associated with a common area of increased activation (anterior insula and medial caudate). Self-ratings of affective valence and arousal being experienced by the participants during the task showed that anticipating gains increased positivity and arousal, whereas loss anticipation resulted in greater negativity along with increased arousal. Interestingly though, valence responses (feeling good or bad) were stronger when people actually received the results of a trial (experienced a loss or a gain) compared to anticipating. In contrast, arousal was largely unaffected by experiencing losses or gains. Arousal would appear to be key to anticipation, albeit with differing valence depending on whether the contemplated outcome is positive or negative. The lesser impact of anticipation on emotional valence, compared to the impact that actual outcomes have, also suggests that the positivity or negativity of anticipatory affect might be a relatively subtle phenomenon, but nonetheless important because it 'colours in' the arousal experienced.

Hope and fear

Hope and fear are the archetypal emotions experienced in the moment when contemplating future negative and positive events, respectively (Kirkland & Cunningham, 2012). Fear and anxiety are obviously very closely related, with the terms often used interchangeably, although they also may be distinguishable in some ways, such as how specific the object of the anxiety is, or the coping responses available (Öhman, 2008). As indicated in Chapter 2, thinking about future possible personal threats is a key feature of the anxiety disorders. Barlow (2004) suggests that anxious apprehension, a mental state focused on contemplating the possibility of future threatening events, is the fundamental process underlying all anxiety disorders. The affective component of anxious apprehension consists of high levels of experienced negative affect and arousal, the function of which is to be prepared to cope with upcoming negative events. In anxiety disorders, anxious apprehension is also typically accompanied by a sense of uncontrollability (Barlow, 2004). What differentiates the different anxiety disorders from each other is the nature of the threat. For example, in panic disorder, anxiety arises through the fear of having future panic attacks, whereas in social anxiety, the concern is about being evaluated negatively by others. Sometimes the anxiety is focused on a specific feared object, as in the case of simple phobias, and other times, for example in generalized anxiety disorder, the apprehension is more diffuse. In all cases, the thought is about future harm, accompanied by anxious feelings in the here-and-now.

The anticipatory emotional component of anxiety is very apparent. In the case of depression, the involvement of anticipatory feeling is less obvious because what appears to characterize depression is a lack of positive anticipatory feeling—it is what is missing that is important. The two key symptoms given pre-eminence in the diagnosis of major depressive episode or major depressive disorder (American Psychiatric Association, 2013) are low mood and loss of interest, both of which reflect the loss or absence of affective elements that are normally present. Both may also crucially involve lack of anticipatory feelings. It is as if when people are depressed they do not experience the spark of feeling that comes from contemplating the future, and that the presence of this spark of feeling is essential to motivate current behaviour

People who are depressed may fail to experience a spark of feeling when they contemplate the future for several reasons. First, they perceive positive future events to be relatively unlikely and don't anticipate them happening (Chapter 2). Second, they may anticipate feeling less good, even if those events did happen, (Chapter 4). Finally, their affective systems are just more likely to be generally dampened and less responsive (Chapter 4). All of these effects would result in a lack of anticipatory positive affect—a failure to experience in the moment positive affect when contemplating the future. Furthermore, not being able to envisage future positive events in a specific, detailed way, which will be discussed more fully in Chapters 6, 7, and 8, might be an important part of this overall picture. Raffard, Esposito, Boulenger, and Van der Linden (2013) found that, compared with a control group, participants diagnosed with schizophrenia (who were also elevated in depression) showed less specific, detailed representations of future events. Importantly for the present discussion, one particular aspect of representations of positive future events, which included a sense of pre-experiencing the event and having a feeling of emotion when the event was thought about, correlated with level of apathy experienced by participants. Apathy was higher when participants had representations of future events that they described as lower in a sense of pre-experiencing the event, and lower in emotion when they thought of it. This finding fits with the idea of feelings in the here-and-now when thinking about future events being a necessary ingredient in motivating and energizing behaviour. It should be noted, however, that the group difference in quality of representations was not replicated when participants were asked to describe three personally significant future events (Raffard et al., 2015), so future work needs to establish under what conditions these effects occur.

Chapter 2 discussed how one particular facet of depression—hopelessness—is key for suicidality. Hopelessness is, literally, lack of hope. There has been some debate about how hope is best conceptualized. Snyder's influential model of hope (Cheavens Feldman, Gum, Michael, & Snyder, 2006; Snyder, Harris, Anderson, Holleran, Irving et al., 1991) views it largely as a cognitive-motivational construct consisting of two elements, agency and pathways. Agency describes the belief that one is capable of achieving goals (e.g. 'I meet the goals that I set for myself), and pathways refers to a belief that there are routes to achieving goals and overcoming setbacks (e.g. 'There are lots of ways round any problem). Conceived of in this way, hope does not have much of an emotional component at all. In contrast, others have argued that hope is primarily an emotional state, one that is associated with the anticipation of a positive outcome (Averill, Catlin, & Chon, 1990). Averill et al. (1990) distinguish hope from optimism by suggesting that the latter reflects an appraisal about the likelihood of a future event, whereas hope is a feeling state accompanying it. In analysing how people commonly use the term, they conclude that hope requires the outcome to have a realistic probability of occurrence (although not be certain) and be personally important. In one sense, these differing views of hope are semantic disagreements, but semantics matter for conceptual clarity, especially being clear about what *constitutes* a construct as opposed to the different question of what other constructs are associated with it. Efficacy and pathways beliefs being related to hope should not expand the definition of hope by concluding that this is what hope consists of. Bruininks and Malle (2005) also point out that the Snyder conceptualization does not account for the fact that people can experience hope for things that they don't have any control over but nevertheless matter to them. Hoping for a good recovery for an elderly relative who is ill or, more mundanely, for good weather for a family outing would be clear examples of hope in the absence of control, efficacy, and plans, but there are many others. It would be fair to say that hope is used in different ways by different researchers, but it seems most obviously to be an emotional state that is directed towards a desired future outcome that has a possibility of happening and where the outcome matters.

Psychological measures of anticipatory feeling

Separating out anticipatory emotions from anticipated emotions and other judgements using psychological measures is not a simple task. It is quite easy for self-report questions to be unclear about whether they are referring to anticipatory, as opposed to anticipated emotions, or even some other variable. For example, Baumgartner, Pieters, and Bagozzi (2008) utilized a naturally occurring event, the Y2K problem, the concern that the change in the clocks in moving to a new millennium could give rise to serious problems in multiple computing systems. It seems strange looking back on it now, but it was the case that at least some people were worried about the virtual breakdown of civilization as a result. Baumgartner et al. (2008) attempted to measure anticipated and anticipatory emotion about the Y2K problem, relating them to other variables such as perceived likelihood of the problem and behaviour taken to prepare for the problem (e.g. stocking up on food). Anticipatory emotion was operationalized through questions about how hopeful, optimistic, and worried people felt, as well as how confident they felt that there would be no bad outcomes for them. It is easy to see that these questions could easily have been interpreted by respondents as an appraisal or judgement about the future event, for example how likely the event was or how badly they thought it would affect them, rather than asking for their emotional state in that moment when they thought about the future event. Unfortunately for the study, it turned out that people were not really very worried about Y2K at all (on average less than two on a seven-point scale), which limited the findings, but the main point being illustrated here is the potential for questions to confuse anticipatory feeling with anticipated feeling, or even other judgements about the event. Barsics, Van der Linden, and D'Argembeau (2016) utilized a similar self-report methodology but, using a naturalistic thought sampling method, asked participants to record future-oriented thoughts that were accompanied by a feeling state. Participants rated both the emotion felt at the time and the emotion they anticipated they would feel when the situation the future-thought related to occurred. Of the example emotions they were given (fear, joy, pride, anger, shame, and sadness), fear and joy were by far the most common emotions rated as occurring at the time. Interestingly, fear was significantly more prevalent in anticipatory than anticipated feeling ratings, whereas joy, although the most common anticipatory emotion, was even more common in the ratings of how people thought they would feel in the future (i.e. anticipated). It is worth noting that the correlation between anticipated and anticipatory ratings was extremely high ($r = .78$). This correlation can be taken as indicating that the two concepts are very closely connected, or that participants found it difficult to make the distinction very clearly, especially considering that sometimes the ratings were done in retrospect rather than at the time of the thought occurring. It is quite possible that there is truth in both of these interpretations.

A different kind of approach to distinguishing anticipatory and anticipated feelings is through utilizing an experimental method, giving greater control over both outcomes being thought about, and measures. Schlösser, Dunning, and Fetchenhauer (2013) described a set of gambling studies where participants were given $5 and could choose to keep it or gamble it, for example, on a 50% chance of winning $10. Participants were asked to estimate how they would feel about each of the four possible outcomes if they happened (e.g. if they chose to gamble and lost) and also asked to say how they felt right now when considering what to choose. Anticipatory feelings (how they felt now when contemplating the gamble) predicted choice over and above perceived probability of winning/losing and estimations of how they would feel about outcomes after they happened.

One of the most systematic attempts to isolate and measure psychologically the anticipatory emotion system is a series of studies by Van Boven and Ashworth (2007), mentioned in Chapter 1. Van Boven and Ashworth (2007) were interested in how people felt in the here-and-now when they recalled past events or anticipated similar events in the future. For example, people remembered or anticipated Thanksgiving, and reported on how they felt while doing that. In one of the studies, participants rated their right-now feelings on 15 different emotions. Participants also had to rate their remembered feelings at the time of the event or the feelings that they anticipated they would feel in the future when the event occurred, further helping them to recognize the distinction between anticipatory and anticipated feelings. A range of different events were used, including real life events (Thanksgiving, menstruation), a hypothetical event (ski vacation), and experimentally manipulated events (annoying noises that they either had already experienced or were going to experience in the future having already been given a taster of the noises). Reported current mood was consistently better (e.g. Thanksgiving) and worse (e.g. menstruation) when people anticipated, compared to when they remembered. In other words, anticipation had a greater impact on current mood than did remembering, a consistent finding across the other studies. These findings further support the distinction between anticipatory and anticipated (as well as remembered) emotion, and suggest that people are able to report on their anticipatory emotions.

As a final example of measuring the experience of anticipatory emotions, Gard, Gard, Kring, and John (2006) designed a self-report measure—the Temporal Experiences of Pleasure Scale (TEPS)—to assess trait-like aspects of anticipatory, as distinct from consummatory pleasure. Sample items are shown in Table 5.1. Patients diagnosed with schizophrenia or schizoaffective disorder showed reduced anticipatory pleasure compared to controls (Gard, Kring, Gard, Horan, & Green, 2007), supporting the idea of anticipatory deficits being salient for this group (Raffard et al., 2013). The groups did not differ on consummatory pleasure. Consistent with the between-group effects, clinical ratings of anhedonia were correlated with anticipatory but not consummatory pleasure. A note of caution is that a number of items on the anticipatory

Table 5.1 The three highest loading items on the anticipatory and consummatory pleasure subscales from the Temporal Experiences of Pleasure Scale

Anticipatory pleasure	Consummatory pleasure
◆ When I think about eating my favorite food I can almost taste how good it is.	◆ The sound of crackling wood in the fireplace is very relaxing.
◆ When I think of something tasty, like a chocolate chip cookie, I have to have one.	◆ The smell of freshly cut grass is enjoyable to me.
◆ When ordering something off the menu I imagine how good it will taste.	◆ I appreciate the beauty of a fresh snowfall.

Adapted from Journal of Research in Personality, 40 (6), Gard, D. E., Gard, M. G., Kring, A. M., & John, O. P., Anticipatory and consummatory components of the experience of pleasure: A scale development study, 1086–1102, Copyright 2006, with permission from Elsevier.

pleasure subscale, including the three highest loading items, are related to food, whereas none of the items on the consummatory pleasure subscale are food related. Rather, the latter scale is largely about appreciation of sounds, smells, and sights in nature (none of the anticipatory items had such content). These content differences make the findings more difficult to interpret. For example, it is not clear how results would look if the consummatory pleasure scale contained items such as 'When I put the first forkful of a good meal in my mouth I really love it'.

Emotional avoidance

An important aspect of anticipatory affect is how people respond to it, something that may be particularly important in the case of negative anticipatory affect. Avoidance is an obvious consequence of feelings of anxiety about a future threat, and dealing with avoidance is a key ingredient of the treatment of anxiety (Barlow, 2004). Aside from behavioural avoidance (e.g. staying at home to avoid a panic attack, refusing social invitations to avoid feelings of acute self-consciousness, leaving someone else to do the garden to avoid encountering any spiders), people may also find internal ways of directly avoiding the negative feeling states themselves. When people experience feelings of anxiety upon contemplating the future, for example, they may well try to suppress or avoid or minimize them. It is not difficult to see that this is a natural response—who likes to feel bad? Increasingly it is being recognized and argued that this emotional avoidance is a fundamental problem in itself, and, in fact, can even become more of a problem than the primary (usually negative) emotional states to which it is a response. Within a behavioural framework, avoidance of internal, unpleasant states, such as feelings of anxiety, is thought to reduce exposure and therefore limit the extinction of those states (Foa & Kozak, 1986). Preventing avoidance of unwanted experience is also part of standard CBT treatment (Barlow, Allen, & Choate, 2004) and is also fundamental to third wave cognitive behavioural therapies such as acceptance and commitment therapy (ACT; Hayes, Strosahl, & Wilson, 2011), mindfulness based cognitive therapy (MBCT; Segal, Williams, & Teasdale, 2012) and dialectical behaviour therapy (DBT; Linehan, 1993), where emotional avoidance is contrasted with acceptance, in which someone is willing to tolerate the experience of these unwanted internal states in a non-judgemental way without trying to change them.

Like many of the most intriguing and potentially valuable constructs in psychology, emotional avoidance is difficult to measure. Because the avoidance is of internal psychological states rather than external situations, straightforward behavioural indices are of limited use. Self-report measures are an obvious choice. One commonly used self-report measure of emotional avoidance is the Acceptance and Action Questionnaire (AAQ; Hayes et al., 2004), subsequently revised as the AAQ-II (Bond et al., 2011). The AAQ-II was rebadged as a measure of psychological flexibility/inflexibility, because avoidance is seen as part of the broader concept of psychological (in)flexibility central to ACT, where people are able to choose to pursue valued goals despite emotional discomfort. It is worth noting that in ACT, the term 'flexibility' is used in a particular, idiosyncratic way, incorporating the two elements that are central to ACT: 'the ability to contact the present moment more fully as a conscious human being, and to change or persist in behavior when doing so serves valued ends' (Hayes, Luoma, Bond, Masuda, & Lillis, 2006, p. 7). What is not clear is whether the items on the AAQ-II do measure this broader construct.

The AAQ-II, like some other psychological self-report measures (see Hawkes & Brown, 2015; Nicholls, Licht, & Pearl, 1982), suffers from the difficulty of separating the variable it is interested in, in this case avoidance (or, in terms of the model, avoidance as part of inflexibility), from the construct that the variable is intended to explain—ongoing psychological difficulties characterized by distress. For example, some of the items from the AAQ-II could, if presented on their own, be taken for items measuring straightforward psychological distress. Items such as 'emotions cause problems in my life' or 'my painful memories prevent me from having a fulfilling life', are items intended to measure *responses* to negative feelings rather than the presence of negative feelings themselves. Such a subtle distinction, while possibly clear when seen through the lens of an expert in the area, may well be lost on participants simply asked to read and rate themselves on these statements. Participants have been shown to find it hard even to distinguish between behavioural avoidance, which is obviously more concrete than emotional avoidance and distress (Gamez, Kotov, & Watson,

2010). It is quite possible that someone could score highly on the AAQ-II simply through having a lot of negative feelings. Responding strongly to 'I'm afraid of my feelings' could arise because I experience a lot of strong negative feelings, such that anyone who had them would be afraid of them, something that is not the intended target of the measure. Alternatively, it could be that I have the usual sort of amount of negative feelings but respond with excessive fear, which does now reflect the aim of the measure. There is no way of telling which of these two outcomes the measure actually assesses. Similarly, someone scoring low on this item might reflect the fact that they simply do not experience much in the way of negative feelings, so there is nothing to be afraid of, as opposed to it being the case that they do have negative feelings but respond in an unafraid, accepting way. Hawkes and Brown (2015) point out that with low scores on such double-barrelled items there is no way of distinguishing between the two possibilities. On a separate point, it is also worth noting that an item about being afraid of feelings does not actually measure avoidance; it is one step removed, simply measuring something that is assumed to be a precursor to avoidance.

Despite the aforementioned problems the AAQ and AAQ-II have been widely used, but the measurement problems have been recognized (Gamez et al., 2010; Wolgast, 2014). Wolgast (2014) highlighted the problem of process and outcome overlap by constructing new items that separated out the mixed content of the AAQ-II items. These new items either contained just the distress element (e.g. I have lots of painful memories) or just the acceptance/non-acceptance element (I do the things I want to do even if it makes me feel nervous or anxious). AAQ-II items loaded clearly onto a factor with distress items whereas five of the seven acceptance/non-acceptance items loaded onto a separate factor. Perhaps the most interesting finding to emerge from the factor analysis, however, was that two of the items constructed to measure acceptance/non-acceptance loaded onto neither of the two main factors but formed a third factor on their own. Those two items—"I do the things I want to do even if it makes me feel nervous or anxious" and "When I feel anxious, worried, or depressed I note those feelings but live my life the way I want to"—arguably get most clearly to the heart of psychological flexibility as contained in ACT, that is the ability to pursue valued goals despite the presence of inner discomfort.

Other measures have been developed that try to measure avoidance in a more specific way (Gámez, Chmielewski, Kotov, Ruggero, Suzuki et al., 2014; Gámez, Chmielewski, Kotov, Ruggero, & Watson 2011; Stapinski, Abbott, & Rapee, 2014). Stapinski et al. (2014) developed the Affect Intolerance Scale, consisting of two subscales. The avoidance/suppression subscale, with items such as 'I try to avoid negative feeling' and 'I try to avoid anything that will trigger my negative feelings' clearly maps onto the idea of emotional avoidance, although still suffers from the same issue of greater experiencing of negative feelings potentially being at the root of any avoidance. In contrast, the other subscale—threat expectancy (e.g. 'my negative feelings could spiral out of my control', 'I experience negative emotions more intensely than others')—has a very strong element of the primary experience of negative feelings—but clearly does not fit well in an overall measure labelled as a measure of emotional intolerance. Finally, Gamez and colleagues (Gámez et al., 2011, 2014) developed a scale to reflect the multidimensional nature of emotional avoidance, as well as to address the overlap with negative emotionality. The measure has subsequently been condensed into a brief version, containing items such as 'I work hard to keep out upsetting feelings' or 'I rarely do things that might upset me'. Such statements certainly hone in much more clearly on emotional avoidance and empirically have been shown to have lower (but still medium sized) correlations with self-reported neuroticism than does the AAQ-II. It is, however, difficult, to get away entirely from the fact that response to these items may be influenced, strongly influenced in some cases, by the extent or degree of the negative emotions felt rather than the response to them.

A final point to mention is that there may well be cultural differences in the desire to avoid negative emotions, even among countries where there is some historical connection. Koopman-Holm and Tsai (2014) compared European Americans with a matched group of Germans on their actual experience of, and their desire to avoid, negative emotions. While there was little difference between the groups from the two countries on experienced negative emotion, the American group showed a significantly greater desire to avoid negative emotions. Moreover, an analysis of sympathy cards from the two countries showed less negative (e.g. "We mourn the loss") and more positive (e.g. "Hold on to hope") content in the American cards than in those from Germany.

Worry as avoidance

Avoidance of negative emotions is widely accepted as a secondary problem that contributes to a person's difficulties by maintaining or even exacerbating their negative emotions. Taking things a step further, worry, previously seen as a primary, future-oriented, anxiety-related problem that causes distress, has itself been cast in the role of an avoidance behaviour (Borkovec & Hu, 1990). Part of the rationale for this repositioning of worry is that (a) worry is primarily verbal rather than imagery based, (b) imagery is associated with stronger affective responses, therefore (c) it is possible that worry could be an avoidance of the more emotionally upsetting imagery that someone might experience in relation to future negative events. Of course, in purely logical terms this does not necessarily follow, but data have been presented in support of the idea that worry does function in this way. Probably the strongest pillar upon which the idea is built is evidence that involves people engaging in worry about a threat, then confronting an image related to the threat. The exposure to the image is intended to mimic the experience of what it is like to actually encounter the threat. An influential study by Borkovec and Hu (1990) had participants, all of whom were fearful of public speaking, worry about public speaking, think neutral thoughts, or think relaxing thoughts, then subsequently bring to mind images of themselves in a public speaking situation (e.g. standing before a large audience, feeling their mouth go dry, etc.). The increase in heart rate upon entering the imagery phase was lowest in those who had spent their thinking period worrying, and largest in those who had spent the time thinking relaxing thoughts. Strangely, Borkovec and Hu (1990) compared the rise in anxiety from the thinking period to the imagery period rather than comparing heart rate in the imagery phase to baseline heart rate before participants engaged in worrying, relaxing or neutral thinking. When that comparison is made, rather than using change from the thinking period, the effect is no longer present (Peasley-Miklus & Vrana, 2000). Figure 5.1 illustrates in a schematic way the general

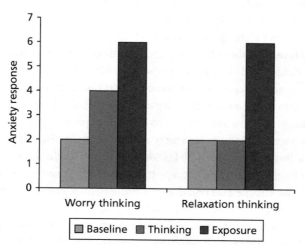

Figure 5.1 A schematic representation of what happens in experiments where baseline anxiety ratings (subjective, physiological) are taken, people are asked to think either worrisome or relaxing thoughts, and then are exposed to a threat image. Engaging in worry thinking before exposure produces a stepped change in anxiety that is inconsistent with worry as avoidance, and explains why there is a more dramatic change in the relaxation group.

pattern that appears to hold in studies of this type. The attenuated increase from the thinking stage to where threat is imagined appears to be due to the fact that people asked to worry start to experience some physiological and subjective feelings of anxiety as a result of worrying. Not surprisingly, they then show less additional *incremental* change when asked to bring to mind images of a feared event (see Newman & Llera, 2011). In contrast, those who have been thinking relaxing thoughts, when then asked to contemplate threatening images understandably show a spike in anxious responding. If absolute levels of anxious responding (either physiological or subjective) during the exposure phase are used then there is no difference between those asked to worry and those asked to relax (Newman & Llera, 2011). In fact, there is overwhelming evidence that during worry people do experience increased physiological reactivity as well as increased subjective states of negative affect (see Newman & Llera, 2011), raising serious doubts about whether there is any reason to think of worry as avoidance.

The data would appear to support the traditional view of worry as causing (or being a component) of negative emotional states rather than being an attempt to suppress them. Worrying may well have a functional role, but rather than being about warding off negative images in order to limit arousal, it is likely to be about bracing oneself for a 'hit', as well as thinking about possible steps that might be taken to minimize or avoid the situation. Newman and Llera (2011) have elaborated on this traditional view of worry by suggesting that worry is indeed about bracing. Their Contrast Avoidance Model of worry (Newman & Llera, 2011) argues that people with GAD and high anxiety prefer to have ongoing negative emotional states rather than have a sudden spike of anxiety due to encountering a negative event. Take the example of public speaking anxiety. Someone who is anxious about public speaking might prefer to have a week of increasing worry and consequent discomfort leading up to the occasion, accompanied by less dramatic increase in their anxiety when they come to give their talk (because it is quite high already), rather than feel relaxed and be knocked off balance by a sudden, overwhelming wave of anxiety at the time of the talk. For Newman and Llera (2011) it is not avoidance of emotions so much as avoidance of a rapid increase in negative emotion that motivates worry. This is an interesting interpretation, and is certainly consistent with my own experience of working with chronic worriers in the clinic, who commonly talk about the worst scenario being where they drop their guard (stop worrying) and are then taken by surprise by the worried-about event happening.

The Contrast Avoidance Model has intuitive appeal, but it is worth remembering that what underpins the theory is the basic finding that worrying makes people more (rather than less) anxious. It is then a matter of interpretation to say that worry is a motivated behaviour, chosen to minimise the potential increase in anxiety that would occur should the person encounter a negative life situation in the future. This is, of course possible, and it has some plausibility, but there are two challenges to the view. The first is that typically, people who worry a lot report little control over their worry (Barlow, 2004), indicating that it is, at least subjectively, not a consciously chosen strategy. A bigger challenge is the consistent finding discussed in Chapter 2, that anxiety and worry are associated with an elevated belief in the likelihood of negative events happening. It is plausible that it is simply this increased sense of future threats being likely that gives direct rise to worry, rather than it being the case that some people are particularly sensitive to large increases in future anxiety, and that worry (through raising anxiety now) functions to minimise that. The Contrast Avoidance Model would be more persuasive if it could be shown that worry does not simply coexist as function of perceived future threat. This is the problem faced by any secondary process model (i.e. one that attempts to explain a phenomenon by people's reactions to a basic primary problem): parsimony would dictate accepting the primary problem (e.g. thinking bad things are likely to happen) as an account of the phenomenon (anxious worry) with little need for further explanation by reference to a secondary problem (how someone responds to thinking bad things are likely to happen and the associated feelings of anxiety). This is not to say that secondary responses do not have an important role to play, for example, in maintenance or exacerbation of a problem. On a practical note, it might also be the case that secondary processes are more amenable to change than are primary processes, and to that extent they represent important targets of intervention.

Summary and conclusion

Emotional states are not simply responses to events that have happened in the past or are happening in the present but often arise in relation to events that are yet to happen. These anticipatory emotions have sometimes been confused with anticipated, or predicted emotions (to which they may be linked), but they are distinct because they are about feeling states in the here-and-now. These present moment anticipatory feeling states are mediated through distinct neural systems that are different from those underlying emotional states arising in response to events having already occurred. Anticipatory feelings are important guides to action, and, arguably, represent the spark that is often needed for any animal, including humans, to take action towards desired, or avoid undesired, future states. Hope and fear represent the typical anticipatory emotional states, with links to depression and anxiety representing a deficit and excess of hope and fear, respectively. Measuring anticipatory emotions psychologically has proven to be something of a challenge, partly because of the difficulty separating it from other variables, such as judgements about the future. Work remains to be done on how anticipatory emotions can be measured at the psychological level. Avoidance of emotional states, of which anticipatory emotions are an important example, has come to be seen as central to psychological distress but has proven to be elusive to measurement. Emotional avoidance is an intriguing notion with a lot of clinical plausibility, but it is not straightforward to devise measures that are able to identify it as something distinct from participants' primary experience of the emotion that is assumed to be being avoided. In an interesting twist, worry, which has traditionally been seen as the cognitive element of anticipatory anxiety, has been recast in the role of an activity functioning to avoid negative emotion, although the data do not support such a reconceptualization.

References

American Psychiatric Association (2013). *Diagnostic and statistical manual of mental disorders.* (5th edition). Washington, DC: Author.

Averill, J. R., Catlin, G., & Chon, K. K. (1990). *Rules of hope.* New York: Springer.

Barlow, D. H. (2004). *Anxiety and its disorders: The nature and treatment of anxiety and panic* (2nd edition). New York: Guilford Press.

Barlow, D. H., Allen, L. B., & Choate, M. L. (2004). Toward a unified treatment for emotional disorders. *Behavior Therapy*, **35**(2), 205–230. http://doi.org/10.1016/S0005-7894(04)80036-4

Barsics, C., Van der Linden, M., & D'Argembeau, A. (2016). Frequency, characteristics, and perceived functions of emotional future thinking in daily life. *The Quarterly Journal of Experimental Psychology*, **69**(2), 217–233. http://doi.org/10.1080/17470218.2015.1051560

Baumgartner, H., Pieters, R., & Bagozzi, R. P. (2008). Future-oriented emotions: Conceptualization and behavioral effects. *European Journal of Social Psychology*, **38**(4), 685–696. http://doi.org/10.1002/ejsp.467

Bechara, A., Damasio, A. R., Damasio, H., & Anderson, S. W. (1994). Insensitivity to future consequences following damage to human prefrontal cortex. *Cognition*, **50**(1–3), 7–15. http://doi.org/10.1016/0010-0277(94)90018-3

Bechara, A., Damasio, H., Tranel, D., & Damasio, A. R. (1997). Deciding advantageously before knowing the advantageous strategy. *Science*, **275**(5304), 1293–1295. http://doi.org/10.1126/science.275.5304.1293

Bechara, A., Dolan, S., & Hindes, A. (2002). Decision-making and addiction (part II): Myopia for the future or hypersensitivity to reward? *Neuropsychologia*, **40**(10), 1690–1705. http://doi.org/10.1016/S0028-3932(02)00016-7

Berridge, K. C. & Kringelbach, M. L. (2013). Neuroscience of affect: Brain mechanisms of pleasure and displeasure. *Current Opinion in Neurobiology*, **23**(3), 294–303. http://doi.org/10.1016/j.conb.2013.01.017

Berridge, K. C., Robinson, T. E., & Aldridge, J. W. (2009). Dissecting components of reward: 'Liking', 'wanting', and learning. *Current Opinion in Pharmacology*, **9**(1), 65–73. http://doi.org/10.1016/j.coph.2008.12.014

Bond, F. W., Hayes, S. C., Baer, R. A., Carpenter, K. M., Guenole, N., Orcutt, H. K., Waltz, T., & Zettle, R. D. (2011). Preliminary psychometric properties of the Acceptance and Action Questionnaire–II: A revised measure of psychological inflexibility and experiential avoidance. *Behavior Therapy*, **42**(4), 676–688. http://doi.org/10.1016/j.beth.2011.03.007

Borkovec, T. D. & Hu, S. (1990). The effect of worry on cardiovascular response to phobic imagery. *Behaviour Research and Therapy*, **28**(1), 69–73. http://doi.org/10.1016/0005-7967(90)90056-O

Brevers, D., Bechara, A., Cleeremans, A., & Noël, X. (2013). Iowa Gambling Task (IGT): Twenty years after—gambling disorder and IGT. *Frontiers in Psychology*, **4**. http://doi.org/10.3389/fpsyg.2013.00665

Bruininks, P. & Malle, B. F. (2005). Distinguishing hope from optimism and related affective states. *Motivation and Emotion*, **29**(4), 324–352. http://doi.org/10.1007/s11031-006-9010-4

Cheavens, J. S., Feldman, D. B., Gum, A., Michael, S. T., & Snyder, C. R. (2006). Hope therapy in a community sample: A pilot investigation. *Social Indicators Research*, **77**(1), 61–78. http://doi.org/10.1007/s11205-005-5553-0

Damasio, A. (2005). *Descartes' error: Emotion, reason, and the human brain* (Reprint edition). London: Penguin Books.

Fernie, G. & Tunney, R. J. (2013). Learning on the IGT follows emergence of knowledge but not differential somatic activity. *Frontiers in Psychology*, **4**. http://doi.org/10.3389/fpsyg.2013.00687

Foa, E. B. & Kozak, M. J. (1986). Emotional processing of fear: Exposure to corrective information. *Psychological Bulletin*, **99**(1), 20–35. http://doi.org/10.1037/0033-2909.99.1.20

Gámez, W., Chmielewski, M., Kotov, R., Ruggero, C., Suzuki, N., & Watson, D. (2014). The Brief Experiential Avoidance Questionnaire: Development and initial validation. *Psychological Assessment*, **26**(1), 35–45. http://doi.org/10.1037/a0034473

Gámez, W., Chmielewski, M., Kotov, R., Ruggero, C., & Watson, D. (2011). Development of a measure of experiential avoidance: The Multidimensional Experiential Avoidance Questionnaire. *Psychological Assessment*, **23**(3), 692–713. http://doi.org/10.1037/a0023242

Gamez, W., Kotov, R., & Watson, D. (2010). The validity of self-report assessment of avoidance and distress. *Anxiety, Stress & Coping: An International Journal*, **23**(1), 87–99. http://doi.org/10.1080/10615800802699198

Gard, D. E., Gard, M. G., Kring, A. M., & John, O. P. (2006). Anticipatory and consummatory components of the experience of pleasure: A scale development study. *Journal of Research in Personality*, **40**(6), 1086–1102. http://doi.org/10.1016/j.jrp.2005.11.001

Gard, D. E., Kring, A. M., Gard, M. G., Horan, W. P., & Green, M. F. (2007). Anhedonia in schizophrenia: Distinctions between anticipatory and consummatory pleasure. *Schizophrenia Research*, **93**(1–3), 253–260. http://doi.org/10.1016/j.schres.2007.03.008

Hawkes, N. & Brown, G. P. (2015). Toward a validity framework for cognitive-behavioral therapy self-report assessment. In G. P. Brown & D. A. Clark (Eds.), *Assessment in cognitive therapy.* (pp. 243–267). New York: Guilford Press.

Hayes, S. C., Luoma, J. B., Bond, F. W., Masuda, A., & Lillis, J. (2006). Acceptance and commitment therapy: Model, processes and outcomes. *Behaviour Research and Therapy,* 44(1), 1–25. http://doi.org/10.1016/j.brat.2005.06.006

Hayes, S. C., Strosahl, K. D., & Wilson, K. G. (2011). *Acceptance and commitment therapy: The process and practice of mindful change* (2nd edition). New York: Guilford Press.

Hayes, S. C., Strosahl, K., Wilson, K. G., Bissett, R. T., Pistorello, J., Toarmino, D., Polusny, M. A., Dykstra, T. A., Batten, S. V., Bergan, J., Stewart, S. H., Zvolensky, M. J., Eifert, G. H., Bond, F. W., Bond, F. W., Forsyth, J. P., Karekla, M., & McCurry, S. M. (2004). Measuring experiential avoidance: A preliminary test of a working model. *The Psychological Record,* 54(4), 553–578.

Kirkland, T. & Cunningham, W. A. (2012). Mapping emotions through time: How affective trajectories inform the language of emotion. *Emotion,* 12(2), 268–282. http://doi.org/10.1037/a0024218

Knutson, B. & Greer, S. M. (2008). Anticipatory affect: neural correlates and consequences for choice. *Philosophical Transactions of the Royal Society B: Biological Sciences,* 363(1511), 3771–3786. http://doi.org/10.1098/rstb.2008.0155

Koopmann-Holm, B., & Tsai, J. L. (2014). Focusing on the negative: Cultural differences in expressions of sympathy. *Journal of Personality and Social Psychology,* 107(6), 1092–1115. http://doi.org/10.1037/a0037684

Kringelbach, M. L. & Berridge, K. C. (2012). The joyful mind. *Scientific American,* 307(2), 40–45.

Linehan, M. M. (1993). *Cognitive-behavioral treatment of borderline personality disorder.* New York: Guilford Press.

Newman, M. G. & Llera, S. J. (2011). A novel theory of experiential avoidance in generalized anxiety disorder: A review and synthesis of research supporting a contrast avoidance model of worry. *Clinical Psychology Review,* 31(3), 371–382. http://doi.org/10.1016/j.cpr.2011.01.008

Nicholls, J. G., Licht, B. G., & Pearl, R. A. (1982). Some dangers of using personality questionnaires to study personality. *Psychological Bulletin,* 92(3), 572–580. http://doi.org/10.1037/0033-2909.92.3.572

Öhman, A. (2008). Fear and anxiety: Overlaps and dissociations. In M. Lewis, J. M. Haviland-Jones, & L. F. Barrett (Eds.), *Handbook of emotions* (3rd edition). (pp. 709–728). New York: Guilford Press.

Peasley-Miklus, C. & Vrana, S. R. (2000). Effect of worrisome and relaxing thinking on fearful emotional processing. *Behaviour Research and Therapy,* 38, 129–144. http://doi.org/10.1016/S0005-7967(99)00025-X

Raffard, S., Bortolon, C., D'Argembeau, A., Gardes, J., Gely-Nargeot, M.-C., Capdevielle, D., & Van der Linden, M. (2015). Projecting the self into the future in individuals with schizophrenia: a preliminary cross-sectional study. *Memory,* 1–12. http://doi.org/10.1080/09658211.2015.1057152

Raffard, S., Esposito, F., Boulenger, J.-P., & Van der Linden, M. (2013). Impaired ability to imagine future pleasant events is associated with apathy in schizophrenia. *Psychiatry Research*, **209**(3), 393–400. http://doi.org/10.1016/j.psychres.2013.04.016

Schlösser, T., Dunning, D., & Fetchenhauer, D. (2013). What a feeling: The role of immediate and anticipated emotions in risky decisions. *Journal of Behavioral Decision Making*, **26**(1), 13–30. http://doi.org/10.1002/bdm.757

Segal, Z. V., Williams, J. M. G., & Teasdale, J. D. (2012). *Mindfulness-based cognitive therapy for depression* (2nd edition). New York: Guilford Press.

Snyder, C. R., Harris, C., Anderson, J. R., Holleran, S. A., Irving, L. M., Sigmon, S. T., Yoshinobu, L., Gibb, J., Langelle, C., & Harney, P. (1991). The will and the ways: Development and validation of an individual-differences measure of hope. *Journal of Personality and Social Psychology*, **60**(4), 570. http://doi.org/10.1037/0022-3514.60.4.570

Stapinski, L. A., Abbott, M. J., & Rapee, R. M. (2014). Development and validation of the Affect Intolerance Scale to assess maladaptive beliefs and avoidance of emotion. *Behaviour Change*, **31**(3), 205–221. http://doi.org/10.1017/bec.2014.13

Van Boven, L. & Ashworth, L. (2007). Looking forward, looking back: Anticipation is more evocative than retrospection. *Journal of Experimental Psychology: General*, **136**(2), 289–300. http://doi.org/10.1037/0096-3445.136.2.289

Wolgast, M. (2014). What does the Acceptance And Action Questionnaire (AAQ-II) really measure? *Behavior Therapy*, **45**(6), 831–839. http://doi.org/10.1016/j.beth.2014.07.002

Chapter 6

Memory

Autobiographical memory and emotional disorders

As already mentioned in Chapter 2, Mark Williams and I, while working at the Medical Research Council Applied Psychology Unit in Cambridge, were keen to understand more about the hopelessness for the future that characterizes people who are suicidal. We developed two ways of examining future-directed thinking in more detail. The Future-thinking Task (or Future Fluency Task) has already been described in Chapter 2. The second method we constructed was derived from the research literature on memory in emotional disorders, which had developed over the preceding five or ten years.

Empirical findings had confirmed, not surprisingly, that when people are in a depressed mood they remember the past differently than when in a happier mood; for example, they are less likely to remember happy memories and be slower to do so (Clark & Teasdale, 1982; Teasdale & Fogarty, 1979). Less intuitively obvious was a finding that Mark Williams and Keith Broadbent reported (Williams & Broadbent, 1986). In looking at retrieval of positive and negative memories in people who were suicidal, an interesting qualitative difference emerged from their data: asked to think of specific memories in response to a mix of positive and negative cue words (e.g. 'sorry', 'successful'), suicidal participants did produce memories, even to positive cue words, but their memories tended to be of a different kind. Despite being asked to provide specific memories (something that happened at a particular time and place and lasted less than one day), they were more likely than matched control groups to volunteer memories that were less specific on the details of what they described, often describing a general class of events rather than one particular event (Williams & Broadbent, 1986). For example, upon being read aloud the cue word 'safe', someone might respond with 'at my mum's', rather than 'when I stayed over at my mum's last Saturday', which is what the task instructions ask for. The suicidal participants appeared to find it more difficult, at least as indicated by not giving the 'correct' response that was asked for, to provide specific memories.

Since that initial finding, there have been many studies examining overgeneral memory in clinical problems, particularly depression and post-traumatic stress disorder (PTSD). It is a very consistent finding that depression, either at clinical or sub-clinical levels, is associated with overgeneral memory, both to positive and negative cue words (see Williams et al., 2007 for a review). The majority of studies have also found an association between overgeneral memory and a history of trauma, particularly in the presence of PTSD, although the relationship is not often found at lower levels of trauma symptomatology. In contrast, studies comparing generality of memories in a variety of anxiety disorders or those high in trait anxiety have shown little difference to control participants, indicating disorder specificity (Williams et al., 2007).

Overwhelmingly, the reduced specificity of autobiographical memory in depression and other psychological problems has used the Autobiographical Memory Test already described, where participants are given a single cue word and asked to think of a memory that the word reminds them of. Results have been more equivocal using other methods. In recognizing that levels of specificity were very high in community samples, Raes and colleagues devised the Sentence Completion for Events from the Past Test (SCEPT; Raes, Hermans, Williams, Eelen, 2007), intended to be more sensitive to variations in overgenerality in non-clinical groups. The task presents participants with sentences like 'Last year I …', and 'I can still picture how …'. Participants are asked to complete the sentences, and, upon completion, are re-presented with their responses and asked to code them in relation to specificity. Within a non-clinical sample, Raes et al. (2007) found that overgeneral responding on the SCEPT correlated with depression scores, whereas the frequency of overgeneral memories to the standard word cuing method did not. However, using the same methodology, also in a non-clinical sample, Robinaugh and McNally (2013) found no relationship between depression and overgenerality of memories. Sumner, Mineka, and McAdams (2013) adopted a different approach by coding participants' narratives of self-defining memories for specificity. Self-defining memories are frequently recalled memories of events that have particular personal ongoing significance for how an individual sees themselves as a person. Such memories also have the power to evoke strong feeling. These authors found no relationship between depression symptoms and coders' ratings of specificity of these self-defining memories but did, somewhat surprisingly, find that specificity predicted depression symptoms ten weeks later, an overall pattern of findings that is difficult to interpret.

Söderlund et al. (2014) used a method that relied on coding of a fuller description of memories using the Autobiographical Interview, which had been developed by Levine, Svoboda, Hay, Winocur, and Moscovitch (2002). Closely analogous to the distinction between specific and general memories is what Levine et al. (2002) referred to as internal versus external details of personal memories, a distinction that also maps onto the one between epi-sodic and semantic memory. These authors devised a method of looking at personal memories, where, rather like the Autobiographical Memory Test, participants are given cue words and asked to recall personal memories that the words bring to mind. The respondents then have to elaborate on the mem-ory, providing as much detail as possible, and these elaborated responses are coded by independent raters. Responses are divided into segments and cat-egorized as describing internal or external details. Internal details are those that relate to a particular episode, where, by providing details about particular time and place as well as sensations and emotions experienced, the person conveys a sense of re-experiencing the event (e.g. 'On that first Monday we were there, we went for a long walk along the beach. I loved the feeling of the breeze in my face'). External details cover a wide range of non-specific, non-detailed comments, including general semantic information (it's the longest beach in Mexico), personal observations (I love going to the beach), and information referring to multiple experiences or experiences taking place over a period of time (we went swimming lots), as well as unrelated com-ments. In other words, external details refer to information that is not spe-cific to the particular experience of the person as they were having it at that moment in time, and do not convey a strong sense of the person re-experienc-ing the event. Using the Autobiographical Interview Söderlund et al. (2014), found that, compared to non-depressed controls, depressed patients produced fewer internal details of memories across a range of time periods, from the previous two weeks to the past ten years, with no difference on the number of external details provided.

Overall, there is clear evidence from a variety of methodologies that when depressed people are asked to provide memories of past experiences, they volunteer memories that are less likely to represent a distinctive experienced episode. Instead, they provide memories that describe past experiences in a more general way. Williams et al. (2007) suggest three explanations for this phenomenon. The first explanation—functional avoidance—is built around the idea that specific detailed memories are more likely than general memories to produce current feeling states upon being recalled. Someone prone to nega-tive mood may block the retrieval of specific memories as a way of avoiding negative feeling states. Because it would be very difficult to selectively inhibit negative memories, and because any memories, even positive ones, have the potential to create negative mood, for example, through a contrast effect ('I was so happy then, what's happened to me?'), then specific memories of all types are inhibited. Second, because those who are depressed are prone to rumina-tion focused on understanding themselves and their feelings, initial attempts at generating memories may be captured by highly activated self-schemas. These self-schemas draw the attempt at recall into the more general, ruminative thinking that the depressed person is prone to engage in about themselves and their problems. For example, a cue word like 'success' might prompt more global thoughts about why they have always failed at whatever they tried. The final mechanism is about having reduced cognitive resources to direct the retrieval of memories. Retrieval of specific memories is thought to involve a generative, effortful type of process where resources have to be allocated to retrieving a memory through different layers of specificity (Conway & Pleydell-Pearce, 2000). When people are depressed, their capacity for these effortful, executive operations is reduced, and as a result they are more likely to get stuck at the initial stages. Dalgleish et al. (2007) have argued for this last explanation, showing that both performance on retrieving specific memories, and depression were related to measures of executive control. In one of their reported studies, the correlation between depression and specificity was reversed if participants were instructed to retrieve general rather than specific memories. The implication is that the control participants were now able to exercise their superior executive resources in producing general memories, whereas in the standard autobiographical memory test requiring specificity, they applied their resources to producing specific memories. A number of caveats should be noted about the Dalgleish et al. (2007) findings: (1) other studies using different measures of executive control (see Non-episodic factors in future-thinking section later in this chapter) have not found that executive processes correlate with memory specificity, (2) the results are based on correlations within a non-clinical sample, where the norm is to find no relationships between depression and memory specificity on the autobiographical memory test, and (3) the same reverse correlation has not been found in a PTSD sample (Dalgleish, Rolfe, Golden, Dunn, & Barnard, 2008), although it could be argued that different mechanisms produce overgenerality in depression and PTSD.

Specificity of future-thinking and emotional disorder

To try to get at future-directed thinking in more detail, Williams et al. (1996) adapted the standard word cuing memory task to looking at future-thinking. In trying to adapt this method to future-thinking it became clear that people found it more difficult to think of future personal events to single cue words than they did to retrieve memories to those same words. Accordingly, we adapted the method to embed the cue words in a sentence, for example, rather than being given the cue word 'proud', participants were presented with 'think of a time in the future when you will feel proud'. In the first study to use this method we gave this future-oriented adaptation of the Autobiographical Memory Test (sometimes called the Future Events Test) to a group of individuals who had very recently been admitted to hospital following a deliberate overdose, as well as to suitably matched control participants. Not surprisingly, given the greater uncertainty inherent in events that have not yet happened, the responses people gave when thinking about the future were typically less specific and clear cut than those from studies on autobiographical memory, where a memory can quite clearly be judged as referring to a specific incident. We therefore scored the future memories on a three-point scale of specificity, illustrated in Table 6.1. Participants also completed the memory version, with cue words embedded in comparable, but past-focused, sentences to make the two tasks similar. Alongside confirming the phenomenon of more general memories in the suicidal group, we found the same overgeneral thinking represented in their thoughts about future events. The results for both conditions were highly similar, with the deliberate self-harm patients giving fewer specific memories and less specific future events than controls, and this was true whether the cue words were positive, negative, or neutral (Williams et al., 1996, Study 1).

Since that initial study there have been other studies with a variety of clinical groups, examining specificity of future-thinking in response to word cues. The procedure has varied slightly, with some studies using only neutral cue words, some modelling their future condition on the standard memory condition and cuing with single words rather than words embedded in a sentence, and

Table 6.1 Examples of general, specific, and intermediate future event responses to positive and negative cue words

'Try to picture a situation in the future where you make a mistake.'		
General	**Intermediate**	**Specific**
'I'll always be making mistakes.'	'Perhaps giving a friend the wrong advice.'	'My law exams in October.'
'Try to picture a situation in the future where someone pays you a compliment.'		
General	**Intermediate**	**Specific**
'A friend could.'	'Someone at work may say I've lost weight.'	'Next week from my husband when I have my hair cut again.'

Memory & Cognition, The specificity of autobiographical memory and imageability of the future, 24, 1996, 116–125, Williams, J. M. G., Ellis, N. C., Tyers, C., Healy, H., Rose, G., & MacLeod, A. K., (Copyright © 1996, Psychonomic Society, Inc.) With permission of Springer.

some simply coding responses as either specific or general rather than uti-lizing a scale of specificity. The results, though, are very consistent: clinical groups show reduced specificity of future responses. This reduced specificity of future responses has been found in a diverse range of groups, including people meeting a diagnosis of schizophrenia (D'Argembeau, Raffard, & Van der Linden, 2008), depression (Belcher & Kangas, 2014; Hach, Tippett, & Addis, 2014), bipolar disorder (Boulanger, Lejeune, & Blairy, 2013), compli-cated grief (Robinaugh & McNally, 2013), autistic spectrum disorder (Lind & Bowler, 2010), and post-traumatic stress disorder (PTSD; Brown et al., 2013; Kleim Graham, Fihossy, Stott & Ehlers, 2015). Where positive and negative cue words have been used and examined separately, the overgen-erality has not been dependent upon the valence of the cue word, as par-ticipants in the clinical groups have shown overgeneral responding to both positive and negative cue words (an exception was Kleim et al. (2015), where the PTSD group showed the effect only for positive cue words). Robinaugh and McNally (2013) cued their bereaved participants to think of responses (memory and future) either related or unrelated to the partner they had lost. These authors found that the overgenerality was restricted to responses related to the deceased, suggesting that there may at least be some cases where the specific content of the memory matters rather than there being a global effect. It remains to be seen whether this sort of very particular effect from complicated grief is transferable to other problems that might also have such a discrete focus.

Most studies have relied on the same, or similar, procedure devised in the initial Williams et al. (1996) study. However, other methods of examining the specific, detailed episodic nature of memories have also been adapted to looking at future-thinking. Addis, Wong, and Schacter (2008) extended the Autobiographical Interview to look at future thoughts, where single words are used to elicit both memories and episodic future thoughts, and participants then elaborate on each event that they bring to mind. Participants' responses are then coded using the standard Autobiographical Interview scoring procedure. Using the Addis et al. (2008) method in their group of war veterans, Brown et al. (2014) found that those veterans suffering from PTSD provided fewer internal details and more external details in their episodic future thoughts, compared to the non-PTSD group, and severity of PTSD symptoms within the traumatised group correlated with fewer internal and more external details. Also utilizing the adapted Autobiographical Interview, King and colleagues found that, rela-tive to controls, those diagnosed with bipolar disorder (King et al., 2011b) and those diagnosed with major depressive disorder (King, MacDougall, Ferris,

Herdman, & McKinnon, 2011a) reported fewer internal details, with no accompanying group differences on number of external details.

Specificity of memory and future-thinking

Most of the studies discussed in the preceding section showing reduced specificity in future-thinking also measured autobiographical memory retrieval alongside future event generation, allowing direct comparison between the pattern of findings for past- and future-thinking. In all of these studies the patterns for the past and future conditions have been strikingly similar. On some occasions the extent of overgenerality may vary. For example, D'Argembeau et al. (2008) did find that the difference between their schizophrenic and control groups was especially marked on future responses, and Hach et al. (2014) found a similar pattern in a depressed sample, but other studies have found a main effect of group in the absence of a group by condition interaction.

Furthermore, where correlations between memory and future specificity scores are reported, they are typically very high. In their initial study, Williams et al. (1996) found correlations of $r = .52$ and $r = .60$ in their patient and control samples, respectively. Other correlations have been higher (Lind & Bowler, 2010, $r = .72$ in their control sample) or lower (Hill & Emery, 2013, $r = .42$ in an unselected student sample) or in one unique case (non-significantly) negative (Lind & Bowler, 2010, $r = -.25$ in their ASD sample). Overall, it is clear that there is a strong relationship between the degree of specificity in both tasks. Using the Autobiographical Interview to elicit past and future episodic details, Brown et al. (2013), in their PTSD sample, reported correlations of $r = .80$ and $r = .81$ between the number of internal details provided for past and future episodes within each of their groups.

The parallel effects of reduced specificity of memory and episodic future-thinking have also been shown in other groups who are already known to show reduced specificity of episodic memories. In their development study of the Autobiographical Interview, Levine et al. (2002) found that older, compared to younger, adults provided less internal and more external detail in their retrieved memories. Addis et al. (2008), in extending the measure to include a future time frame, replicated those memory effects and also found that older adults demonstrated reduced internal detail and more external detail on the future-focused condition of the task that paralleled their performance on the memory version of the task. Moreover, past and future internality scores were highly correlated. A similar study with Alzheimer disease patients again produced comparable effects of fewer internal details for both past and future conditions, compared to non-Alzheimer disease controls (Addis, Sacchetti, Ally, Budson, & Schacter,

2009b). Again, there was a strong correlation between internality scores on past and future conditions.

Other similarities between past-and future-thinking

It appears that the specificity with which people think about their personal futures mirrors the specificity of the personal memories that they retrieve from their pasts. This is not the only way in which episodic future-thinking parallels episodic memory. Studies have examined the phenomenological properties of both retrieved past episodes and imagined future episodes. In these studies, participants are asked to retrieve specific memories and imagine episodic future events, normally using a standard word cuing method, and subsequently asked to rate the responses they have produced on a range of different dimensions. In one of the early studies to examine both past and future in this way, D'Argembeau and Van der Linden (2004) cued people with positive or negative words and asked them to retrieve memories from the recent (past year) or more distant (past five to ten years) past, and also think of plausible specific events that might happen to them in the next year or next five to ten years. Close events, compared to distant events, and positive, as opposed to negative events, were rated as having more sensory details and a stronger feeling of being experienced when they were thought about. Importantly for the discussion here, this was equally true for memories and episodic future thoughts. The two processes of retrieving episodic memories and generating episodic events also appear to emerge around the same time (Atance & O'Neill, 2005; Busby & Suddendorf, 2005) and, as already indicated, show similar age-related decline (Addis et al., 2008) The emergence of self-narrative ability (providing a life story for oneself) for past and future also develops in parallel, although with some indication of a slightly earlier emergence for memories than future narratives (Bohn & Berntsen, 2013). The temporal distribution of memories and episodic future thoughts is also similar, with the largest number of events being close to the present and tapering as the distance from the present increases, something that is true both for short (Conway, Loveday, & Cole, 2016) and longer time frames (Spreng & Levine, 2006).

So far in this chapter I have discussed existing memory measures being adapted to examine future-thinking. The Future-thinking Task, discussed in detail in Chapter 2, which was designed specifically to examine future-thinking has also been adapted to measure past positive and negative memories. Findings again show strong parallels between memory and future-thinking. MacLeod, Tata, Kentish, and Jacobsen (1997) administered the standard task asking depressed patients, panic disorder patients, and controls to think of things they were looking forward to and things they were not looking forward to for different time periods in the future (next week, next year, next five to ten years). The memory condition asked people to think of positive experiences and negative experiences that had occurred to them in comparable past time frames (past week, past year, past five to ten years). The results, averaged across the different time periods and shown in Figure 6.1, illustrate the striking similarities between past and future responses. The anxious and depressed groups showed very distinctive profiles, and these profiles were almost identical for past- and future-thinking. Relative to controls, depression was associated only with a reduced number of positive memories and anticipated future events, whereas anxiety was associated only with increased negative memories and expectancies. Similar parallel memory and future-thinking effects have been found in dysphoric compared to non-dysphoric adolescents (Miles, MacLeod, & Pote, 2004), and Hill and Emery (2013) reported very high correlations between number of past and future events generated in a student sample, an effect that was not explained by variations in general verbal fluency.

Finally, fMRI analysis points to similar neural circuits involved in recalling the past and imagining the future (Addis, Wong, & Schacter, 2007; Schacter et al., 2012). In both types of activity an extended but highly interconnected

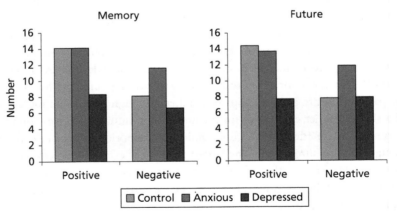

Figure 6.1 Anxious, depressed, and control participants' number of positive and negative memories and future thoughts. Depression was associated specifically with fewer positive thoughts and anxiety with more negative thoughts, and the pattern was almost identical for the memory and future-thinking conditions.

Affect, Emotional Disorder, and Future-directed Thinking, MacLeod, A. K., *Cognition and Emotion*, 1996, Routledge, reprinted by permission of the publisher (Taylor & Francis Ltd, http://www.tandfonline.com).

set of neural structures are active. These areas include the medial prefrontal cortex, retrosplenial cortex, posterior cingulate, medial and lateral temporal areas, and some areas of the parietal lobes, which have been referred to as the *core network* underlying thinking about the personal past and future (Addis, Pan, Vu, Laiser, & Schacter, 2009a). This core network in turn overlaps substantially with the functional network known as the *default network*, or *default mode network*. It had previously been observed in experimental studies that activity reliably increased in this set of interconnected structures while people were in resting phases between experimental tasks. In contrast, during directed tasks, activity in other brain areas increased, while default network activity was dampened. Initially seen as a system representing resting, or off-task, states, it has increasingly been recognized that activation of the default network represents mental activity of a different sort, focused more on internal self-generated, especially self-relevant, thought (Andrews-Hanna, Reidler, Huang, & Buckner, 2010; Schacter et al., 2012). Autobiographical remembering and future-thinking clearly fit into this category of thought and it is therefore not surprising that both are associated with regions that strongly overlap with the default network. The evidence that people are often engaged in thinking about themselves, especially in relation to the future during the 'mind wandering' that takes place in off-task processing (see Chapter 9) also fits clearly with the idea of memory and future-thinking being related to default network activity.

Some differences in neural activation between episodic memory and future-thinking have also been observed, although these are not always consistent and are less striking than the similarities (Schacter et al., 2012; Stawarczyk & D'Argembeau, 2015). Future-thinking appears to involve a wider neural network than does recalling memories, probably due to the greater degree of cognitive processing involved in thinking about events that have not yet occurred (Addis et al., 2007). Areas that are involved in processing contextual and visual information (e.g. parahippocampal cortex and posterior visual cortex) do, however, show greater activation during memory than imagining (Addis et al., 2009a; Gilmore, Nelson, & McDermott, 2014).

Differences between past and future episodic thought

Alongside the similarities outlined in the previous section, a range of differences between past and future thoughts have also been identified. Not surprisingly, people think about the future in a more abstract and less detailed way than they recall the past. This sort of difference has been demonstrated using the Autobiographical Memory Test (e.g. Hill & Emery, 2013), but has also been shown using other measures. Anderson and Dewhurst (2009) extended the SCEPT (Raes et al., 2007) by adapting the wording of sentences to create a future tense condition (e.g. 'Next year I …'; 'At some time I will …'). Responses were coded as specific or non-specific in the standard way. The memory version of the measure produced 39% specific responses compared to 23% of specific responses in the future-tense version, largely due to the presence of more extended events in the future-tense version (i.e. events, such as 'have a good summer', that covered a period of more than one day and would therefore not qualify as specific). Using the extended version of the Autobiographical Interview future episodes have been found to be described with fewer internal (i.e. specific) details compared to memories (Addis et al., 2008).

D'Argembeau, Lardi, and van der Linden (2012) adapted the concept of self-defining memories to try to elicit self-defining future thoughts. Participants were able to generate self-defining future thoughts, which is an interesting finding in itself, but, consistent with other measures, responses were less specific than those produced for self-defining memories. Self-ratings of vividness and sensory detail also follow the same pattern as independent ratings of specificity or internality, with participants rating their memories as more vivid and containing more sensory detail than their future thoughts (Berntsen & Bohn, 2010; D'Argembeau, Ortoleva, Junentier, & Van Der Linden, 2010). This difference in vividness and sensory detail is true when people are cued by the usual sorts of words but is even more marked when people were simply asked to think of important things in the past or the future (Berntsen & Bohn, 2010).

In addition to differences in level of detail or specificity, there are also other differences between past and future representations. People consistently rate their future episodes as more positive and more personally important or significant than past episodes (Berntsen & Bohn, 2010), although on fluency measures they generate a greater number of memories than future events (D'Argembeau & Mathy, 2011; Hill & Emery, 2013). Content differences have not been widely examined but Pillemer, Thomsen, Kuwabara, and Ivcevic (2013) found that whereas memories of feeling good have been found to be associated with achievement, and memories of feeling bad with interpersonal themes, this matching of valence and theme was less clear-cut for future events. It was indicated earlier that the temporal pattern of generated past and future events follows a broadly similar pattern, with a tapering of number of events with increasing distance from the present. However, within that broad pattern, people generally think less far into the future than they think back to the past (Anderson, Dewhurst, & Nash, 2012; Berntsen & Bohn, 2010). Interestingly, Berntsen and Bohn (2010) found that this temporal difference was influenced

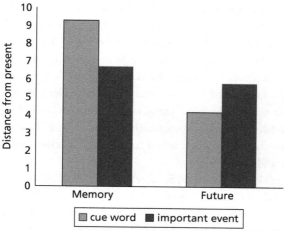

Figure 6.2 Age of memory and future episode expressed as distance (years) from the present, prompted by a cue word or by a request for an important event. Future events are generally closer than memories, but important future events are further away than those prompted by a cue, whereas the opposite is the case for memories. *Memory & Cognition*, Remembering and forecasting: The relation, **38** (3), 2009, 265–278, Bohn, A, Berntsen, D, With permission of Springer.

by how people were cued: participants produced more distant memories when cued by single words than when asked for an important memory, whereas the opposite was the case for future responses, where important future events were further into the future compared with events produced in response to a single cue word (see Figure 6.2).

The constructive episodic simulation hypothesis

Notwithstanding the differences between past and future thought, Dan Schacter and Donna Rose Addis recognized the similarities between past and future episodic thought and suggested that episodic future thoughts are constructed from the elements of episodic memories. This causal link is consistent with the overlap between the two phenomena but is also supported by the fact that experimental manipulations of memory specificity produce effects on episodic future specificity (Williams et al., 1996). In one study, Williams et al. (1996) manipulated memory specificity by giving participants the standard cue words and instructing them to generate either specific (particular events that happened to them on one day) or generic (the sorts of things that have happened or do happen to them) responses. Those who were asked for specific memories subsequently produced more specific responses when asked for episodic future events compared to those who had the generic memory induction. A similar, in fact much stronger, effect was found with a less obvious manipulation not so open to demand characteristics, where either high or low imageability cue words were used to prompt memories. High imageability cue words (e.g. 'fire') are known to facilitate more specific recall than are low imageability words (e.g. 'attitude'). Compared to those who had been given low imageability cue words in their autobiographical memory task, those who had been given the high imageability cue words subsequently produced significantly more specific episodic future thoughts when asked to generate specific future episodes in response to standard cue words.

Putting the evidence together, Schacter and Addis (2007) proposed the *constructive episodic simulation hypothesis*. In this view, one of the main roles of episodic memory is to facilitate the construction of imagined future events through the retrieval and recombination of stored elements of episodes from the past. This is not memory influencing future-thinking by the retrieval of specific memories to influence *judgements* about the future likelihood of those events, as in the *simulation heuristic* (Kahneman & Tversky, 1982); rather, it is a process of utilizing stored information in a constructive way to create new representations of future outcomes. Where episodic memory is impaired, as in clinical disorders, ageing, degenerative neurological conditions, and so on, then future-thinking will be impaired because people do not have at their disposal the raw materials contained in the episodic system with which to construct future episodes. By implication, where specific episodic memory can be facilitated, for example, in the manipulations by Williams et al. (1996), then episodic future-thinking will be enhanced. The hypothesis therefore makes sense of many of the findings. The fact that there are differences between past- and future-thinking is not necessarily problematic for this hypothesis. Thoughts of the future are naturally less specific than those of the past because the future has not yet happened, and therefore there is just simply less sensory detail and more uncertainty about the specifics of future events (MacLeod, 2016). Just as in affective forecasting, where the fact that anticipated feelings are typically higher than the experience people have when the events happen, does not undo their connection (see Chapter 4), so differences between past recall and future imagination simply reflect the fact that they are not identical phenomena.

One challenge that does emerge for the episodic simulation hypothesis comes from studies that, as well as asking people to recall specific memories or generate specific episodic future events in detail, also ask participants to construct scenes that are not particularly personal and are not located in any temporal context. If groups who had difficulty in episodic retrieval and construction also had difficulties in constructing these scenes, it would suggest a more diffuse difficulty, that is, of course, assuming that the scene construction did not also rely on epi-sodic information. For example, Hassabis, Kumaran, Vann, and Maguire (2007) reported that patients with bilateral hippocampal damage, who have difficulty providing episodic detail, also found it difficult to provide detailed descriptions of internal details to fictitious scenes (e.g. 'Imagine you are lying on a beauti-ful sandy beach in a white tropical bay'). These findings suggest that there can exist a more widespread difficulty in generating detail. Other groups have also been compared on fictitious scene construction. Lind, Williams, Bowler, and Peel (2014) found that participants on the autistic spectrum were as impaired on details when imagining fictitious scenes as they were when recalling spe-cific memories or generating future episodes in response to cues, and Raffard, D'Argembeau, Bayard, Boulenger, and Van der Linden (2010) reported similar findings when comparing patients diagnosed with schizophrenia with matched non-schizophrenic controls.

Studies comparing younger and older adults have also yielded findings that appear not to support the constructive episodic simulation hypothesis. Rendell et al. (2012) compared younger and older adults' autobiographical memories using the modified Autobiographical Interview method for scoring partici-pants' responses. People were required to describe in detail a fictitious scene, like the ones used by Hassabis et al. (2007), a future scenario (e.g. 'Imagine how you will spend next Christmas') and a narrative condition that involved describing walking through a medieval castle. Older adults showed reduced detail for all three conditions, although the reduced amount of specific detail was most marked on the future condition. It is quite difficult to eliminate pos-sible episodic influences from the fictitious scene construction—for example, someone may, if they are lucky, have spent time on a deserted sandy beach in a beautiful tropical bay or spent some time wandering around a medieval cas-tle, or, more generally, have relevant episodic information derived from past experiences. However, even on a simple description task, older adults exhibit reduced specificity. Gaesser, Sacchetti, Addis, and Schacter (2011) presented older and younger adults with pictures of common scenes, for example, an air-port, and asked them to either simply describe the picture in words, imagine a personal event that could occur in the next few years, using the picture as a context, or (Study 2) recall a past event cued by the picture. Scoring based on an adaptation of the Autobiographical Interview showed that the older adults provided fewer internal and more external details on all three conditions.

All of these results raise the possibility that the findings already described, of difficulties encountered by a variety of groups in constructing future per-sonal events, are not due to episodic memory difficulties per se but, rather, due to a broader problem in putting details together to create a coherent scene, or perhaps even reflect a communicative or narrative style difference in how representations are described. To test the latter of these possibilities, Madore, Gaesser, and Schacter (2014) devised an experimental manipulation designed to increase specific thinking, and observed effects of this induction on retrieval of personal memories and generation of episodic future events. During the specificity induction, participants watched a video of a routine scene of people performing everyday activities in a kitchen and interacting with each other, followed by guided recall of the video using prompts from the Cognitive Interview. The Cognitive Interview is a widely used procedure within the legal system for enhancing detailed recall of scenes in people who have witnessed an incident (Memon, Meissner, & Fraser, 2010). To help with specific recall of the scene they had watched, participants were asked to close their eyes and imagine the video, and then report in detail everything they could remember. Probes were used to facilitate the recall. A comparison group was shown the same video but instead of being asked to recall specific details were asked for their general impressions of the video (Study 1), or completed a more neutral filler task (Study 2). Participants, who were groups of younger and older adults, completed both conditions but one week apart to minimize interference from doing both conditions. Following the inductions, participants completed the same memory, future-thinking, and picture description tasks used by Gaesser et al. (2011). The specificity induction resulted in participants giving more internal details on the memory and future conditions, but critically, scores on the picture description were no different between specificity induction and control conditions. These effects were found for both age groups. The effect has been replicated where participants are cued with words rather than pictures, and where a verbal control task was used that required more generative search than simply describing pictures (Madore & Schacter, 2016). Madore et al. (2014) concluded that the reduced specificity shown by older adults cannot be accounted for by a narrative or communicative style. Being able to increase the specificity of episodic memory and episodic future-thinking in this way, in the absence of any effect on the specificity of picture description, provides support for a direct link between episodic memory and episodic future-thinking, consistent with the constructive episodic simulation hypothesis.

In a related study, Madore and Schacter (2014) replicated the effects of the induction on internal details for memories and future events, again in samples of younger and older adults. This second study also examined the effects of the induction on the Means End Problem Solving Task (MEPS; Platt & Spivack, 1975), in which participants are given a set of problems and a solution for each one, with the requirement to complete an account of how the problem was solved. Additionally, participants were given a selection of problems previously generated by comparable groups as being relevant for the study population, for example, exercising more or making more time for family. The specificity induction enhanced performance on the MEPS, both the standard items and the items generated for this particular study. Both younger and older participants in the specificity induction produced more relevant means to get to the solution than those in the control induction, and there was no difference between the groups on irrelevant means (i.e. steps that would not lead to the solution). Interestingly, the Autobiographical Interview scoring was also applied to the MEPS responses and showed more internal details in the induction groups, although the correlation between internal details and number of relevant steps was extremely high ($r = .80$) suggesting that both types of scoring are picking up on very similar qualities. Madore and Schacter (2014) suggest that the specificity induction works through directing people to attend to episodic-like details, such as people, places, and actions, which then helps in tasks that involve constructing a coherent scene utilizing those kinds of details.

Non-episodic factors in future-thinking

There is clearly enough evidence to accept that episodic memories play a role in episodic future-thinking. The findings already discussed about some of the differences between memory and future-thinking do not necessarily undermine that connection, because the two are not identical phenomenon and therefore there will inevitably be some differences between them. For example, the consistent difference in specificity simply reflects the fact that the future has not yet happened, and is therefore less detailed and particular, whereas memories are about events that have already been experienced directly, with details already laid down. In addition to some of the findings already outlined, however, there are other important pieces of evidence to suggest that factors other than specific episodic knowledge play a significant role when people think about personal events in the future.

Amnesic patients who show both impaired episodic memory and impaired episodic future-thinking are often cited as evidence consistent with the connection between the two systems (Schacter, 2012). But, if it could be shown that there are situations where episodic memory was intact yet episodic future-thinking was impaired, that would, at a minimum, add an important qualification to a simple causal link between the two systems. Semantic dementia is a neurodegenerative condition characterized by relatively intact episodic memory in the presence of severely impaired semantic memory, in contrast to Alzheimer's disease, which shows much milder semantic impairments, normally alongside profound disturbance of episodic memory. Irish, Addis, Hodges, and Piguet

(2012) compared semantic dementia patients, Alzheimer's disease patients, and a matched control group on past and episodic future-thinking, using the Autobiographical Interview method already outlined. Participants were cued to retrieve specific instances with single words, asked to elaborate on each instance, and responses were rated for internality or externality. The results, which are illustrated in Figure 6.3, were very clear. The Alzheimer's group showed the expected lack of internal details in both memory and future conditions. The semantic dementia group, despite their episodic memory largely being spared, when asked to describe future episodes, showed equivalent lack of internal details to the Alzheimer group. Similar findings were reported by Duval et al. (2012). A small group ($N = 8$) of semantic dementia patients and matched controls were asked to complete a number of self-identity statements, which were present-focused (e.g. 'I am …'), past-focused (e.g. 'I was …'), or future-focused (e.g. 'I will be …'). Following selection of two statements from each condition, participants then had to generate specific instances to support each statement, and these instances were scored for specificity. The patients performed relatively well on the first stage of generating the statements, indicating that this sort of autobiographical self-knowledge was spared but did less well on the specific instances stage. Importantly, this difficulty with specific instances was especially marked for the

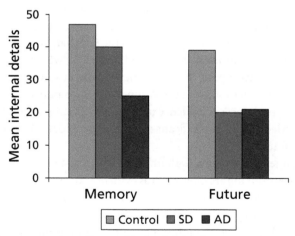

Figure 6.3 Average number of internal (episodic) details generated across the three participant groups: control, semantic dementia (SD), and Alzheimer's disease (AD) on past and future conditions (Irish et al., 2012). The semantic dementia patients showed intact memory but impaired episodic future-thinking.

future condition. These data point to the importance of semantic information in future-thinking. Irish et al. (2012) suggest that semantic knowledge provides a framework, or scaffold, within which representations of the future containing episodic information can be constructed.

Further evidence for the role of semantic information comes from links between measures of strategic processing and recall of past, and generation of future, specific episodes. It is commonly assumed that there are two pathways to retrieving memories: they can either be retrieved directly, such as when they come to mind spontaneously, typically prompted by some environmental cue, or they can be retrieved through an effortful, generative search (e.g. Conway & Pleydell-Pearce, 2000). The generative search might start with a more semantic level that can also include personal semantic knowledge and proceed to more specific representations. For example, if presented with the cue word 'friend', someone may think first who their friends are and then think about what they do with their friends. This process might lead onto a specific episode. In the case of memories, this process might be redundant because of the direct availability of specific instances that just 'pop into one's' mind. Of course, this can happen in future-thinking too; as I am writing this the cue word 'friend' brought to mind fairly effortlessly my arrangement to meet my friend Richard in London this Thursday. But, given the greater uncertainty about the future compared with the past, it is quite plausible that spontaneous retrieval would take place more often for memories, whereas future episodes would be more dependent on generative search. There is both direct and indirect evidence that this is the case.

Anderson et al. (2012) used high (e.g. butterfly) and low (e.g. attitude) imagery cues to prompt specific memories and future events. Low imagery cues, being difficult, are thought to prompt generative search, whereas memories to high imagery cues are more likely to be easily and directly retrievable. Specificity, and also latency, to provide a response showed little difference between past and future conditions for low imagery cues, but with high imagery cues memories were faster to come to mind and more specific compared to future events. It appears that memories were able to benefit from the opportunity afforded by high imagery cues to access a representation directly in a way that episodic future events were not, presumably because there are just fewer such future events available. The idea that specific episodic future events depend more on generative retrieval than do memories is also supported by the stronger relationship of executive processes to future-thinking than to memory. For example, both Hill and Emery (2013) and D'Argembeau et al. (2010) found that measures of working memory correlated with future event specificity but not with autobiographical memory specificity. In addition, future-oriented off-task thoughts that occur during a routine choice reaction time task are reduced by about half when, instead, the task is a more demanding, working memory task, but the number of past-oriented off-task thoughts is unaffected (Smallwood et al., 2011). It would appear that spontaneous thinking about the future requires greater availability of executive processing than does spontaneous thinking about the past. The working memory task ties up executive capacity, thus reducing future-directed thoughts but not past-oriented thoughts. D'Argembeau et al. (2010) conclude that bringing to mind mental representations of specific future episodes creates more demand on executive processes because of the greater reliance on generative retrieval, an interpretation that is also very plausible given the greater uncertainty of the future compared to the past. Put very simply, it is harder to think about the future than it is the past.

Finally, some direct evidence of a greater role of non-episodic information in future-thinking was provided by D'Argembeau and Mathy (2011). In an attempt to understand the processes involved in trying to retrieve past and generate future episodic events, participants were given the standard word cuing tasks (memory and future) but with the additional requirement of having to think aloud while doing the tasks. Participants' responses generated during thinking aloud were broken down into units and coded as semantic information, general events, or specific thoughts. For example, in response to being asked to think of a future episode using the cue word 'friend' someone might say 'Aisha is my closest friend' (semantic), 'we are planning on going to Pakistan this summer' (general event), 'I can imagine arriving at Aisha's aunt's house on the first day we arrive' (specific event). Typically, as in the example just given, people moved from semantic and general event knowledge being more prominent in the early steps of the thinking they described, becoming more specific as their thoughts progressed. Importantly, the memory and future conditions differed, with memory responses being more specific at Steps 1 and 2. So, for example, someone would be more likely to go straight to a past memory of arriving at Aisha's aunt's house than they would be to imagine it happening in the future, in the latter case, being more likely to go through the earlier stages of the process first. Only 27% of memories were specific at the first step, indicating that even for memory, very direct retrieval occurs only in a minority of cases (at least in this task).

In a follow-up study, cuing people with words related to their personal goals, compared to familiar locations or people, produced more specific memories and future episodes at an earlier stage of the process, but the difference between the two conditions remained. That is, personal goal cues facilitated retrieval and generation of future episodes, but did so in a consistent way. It appears, therefore, that when given single cue words and asked to think of specific future episodes, as opposed to being asked for memories, people have to engage more in a process of inference that goes from semantic through to episodic information. However, it should be noted that, in contrast, Jeunehomme and D'Argembeau (2016) also provided some evidence that many memories and future episodes may be produced directly rather than as the result of generative search. In a series of studies where people were not constrained by providing novel events (as they were in D'Argembeau and Mathy, 2011), participants' self-reports, as well as ratings of think aloud protocols by an independent judge, indicated that a high proportion of both memory and future responses to cue words came to mind directly, rather than through generative search. Most of the future events that were direct were reported as having been thought about before, indicating that, when the task allows it, people produce previously-formed representations of future events. That is, people often have memories of previously constructed representations of events that are yet to happen in the future. This latter finding should come as no surprise, given how much time people spend thinking about the future (see Chapter 1).

Future thoughts as hybrid representations

The future is inevitably more uncertain and abstract than the past, for example, future episodic thoughts are reported as being less vivid compared to memories (Arnold, McDermott, & Szpunar, 2011). It is therefore not really surprising that semantic memory might play a particularly important role in how people think about the future. As outlined in Chapter 1, Szpunar, Spreng, and Schacter (2014) distinguished four aspects of future-directed thinking—simulation, prediction, intention, and planning. Importantly, these authors suggest that all four aspects can have contributions from both semantic and episodic knowledge, and many representations about the future will be hybrid representations containing a mixture of semantic and episodic information extracted from memory. From the evidence and argument presented so far in this chapter, it would appear that semantic knowledge may play a bigger role in thoughts about the future than it does in memories of the past.

Klein (2013) has gone as far as to suggest that not only is semantic memory necessary for future-thinking, but that much of the thinking that is needed for the future can be constructed from the semantic memory system alone[1];

---

[1] Klein suggests that it is the autonoetic (i.e. sense of experiencing) aspect of episodic memory rather than the episodic nature of the memories that allows a sense of pre-experiencing the future, although it is not entirely clear how episodicity and autonoetic awareness can be easily separated.

he argues that it is possible to get by in thinking about the future by using only semantic information from memory. This may or may not be the case, but if mentally constructing specific (as opposed to general) future episodes depends on episodic memory, then many important aspects of future-thinking would not be possible without the involvement of episodic memory. Semantic knowledge would take us so far but would fail to deliver some of the important aspects of future-thinking. For example, specific episodes, or hybrid representations with strong episodic elements, have greater power than general thoughts to elicit feelings (Renoult, Davidson, Palombo, Moscovitch, & Levine, 2012) probably linked to their greater imagery and vividness. Obviously, in the case of anxiety, episodic future-thinking can produce deleterious well-being consequences, where people can quite effortlessly construct detailed future episodes in which they are having a panic attack in the supermarket or where they are being humiliated at work by their boss or where their flight crashes. These vivid and compelling future representations need to be worked with therapeutically to undo or minimize their anxiety-provoking and paralysing effects. The way this therapeutic work is normally carried out is to allow the dysfunctional representation to be replaced with a more functional, but equally episodic, representation. This replacement episodic future thought is, where possible, derived from behavioural experiments where the person tests out the negative beliefs and allows them to be disconfirmed experientially (Bennett-Levy et al., 2004). However, it is not only the presence of specific episodic future-thinking that is detrimental to well-being. The absence of such thinking can also be harmful. In the case of depression, it may be that the absence of specific episodic thinking about the future rewarding experiences means a loss of an important source of well-being that arises from being able to anticipate and have a feeling of looking forward to specific positive future experiences (see Chapter 2).

Furthermore, it is clear that a binary division of memory into semantic and episodic components does not capture some of the important ways in which memory representations differ (Klein, 2013; Renoult et al., 2012; Szpunar et al., 2014). In particular, representations that are not episodic can be quite varied (Conway & Pleydell-Pearce, 2000). Autobiographical facts (e.g. knowing that I come from Scotland), self-knowledge (e.g. I am a fair person), and repeated events (e.g. holidays to the south of France) are all non-episodic and would be discounted as examples of what is required in the various tasks described in this chapter. However, these are clearly quite different from each other. For example, in terms of neuropsychological correlates, autobiographical facts are like general semantic memory, whereas repeated episodes appear to be more like episodic memories (Renoult et al., 2012). This is not to say that repeated

episodes and episodic memories do not differ from each other, for example, episodic memories are more emotional and vivid than repeated general memories
(Renoult et al., 2012). Therefore, not only will future thoughts vary in the balance of semantic and episodic knowledge they contain, but the type of semantic
knowledge involved will also vary.

A second dimension of complexity arises from mental representations about
the future varying considerably from each other. One obvious dimension of
variation is the time frame. Consider two responses to prompts for future episodes: 'taking the car to the garage on Thursday' and 'getting married when
I am in my 30s'. Both are future-directed thoughts but they represent quite different kinds of thought. The first one is very specific, imminent, and relatively
unimportant; in contrast, the second thought is quite general, more distant,
and relates to something much more positive and important[2]. As already discussed, future events tend to be less specific yet rated as more important than
memories, and the more distant they are the more positively they are rated.
Grysman, Prabhaker, Anglin, and Hudson (2013) asked students to write about
recent (one month to one year) and distant (five to ten years) past and future
events and subsequently rate each of their responses on numerous dimensions.
Figure 6.4 shows the valence (how positively participants rated their responses
for each of the time periods. There is a clear linear tendency where, interestingly,
memory and future thoughts diverge, with distant past thoughts least positive
and distant future thoughts rated as most positive. Also shown are ratings of
the quality of the representations, a combined score consisting of vividness,
sensory detail, coherence, and so on. Quality ratings decline with increasing
distance from the present, but this is particularly marked with future thoughts.

As well as self-ratings of thoughts, Grysman et al. (2013) categorized participants' responses as to whether they belonged to cultural life scripts. The life
scripts were derived from a study by Rubin, Berntsen, and Hutson (2009), who
identified 24 items that occurred commonly when people were asked to list the
seven most important things to happen to people in their lives (e.g. starting
school, getting married, having children, death of parents). More distant future
events were more likely to belong to one of the cultural life script categories
compared to the other three conditions, which were no different from each
other. Interestingly, de Vito et al. (2015) asked participants to think of desirable

---

[2] It is worth noting that 'importance' could be interpreted in at least two different ways: it
could mean how important an event is in the scheme of one's life, or it could mean how
important it is right now. In the former meaning, getting married would be rated as more
important, but in the latter sense, taking the car to the garage might well be rated as more
important.

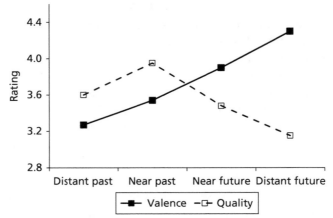

Figure 6.4 Valence ratings and quality ratings by near and distant, past and future, data from Grysman et al. (2013). The clear linear progression for valence indicates more positive ratings of responses running from distant past to distant future, whereas quality ratings are lower for future representations, especially distant future.

Data from Grysman, A., Prabhakar, J., Anglin, S. M., & Hudson, J. A. (2013). The time travelling self: Comparing self and other in narratives of past and future events. *Consciousness and Cognition*, **22**(3), 742–755.

and undesirable future episodes separately, and found that desirable events contained more specific information (internal details) but also corresponded more to common themes or life scripts, whereas negative future thoughts were more idiosyncratic and participants were more likely to report them as being linked to a particular negative memory. Using a different method to elicit future thoughts, Bohn and Berntsen (2013) asked 10–14-year-old students to write down their future life stories. The main aim of the study was to examine whether the reminiscence bump (the tendency to recall more memories in the young adulthood period (aged 15 to 30) would also be shown prospectively, which it was. These 10–14-year-olds produced more content related to young adulthood than to any other period, showing that the reminiscence bump is not simply a recall effect. What is of main interest for the discussion here, though, is that the large majority of event content (79%) corresponded to life scripts, most of those also clustering in young adulthood.

In contrast to the life story responses, which were distant and script-like, when the participants were given word cues and asked to write down future events from their own lives that were prompted by the cue, very few of the responses (7%) were script-related, and they clustered in the near future. This difference between the two methodologies also highlights that the nature of future thoughts that are elicited will depend on the method used to elicit those thoughts. Prompting future thoughts from word cues has been adopted from the memory literature and has been extremely useful in comparing memories and episodic future thoughts. It is possible, however, that word cues, which tend to rely on connecting with a fragment of a remembered experience may be less sensitive to capturing a lot of future-thinking because future events, compared to memories, have less of that sort of specificity inherent in them, especially with representations that are located further into the future.

It appears, therefore, that the distant future is where the majority of people's important and positive events reside, at least in the predominantly young samples that have been studied to date. Such future representations are probably episodic in the sense of having a feeling of belonging to the person and being part of their (anticipated) life, but they are not at all episodic in the sense of having detail and context, in the way that even distant memories can have. Instead, they rely on cultural life scripts. In contrast, near future events, say over the next week, are more definite, more specific, have more contextual information about people, place, time, and so on. In short, they are more like episodic memories. Such representations may well be more likely to draw on episodic knowledge. For instance, the example I gave earlier in this chapter about meeting my friend Richard is full of specific information—meeting at the bookshop in Victoria train station at 6.30pm on Thursday. Episodic memory feeds into this representation based on previous episodes of meeting Richard, previous times of being at Victoria station, and so on. One methodological caveat to this conclusion is that it is difficult to separate how far extended into the future the event is and the type of response participants might think a researcher is interested in. If asked to think of a future event in the next week someone might say 'having dinner with my family on Friday night', and be able to provide lots of internal detail about that. Asked to think of an event in the next one to five years and they are unlikely to say 'enjoying having dinner with my family on a Friday night three years from now', perhaps because it would not occur to them to think that was the sort of thing that the researcher was asking for. But asked to describe a Friday night in three years' time, they might well be able to provide a detailed episode. Whether there is a methodological artefact underlying the issue just described or whether it simply reflects how people just do think about the near and the distant future, is not entirely clear at this point.

Further issues

Extending frameworks and methods from memory to studying future-thinking has been very valuable, especially in establishing the connection between episodic memory and future-thinking. It is now clear that although both memories and future-representations are often semantic–episodic hybrids it does seem to be the case that there is a higher element of semantic knowledge involved in thinking about the future than there is in remembering the past. This difference is especially marked in representations about future distant outcomes. There is scope for developing methods that are sensitive to the important dimensions of future-thinking that may not be captured by memory frameworks, where the emphasis is on the presence or absence of specificity. Applying criteria used for categorizing memories might not always work in the same way for future thoughts either. Take, for example, someone responding to the cue word 'happy' with 'my wedding day'. If a memory was being asked for, it is quite reasonable to infer that someone is remembering that in an episodic way—what it was like for them to be there, the scene, how they felt, and so on—and under normal scoring guidelines this would qualify as a specific event: it is a very distinct event that happened at a particular time and place. If the same response was produced as a request for a future event, applying the same rules would also classify the response as specific. But there is more ambiguity in the case of a future response. It could be a specific representation with lots of detail, that the person has thought about and perhaps even planned, and might even be imminent. Or it could be a very script-like response from the participant based on the idea that one day they will get married and that will be a happy event. The Autobiographical Interview does go some way towards dealing with this difficulty by eliciting more detail and coding it in a much more thorough way, but there is scope for further development of methods that are sensitive to hybrid responses in all their various forms.

A second area worth addressing, which is related to the previous point, is developing ways of measuring the subjective sense of experiencing a future event. It is possible to give responses to requests for past and future events that vary in the extent to which they are being subjectively experienced as the response is given. In other words, as they describe it, someone can have a sense of themselves re-experiencing a past event or pre-experiencing a future event, but it is also quite possible to provide responses with this subjective sense absent or only weakly present. In the case of memories, specificity is often, quite reasonably, used as an indicator of re-experiencing (i.e. of whether someone is describing an episodic experience). Klein (2013) has questioned whether there is actually any equivalent to re-experiencing in future-thinking, that is, whether pre-experiencing is possible at all. Clearly, future events can be pre-experienced, otherwise the world would largely be an anxiety-free place, for example, although much more research is needed to understand this phenomenon more fully, and methods for measuring it, alongside the obvious self-ratings of phenomenological experience, would be valuable if they could be developed.

Summary

Personal knowledge, and therefore memory, is clearly the basis that people possess for forming thoughts about the future. Memory for personal episodes appears to be the most obvious basis for having thoughts about one's own personal future and there is strong evidence from a wide range of sources that episodic memories are directly linked to being able to form episodic future representations. Importantly, in the case of well-being, those with emotional difficulties, notably those who are depressed, show similar lower levels of specificity about the future as they do about the past. This lack of specificity is likely to lead to both a lack of positive emotion in the moment when contemplating a future event, and also a lack of motivation to pursue events because it is difficult to predict positive feelings where detail about the event is missing. There is also evidence that thinking about the future is, on the whole, less specific and detailed than remembering the past. There is good evidence, again from a variety of sources, that semantic memory plays more of a role when someone thinks about their personal future than it does when they recall their past. This effect is particularly marked in thinking about more distant future events, where there is greater reliance on cultural scripts than there is in thinking about details of specific episodes. However, future representations such as 'getting married' or 'retiring' may well still be autobiographically important and contribute to some aspects of a person's well-being, despite having little in the way of episodic detail. For example, such representations might be connected with a sense of purpose, direction, and meaning, rather than necessarily having strong affective qualities. It remains for future research to try to understand how episodic and non-episodic knowledge produce varieties of hybrid representations of future outcomes and the significance of these different kinds of representations for different facets of a person's well-being and mental health.

References

Addis, D. R., Pan, L., Vu, M.-A., Laiser, N., & Schacter, D. L. (2009a). Constructive episodic simulation of the future and the past: Distinct subsystems of a core brain network mediate imagining and remembering. *Neuropsychologia*, **47**(11), 2222–2238. http://doi.org/10.1016/j.neuropsychologia.2008.10.026

Addis, D. R., Sacchetti, D. C., Ally, B. A., Budson, A. E., & Schacter, D. L. (2009b). Episodic simulation of future events is impaired in mild Alzheimer's disease. *Neuropsychologia*, **47**(12), 2660–2671. http://doi.org/10.1016/j.neuropsychologia.2009.05.018

Addis, D. R., Wong, A. T., & Schacter, D. L. (2007). Remembering the past and imagining the future: Common and distinct neural substrates during event construction and elaboration. *Neuropsychologia*, **45**(7), 1363–1377. http://doi.org/10.1016/j.neuropsychologia.2006.10.016

Addis, D. R., Wong, A. T., & Schacter, D. L. (2008). Age-related changes in the episodic simulation of future events. *Psychological Science*, **19**(1), 33–41. http://doi.org/10.1111/j.1467-9280.2008.02043.x

Anderson, R. J. & Dewhurst, S. A. (2009). Remembering the past and imagining the future: Differences in event specificity of spontaneously generated thought. *Memory*, **17**(4), 367–373. http://doi.org/10.1080/09658210902751669

Anderson, R. J., Dewhurst, S. A., & Nash, R. A. (2012). Shared cognitive processes underlying past and future thinking: The impact of imagery and concurrent task demands on event specificity. *Journal of Experimental Psychology: Learning, Memory, and Cognition*, **38**(2), 356–365. http://doi.org/10.1037/a0025451

Andrews-Hanna, J. R., Reidler, J. S., Huang, C., & Buckner, R. L. (2010). Evidence for the default network's role in spontaneous cognition. *Journal of Neurophysiology*, **104**(1), 322–335. http://doi.org/10.1152/jn.00830.2009

Arnold, K. M., McDermott, K. B., & Szpunar, K. K. (2011). Imagining the near and far future: The role of location familiarity. *Memory & Cognition*, **39**(6), 954–967. http://doi.org/10.3758/s13421-011-0076-1

Atance, C. M., & O'Neill, D. K. (2005). The emergence of episodic future thinking in humans. *Learning and Motivation*, **36**(2), 126–144. http://doi.org/10.1016/j.lmot.2005.02.003

Belcher, J. & Kangas, M. (2014). Reduced goal specificity is associated with reduced memory specificity in depressed adults. *Cognition and Emotion*, **28**(1), 163–171. http://doi.org/10.1080/02699931.2013.807776

Bennett-Levy, J., Butler, G., Fennell, M., Hackmann, A., Mueller, M., Westbrook, D., & Rouf, K. (2004). *Oxford guide to behavioural experiments in cognitive therapy*. Oxford: Oxford University Press.

Berntsen, D. & Bohn, A. (2010). Remembering and forecasting: The relation between autobiographical memory and episodic future thinking. *Memory & Cognition*, **38**(3), 265–278. http://doi.org/10.3758/MC.38.3.265

Bohn, A. & Berntsen, D. (2013). The future is bright and predictable: The development of prospective life stories across childhood and adolescence. *Developmental Psychology*, **49**(7), 1232–1241. http://doi.org/10.1037/a0030212

Boulanger, M., Lejeune, A., & Blairy, S. (2013). Overgenerality memory style for past and future events and emotions related in bipolar disorder. What are the links with problem solving and interpersonal relationships? *Psychiatry Research*, **210**(3), 863–870. http://doi.org/10.1016/j.psychres.2013.06.029

Brown, A. D., Addis, D. R., Romano, T. A., Marmar, C. R., Bryant, R. A., Hirst, W., & Schacter, D. L. (2014). Episodic and semantic components of autobiographical memories and imagined future events in post-traumatic stress disorder. *Memory*, **22**(6), 595–604. http://doi.org/10.1080/09658211.2013.807842

Brown, A. D., Root, J. C., Romano, T. A., Chang, L. J., Bryant, R. A., & Hirst, W. (2013). Overgeneralized autobiographical memory and future thinking in combat veterans with posttraumatic stress disorder. *Journal of Behavior Therapy and Experimental Psychiatry*, **44**(1), 129–134. http://doi.org/10.1016/j.jbtep.2011.11.004

Busby, J., & Suddendorf, T. (2005). Recalling yesterday and predicting tomorrow. *Cognitive Development*, **20**(3), 362–372. http://doi.org/10.1016/j.cogdev.2005.05.002

Clark, D. M. & Teasdale, J. D. (1982). Diurnal variation in clinical depression and accessibility of memories of positive and negative experiences. *Journal of Abnormal Psychology*, **91**(2), 87–95. http://doi.org/10.1037/0021-843X.91.2.87

Conway, M. A., Loveday, C., & Cole, S. N. (2016). The remembering–imagining system. *Memory Studies*, **9**(3), 256–265. http://doi.org/10.1177/1750698016645231

Conway, M. A. & Pleydell-Pearce, C. W. (2000). The construction of autobiographical memories in the self-memory system. *Psychological Review*, **107**(2), 261–288. http://doi.org/10.1037/0033-295X.107.2.261

Dalgleish, T., Rolfe, J., Golden, A.-M., Dunn, B. D., & Barnard, P. J. (2008). Reduced autobiographical memory specificity and posttraumatic stress: Exploring the contributions of impaired executive control and affect regulation. *Journal of Abnormal Psychology*, **117**(1), 236–241. http://doi.org/10.1037/0021-843X.117.1.236

Dalgleish, T., Williams, J. M. G., Ann-Marie J. Golden, Perkins, N., Barrett, L. F., Barnard, P. J., Yeung, C. A., Murphy, V., Elward, R., Tchanturia, K., and Watkins, E. (2007). Reduced specificity of autobiographical memory and depression: The role of executive control. *Journal of Experimental Psychology: General*, **136**(1), 23–42. http://doi.org/10.1037/0096-3445.136.1.23

D'Argembeau, A., Lardi, C., & van der Linden, M. (2012). Self-defining future projections: Exploring the identity function of thinking about the future. *Memory*, **20**(2), 110–120. http://doi.org/doi: 10.1080/09658211

D'Argembeau, A. & Mathy, A. (2011). Tracking the construction of episodic future thoughts. *Journal of Experimental Psychology: General*, **140**(2), 258–271. http://doi.org/doi: 10.1037/a0022581.

D'Argembeau, A., Ortoleva, C., Jumentier, S., & Van Der Linden, M. (2010). Component processes underlying future thinking. *Memory and Cognition*, **38**(6), 809–819. http://doi.org/doi: 10.3758/MC.38.6.809.

D'Argembeau, A., Raffard, S., & Van der Linden, M. (2008). Remembering the past and imagining the future in schizophrenia. *Journal of Abnormal Psychology*, **117**(1), 247–251. http://doi.org/10.1037/0021-843X.117.1.247

D'Argembeau, A. & Van der Linden, M. (2004). Phenomenal characteristics associated with projecting oneself back into the past and forward into the future: Influence of valence and temporal distance. *Consciousness and Cognition*, **13**(4), 844–858. http://doi.org/10.1016/j.concog.2004.07.007

de Vito, S., Neroni, M. A., Gamboz, N., Della Sala, S., & Brandimonte, M. A. (2015). Desirable and undesirable future thoughts call for different scene construction processes. *The Quarterly Journal of Experimental Psychology*, **68**(1), 75-82. https://doi.org/10.1080/17470218.2014.937448

Duval, C., Desgranges, B., de La Sayette, V., Belliard, S., Eustache, F., & Piolino, P. (2012). What happens to personal identity when semantic knowledge degrades? A study of the self and autobiographical memory in semantic dementia. *Neuropsychologia*, **50**(2), 254–265. http://doi.org/10.1016/j.neuropsychologia.2011.11.019

Gaesser, B., Sacchetti, D. C., Addis, D. R., & Schacter, D. L. (2011). Characterizing age-related changes in remembering the past and imagining the future. *Psychology and Aging*, **26**(1), 80–84. http://doi.org/10.1037/a0021054

Gilmore, A. W., Nelson, S. M., & McDermott, K. B. (2014). The contextual association network activates more for remembered than for imagined events. *Cerebral Cortex.* http://doi.org/10.1093/cercor/bhu223

Grysman, A., Prabhakar, J., Anglin, S. M., & Hudson, J. A. (2013). The time travelling self: Comparing self and other in narratives of past and future events. *Consciousness and Cognition*, **22**(3), 742–755. http://doi.org/10.1016/j.concog.2013.04.010

Hach, S., Tippett, L. J., & Addis, D. R. (2014). Neural changes associated with the generation of specific past and future events in depression. *Neuropsychologia*, **65**, 41–55. http://doi.org/10.1016/j.neuropsychologia.2014.10.003

Hassabis, D., Kumaran, D., Vann, S. D., & Maguire, E. A. (2007). Patients with hippocampal amnesia cannot imagine new experiences. *Proceedings of the National Academy of Sciences*, **104**(5), 1726–1731. http://doi.org/10.1073/pnas.0610561104

Hill, P. F. & Emery, L. J. (2013). Episodic future thought: Contributions from working memory. *Consciousness and Cognition*, **22**(3), 677–683. http://doi.org/10.1016/j.concog.2013.04.002

Irish, M., Addis, D. R., Hodges, J. R., & Piguet, O. (2012). Considering the role of semantic memory in episodic future thinking: Evidence from semantic dementia. *Brain*, **135**(7), 2178–2191. http://doi.org/10.1093/brain/aws119

Jeunehomme, O. & D'Argembeau, A. (2016). Prevalence and determinants of direct and generative modes of production of episodic future thoughts in the word cueing paradigm. *The Quarterly Journal of Experimental Psychology*, **69**(2), 254–272. http://doi.org/10.1080/17470218.2014.993663

Kahneman, D. & Tversky, A. (1982). The simulation heuristic. In D. Kahneman, P. Slovic, & A. Tversky (Eds.), *Judgement under uncertainty: Heuristics and biases.* (pp. 201–208). New York: Cambridge University Press, USA.

King, M. J., MacDougall, A. G., Ferris, S., Herdman, K. A., & McKinnon, M. C. (2011a). Episodic simulation of future events is impaired in patients with major depressive disorder. *Psychiatry Research*, **187**(3), 465–467. http://doi.org/10.1016/j.psychres.2011.02.002

King, M. J., Williams, L. A., MacDougall, A. G., Ferris, S., Smith, J. R. V., Ziolkowski, N., & McKinnon, M. C. (2011b). Patients with bipolar disorder show a selective deficit in the episodic simulation of future events. *Consciousness and Cognition*, **20**(4), 1801–1807. http://doi.org/doi: 10.1016/j.concog.2011.05.005.

Kleim, B., Graham, B., Fihosy, S., Stott, R., & Ehlers, A. (2015). Reduced specificity in episodic future thinking in posttraumatic stress disorder. *Clinical Psychological Science.* http://doi.org/doi.org/10.4135/9781473915640

Klein, S. B. (2013). The complex act of projecting oneself into the future. *Wiley Interdisciplinary Reviews: Cognitive Science*, **4**(1), 63–79. http://doi.org/10.1002/wcs.1210

Levine, B., Svoboda, E., Hay, J. F., Winocur, G., & Moscovitch, M. (2002). Aging and autobiographical memory: Dissociating episodic from semantic retrieval. *Psychology and Aging*, **17**(4), 677–689. http://doi.org/10.1037/0882-7974.17.4.677

Lind, S. E., & Bowler, D. M. (2010). Episodic memory and episodic future thinking in adults with autism. *Journal of Abnormal Psychology*, **119**(4), 896–905. http://doi.org/10.1037/a0020631

Lind, S. E., Williams, D. M., Bowler, D. M., & Peel, A. (2014). Episodic memory and episodic future thinking impairments in high-functioning autism spectrum disorder: An underlying difficulty with scene construction or self-projection? *Neuropsychology*, **28**(1), 55–67. http://doi.org/10.1037/neu0000005

MacLeod, A. K. (2016). Prospection, well-being and memory. *Memory Studies*, **9**(3), 266–274. http://doi.org/10.1177/1750698016645233

MacLeod, A. K., Tata, P., Kentish, J., & Jacobsen, H. (1997). Retrospective and prospective cognitions in anxiety and depression. *Cognition and Emotion*, **11**(4), 467–479. http://doi.org/10.1080/026999397379881

Madore, K. P., Gaesser, B., & Schacter, D. L. (2014). Constructive episodic simulation: Dissociable effects of a specificity induction on remembering, imagining, and describing in young and older adults. *Journal of Experimental Psychology: Learning, Memory, and Cognition*, **40**(3), 609–622. http://doi.org/10.1037/a0034885

Madore, K. P. & Schacter, D. L. (2014). An episodic specificity induction enhances means-end problem solving in young and older adults. *Psychology and Aging*, **29**(4), 913–924. http://doi.org/10.1037/a0038209

Madore, K. P. & Schacter, D. L. (2016). Remembering the past and imagining the future: Selective effects of an episodic specificity induction on detail generation. *The Quarterly Journal of Experimental Psychology*, **69**(2), 295–298. http://doi.org/10.1080/17470218.2014.999097

Memon, A., Meissner, C. A., & Fraser, J. (2010). The Cognitive Interview: A meta-analytic review and study space analysis of the past 25 years. *Psychology, Public Policy, and Law*, **16**(4), 340–372. http://doi.org/10.1037/a0020518

Miles, H., MacLeod, A. K., & Pote, H. (2004). Retrospective and prospective cognitions in adolescents: Anxiety, depression, and positive and negative affect. *Journal of Adolescence*, **27**(6), 691–701. http://doi.org/10.1016/j.adolescence.2004.04.001

Pillemer, D. B., Thomsen, D., Kuwabara, K. J., & Ivcevic, Z. (2013). Feeling good and bad about the past and future self. *Memory*, **21**(2), 210–218. http://doi.org/10.1080/09658211.2012.720263

Platt, J. J., & Spivack, G. (1975). *The Means End Problem Solving Procedure manual.* Philadelphia, PA: Hahnemann University Press.

Raes, F., Hermans, D., Williams, J. M. G., & Eelen, P. (2007). A sentence completion procedure as an alternative to the Autobiographical Memory Test for assessing overgeneral memory in non-clinical populations. *Memory*, **15**(5), 495–507. http://doi.org/10.1080/09658210701390982

Raffard, S., D'Argembeau, A., Bayard, S., Boulenger, J.-P., & Van der Linden, M. (2010). Scene construction in schizophrenia. *Neuropsychology*, **24**(5), 608–615. http://doi.org/10.1037/a0019113

Rendell, P. G., Bailey, P. E., Henry, J. D., Phillips, L. H., Gaskin, S., & Kliegel, M. (2012). Older adults have greater difficulty imagining future rather than atemporal experiences. *Psychology and Aging*, **27**(4), 1089–1098. http://doi.org/10.1037/a0029748

Renoult, L., Davidson, P. S., Palombo, D. J., Moscovitch, M., & Levine, B. (2012). Personal semantics: At the crossroads of semantic and episodic memory. *Trends in Cognitive Sciences*, **16**(11), 550–558. http://doi.org/doi: 10.1016/j.tics.2012.09.003

Robinaugh, D. J. & McNally, R. J. (2013). Remembering the past and envisioning the future in bereaved adults with and without complicated grief. *Clinical Psychological Science*, **1**(3), 290–300. http://doi.org/10.1177/2167702613476027

Rubin, D. C., Berntsen, D., & Hutson, M. (2009). The normative and the personal life: Individual differences in life scripts and life story events among USA and Danish undergraduates. *Memory, 17*(1), 54–68. http://doi.org/10.1080/09658210802541442

Schacter, D. L. (2012). Adaptive constructive processes and the future of memory. *The American Psychologist, 67*(8), 603–613. http://doi.org/10.1037/a0029869

Schacter, D. L. & Addis, D. R. (2007). The cognitive neuroscience of constructive memory: Remembering the past and imagining the future. *Philosophical Transactions of the Royal Society of London (B), 362,* 773–786. http://doi.org/10.1098/rstb.2007.2087

Schacter, D. L., Addis, D. R., Hassabis, D., Martin, V. C., Spreng, R. N., & Szpunar, K. K. (2012). The future of memory: Remembering, imagining, and the brain. *Neuron, 76*(4), 677–694. http://doi.org/10.1016/j.neuron.2012.11.001

Smallwood, J., Schooler, J. W., Turk, D. J., Cunningham, S. J., Burns, P., & Macrae, C. N. (2011). Self-reflection and the temporal focus of the wandering mind. *Consciousness and Cognition, 20*(4), 1120–1126. http://doi.org/10.1016/j.concog.2010.12.017

Söderlund, H., Moscovitch, M., Kumar, N., Daskalakis, Z. J., Flint, A., Herrmann, N., & Levine, B. (2014). Autobiographical episodic memory in major depressive disorder. *Journal of Abnormal Psychology, 123*(1), 51–60. http://doi.org/10.1037/a0035610

Spreng, R. N., & Levine, B. (2006). The temporal distribution of past and future autobiographical events across the lifespan. *Memory & Cognition, 34*(8), 1644–1651.

Stawarczyk, D. & D'Argembeau, A. (2015). Neural correlates of personal goal processing during episodic future thinking and mind-wandering: An ALE meta-analysis. *Human Brain Mapping, 36*(8), 2928–2947. http://doi.org/10.1002/hbm.22818

Sumner, J. A., Mineka, S., & McAdams, D. P. (2013). Specificity in autobiographical memory narratives correlates with performance on the Autobiographical Memory Test and prospectively predicts depressive symptoms. *Memory, 21*(6), 646–656. http://doi.org/10.1080/09658211.2012.746372

Szpunar, K. K., Spreng, R. N., & Schacter, D. L. (2014). A taxonomy of prospection: Introducing an organizational framework for future-oriented cognition: Fig. 1. *Proceedings of the National Academy of Sciences, 111*(52), 18414–18421. http://doi.org/10.1073/pnas.1417144111

Teasdale, J. D. & Fogarty, S. J. (1979). Differential effects of induced mood on retrieval of pleasant and unpleasant events from episodic memory. *Journal of Abnormal Psychology, 88*(3), 248–257. http://doi.org/10.1037/0021-843X.88.3.248

Williams, J. M. G., Barnhofer, T., Crane, C., Herman, D., Raes, F., Watkins, E., & Dalgleish, T. (2007). Autobiographical memory specificity and emotional disorder. *Psychological Bulletin, 133*(1), 122–148. http://doi.org/10.1037/0033-2909.133.1.122

Williams, J. M. G. & Broadbent, K. (1986). Autobiographical memory in suicide attempters. *Journal of Abnormal Psychology, 95*(2), 144–149. http://doi.org/10.1037/0021-843X.95.2.144

Williams, J. M. G., Ellis, N. C., Tyers, C., Healy, H., Rose, G., & MacLeod, A. K. (1996). The specificity of autobiographical memory and imageability of the future. *Memory & Cognition, 24*(1), 116–125.

Chapter 7

Goals

What are goals?

Table 7.1 contains a selection of verbatim responses from a variety of participants in a study where people were simply asked to list their goals. In this study (Sherratt & MacLeod, 2013) participants were given little in the way of instruction; the researcher simply explained that she would like participants to think about their goals for the future, given the prompt 'In the future it will be important for me to …' and asked people to list as many completions of that sentence as possible. The responses clearly vary in many ways—how specific they are, how near or far into the future they go, the life domains they cover, whether they represent preserving things as they are, as opposed to gaining new things, or avoiding unwanted experiences, whether they have an internal focus on thoughts and feelings, or are more externally focused about outcomes in the world, and so on. This chapter will discuss these different dimensions and how they relate to well-being. Before getting onto the key questions that the chapter addresses, the present section will discuss how the term 'goals' has been defined in the psychological literature in order to clarify exactly what is being talked about under the goals heading.

In the psychological literature one commonly cited definition of goals is 'internal representations of desired states, where states are broadly construed as outcomes, events, or processes' (Austin & Vancouver, 1996, p. 338). This description is extremely broad and could apply to a very diverse array of different kinds of phenomena, from simple actions like reaching for a door handle through to large-scale personal life goals, such as being a mother or being happy. Even when talking about the personal domain involving the self, goals can mean quite different kinds of things. For example, Markus and Ruvolo (1989), in discussing goals, talk about routine activities like getting dressed in the morning alongside more complex aspirations such as gaining tenure in a profession. Although the term is flexible enough to be used in all these different ways, it then becomes questionable how useful such a broad concept is. The focus in the present chapter is on the everyday use of the term, defined by the sorts of descriptions that people give when they are asked what their goals are, as illustrated in Table 7.1.

Table 7.1 Sample of personal goals given by participants

- *Meet someone and fall in love*
- *To get at ease with myself/love myself*
- *To be a nicer person*
- *To be happy*
- *Make time for activities with good friends*
- *Have a bath in a bathroom, not just a shower*
- *Be a good grandparent*
- *To get a new job which I find challenging and rewarding*
- *Keep volunteering and be there for others*
- *Pay off debts*
- *Travel more*
- *To relax more*
- *To be less negative*
- *Learn a new language*
- *To have children and a family*
- *To be loved*
- *Stay close to my family*
- *Make the most of my opportunities*
- *Learn how to drive*
- *To keep in touch with my children no matter how difficult it is to bypass my ex*
- *Losing 2kg*
- *Looking for a school for my son*
- *Lose anger*
- *Tell my husband what I am going to buy before I go shopping*
- *Not to become my Mum*

Cochran and Tesser (1996) furnish a fuller definition that captures some of the more specific elements constituting a goal: 'a cognitive image of an ideal stored in memory for comparison to an actual state; a representation of the future that influences the present; a desire (pleasure and satisfaction are expected from goal success); a source of motivation, an incentive to action' (Cochran & Tesser, 1996, p. 100). This definition does much better at capturing the fact that, rather than simply being an idea of something desirable, goals motivate behaviour and imply commitment, and working towards an outcome, something that is captured by the simple dictionary definition: 'the object of a person's ambition or effort'[1], as well as by Little's concept of *personal projects* (Little, Salmela-Aro, & Phillips, 2006), or Emmons' *personal strivings* (Emmons, 1986). Essential to this latter aspect, although not spelled out in the Cochran and Tesser definition, is that goals must be perceived as possible, although not certain. People have and work towards goals that

---

[1]   http://www.oxforddictionaries.com/definition/english/goal, accessed 16 June 2015.

they believe have some likelihood of being realized, although there has to be some degree of uncertainty about the outcome, at least to the point of depending on the person's effort. Goals are distinct from fantasies about future outcomes, which need not be constrained by probabilities, nor do they need any element of working towards the positive outcome that is imagined (Oettingen, 2012).

In essence, goals are mental representations of a desired future state that people are either actively engaged in working towards or have some intention of taking action to realize, and which they believe have some likelihood (without certainty) of coming about.[2] Getting dressed in the morning could qualify as a goal, but only under special circumstances, for example, in the case of someone undergoing rehabilitation where it was an identified meaningful target for them, or for a child learning to get themselves ready for school in the morning rather than being dressed by their parents. In these cases, getting dressed in the morning is the desired object of effort or ambition (in the latter example, the object of effort for the child and desired by the parent!), but for most people in most circumstances it would not be a meaningful object of ambition requiring effort, with uncertainty about the outcome, and therefore it would not fall under what we are discussing in this chapter.

Other aspects of personal future-thinking also do not comfortably fit the use of the term goal. If I am looking forward to seeing my son when he comes back from a school trip to Spain, or going on holiday to Scotland, these thoughts are representations of desired future states but are not goals in the everyday use of the term. I do not have a *goal* to see my son and it would sound strange to say that because there is no sense of uncertainty about it and neither do I have to put in any effort to make it happen. So, although sometimes goals are talked about as if they are synonymous with future-directed thinking, it should be borne in mind that there are other important thoughts about the future that are not properly described as goals, for example, expectancies and anticipation (see Chapters 2 and 3). Within Szpunar and colleagues' taxonomy of future-directed thinking discussed in Chapter 1, goals refer to one of four dimensions of future thought, the other three being prediction, simulation, and planning (Szpunar,

---

[2] People are typically aware of goals, at least in the way the term is being used here, but findings have also been reported showing unconscious influences in personal goal-related behaviour (see Dijksterhuis & Aarts, 2010). There is ongoing debate about how replicable some of the reported social priming findings are (e.g. Shanks, Newell, Lee, Balakrishnan, Ekelund et al., 2013), but in any case, the focus on this chapter will be on goals that people are aware of having to the extent of being able to describe them.

Spreng, & Schacter, 2014). The last of these dimensions is closely related to goals and will be discussed in Chapter 8.

Goals are, however, undoubtedly a hugely important aspect of future-oriented thinking. D'Argembeau and Mathy (2011) have suggested that thoughts about the future are organized around goals, and others (e.g. Conway & Pleydell-Pearce, 2000) have argued that memory is similarly structured, although it is likely that future-thinking is particularly connected to goals. Cole and Berntsen (2016) found that mind wandering during a monotonous task, where the content of thoughts was about the future, was more strongly related to participants' current concerns (goals) than were mind wandering episodes where people were recalling memories. Within theories of motivation, goals are seen as a way of describing a middle level of analysis within a multi-level hierarchy, providing a bridge between higher level motivations—values and needs—and lower level, more specific behaviours (Emmons, 1986). For example, a higher level motivation like affiliation might be served by a goal of 'becoming closer to my brother'. This goal might then be connected to particular behaviours, such as the person arranging to play golf with his or her brother every Sunday, which could be served by a specific behavioural plan, ('calling my brother this evening to arrange to play this Sunday'). Any level in this hierarchy can be described as a goal and, because of the hierarchical and interconnected nature of the different levels, can also represent a plan to reach the goal on the level above, a point which will be returned to in Chapter 8.

Goals and well-being

It is widely accepted in the psychological literature that goals are central to well-being. Underpinning this belief is the view that human beings are essentially goal-directed organisms (e.g. Carver & Scheier, 1990; Emmons, 1986) and, as such, their well-being must be connected with having and pursuing goals. Theoretical approaches that emphasize the centrality of goals to human functioning and well-being have been called 'telic theories', referring to purposiveness focused on an end point (Diener, 1984). According to telic theories, people experience well-being when they are actively engaged in striving towards valued goals (Schmuck & Sheldon, 2001). This purposive future orientation is often embedded in some of the definitions of well-being themselves, that is, goals are often represented in the list of goods drawn up by list theorists as defining well-being (see Chapter 1). For example, Ryff's multidimensional model of well-being has purpose in life as one of its dimensions, with a high scorer on the dimension having 'goals in life and a sense of directedness', in contrast to someone at the low end who 'lacks a sense of meaning in life, has few goals or aims' (Ryff, 1989, p. 1072). An empirical stance is also possible if goals are seen as something distinct from well-being. A subjective account of well-being allows empirical examination of whether goals are related to life satisfaction as well as to positive and negative affect.

How might goals be related to well-being? Goals reflect engagement in life and engagement is linked to, or perhaps just an inherent element of, a life that is good for a person, depending on the concept of well-being that is adopted (Seligman, 2011). As well as motivating engagement in life tasks, goals also guide behaviour, thus providing a structure that directs actions (Cantor & Sanderson, 1982) and provides reasons for that action. In this kind of view, goals are inherently valuable; their value does not reside in their end point. In other words, someone does not have to achieve their goals to derive well-being benefit from them. A participant, in one goal-setting and planning skills group (see Chapter 10) that I ran once, commented when another member was lamenting his lack of achievement, 'the path is the goal', a concept present in Buddhist teaching (Trungpa, 2011).

Another possibility is that goals derive well-being benefit from being achieved. Achievement is rewarding, creating positive affect as well as other good feelings, such as a sense of efficacy or attainment. It just feels good to succeed, especially having worked and struggled to achieve a goal. Carver and Scheier (1990) suggest, however, that the attainment of goals is not what really matters for well-being. In fact, they suggest that attaining a goal can lead to a feeling of emptiness if it does not open up the possibility of another goal. In their influential model, a sense of progressing towards goals is the direct source of subjective well-being. According to Carver and Scheier (1990), people are constantly self-regulating, comparing themselves where they are now against their goals. Where there is a discrepancy, behaviour is implemented to move towards the goal and close the gap. A second monitoring system tracks the rate of progress towards the goal. Positive feelings arise when the rate of progress is perceived to be good, and, conversely, negative feelings result from lack of progress, or progress that is too slow, and indicate that something needs to change. Oatley and Johnson-Laird (1987) also proposed a similar self-regulatory model with an emphasis on the signalling properties of affect. For Oatley and Johnson-Laird (1987) positive emotions signal that goals are going well and that behaviour should continue in the way it has been, whereas negative emotions signal difficulties with goal progress and direct the person towards efforts to solve the difficulties or to reappraise the goal. If the goal signalling account of affect is correct, the feelings arising from progress towards goals could be of different kinds. Someone could derive a sense of satisfaction directly from each of the steps taken towards the goal. Alternatively, positive feelings could be in the form of anticipatory affect (see Chapter 5), arising from a sense that the goal is becoming closer and more likely to be achieved. This pre-goal attainment positive affect (see Chapter 5) is hypothesized to be a core feature of motivated behaviour (Davidson, 1998).

The different ways that goals might link to well-being are not mutually exclusive. It may be good simply to have goals because they provide structure and shape to life, direct action, and give a sense of meaning and purpose. Additionally, achieving goals provides different elements of well-being—a sense of mastery, achievement and satisfaction, and progress provides both satisfaction at progress made and anticipatory affect at the prospect of the goal getting closer. Adopting a multidimensional concept of well-being, as outlined in Chapter 1, opens up possibilities for examining whether different aspects of goals influence distinct aspects of well-being. The rest of this chapter will review the evidence in relation to whether goals are related to well-being, as well as evidence in relation to some of the linking mechanisms that have been suggested.

Goal progress and attainment

Aside from having goals, is it important to achieve them, or, at least to have a sense of making progress towards them? There is a substantial literature examining goal progress or attainment and their relationship to well-being. Klug and Maier (2015) conducted a systematic review and meta-analysis, including data from 85 different reports, with more than 20,000 participants. There was evidence of a significant link between goal striving and well-being. Higher levels of well-being were associated with attaining goals, but interestingly the link between goals and well-being was strongest when the goal outcome variable was defined as a sense of progressing towards them, rather than a measure of actual goal attainment. Klug and Maier (2015) conclude that goal achievement does matter for well-being but not as much as having a goal and feeling that one is progressing towards it. Results also varied by different facets of well-being, in that well-being measured as the presence of positive experience (e.g. positive affect) proved to be more strongly related to goal progress than when it was measured as the absence of negative experience (e.g. negative affect). A note of caution was that the effects were strongest for student samples, indicating restraint in generalizing effects beyond the typical university student population, which is what the vast majority of studies rely upon. A major conclusion from the Klug and Maier (2015) review is that the link between goals and well-being does not simply depend on the actual achievement of goals but is more closely connected to a sense of progress. This makes motivational sense in that many goals are longer-term and persistence would be difficult if there was little or no feedback and reward during the goal pursuit process. A sense of goal progress is likely to be intrinsically rewarding, with many small steps giving rise to feelings of satisfaction. However, the fact that positive affect, which is characterized strongly by anticipatory states such as excitement and energy, shows the strongest effect indicates that anticipatory affect (see Chapter 5) in response to the goal becoming closer is likely to be an important source of well-being from goal progress.

A sense of progress is distinct from a feeling that the goal is increasingly likely, but it is closely related to it. Clinical groups, notably those who are depressed, have been found to show lower likelihood estimates of future positive events (see Chapter 2). This reduced expectancy for future positive events is found when participants are asked to rate the subjective probability of a list of hypothetical future positive events, some of which are presumed to overlap with their own goals. In addition, depressed and suicidal individuals are less able than controls to think of events that they are looking forward to (see Chapter 2), and when they are asked to rate the likelihood of those events, give lower estimates of the ones that they do manage to think of (MacLeod & Salaminiou, 2001). Some of the sorts of events that depressed or suicidal people are lacking, particularly the short-term ones (e.g. 'seeing friends tomorrow night', 'having some time to myself this weekend') are not what could be described as goals in the sense outlined at the beginning of this chapter, but the longer-term ones that they are missing (e.g. 'getting married', 'finding a job I like') are more goal-like. More direct evidence about likelihood beliefs in relation to goals comes from studies where participants identify their own goals and rate their degree of belief in them coming about. For example, Dickson, Moberly, and Kinderman (2011) asked depressed patients and matched non-depressed controls to write down as many things as possible that they would typically be trying to achieve in the future. The groups did not differ in the number of goals they generated but when asked to rate how likely the goals were to be achieved, the depressed group showed significantly lower estimates than controls. The depressed group also showed lower ratings of control over the goal outcomes. Comparable levels of goal importance (Dickson et al., 2011) and goal commitment (Vergara & Roberts, 2011) have been reported in depressed and non-depressed participants, suggesting intact aspects of basic underlying motivation. At the extreme low end of well-being, suicidal patients have also been found to be able to describe personal goals, but show markedly lower subjective estimates of the goals ever coming about (Danchin, MacLeod, & Tata, 2010; Vincent, Boddana, & MacLeod, 2004). For example, Figure 7.1 shows the number of goals participants were able to generate along with ratings of their perceived likelihood and control in relation

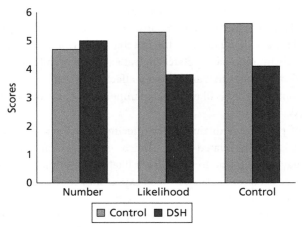

Figure 7.1 Number of goals generated, with perceived likelihood of the goals occurring, and perceived control (both on seven-point scales) over the outcomes, in control and deliberate self-harm (DSH) groups. The groups differed significantly in likelihood and control but not in number.

Data from Vincent, P. J., Boddana, P., MacLeod, A. K, *Clinical Psychology & Psychotherapy* **4**(1), 15–24. Copyright © 2004 by John Wiley Sons, Inc. Reprinted by permission of John Wiley & Sons, Inc.

to those goals (Vincent et al., 2004). In this study, we recruited participants who presented at hospital following an episode of self-harm (predominantly overdose), and compared them with a matched, non-suicidal control group. Such lowered likelihood estimates, along with a perceived lack of control, are arguably strong proxies for a sense of lack of progress, or anticipated progress, towards goals. In the terms already discussed, those who are suicidal are able to describe goals but are not able to derive satisfaction from a sense of progress or experience anticipatory well-being benefit from those goals due to the lack of a sense of the goal coming any closer.

Progress, attainment, and motivation

So far, goals that might confer a well-being benefit have been defined simply by what people describe as their goals, with no qualification. However, evidence suggests that the idea of goal progress as related to well-being needs to be tempered by an understanding of the underlying motivation that people have for the goals. The point is that it is possible to have goals and be making progress, or even achieve the goals, without that necessarily conferring a well-being benefit. The first qualification refers to a generic aspect of underlying motivation—the extent to which people freely choose the goals they have. Sheldon and Elliot (1999) found that those who pursued goals because of more internal motives (because they enjoyed them or valued them, known as high self-concordance) showed more goal progress and greater increases in well-being from progress, whereas those who pursued their goals because they felt someone else wanted them to, or they would feel bad if they didn't (low self-concordance), did not. In many subsequent studies, an index of self-concordance has been derived by subtracting the first two sources of motivation (autonomous motivation) from the latter two (controlled motivation). There is evidence, however, that the negative correlation between the two is not strong and that goal progress has been found to correlate with autonomous motivation but show no relationship to controlled motivation (Koestner, Otis, Powers, Pelletier, & Gagnon, 2008). However, in clinical samples, controlled motivation appears to be important. Joanne Dickson and Nick Moberly, who have conducted much of the recent research on goals and mental health, compared anxious adolescents to a non-anxious control group (Dickson & Moberly, 2013a). The anxious adolescents showed greater endorsement of pursuing their goals because of feelings of shame, anxiety, or guilt (introjected reasons) if they did not, or because they felt other people wanted them to or the situation demanded it. Winch, Moberly, and Dickson (2015), in a student sample, also found correlations between anxiety and reasons for pursuing both approach and avoidance goals; in contrast, depression showed a unique relationship to lack of internal reasons for pursuing approach goals (i.e. because they were enjoyable or stimulating). In looking at recovery from depression following interpersonal therapy, McBride et al. (2010) reported that more controlled motivation (obligation, avoiding feeling bad) for taking part in treatment predicted lower symptom remission at the end of treatment, whereas levels of autonomous motivation towards treatment were unrelated to outcome. There is thus, evidence of the importance of both main aspects of motivation, although the details of how and when they are important for well-being remain to be mapped out.

A second aspect of underlying motivation that has been highlighted is the connection between the type of goals and the nature of the person's underlying needs or motives. Brunstein, Schultheiss, and Grässman (1998) found that well-being benefit was only present when people were pursuing goals that were congruent with underlying motivations of agency (need for achievement and power) or communion (need for affiliation and intimacy). Participants who scored higher on a measure of a need for agency did not derive well-being benefit from progressing towards communal goals, but they did derive benefit from agentic goals; communion-motivated participants showed the opposite. However, results from other studies using different kinds of measures of agency and communion have not found any particular well-being benefit from the fit between how agentic and communal a person's goals were, and whether they engaged in agentic or communal behaviours, or how strongly they held agentic or communal goals (Buchanan & Bardi, 2015) Measures of underlying motives can be either implicit, for example, coding of stories that participants write in response to pictures they are shown (e.g. Brunstein et al., 1998), or explicit, based on endorsement of value items on a self-report measure, as in the Buchanan and Bardi (2015) study. These two approaches to measuring motives show little or no correlation with each other (Rawolle, Schultheiss, & Schultheiss, 2013), which, along with the conflicting findings, makes it difficult to draw firm conclusions at this point about the importance of the motive–goal fit, although the idea does carry an intuitive appeal and sense of plausibility.

Goal content

Goal progress is related to well-being. Underlying motivation matters too, in that well-being benefit derives from goals that are freely chosen for autonomous rather than controlled reasons, and possibly it also matters that the goals fit with a person's underlying values or motivations. Following on from these more general aspects of motivational fit is the question of whether any goal, as long as it fits with underlying values or type of motivation, will be equally beneficial. Or, alternatively, are only certain specific kinds of goal content related to well-being. To take an extreme example, if someone has the goal of dominating and exercising power over others, which is freely chosen for reasons of value or enjoyment, and which they are actively and successfully pursuing, can this enhance that person's well-being? It is easy to see how this might enhance subjective feelings of well-being, but potentially it could even increase other more prescribed elements of well-being, for example, feelings of mastery, a sense of purpose, and enhanced autonomy. Obviously there are other, moral reasons why we think it is a bad thing for a person to pursue the goal of dominating others, mainly because it is usually bad for the well-being of those other people, but might it be good for the well-being of the person doing the dominating? Indeed, power is recognized as a value belonging to the category of self-enhancement values, which also include wealth, status, and prestige, opposite in the spectrum to values of self-transcendence, such as benevolence and universalism, which are focused on the welfare of others (Schwartz, 1992),

In an empirical programme of research, Kasser and colleagues (e.g. Kasser et al., 2014; Kasser & Ryan, 2001; Sheldon & Kasser, 1998) adopted a related distinction between goals that are about affiliation, self-acceptance, and community feeling, which they call intrinsic goals, contrasted with extrinsic goals concerned with financial success, appearance, or social recognition. Having achieved, or progressing towards, intrinsic goals or aspirations has been found to be related to well-being, whereas the same is not true for extrinsic goals (Kasser & Ryan, 2001; Sheldon & Kasser, 1998). Adopting a similar sort of distinction, Bauer and McAdams (2004) asked participants to list two major life goals and write a paragraph about each one, including the reasons for having them. The reasons (not the goals) were coded for whether they were intrinsic (concerned with meaningful relationships, contribution to society or future generations) or not. The presence of intrinsic reasons was associated with greater self-reported life satisfaction. In a second study using a very similar methodology, Bauer and McAdams (2010) coded the reasons for participants' two major life goals and measured their subjective well-being at the same time, and again three years later. The presence of what were called *socioemotional growth communal goals* (again, however, it was actually the reasons that were coded rather than the goals) was significantly correlated with well-being at the initial point of measurement and, moreover, predicted increases in well-being three years later after controlling for initial levels of well-being. These goals were defined by aiming for a deeper experience of others and relationships, greater abilities to act fairly or caringly and fostering the growth of others.

At the other end of the spectrum, goals related to wealth and financial success have received particular attention. Kasser et al. (2014) reported results from three longitudinal studies examining changes in well-being and materialistic goals, carried out in the US and Iceland, with time frames varying from six months to 12 years. A reduction in materialistic goals was associated with increases in well-being. For example, those who at follow-up showed reduced endorsement of the importance of goals such as 'to be a very wealthy person' showed improvements in subjective well-being, after controlling for baseline levels of well-being. Dittmar, Bond, Hurst, and Kasser (2014) reported a meta-analysis based on 151 different research reports, yielding over 700 effect sizes from 259 different samples. There was clear evidence of an inverse relationship between materialistic goals ($r = -.16$ to $r = -.24$) and indicators of subjective well-being, although the relationships were strongest for behavioural measures, such as risky health or extreme consumer behaviour, that are not direct measures of well-being; effects were weaker (but still significant) for measures of life satisfaction and affect.

Content and mania

Broadly supportive conclusions can be found from research focusing on the goal-related thoughts and behaviour that are central to bipolar disorder and hypomania (Johnson, Edge, Holmes, & Carver, 2012). An increase in goal-directed activity is one of the symptoms, along with other symptoms like grandiosity, increased talkativeness, racing thoughts, and increased engagement in risky, pleasurable behaviour, that characterizes a manic episode and its less extreme form, a hypomanic episode (American Psychiatric Association, 2013). With the sort of exaggerated goal-directed behaviour of bipolar patients in mind, Johnson and Carver (2006) developed a measure to assess extreme, ambitious goal setting—the elaborately named Willingly Approached Set of Statistically Unlikely Pursuits (WASSUP; Johnson & Carver, 2006). Respondents indicate how likely they are to set a number of goals for themselves on items that make up seven subscales: popular fame (e.g. 'you will appear regularly on TV'), friendships (e.g. 'everyone you know will love you'), world well-being (e.g. 'you will create world peace'), political influence (e.g. 'you will be important in political circles'), family (e.g. 'your children will see you as the perfect parent'), financial success (e.g. 'you will have a million dollars or more'), and creativity (e.g. 'you will create a great work of art, music, or poetry').

Stange et al. (2013) compared a sample of people judged to be vulnerable to onset of bipolar disorder on WASSUP scores. Participants were selected from a screening of almost 10,000 young people based on their scores on self-report measures of behavioural approach that are known to be related to bipolar disorder. Those in the top 15% of scores on these measures were categorized as high risk and were compared with mid-scorers whose scores were in the range of the 40th to 60th centiles. The validity of participants' risk status was subsequently borne out by a significantly higher onset of bipolar disorder within the high-risk group (Alloy et al., 2012). At baseline, the high-risk group showed higher scores on the fame, political influence, and financial success subscales of the WASSUP, but the groups did not differ on the other four subscales. Alloy et al. (2012), following participants up for an average of just over one year, found that the fame and wealth scores predicted the overall likelihood and earlier onset of a first episode bipolar spectrum disorder over and above other risk variables. In a study comparing a sample of people who already had experienced bipolar disorder (although were not highly symptomatic at the time of the study) with controls, Johnson, Carver, and Gotlib (2012) found that the bipolar group scored significantly higher on popular fame, although they did not differ on wealth. Additionally, Johnson et al. (2012) found that the bipolar group scored significantly lower than controls on the friends and the family subscales, although other studies have generally not found this inverse relationship between measures of mania and any WASSUP subscales.

It therefore appears that the extreme goal-oriented thoughts and behaviour in bipolar disorder and hypomania are connected specifically with the more extrinsic type of goals, further supporting the idea that extrinsic goals are related to low well-being. An important caveat is that this measure does not ask for actual goals, but instead, participants are asked to rate the likelihood of setting an item as a future goal (from 'no chance' through to 'definitely will'). It is possible that the way the items and response scales are phrased might encourage participants to treat them as judgements of the likelihood of the events themselves happening (which is, in fact, how the scale started out—see Johnson & Carver, 2006, Study 1), rather than the likelihood of setting them as goals in the future, which is, after all, an unusual sort of judgement to be asked to make. If this was the case it suggests that those at risk, or having experienced bipolar disorder, judge these kinds of events to be more likely, which nevertheless is also an important aspect of goal-directed behaviour.

The content—well-being link

The benefits of intrinsic goals have been understood with reference to Self Determination Theory (SDT; Deci & Ryan, 2000). SDT posits three underlying needs—autonomy, competence and relatedness—that reflect a fundamental, universal human nature. Intrinsic goals are good for well-being because they relate more closely to these basic underlying needs than do extrinsic goals, and are more likely to satisfy those needs. Materialistic goals are interpreted as having limited, or even negative, capacity to enhance well-being because they do not foster the satisfaction of more fundamental sources of well-being such as relatedness (Dittmar et al., 2014), although it is less clear how extrinsic goals are necessarily unrelated to the sorts of competence (achievement) and autonomy (independence) dimensions of SDT. In support of the SDT interpretation, Sheldon et al. (2010) reported some evidence that participants who made good progress at pursuing goals focused on enhancing autonomy, competence and relatedness showed increases in well-being, compared to those asked simply to pursue goals to improve their life circumstances (see Chapter 10 for a fuller description of the study). If the SDT interpretation is correct, it does raise a question of why so many individuals appear to pursue materialistic goals and why many societies appear to value them, a question that is beyond the scope of the present discussion. There is also an apparent paradox in that it is clear there is a positive relationship between wealth and well-being, one that may well be stronger than initially thought and one that may also be true for absolute, not only for comparative wealth (Sacks, Stevenson, & Wolfers, 2012). It would appear that having money, at least up to a point, is related to well-being, whereas pursuing it is not.

The findings by Sheldon et al. (2010) support the idea that having and working towards certain goals can *cause* levels of well-being. Along with colleagues (e.g. MacLeod, Coates, & Hetherton, 2008), I have also reported a number of findings in support of a causal relationship between goals and well-being. Those who took part in an intervention package designed to help them to identify goals, form plans, and implement steps to move towards goals (described more fully in Chapter 10) increased in well-being, compared to those who did not. In these studies, participants generated a list of goals and selected ones to work on that were self-concordant and approach-oriented. Kasser et al. (2014) reported mixed outcomes for a programme specifically targeted on reducing materialism in families. Those receiving the programme showed, as would be expected, a reduction in materialistic goals compared to a control group who did not receive the intervention. This reduction in materialistic goals was accompanied by enhanced well-being, but only in those who started with the highest levels of materialistic goals, and only significantly so for self-esteem (changes in life satisfaction and anxiety were both non-significant even in the stratified analysis); so, taken as a whole, the results do not provide strong support for changes in materialism leading to enhanced well-being. Even accepting that there is a general causal link flowing from goals to well-being, this does not preclude reverse causality. It is not difficult to picture that being unhappy might well lead someone to grasp at goals about getting money and recognition, which are seen as the most obvious route to escape from their unhappiness. Nevertheless, if such goals are limited in their capacity for well-being enhancement, then there is a negative cycle where those low in well-being try to pursue goals to improve their situation, not realizing that the goals they are pursuing have little of that capability as well as having the concurrent effect of crowding out more intrinsic goals that do have the potential to enhance their well-being.

Like all group-based results that describe what is true on average for groups rather than for individuals, caution needs to be adopted in applying the findings to individuals. It may well be the case that certain individuals can enhance their well-being through having financial goals or popularity goals, or other types of goals that would not be described as intrinsic. This idea is made more convincing by the fact that well-being is probably not a unitary concept, and some aspects of it may be more linked to intrinsic goals, but other aspects may be served by extrinsic goals. For example, being financially independent may increase a person's sense of autonomy and reduce negative affect/anxiety, but do little to enhance the quality of relationships with others, or increase positive affect. A second point to bear in mind, as already discussed in this chapter, is that it is likely to be what the goal serves, rather than the goal content itself, that is important. Although there may often be a clear link between the two, this is not necessarily so. So, someone may have what appears to be an extrinsic goal (making a lot of money before they are 35) but that goal could serve a variety of possible motives (to provide security and care for their elderly parents, or gaining the admiration of their peers, or settling down so that they can have a family). Because goals are part of a hierarchy, it is not always possible to detect the underlying motive from the surface content of the goal. Kasser et al. (2014) attempted to deal with the motivation issue by measuring both goal content and motives, finding that each independently predicted changes in well-being. However, their conception of motives was in terms of whether the motives were autonomous, as opposed to controlled, measured by questions about goal self-concordance. Whether someone pursues a goal because they value it, as opposed to because they would feel guilty if they did not, is different from the actual content or nature of the motive. For example, someone (1) may have the goal of becoming wealthy, (2) so that they can care for their parents, (3) because they value that highly. The Kasser et al. (2014) studies measured levels (1) and (3) but not the actual content of the motive at level (2), which paints quite a different picture. The methodology employed by Bauer and McAdams (2004, 2010), where richer descriptions of motives are obtained and then independently coded for content, enables measurement of the underlying reasons behind goals, and offers a promising way forward to understand more about the nature of goals, motives, and their potential effects on well-being.

Happiness as a goal

Some goals, as can be seen in the list in Table 7.1 at the beginning of this chapter are about feeling states rather than states in the world, for example, 'to get at ease with myself/love myself', 'to be happy', and 'to relax more'. Such goals are abstract in that they typically do not connect with particular events or relate to particular times and places, and they describe outcomes that are essentially global affective states. 'To be happy' is perhaps the paradigm case of this kind of goal.

There are indications from the empirical literature that having positive thoughts about the future that are focused on feeling states is linked to lower levels of well-being. For example, Godley, Tchanturia, MacLeod, and Schmidt (2001) found that a group of participants diagnosed with anorexia nervosa showed overall levels of positive thoughts about the future that were comparable to controls, but a significantly greater proportion of those thoughts were intrapersonal, that is, concerned with their own internal mental states, including being happy. A group diagnosed with bulimia nervosa also showed this elevated number of intrapersonal positive future thoughts, despite being lower than controls on number of positive thoughts overall. The study by O'Connor, Smyth, and Williams (2015) referred to in Chapter 2, followed up a sample of hospitalized suicide attempters over a period of 15 months, and found that having more intrapersonal positive thoughts about the future was related to further suicidal behaviour.

Mauss and colleagues have argued that it is counterproductive to have the goal of happiness. In fact, they go further and suggest that valuing happiness highly has paradoxical effects on experienced happiness because it sets up high standards for feeling happy, which then magnify any discrepancy when someone is not feeling as happy as they think they should. The result is even lower happiness (Mauss, Tamir, Anderson, & Savino, 2011). The Valuing Happiness Scale (VHS; Mauss et al., 2011) was developed to measure this construct, and consists of seven statements, for example 'I am concerned about my happiness even when I feel happy' and 'I would like to be happier than I generally am'. VHS scores were measured in a community sample of women, some of whom had experienced a stressful event in the last six months. Having experienced a stressful event was, as might be expected, related to lower well-being scores. Being high or low on VHS scores made no difference in this stressed group, presumed to result from VHS levels being overridden and made redundant by the presence of an external reason for being unhappy. However, in those without a stressor, the general effect of being higher in well-being was dampened in those scoring highly on the VHS measure. The findings are interpreted as the result of valuing happiness highly, exerting pressure on the person to be happy, which, in the absence of an obvious external explanation for any lack of happiness the person might feel, results in lower happiness. In a parallel finding, priming the value, and by implication the goal, of happiness by reading an article extolling the benefits of being happy, was associated with less happy responding to a subsequent amusing film clip, whereas such priming made no impact on responses to a sad film clip. Participants in the happiness induction subsequently reported trying harder to be happy during the amusing film clip. Studies have found that VHS scores correlate with depressive symptoms and are higher in remitted depressed patients compared to controls (Ford, Shallcross, Mauss, Floerke, & Gruber, 2014) and correlate with mild hypomanic symptoms as well as being higher in those who met criteria for bipolar disorder (Ford, Mauss, & Gruber, 2015).

The suggestion that it is not a good idea to have the goal of happiness, or to value happiness appears at odds with widely held views about what constitutes a good life (e.g. MacLeod, 2015). For example, it is a fairly uncontroversial claim that what parents most want for their children is for them to be happy: 'First a quiz: In two words or less, what do you most want for your children? If you are like the hundreds of parents I've asked, you respond, "Happiness, Confidence, Contentment, Balance, Good stuff, Kindness, Health, Satisfaction, and the like". In short, you most want well-being for your children' (Seligman, Ernst, Gillham, Reivich, & Linkins, 2009, p. 293). Empirically, Bastian, Kuppens, De Roover, and Diener (2014) found in a survey of college students in 47 different countries around the world, that life satisfaction was higher for those who lived in countries where survey respondents also reported valuing positive emotions highly (e.g. Belgium, Venezuela), than for those where positive emotions were reported as being relatively unvalued (e.g. Turkey, Hong Kong). Mauss et al. (2011) do suggest that the VHS might be measuring an extreme valuing of happiness, but it seems equally plausible that it is picking up something more like a preoccupation with happiness, along with a tone of dissatisfaction, that leads to focusing on happiness and thinking about it a lot. Having a goal and thinking a lot about the goal are different things and may often be incompatible. My goal, as I am writing this section, is to complete this chapter by the end of the week. If I keep thinking about that goal—'is it getting done?' 'am I progressing quickly enough?', 'will I finish it?'—it will impede my progress. The best way to achieve my goal is, having formed it, to put it to the back of my mind and lose myself in the material that I am working on, perhaps now and then checking in with my goal to see if there is anything I need to be doing differently. There is no real reason to suppose that the goal of happiness is unique in this way. Constantly thinking about whether your goal of happiness is being realized will impede your attainment of happiness, just in the same way that constantly thinking about any goal will hamper it being achieved. Further support for this distinction between valuing and pursuing an outcome versus thinking about it a lot comes from the fact that the remitted depressed participants in the Ford et al. (2014) study who scored higher on VHS scored no higher than controls on a straightforward measure of how much they would ideally like to experience a range of positive emotions.

The fact that people who are depressed, or suicidal, or prone to bipolar disorder show more current concern with emotion goals, in particular, feeling happy, is also easily understood by the fact that many of them will currently be feeling very unhappy. In the same way that someone who is hungry will constantly think about food and prioritize its value, those who are unhappy will do the same about happiness. Unfortunately, the vicious cycle that is often prevalent in mood disorders also operates here, in that this preoccupation with good feeling states is likely to interfere with the ability to experience them. In short, highly valuing and holding the goal of happiness as a distal or even ultimate goal is not itself problematic, but constantly thinking about it as a proximal goal, rather than being engaged and focused on what may produce it, will likely impede it being realized. In this way, the goal of happiness is no different from most other goals.

Goal orientation—approach and avoidance goals

One major distinction that has been drawn in the goals literature is between approach goals and avoidance goals (Elliot, Sheldon, & Church, 1997). The typical approach goal is focused on moving towards a positive outcome; the emphasis is on attaining a new desired outcome that does not currently exist (e.g. 'to get a new job which I find challenging and rewarding'). Avoidance goals, in contrast, are about preventing future outcomes that the person does not want to happen (e.g. 'to be less negative'). This simple distinction does not capture all of the relevant nuances. For example, Elliot, Thrash, and Murayama (2011) include within their definition of approach goals those aimed at preserving an existing positive state, as well as those targeted on bringing about a new positive state. From the list in Table 7.1, these two categories would be represented by 'stay close to my family' and 'meet someone and fall in love', respectively. Although both are connected to a desirable outcome, goals focused on acquiring new desired outcomes and those concerned with preserving existing valued ones may well turn out to be psychologically distinctive and related to different aspects of well-being. Penningroth and Scott (2012), in a study comparing goals of younger and older adults, did define three categories of goals—gain, maintenance, and loss prevention. In this study, the authors combined maintenance and loss prevention categories, due to low numbers of loss prevention goals; older adults showed fewer gain and more maintenance/loss prevention goals, compared to younger adults. Further work could usefully be carried out distinguishing between these different types of goals, particularly between gain and maintenance, and also distinguishing between goals that are about getting rid of unwanted current conditions (e.g. 'lose anger') and avoiding the occurrence of new ones in the future (e.g. 'not to become my mum!'). Nevertheless, the simple division into approach and avoidance has proven to be useful and corresponds to the longstanding separation in the motivational literature between approach-oriented and avoidance-oriented motivational systems (e.g. Fowles, 1994; Gray & McNaughton, 2003), where depression is linked to a primary deficit in the approach system, with anxiety having stronger connections to the avoidance system (see Chapter 2).

The evidence on the relationship of approach and avoidance goals to well-being is mixed. Studies with student samples have found a greater proportion of avoidance relative to approach goals to be associated with lower levels of subjective well-being, both at a single point in time and longitudinally over the course of a semester (Elliot et al., 1997; Elliot et al. 2011). Taking a proportion of approach to avoidance goals establishes a possible relationship to well-being but does not enable the different contributions of approach versus avoidance goals to be assessed. Is it the prevalence of approach goals or the absence of avoidance goals, or both, that is linked to well-being? Joanne Dickson and I (2004a, 2004b, 2006) reported a series of studies that assessed the relationships of sub-clinical levels of anxiety and depression to approach and avoidance motivation. Participants (students or adolescents) were asked to generate approach goals (in the future it will be important for me to …) and avoidance goals (in the future it will be important for me to avoid …). The task was to think of as many goals as possible of each type. In two studies (Dickson & MacLeod, 2004a, 2004b) depression was significantly associated with fewer approach goals, whereas anxiety was related to having more avoidance goals. In the other study, we found that a combination of high approach and low avoidance goals distinguished control from depressed participants, although neither type of goal differed significantly on their own between the groups (Dickson & MacLeod, 2006).

However, studies using diagnosed samples have not produced equivalent findings. Dickson et al. (2011) found no difference in numbers of approach or avoidance goals in depressed patients compared to controls. Similar findings were replicated in another sample of depressed patients (Dickson & Moberly, 2013b) and in depressed volunteers who met diagnostic criteria for major depressive disorder (Belcher & Kangas, 2014). Both these latter two studies found the goals generated by depressed participants to be lower in specificity (cf. Chapter 6), but this lack of specificity was equally true of approach and avoidance goals. To complicate matters further, Vergara and Roberts (2011), after screening a large number of students, compared a group who met criteria for remitted depression (i.e. had experienced at least one episode of depression in the past but were not currently depressed) with those who had never been depressed. There was no difference on number of approach goals, but the previously depressed group did generate more avoidance goals.

The reason for the discrepancy in findings is unclear, although some of it might be the result of variations in severity of symptoms, or the age of the samples. One complication in trying to elicit approach and avoidance goals is that goals can be provided in response to approach or avoidance prompts, and may have the appearance of being those types of goals but actually reflect different underlying motivation. The hierarchical organization of the motivational system discussed earlier means that there are multiple levels related to any given goal. So, for example, an approach goal (e.g. being promoted at work) might reflect an underlying approach motivation (so that I can buy my own house), or it could potentially mask an underlying avoidance motivation (so that my parents will stop thinking I am a failure). The situation is even more complicated because (a) those underlying motivations may in turn have a further level, or even more than one level, of motivation underlying them, and (b) people may well have mixed motivations for the one goal that could include both approach and avoidance motives. Some people may, for example, want to buy their own house because they don't want to start feeling that life is passing them by (avoidance), as well as because they want to have somewhere they can invite friends to stay (approach). The discordance between how a goal appears and the underlying motivation is perhaps easier to envisage for approach goals but could potentially also arise for avoidance goals. This recognition of underlying levels of motivation is present in Bauer and McAdams' (Bauer & McAdams, 2004, 2010) methodology described earlier in the chapter, which coded the underlying reasons people gave for having their goals, rather than the goals themselves. Similarly, Higgins (Higgins, 1997, 2013) has suggested that people can have either a *promotion* or a *prevention* orientation to what appears to be the same goal. Promotion orientation is like approach motivation, in that the main focus is on gaining something desirable, whereas a prevention orientation sees the main value of goal attainment as leading to the prevention of something undesirable that would occur if the goal was not attained. For example, the goal of winning the lottery might have an underlying promotion focus, such as being able to travel the world, or a prevention focus, such as stopping the house being repossessed.

Going some way towards getting at the different levels, Dickson and Macleod (2004a) asked participants to generate approach and avoidance goals, and then asked them to describe the most important consequence associated with achieving or not achieving their two most important goals. These consequences were themselves coded as approach or avoidance. Using the coding of the consequences rather than the coding of the goals increased the strength of the relationships of approach and avoidance motivation to depression and anxiety, respectively.

Kate Sherrat and I (2013) wanted to explore this issue of underlying motivation more fully. We asked depressed patients and matched controls to generate approach and avoidance goals in the standard way. Participants were then re-presented with the two goals they had rated as most important and asked to describe reasons why the goal mattered, and why they wanted it to happen. Those reasons were then coded as approach or avoidance. So, for the goal of getting a new job that is challenging and rewarding, someone might say that is important to them because they want to learn new skills (approach), or because they want to stop being bored (avoidance). Consistent with the other findings on patient samples, the groups did not differ on the straightforward number of approach and avoidance goals. In contrast, for underlying reasons, the depressed participants gave relatively more avoidance reasons and fewer approach reasons for approach goals (see Figure 7.2): whereas for controls, only 10% of their reasons underlying approach goals were avoidance-driven, for the depressed group that figure was 39%. The approach goals of the depressed participants were relatively more likely to be driven by underlying avoidance motivation and therefore only have the surface appearance of approach goals. Avoidance goals did not show comparable divergence on underlying motivation. Thus, there does appear to be some evidence that approach and avoidance orientations to goals are related to depression and anxiety, but it may sometimes be necessary to dig down to deeper levels of motivation in order to find those relationships.

A final point to note in relation to approach and avoidance goals is that there may well be individual and cultural differences in how they relate to well-being. Tamir and Diener (2008) have suggested that within individualistic cultures, well-being may be linked to more approach and fewer avoidance goals, but that in collectivist cultures this pattern may not hold up to the same degree. In addition, individual differences in preference for type of goal may well moderate the

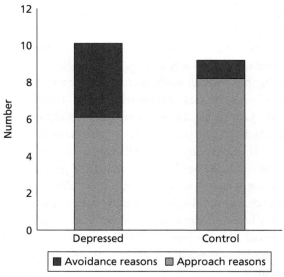

Figure 7.2 Number of reasons of each type (approach or avoidance) given for approach goals by depressed and control participants. The overall number of reasons given does not differ between groups but there is a significantly greater proportion of avoidance reasons given by the depressed group.
Data from Sherratt, K.A.L., MacLeod, A.K. *Cognition & Emotion*, 27(8), 1432 -1440. 2013 Taylor & Francis.

relationship—where people have preferences for avoidance goals, for example, then their well-being will not be best served by having a high preponderance of approach goals.

Goal structure—overvaluing goals

As has already been described, goals are organized in an interlinked way so that they serve higher order levels of motivation, and are in turn supported by sub-goals, the attainment of which will contribute to the goal being achieved. In a well-functioning system these different levels are consistent with each other. However, it has also been suggested that this linkage between levels has the potential to be dysfunctional if the different levels become overly identi-fied with each other. The idea is that connection is good, but that the system should have some degree of flexibility, so that, for example, a higher order goal of being happy or feeling loved does not depend solely and inflexibly on a par-ticular lower level goal being achieved. People who display a very high degree of connection between the different levels have been called *linkers* (McIntosh, 1996) or *conditional goal setters* (Street, 2002). Street (2002) measured condi-tional goal setting by the extent to which people endorsed 'I can only be happy/ fulfilled/have self-worth if …', where each sentence is completed in relation to goals that the person has described. High levels of conditional goal setting— seeing attainment of lower level goals (e.g. 'being together with Karl') as neces-sary for attaining higher level goals, such as happiness—have been found to be related to depression (Crane, Barnhofer, Hargus, Amarasinghe, & Winder, 2010; Street, 2002) and levels of hopelessness within a chronic depression sam-ple (Hadley & MacLeod, 2010), as well as being elevated in those with a recent suicide attempt (Danchin et al., 2010). Danchin et al. (2010) found that their suicidal group showed elevated levels of conditional goal setting compared to an anxious/depressed patient sample, as well as to a non-clinical control group, despite showing comparable levels of depression to the patient group. The sui-cidal group did, however, show higher levels of self-reported hopelessness, which is consistent with the finding from Hadley and MacLeod (2010) that self-reported hopelessness was more strongly related than depression to con-ditional goal setting.

As mentioned at various points throughout this book, it is not difficult to find that people who are feeling low will endorse negatively valenced or worded items on a self-report measure, whatever the content of the items, an issue that will be returned to in Chapter 11. Conditional goal-setting items may well also suffer from this problem. Danchin et al. (2010) reversed the questions so that people were asked to rate how happy/fulfilled and how much of a sense of self-worth they *would* feel if the goal *was* achieved. The suicidal patients showed higher endorsement of these positive statements than did either of the other two groups, that is, they reported thinking that they would experience higher levels of happiness upon their goals being achieved, than did either of the other two groups. In an attempt to look at this issue using something other than a single self-report judgement, Kate Coughlan, Philip Tata and I (Coughlan, Tata, and MacLeod, 2016) examined this issue more directly. Suicidal patients and non-suicidal controls completed standard well-being measures, then spent some time contemplating and envisaging their most important goal being achieved, before finally completing the same well-being measures again, this time under instructions to provide ratings that they anticipated they would feel with the goal achieved. Obviously, the suicidal group was significantly lower on actual well-being scores, but after envisaging achieving their goals they gave antici-pated well-being ratings that were equivalent to those of the controls. Figure 7.3 shows the current and anticipated levels for two of the varied well-being scores measured. Thus, using a different methodology, the findings suggest that those who have just recently deliberately self-harmed and have very high levels of depression and hopelessness, believe that their goals being achieved will be sufficient to bring them a 'normal' level of well-being. These findings reinforce

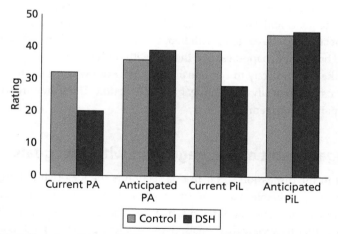

Figure 7.3 Deliberate self-harm (DSH) and control group current and anticipated scores on two well-being measures (Positive Affect, PA; Purpose in Life, PiL). The DSH group are significantly lower than controls on both variables when measured as current well-being, but the groups do not differ in their anticipated levels of well-being upon a major goal being achieved.

Data from Coughlan, K., Tata, P., & MacLeod, A. K. (2016) Personal goals, well-being and deliberate self-harm. *Cognitive Therapy and Research*. With permission of Springer.

the idea of specific goals being identified with higher level goals to such a degree that they are not only seen as necessary but also as sufficient to bring about the higher level goal of well-being, and that even those lowest in well-being can, in their imagination, think of a future where they feel good.

Rather like a rigid structure that has no give in it to absorb shocks, identifying higher level goals such as happiness or self-worth, or other aspects of well-being with particular low level goals, leaves a person vulnerable should they be put under stress, notably, when the goal seems to recede or even move out of reach altogether. As discussed earlier in this chapter, those low in well-being, even at the extremes of being suicidal, are able to describe personal goals, but they show a lowered perception in the likelihood of those goals coming about. This lowered belief in their goals' likelihood, combined with a higher dependence on them happening as the route to happiness does produce a particularly pernicious psychological state, which we have called *painful engagement* (Danchin et al., 2010; MacLeod & Conway, 2007), seen at its most extreme in those who are suicidal. Rather than being disengaged from the future, those who are high in hopelessness and suicidal, do have personal goals for the future; those goals are seen as necessary, and even sufficient, for a happy life, but they are perceived as relatively unlikely to happen. Chapter 8 will examine some of the reasons why people might have problems seeing their goals as likely to come about, but, given that their goals are perceived in this way, why do people not disengage from those goals and find new ones? The answer lies in the identification of those specific lower level goals with happiness. If someone thinks that life with Karl will bring them happiness and that life without Karl means a life of unhappiness, they are unlikely to relinquish that goal, even when it seems unlikely, because psychologically they simply have little option. Thus, they are stuck in a state of painful engagement.

Disengagement and engagement with new goals

Implicit in the discussion so far in this section is the idea that although goal engagement is valuable, there are times when it might be better to abandon goals and seek new ones, and that this may be difficult for some people because of the way that they view their goals. Some studies have attempted to measure difficulty in disengaging from goals that are not being attained, and problems engaging with new, different goals. Concepts such as tenacious goal pursuit versus flexible goal adjustment (Brandtstädter & Renner, 1990) have been applied to aging. In recognition that some goals become more difficult to obtain with aging, and that in these cases both perseverance and flexibility are important, each orientation is thought to have well-being value (e.g. Henselmans et al.,

2011). The Goal Adjustment Scale (Wrosch, Scheier, Miller, Schulz, & Carver, 2003) has a somewhat different emphasis because it assesses two dimensions of how people respond when it is clear that they are forced to stop pursuing the goals they have set. Goal disengagement is measured by items such as 'It's easy for me to reduce my effort towards the goal' and 'I find it difficult to stop trying to achieve the goal', the latter being reverse scored. 'I think about other new goals to pursue' would be a typical re-engagement item. To clarify, the re-engagement scale is actually about *new* engagement and not about re-engaging with the same goals after a break from them.

On the whole, the link to subjective well-being and depressive symptoms has proven to be stronger with the disengagement, than with the re-engagement scale (Dunne, Wrosch, & Miller, 2011). Those who score low on disengagement, that is, report not being able to disengage from goals that are not succeeding, score lower on well-being and higher on depressive symptoms. In contrast, two studies by O'Connor and colleagues found more pronounced effects for re-engagement in suicidal individuals: low scores on the goal re-engagement scale predicted persistence of suicidal symptoms ten weeks after a suicidal episode (O'Connor, Fraser, Whyte, MacHale, & Masterton, 2009) and also predicted repetition over a longer follow-up period (O'Connor, O'Carroll, Ryan, & Smyth, 2012). Relationship of suicidality to disengagement was less clear and more difficult to interpret, with some evidence of interactions between disengagement and re-engagement, although in one of the studies that was further qualified by the age of the participants (O'Connor et al., 2012). Dunne et al. (2011) also examined the predictive value of the scales in explaining changes in depressive symptoms over a six-year period in a sample of older adults. Self-reported functional disabilities concerned with daily living were also measured. Disengagement assessed at baseline predicted depressive symptoms at follow-up, after controlling for initial levels of depression. Moreover, disengagement interacted with increasing levels of disability to predict a small but significant amount of variability in follow-up depression levels. This latter effect is theoretically coherent: as participants age, functional decline would mean a reduced ability to do certain things. Being able to accept these inevitable changes and disengage from some goals would be adaptive, rather than exposing oneself to repeated failure and frustration. Re-engagement showed no effects.

One caveat to the results with disengagement is that the disengagement subscale items are expressed in a way that may be inherently depression-sensitive, with phrases like 'It's easy for me to ...' and 'I find it difficult to ...'. People who are depressed, because of their negative view of themselves, will have a tendency to endorse items that express their inability to do something (and the wording of the items and instructions suggests that what is being asked about is a useful thing to be able to do) and be very willing to endorse those items that allow them to say that they find things difficult. Would the same results be found if the items were less affectively sensitive and more neutral ('I don't stop trying to achieve the goal', rather than 'I find it difficult to stop trying to achieve the goals', or 'I reduce my effort towards the goal', rather than 'It's easy for me to reduce my effort towards the goal')? Possibly, the findings would be the same but perhaps not. As already noted in this chapter and returned to in later chapters, this is a problem that is not unique to this particular measure, but the findings would be more compelling without this complication. Nevertheless, the results, especially those of Dunne et al. (2011) and O'Connor and colleagues (O'Connor et al., 2009, 2012), are intriguing in not only suggesting a capacity to disengage from goals and engage with new goals can be adaptive but also through delineating specific sets of circumstances where that is the case.

Summary

This chapter has discussed goals, in the everyday meaning of desired future outcomes that matter to us, that we believe are possible, and that we are willing to put some effort into achieving. Personal goals vary in all sorts of ways, notably which domain of life they represent, whether they are new outcomes that people want to attain, or potential negatives they want to avoid, or simply preservation of a status quo that they already have and value. Goals can also be focused on internal states, such as happiness, or can be about states of the world, such as owning a home. Some approaches to well-being assume that an orientation towards goals is inherently part of well-being. Although not always explicitly stated, the rationale for this belief would be that a goal-oriented outlook is an expression of an inherent, universal human nature—it is simply how people are, and goals function to motivate behaviour, as well as providing structure and purpose. There is also empirical support for a link between goals and subjective well-being, particularly between goal progress and well-being. Possible mechanisms of this effect include satisfaction derived from steps taken on the route to a goal, and anticipatory affect arising from perceiving the goal as getting closer and more likely to occur, both of which are likely to be disturbed where well-being is low. Even those very low in well-being, for example, people who are suicidal, appear to have personal goals but do not perceive them as likely, therefore will not be able to derive the kinds of affective benefits normally associated with having goals. There are qualifications to the link between goals and well-being. The motivation underlying the goals matter, in that goals held for reasons of enjoyment or value, rather than in response to internal or perceived external pressure, have greater well-being potential. Content also matters. There is evidence that holding goals that are about connection with others, or with their welfare, is more strongly related to well-being than are goals which are easily defined as reflecting narrow self-interests (e.g. wealth, fame), although issues of causality still need to be unpacked. People who are low in well-being are more likely to hold goals that are about feeling states. The link between particular goal content and well-being is plausibly interpreted as bidirectional and may well form a vicious cycle where low well-being leads to certain goals being adopted, but, in fact, those goals have a limited potential to enhance well-being. Approach goals, rather than avoidance goals, are related to well-being, although future work could usefully distinguish between different types of approach and avoidance goals. Finally, the hierarchical nature of goals can mean that there is value in higher and lower levels of the hierarchy working together, but specific, lower level goals can be overidentified, with higher level goals such as happiness, interfering with flexibility to be able to disengage from non-progressing goals and engage with new goals, a capability that is related to well-being.

References

Alloy, L. B., Bender, R. E., Whitehouse, W. G., Wagner, C. A., Liu, R. T., Grant, D. A., Jager-Hyman, S., Molz, A., Choi, J. Y., Harmon-Jones, E., & Abramson, L. Y. (2012). High Behavioral Approach System (BAS) sensitivity, reward responsiveness, and goal-striving predict first onset of bipolar spectrum disorders: A prospective behavioral high-risk design. *Journal of Abnormal Psychology*, 121(2), 339–351. http://doi.org/10.1037/a0025877

American Psychiatric Association. (2013). *Diagnostic and statistical manual of mental disorders*. (5th edition). Washington, DC: Author.

Austin, J. T. & Vancouver, J. B. (1996). Goal constructs in psychology: Structure, process, and content. *Psychological Bulletin*, 120(3), 338–375. http://doi.org/10.1037/0033-2909.120.3.338

Bastian, B., Kuppens, P., De Roover, K., & Diener, E. (2014). Is valuing positive emotion associated with life satisfaction? *Emotion*, 14(4), 639–645. http://doi.org/10.1037/a0036466

Bauer, J. J. & McAdams, D. P. (2004). Growth goals, maturity, and well-being. *Developmental Psychology*, 40(1), 114–127. http://doi.org/10.1037/0012-1649.40.1.114

Bauer, J. J. & McAdams, D. P. (2010). Eudaimonic growth: Narrative growth goals predict increases in ego development and subjective well-being 3 years later. *Developmental Psychology*, 46(4), 761–772. http://doi.org/10.1037/a0019654

Belcher, J. & Kangas, M. (2014). Reduced goal specificity is associated with reduced memory specificity in depressed adults. *Cognition and Emotion*, 28(1), 163–171. http://doi.org/10.1080/02699931.2013.807776

Brandtstädter, J. & Renner, G. (1990). Tenacious goal pursuit and flexible goal adjustment: Explication and age-related analysis of assimilative and accommodative strategies of coping. *Psychology and Aging*, **5**(1), 58–67. http://doi.org/10.1037/ 0882-7974.5.1.58

Brunstein, J. C., Schultheiss, O. C., & Grässman, R. (1998). Personal goals and emotional well-being: The moderating role of motive dispositions. *Journal of Personality and Social Psychology*, **75**(2), 494–508. http://doi.org/10.1037/0022-3514.75.2.494

Buchanan, K. & Bardi, A. (2015). The roles of values, behavior, and value-behavior fit in the relation of agency and communion to well-being. *Journal of Personality*, **83**(3), 320–333. http://doi.org/10.1111/jopy.12106

Cantor, N. & Sanderson, C. A. (1999). Life task participation and well-being: The importance of taking part in daily life. In D. Kahneman, E. Diener, & N. Schwarz (Eds.), *Well-being: The foundations of hedonic psychology.* (pp. 230–243). New York: Russell Sage Foundation.

Carver, C. S. & Scheier, M. F. (1990). Origins and functions of positive and negative affect: A control-process view. *Psychological Review*, **97**(1), 19–35. http://doi.org/10.1037/ 0033-295X.97.1.19

Cochran, W. & Tesser, A. (1996). The 'what the hell' effect: Some effects of goal proximity and goal framing on performance. In L. L. Martin & A. Tesser (Eds.), *Striving and feeling: Interactions among goals, affect, and self-regulation.* (pp. 99–120). Hillsdale, NJ: Lawrence Erlbaum Associates, Inc.

Cole, S. N. & Berntsen, D. (2016). Do future thoughts reflect personal goals? Current concerns and mental time travel into the past and future. *The Quarterly Journal of Experimental Psychology*, **69**(2), 273–284. http://doi.org/10.1080/17470218.2015.1044542

Conway, M. A. & Pleydell-Pearce, C. W. (2000). The construction of autobiographical memories in the self-memory system. *Psychological Review*, **107**(2), 261–288. http://doi. org/10.1037/0033-295X.107.2.261

Coughlan, K., Tata, P., & MacLeod, A. K. (2016). Personal goals, well-being and deliberate self-harm. *Cognitive Therapy and Research*. http://doi.org/10.1007/s10608-016-9769-x

Crane, C., Barnhofer, T., Hargus, E., Amarasinghe, M., & Winder, R. (2010). The relationship between dispositional mindfulness and conditional goal setting in depressed patients. *British Journal of Clinical Psychology*, **49**(3), 281–290. http://doi.org/10.1348/ 014466509X455209

Danchin, C. L., MacLeod, A. K., & Tata, P. (2010). Painful engagement in deliberate self-harm: The role of conditional goal setting. *Behaviour Research and Therapy*, **48**(9), 915–920. http://doi.org/10.1016/j.brat.2010.05.022

D'Argembeau, A. & Mathy, A. (2011). Tracking the construction of episodic future thoughts. *Journal of Experimental Psychology: General*, **140**(2), 258–271. http://doi.org/ doi: 10.1037/a0022581.

Davidson, R. J. (1998). Affective style and affective disorders: Perspectives from affective neuroscience. *Cognition and Emotion*, **12**(3), 307–330. http://doi.org/10.1080/ 026999398379628

Deci, E. L. & Ryan, R. M. (2000). The 'what' and 'why' of goal pursuits: Human needs and the self-determination of behavior. *Psychological Inquiry*, **11**(4), 227–268. http://doi.org/ 10.1207/S15327965PLI1104_01

Dickson, J. M. & MacLeod, A. (2004a). Anxiety, depression and approach and avoidance goals. *Cognition & Emotion*, **18**(3), 423–430. http://doi.org/10.1080/02699930341000013

Dickson, J. M. & MacLeod, A. K. (2004b). Approach and avoidance goals and plans: Their relationship to anxiety and depression. *Cognitive Therapy and Research*, **28**(3), 415–432. http://doi.org/10.1023/B:COTR.0000031809.20488.ee

Dickson, J. M. & MacLeod, A. K. (2006). Dysphoric adolescents' causal explanations and expectancies for approach and avoidance goals. *Journal of Adolescence*, **29**(2), 177–191. http://doi.org/10.1016/j.adolescence.2005.03.007

Dickson, J. M. & Moberly, N. J. (2013a). Goal internalization and outcome expectancy in adolescent anxiety. *Journal of Abnormal Child Psychology*, **41**(3), 389–397. http://doi.org/10.1007/s10802-012-9685-9

Dickson, J. M. & Moberly, N. J. (2013b). Reduced specificity of personal goals and explanations for goal attainment in major depression. *PLoS ONE*, **8**(5). http://doi.org/10.1371/journal.pone.0064512

Dickson, J. M., Moberly, N. J., & Kinderman, P. (2011). Depressed people are not less motivated by personal goals but are more pessimistic about attaining them. *Journal of Abnormal Psychology*, **120**(4), 975–980. http://doi.org/10.1037/a0023665

Diener, E. (1984). Subjective well-being. *Psychological Bulletin*, **95**(3), 542–575. http://doi.org/10.1037/0033-2909.95.3.542

Dijksterhuis, A. & Aarts, H. (2010). Goals, attention, and (un)consciousness. *Annual Review of Psychology*, **61**, 467–490. http://doi.org/10.1146/annurev.psych.093008.100445

Dittmar, H., Bond, R., Hurst, M., & Kasser, T. (2014). The relationship between materialism and personal well-being: A meta-analysis. *Journal of Personality and Social Psychology*, **107**(5), 879–924. http://doi.org/10.1037/a0037409

Dunne, E., Wrosch, C., & Miller, G. E. (2011). Goal disengagement, functional disability, and depressive symptoms in old age. *Health Psychology*, **30**(6), 763–770. http://doi.org/10.1037/a0024019

Elliot, A. J., Sheldon, K. M., & Church, M. A. (1997). Avoidance personal goals and subjective well-being. *Personality and Social Psychology Bulletin*, **23**(9), 915–927. http://doi.org/10.1177/0146167297239001

Elliot, A. J., Thrash, T. M., & Murayama, K. (2011). A longitudinal analysis of self-regulation and well-being: Avoidance personal goals, avoidance coping, stress generation, and subjective well-being. *Journal of Personality*, **79**(3), 643–674. http://doi.org/10.1111/j.1467-6494.2011.00694.x

Emmons, R. A. (1986). Personal strivings: An approach to personality and subjective well-being. *Journal of Personality and Social Psychology*, **51**(5), 1058–1068. http://doi.org/10.1037/0022-3514.51.5.1058

Ford, B. Q., Mauss, I. B., & Gruber, J. (2015). Valuing happiness is associated with bipolar disorder. *Emotion*, **15**(2), 211–222. http://doi.org/10.1037/emo0000048

Ford, B. Q., Shallcross, A. J., Mauss, I. B., Floerke, V. A., & Gruber, J. (2014). Desperately seeking happiness: Valuing happiness is associated with symptoms and diagnosis of depression. *Journal of Social and Clinical Psychology*, **33**(10), 890–905. http://doi.org/doi: 10.1521/jscp.2014.33.10.890

Fowles, D. C. (1994). A motivational theory of psychopathology. In W. D. Spaulding (Ed.), *Integrative views of motivation, cognition, and emotion*. (pp. 181–238). Lincoln, NE: University of Nebraska Press.

Godley, J., Tchanturia, K., MacLeod, A. K., & Schmidt, U. (2001). Future-directed thinking in eating disorders. *British Journal of Clinical Psychology*, **40**(3), 281–295. http://doi.org/ http://dx.doi.org/10.1348/014466501163698

Gray, J. A. & McNaughton, N. (2003). *The neuropsychology of anxiety: An enquiry into the function of the septo-hippocampal system*. Oxford: Oxford University Press.

Hadley, S. A. & MacLeod, A. K. (2010). Conditional goal-setting, personal goals and hopelessness about the future. *Cognition & Emotion*, **24**(7), 1191–1198. http://doi.org/ 10.1080/02699930903122521

Henselmans, I., Fleer, J., van Sonderen, E., Smink, A., Sanderman, R., & Ranchor, A. V. (2011). The tenacious goal pursuit and flexible goal adjustment scales: A validation study. *Psychology and Aging*, **26**(1), 174–180. http://doi.org/10.1037/a0021536

Higgins, E. T. (1997). Beyond pleasure and pain. *American Psychologist*, **52**(12), 1280–1300. http://doi.org/10.1037/0003-066X.52.12.1280

Higgins, E. T. (2013). *Beyond pleasure and pain: How motivation works*. New York: Oxford University Press, USA.

Johnson, S. L. & Carver, C. S. (2006). Extreme goal setting and vulnerability to mania among undiagnosed young adults. *Cognitive Therapy and Research*, **30**(3), 377–395. http://doi.org/10.1007/s10608-006-9044-7

Johnson, S. L., Carver, C. S., & Gotlib, I. H. (2012). Elevated ambitions for fame among persons diagnosed with bipolar I disorder. *Journal of Abnormal Psychology*, **121**(3), 602–609. http://doi.org/10.1037/a0026370

Johnson, S. L., Edge, M. D., Holmes, M. K., & Carver, C. S. (2012). The Behavioral Activation System and mania. *Annual Review of Clinical Psychology*, **8**(1), 243–267. http://doi.org/10.1146/annurev-clinpsy-032511-143148

Kasser, T., Rosenblum, K. L., Sameroff, A. J., Deci, E. L., Niemiec, C. P., Ryan, R. M., Árnadóttir, O., Bond, R., Dittmar, H., Dungan, N., & Hawks, S. (2014). Changes in materialism, changes in psychological well-being: Evidence from three longitudinal studies and an intervention experiment. *Motivation and Emotion*, **38**(1), 1–22. http://doi. org/10.1007/s11031-013-9371-4

Kasser, T. & Ryan, R. M. (2001). Be careful what you wish for: Optimal functioning and the relative attainment of intrinsic and extrinsic goals. In P. Schmuck & K. M. Sheldon (Eds.), *Life goals and well-being: Towards a positive psychology of human striving.* (pp. 116–131). Ashland, OH: Hogrefe & Huber.

Klug, H. J. P. & Maier, G. W. (2015). Linking goal progress and subjective well-being: A meta-analysis. *Journal of Happiness Studies*, **16**(1), 37–65. http://doi.org/ 10.1007/s10902-013-9493-0

Koestner, R., Otis, N., Powers, T. A., Pelletier, L., & Gagnon, H. (2008). Autonomous motivation, controlled motivation, and goal progress. *Journal of Personality*, **76**(5), 1201–1230. http://doi.org/10.1111/j.1467-6494.2008.00519.x

Little, B. R., Salmela-Aro, K., & Phillips, S. D. (Eds.). (2006). *Personal project pursuit: Goals, action, and human flourishing*. Mahwah, NJ: Psychology Press.

MacLeod, A. K. (2015). Well-being: Objectivism, subjectivism or sobjectivism? *Journal of Happiness Studies*, **16**(4), 1073–1089. http://doi.org/10.1007/s10902-014-9561-0

MacLeod, A. K., Coates, E., & Hetherton, J. (2008). Increasing well-being through teaching goal-setting and planning skills: Results of a brief intervention. *Journal of Happiness Studies*, **9**(2), 185–196. http://doi.org/10.1007/s10902-007-9057-2

MacLeod, A. K. & Conway, C. (2007). Well-being and positive future thinking for the self versus others. *Cognition & Emotion*, **21**(5), 1114–1124. http://doi.org/10.1080/02699930601109507

MacLeod, A. K. & Salaminiou, E. (2001). Reduced positive future-thinking in depression: Cognitive and affective factors. *Cognition and Emotion*, **15**(1), 99–107. http://doi.org/10.1080/0269993004200006

Markus, H. & Ruvolo, A. (1989). Possible selves: Personalized representations of goals. In L. A. Pervin (Ed.), *Goal concepts in personality and social psychology.* (pp. 211–241). Hillsdale, NJ: Lawrence Erlbaum Associates, Inc.

Mauss, I. B., Tamir, M., Anderson, C. L., & Savino, N. S. (2011). Can seeking happiness make people unhappy? Paradoxical effects of valuing happiness. *Emotion*, **11**(4), 807–815. http://doi.org/10.1037/a0022010

McBride, C., Zuroff, D. C., Ravitz, P., Koestner, R., Moskowitz, D. S., Quilty, L., & Bagby, R. M. (2010). Autonomous and controlled motivation and interpersonal therapy for depression: Moderating role of recurrent depression. *British Journal of Clinical Psychology*, **49**(4), 529–545. http://doi.org/10.1348/014466509X479186

McIntosh, W. D. (1996). When does goal nonattainment lead to negative emotional reactions, and when doesn't it?: The role of linking and rumination. In L. L. Martin & A. Tesser (Eds.), *Striving and feeling: Interactions among goals, affect, and self-regulation.* (pp. 53–77). Hillsdale, NJ: Lawrence Erlbaum Associates, Inc.

Oatley, K. & Johnson-Laird, P. N. (1987). Towards a cognitive theory of emotions. *Cognition and Emotion*, **1**(1), 29–50. http://doi.org/10.1080/02699938708408362

O'Connor, R. C., Fraser, L., Whyte, M.-C., MacHale, S., & Masterton, G. (2009). Self-regulation of unattainable goals in suicide attempters: The relationship between goal disengagement, goal reengagement and suicidal ideation. *Behaviour Research and Therapy*, **47**(2), 164–169. http://doi.org/10.1016/j.brat.2008.11.001

O'Connor, R. C., O'Carroll, R. E., Ryan, C., & Smyth, R. (2012). Self-regulation of unattainable goals in suicide attempters: A two year prospective study. *Journal of Affective Disorders*, **142**(1–3), 248–255. http://doi.org/10.1016/j.jad.2012.04.035

O'Connor, R. C., Smyth, R., & Williams, J. M. G. (2015). Intrapersonal positive future thinking predicts repeat suicide attempts in hospital-treated suicide attempters. *Journal of Consulting and Clinical Psychology*, **83**(1), 169–176. http://doi.org/10.1037/a0037846

Oettingen, G. (2012). Future thought and behaviour change. *European Review of Social Psychology*, **23**(1), 1–63. http://doi.org/10.1080/10463283.2011.643698

Penningroth, S. L. & Scott, W. D. (2012). Age-related differences in goals: Testing predictions form selection, optimization, and compensation theory and socioemotional selectivity theory. *The International Journal of Aging & Human Development*, **74**(2), 87–111. http://doi.org/10.2190/AG.74.2.a

Rawolle, M., Schultheiss, M., & Schultheiss, O. C. (2013). Relationships between implicit motives, self-attributed motives, and personal goal commitments. *Frontiers in Psychology*, **4**. http://doi.org/10.3389/fpsyg.2013.00923

Ryff, C. D. (1989). Happiness is everything, or is it? Explorations on the meaning of psychological well-being. *Journal of Personality and Social Psychology*, **57**(6), 1069–1081. http://doi.org/10.1037/0022-3514.57.6.1069

Sacks, D. W., Stevenson, B., & Wolfers, J. (2012). The new stylized facts about income and subjective well-being. *Emotion*, **12**(6), 1181–1187. http://doi.org/10.1037/a0029873

Schmuck, P. & Sheldon, K. M. (Eds.). (2001). *Life goals and well-being: Towards a positive psychology of human striving.* Seattle: Hogrefe & Huber Publishing.

Schwartz, S. H. (1992). Universals in the content and structure of values: Theoretical advances and empirical tests in 20 countries. In M. P. Zanna (Ed.), *Advances in experimental social psychology, Vol. 25.* (pp. 1–65). San Diego, CA: Academic Press.

Seligman, M. E. P. (2011). *Flourish: A new understanding of happiness and well-being—and how to achieve them.* London: Nicholas Brealey Publishing.

Seligman, M. E. P., Ernst, R. M., Gillham, J., Reivich, K., & Linkins, M. (2009). Positive education: Positive psychology and classroom interventions. *Oxford Review of Education,* 35(3), 293–311. http://doi.org/10.1080/03054980902934563

Shanks, D. R., Newell, B. R., Lee, E. H., Balakrishnan, D., Ekelund, L., Cenac, Z., Kavvadia, F., & Moore, C. (2013). Priming intelligent behavior: An elusive phenomenon. *PloS One,* 8(4), e56515. http://doi.org/10.1371/journal.pone.0056515

Sheldon, K. M., Abad, N., Ferguson, Y., Gunz, A., Houser-Marko, L., Nichols, C. P., & Lyubomirsky, S. (2010). Persistent pursuit of need-satisfying goals leads to increased happiness: A 6-month experimental longitudinal study. *Motivation and Emotion,* 34(1), 39–48. http://doi.org/10.1007/s11031-009-953-1

Sheldon, K. M. & Elliot, A. J. (1999). Goal striving, need satisfaction, and longitudinal well-being: The self-concordance model. *Journal of Personality and Social Psychology,* 76(3), 482–497. http://doi.org/10.1037/0022-3514.76.3.482

Sheldon, K. M. & Kasser, T. (1998). Pursuing personal goals: Skills enable progress, but not all progress is beneficial. *Personality and Social Psychology Bulletin,* 24(12), 1319–1331. http://doi.org/10.1177/01461672982412006

Sherratt, K. A. L. & MacLeod, A. K. (2013). Underlying motivation in the approach and avoidance goals of depressed and non-depressed individuals. *Cognition & Emotion,* 27(8), 1432–1440. http://doi.org/10.1080/02699931.2013.786680

Stange, J. P., Shapero, B. G., Jager-Hyman, S., Grant, D. A., Abramson, L. Y., & Alloy, L. B. (2013). Behavioral Approach System (BAS)-relevant cognitive styles in individuals with high versus moderate BAS sensitivity: A behavioral high-risk design. *Cognitive Therapy and Research,* 37(1), 139–149. http://doi.org/10.1007/s10608-012-9443-x

Street, H. (2002). Exploring relationships between goal setting, goal pursuit and depression: A review. *Australian Psychologist,* 37(2), 95–103. http://doi.org/10.1080/00050060210001706736

Szpunar, K. K., Spreng, R. N., & Schacter, D. L. (2014). A taxonomy of prospection: Introducing an organizational framework for future-oriented cognition: Fig. 1. *Proceedings of the National Academy of Sciences,* 111(52), 18414–18421. http://doi.org/10.1073/pnas.1417144111

Tamir, M. & Diener, E. (2008). Approach-avoidance goals and well-being: One size does not fit all. In A. J. Elliot (Ed.), *Handbook of approach and avoidance motivation.* (pp. 415–428). New York: Psychology Press.

Trungpa, C. (2011). *The path is the goal: A basic handbook of Buddhist meditation* (Reprint edition). Boston: Shambhala.

Vergara, C. & Roberts, J. E. (2011). Motivation and goal orientation in vulnerability to depression. *Cognition & Emotion,* 25(7), 1281–1290. http://doi.org/10.1080/02699931.2010.542743

Vincent, P. J., Boddana, P., & MacLeod, A. K. (2004). Positive life goals and plans in parasuicide. *Clinical Psychology & Psychotherapy*, 11(2), 90–99. http://doi.org/ DOI: 10.1002/cpp.394

Winch, A., Moberly, N. J., & Dickson, J. M. (2015). Unique associations between anxiety, depression and motives for approach and avoidance goal pursuit. *Cognition and Emotion*, 29(7), 1295–1305. http://doi.org/10.1080/02699931.2014.976544

Wrosch, C., Scheier, M. F., Miller, G. E., Schulz, R., & Carver, C. S. (2003). Adaptive self-regulation of unattainable goals: Goal disengagement, goal reengagement, and subjective well-being. *Personality and Social Psychology Bulletin*, 29(12), 1494–1508. http://doi.org/ 10.1177/0146167203256921

Chapter 8

Plans

What are plans?

Plans represent the route by which goals are to be achieved. They are (i) future-oriented (i.e. refer to actions not yet taken), (ii) entail an intention to act, and (iii) are about steps or strategies aimed at reaching a particular end point, or goal. In short, plans are 'the designs we construct to guide our attempts to reach a goal in a given environment' (Scholnick & Friedman, 1993, p. 146). The distinction between goals and plans is a fine one and may appear to be quite arbitrary. Goals and plans are not necessarily different kinds of things. Whether something is best thought of as a plan or a goal depends on where the focus lies at that point in time. Because of the hierarchical nature of goals, all goals can themselves be seen as plans because their achievement is part of a movement towards a higher level goal which depends upon them. Of course, the final goal—the *finis ultimus*—should there be such a thing, would be the exception to this rule as there would be nothing further towards which it is aimed. As soon as a plan is formed it becomes itself a kind of goal to be achieved, and may require its own planned steps necessary for bringing it about. The goal of getting a promotion at work may be part of the plan to achieve the goal of eventual financial independence, which may, in turn, be a step towards the goal of being autonomous, and so on. So something can be both a plan for a higher level goal and a goal that is supported by plans lower in the hierarchy. Put more succinctly and to paraphrase Paul Simon, 'one plan's goal is another goal's plan'[1].

Table 8.1 shows verbatim responses from two participants in a study we carried out, where people were asked for their goals in a number of different life areas and then had to describe plans for getting from where they were at that moment to a point where the goal was achieved (MacLeod & Conway, 2005). The two goals shown in this table come from the category of leisure goals. Some of the plans look like they would need further planning steps, for example, 'get my husband to go on a fear of flying course' will need some planned steps such

---

[1] One man's ceiling is another man's floor, from the album, There goes Rhymin' Simon. Columbia Records, 1973.

Table 8.1 Examples of goals and plans for goals

Participant 1

Leisure goal: *To go abroad as a family.*

Plan:

- ◆ *Involve all family members in the decision.*
- ◆ *Look at the best/easiest route to take.*
- ◆ *Encourage a trip where there is someone who knows the areas available, e.g. stay with friends in California or go with friends to a shared villa.*
- ◆ *Get the children to lobby their father.*
- ◆ *Get my husband to go on a fear of flying course.*
- ◆ *Start small and build on it.*

Participant 2

Leisure goal: Would like to walk more and see more of the countryside.

Plan:

- ◆ *Put time aside to get away.*
- ◆ *Plan a day's walk/weekend walk in advance so I won't be side tracked.*
- ◆ *Turn off my mobile phone, so can't be side tracked.*
- ◆ *Go on a day that is dry, so I won't stop in a pub somewhere.*
- ◆ *Take food and drink so there's no excuse to stop.*

MacLeod A. K. & Conway, C. (2005). Well-being and the anticipation of future positive experiences: The role of income, social networks, and planning ability. *Cognition & Emotion*, **19**(3), 357–374.

as finding out where such a course runs and thinking about how to persuade him. Any level or sublevel below a nominated goal can be seen as part of a plan to achieve that goal and will be important in the planning process, but arguably the level immediately below the goal—the plans that people are able to think of when asked how they are going to achieve something they have volunteered as a goal—is strongly influential in determining the likelihood of moving towards the goal, and that is the level that will mainly be focused on in the present chapter.

Smith (1996) has pointed out that the literature on planning broadly refers to two quite different activities—planning for discrete tasks and planning for life goals. Planning for discrete tasks is often concerned with solving laboratory-based problems where the parameters are known. A good example is the Tower of London task, where participants are required, in as few steps as possible, to move a set of different sized rings from a starting point on three poles into a particular configuration on the poles (e.g. Carlin et al., 2000). This sort of planning appears, on the face of it, to be quite different to the kind of planning that relates to the pursuit of life goals, where outcomes are much more complex and open-ended (Smith, 1996). In fact, there is now clear fMRI data showing evidence that these two types of planning are distinct, although also with some element of overlap. Spreng, Stevens, Chamberlain, Gilmore, and Schacter (2010) had participants complete the Tower of London task and also an autobiographical planning task. In the autobiographical planning task participants were given goals (e.g. freedom from debt) and two steps towards the goal ('good job' and 'save money'), as well as an obstacle ('have fun'). These goals and associated steps had previously been generated by a different sample of comparable participants and then selected as being likely to be personally relevant to the study participants. Participants were required to integrate the steps and obstacle into a coherent plan for achieving the goal. What was of interest in this study was whether the different tasks would show different patterns of neural activation. As discussed in Chapter 6, the default network is known to be active when people engage in self-referential thinking, including thinking about their future, so the autobiographical planning task was expected to recruit the default network. In contrast, as a discrete task relying on attention to external stimuli, the Tower of London task was expected to rely on activation of the dorsal attention network, which includes the dorsolateral prefrontal cortex, a functional system that shows increased activity in attention-demanding cognitive tasks and which is normally anti-correlated with the default network (Fox et al., 2005). The results showed that both of these predictions were accurate and, in addition, in each task the activated network coupled with the frontoparietal control system, a system that regulates the activity of a range of other neural systems depending on the task at hand (Cole, Repovš, & Anticevic, 2014). Spreng and Schacter (2012) reported similar findings in a study comparing younger and older adults, with the exception that the older adults did not exhibit decoupling of the control and default networks during the Tower of London task.

Planning, of whatever variety, brings together a complex set of mental and behavioural operations, but there are two broad dimensions relevant to the discussion here—planning ability and planning propensity—which play out in whether someone engages in planning or not (Friedman & Scholnick, 1997). Planning ability will depend on cognitive capacity but also on long-term knowledge that is relevant to the particular goal or the planning process. Planning propensity will depend on a wide range of factors, including social and cultural norms. Motivational factors such as belief in the importance and value of the goal and the efficacy of planning will also play an important role in whether someone engages in planning or not. Someone may have planning skills, but if they believe that there is little value in planning because things never work out as they want, or that if they plan for anything it will just set them up for disappointment, then they are unlikely to engage in planning. Such a disinclination to plan could arise for a variety of reasons, for example, having low confidence in one's planning ability or believing that the world is just the sort of place where one's plans never work out, which in turn could be linked to past experience of disappointment.

Plans and well-being

Is there any link between planning and well-being? The literature is not large but from what is known, it appears that there is a link. In an impressively large and diverse sample of American adults, Prenda and Lachman (2001) reported data from a community survey in the US, in which over 3,000 participants reported on their attitude to planning as well as a number of other variables, including life satisfaction. Planning was measured by five questions, each rated on a four-point scale asking to what extent the statements describe the person, for example, 'I like to make plans for the future' (reverse scored) and 'I have too many things to think about today to think about tomorrow'. Planning scores were related to most variables including education and income, but for the purposes of the present chapter, the key point was that planning correlated modestly, but significantly, with life satisfaction ($r = .20$). A note of caution, though, needs to be inserted here. It is possible that the way the items are worded could connect to a dysphoric outlook, independently of any content related to planning. For example, people who are depressed or dissatisfied may well be less likely to endorse *any* statement that begins with 'I like', and having 'too many things to think about today' is the sort of thing that people say when they feel overburdened. In other words, it might be possible to score low on this measure simply because of its underlying affective tone or self-evaluative quality, independently of its specific content on planning.

The European Social Survey (ESS; www.europeansocialsurvey.org) contains probably the largest sample where measures of planning and well-being have been collected. Every two years since 2002, information on the attitudes, beliefs, and behaviours is collected from a random sample of residents of European countries. The third round, which was in 2006, contained two questions on planning. One of the questions was similar to those of Prenda and Lachman (2001): 'I like planning and preparing for my future', answered on a five-point scale anchored by 'strongly agree' and 'strongly disagree'. The second question included in the survey was: 'Do you generally plan for your future or do you just take each day as it comes?', anchored on a ten-point scale by 'I plan for my future as much as possible' at one end, and 'I just take each day as it comes'. A low score in each case indicates high planning. The data are freely available for researchers to analyse, and correlating the first planning question with self-reported life satisfaction produces a correlation of $-.12$, whereas for the second question the correlation is $-.04^2$. With more than 42,000 participants, both correlations are highly significant and, given the large sample size, might be expected to be small, but the fact that arguably, the more affectively balanced question produces a much smaller correlation, does indicate some caution in accepting a relationship between planning propensity and well-being when the question on planning involves a self-evaluative or affective quality.

Nezlek (2001) also used a self-report measure of planning to look at the relationship with well-being but within a different methodology. A sample of students scoring highly on self-report depression scales, completed a daily diary at the end of each day for 21 days, which included mood ratings and a rating of how carefully they had planned their activities that day, along with the extent to which the activities occurred as planned. Those who were elevated on depression scores reported planning their activities for that day less carefully and were less likely to say that their plans had been realized fully, although of course, this relationship does not demonstrate causality. Taking all participants together, anxiety was lower and self-esteem was higher on days that people reported planning more carefully and when their plans had been realized more fully

There is therefore some evidence of self-reported planning being linked to well-being, although how strong this relationship is remains to be fully established. The studies reported so far lean more towards measuring planning propensity. What about planning ability? Clare Conway and I (MacLeod & Conway, 2005) wanted to develop a measure of planning, which we then based on the Means End Problem Solving Task (MEPS; Platt & Spivack, 1975). In the MEPS, participants are presented with the beginning of scenarios where there is a problem (e.g. someone moves to a new area and doesn't know anyone) and the end of the scenario is where the problem is resolved (the person has made friends). The task is to complete the middle portion of the scenario in which the problem gets solved. Various indices of goodness of problem solving can be derived from what people generate, including the number of different problem-solving steps, how specific they are and their effectiveness as solutions, the latter two judged by independent raters (Marx, Williams, & Claridge, 1992). The original MEPS does contain some eccentric items, one of which begins with a man spotting an SS trooper who had tortured and killed his wife and children during the Nazi occupation, and ending with the man killing the SS trooper. Most studies, therefore, use a subset of, or adapted, items from

---

[2] The ESS data are freely available to researchers (www.europeansocialsurvey.org). I conducted these correlations for the present chapter. I am not aware that they have been reported elsewhere.

the MEPS that have more applicability to participants' lives. There are well-established links between poor MEPS performance and depression and suicidality (e.g. Williams, Barnhofer, Crane, & Beck, 2005). In the measure that we developed, participants were first asked to list their goals in a number of different life domains. On being re-presented with some of their goals, participants have to describe how they would get to the goal being achieved, starting from where they are now in their lives. As in the MEPS, various measures are taken such as the number of steps to the goal (where more steps represent good planning), independent ratings of the effectiveness of plans (how likely the plans are to achieve the goal), as well as rater-judged specificity of plan steps. In the first example in Table 8.1 for the goal of going abroad as a family, 'looking at the best/easiest route to take' would be relatively specific, whereas 'start small and build on it' would count as low in specificity. As another example, for the goal of losing weight, a highly specific level of plan would be something like 'take two pieces of fruit to work each day', whereas a general plan would be 'to eat more sensibly'. We found in a community sample that number of planning steps and plan effectiveness correlated with the number of things in the future people could think of that they were looking forward to, which was in turn related to subjective well-being (MacLeod & Conway, 2005).

In a test of the link between planning and well-being in a clinical context, Paula Vincent, Pradeep Boddana, and I (Vincent, Boddana & MacLeod, 2004) used the measure to assess planning towards personal goals in suicidal individuals. A sample of people who had recently been admitted to hospital following an episode of deliberate self-harm, and a matched control group generated a list of their goals. As described in Chapter 7, the groups did not differ in the number of goals they were able to think of. Participants were then re-presented with the three goals that they had identified as their most important and were asked to complete plans starting from where they were now and ending with the goal being achieved. To check that results were not due to any idiosyncratic aspect of personal goals, all participants completed the planning task for three standard goals that had been commonly generated by a similar sample in a previous study ('getting on well with someone close to you', 'feeling good about yourself', 'having an enjoyable job'). The study participants were also asked if they could think of any obstacles that would get in the way of their plans. Figure 8.1 shows the results of the planning variables. The scales of the three variables are very different, so the figure shows the scores of the suicidal group expressed as standard deviations from the control mean for each variable. Also shown for comparison is the number of goals that participants generated. The suicidal participants, although able to provide as many personal goals as the matched controls, generated plans that had fewer steps, and those steps were less specific.

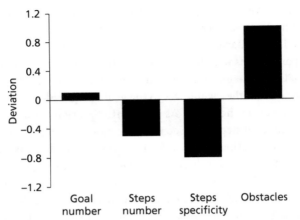

Figure 8.1 Representation of data from Vincent et al. (2004) showing the number of goals, number of planning steps, average specificity of planning steps, and number of obstacles to plans generated by deliberate self-harm participants, expressed in standard deviations from a matched control sample. There was no difference on goal number but the other three effects were all significant when tested as group comparisons.

Adapted from Vincent, P. J., Boddana, P., MacLeod, A. K., *Clinical Psychology & Psychotherapy* **4** (1), 15–24. Copyright © 2004 by John Wiley Sons, Inc. Reprinted by permission of John Wiley & Sons, Inc.

They also described more obstacles. The lack of specificity in planning is very similar to the sort of overgenerality in memory retrieval that was discussed in Chapter 6, and may well be underpinned by it.

This idea of intact goals but impaired planning has also been proposed in other life areas. Oyserman, Johnson, and James (2011) found that family socio-economic status was unrelated to the ability of young people aged 13 to 14 to generate self-goals for the next year, elicited by asking them to say what they expected to be like and to be doing next year[3]. Two-thirds of goals were school-focused, perhaps due to expectations the children perceived from the context, and analysis focused on these goals. Following generation of the goals, participants were asked if they were currently working on each goal, and if so to say what they were doing. Higher socioeconomic status predicted being able to think of more strategies to achieve those goals, and this effect was particularly

---

[3] Note that although the authors described this method as eliciting goals, and that may have been the case, the nature of the question means that it is possible for participants to respond with statements that are not actually goals as defined at the beginning of this chapter.

marked for boys. These authors suggest that the paths being unclear through which goals are to be attained might account for lower levels of educational attainment.

Planning, however, will not necessarily always be associated with feeling good at the time. Oettingen (2012) distinguished between simply having positive fantasies about the future, which she called *indulging*, and having a mindset that mentally contrasts those positive fantasies with present reality. Mentally contrasting the desired future with current reality will stimulate planning, including thinking of obstacles and how to deal with them, and has been found to be associated with greater effort towards, and achievement of, goals. Indulging has the potential to be associated with more pleasant feelings than mentally contrasting because of its purely positive content. Oettingen (2012) suggests that positive fantasies may actually reduce behaviour towards the goal because they prematurely provide the consummatory emotional reward of goal achievement, after which it is difficult to motivate behaviour towards achieving the goal. It is an interesting question whether the process of mentally contrasting would work so well in people who are very low in well-being, such as those who are suicidal, who may well need more help in engaging in mental contrasting in a way that is not counterproductive. Where feelings of efficacy are low and anticipation of obstacles is high, mental contrasting might have a dispiriting effect, unless carried out in a supported way.

The distinction between indulging and mental contrasting has strong parallels with that between outcome simulations and process simulations (Taylor, 2011). Outcome simulations are where someone thinks about what it would be like if they had what they wanted, whereas process simulations are concerned with how to get to that point. Gerlach, Spreng, Madore, and Schacter (2014) asked participants to think about a set of standard goals in two different ways: process (listing four steps to take to reach the goal) and outcome (listing four events or activities associated with having accomplished the goal). For example, process simulation of the goal of going on vacation prompted responses such as going online to compare prices, booking, packing a suitcase, and getting on a plane. In contrast, outcome simulation produced responses such as swimming in a pool, having a meal of local specialities, going snorkelling, sleeping in. Outcome simulations were rated as more detailed, important and desirable than process simulations. Additionally, goals were likely to be endorsed as the person's own personal goals when they were thought about in the outcome condition compared to being thought about in the process condition. Clearly, simulating what it was like to have the outcomes had a more pleasant quality to it, compared with thinking of the planning steps necessary to bring the outcome about. Participants were also scanned while doing the task and fMRI data supported the idea of greater positive emotional response in outcome thinking: whereas process thinking recruited the default network and frontoparietal control regions, in outcome thinking a major node of the default network (the medial prefrontal cortex) coupled with the amygdala, which is known to be involved in reward processing. Interestingly, however, Pham and Taylor (1999) found that students asked to think about a negative event (imminent exam) in a process way showed lower negative emotion (and greater planning) compared to those instructed to think in an outcome way. Gerlach et al. (2014) did not measure emotion directly so it is not possible to say if they would not have found an increase in experienced positive emotion in the outcome simulation group, but it seems plausible. If so, it raises the possibility that outcome and process simulations can have different, perhaps opposite, emotional impact, depending on whether they are directed towards attaining a rewarding, positive goal, or solving a problem and reducing the likelihood of an aversive outcome. Such an account is worthy of further investigation but remains speculative until more data are available.

Intentions

Intentions, which indicate a state of readiness and willingness to engage in a particular behaviour, are closely connected to plans, and have a key role in a number of theories concerned with explaining whether behaviour occurs. In the 'Theory of Planned Behaviour' (Ajzen, 1991) an intention to perform a behaviour is viewed as the part of the chain that best predicts whether a behaviour will occur or not. The theory is mainly concerned with understanding what factors then explain the strength of a person's intention to act, and puts forward three explanatory variables: having beliefs about the value of performing the behaviour (attitude); whether the behaviour is expected, or approved of, by others, particularly important others (subjective norms); and whether the behaviour is seen as something that is easily do-able (perceived behavioural control). So, for example, someone may form an intention to eat more fruit and vegetables if they think it will make them healthier and they value that outcome, people around them think it is good and are doing it, and there is a fruit and vegetable shop around the corner from their house. If a strong intention is formed, then there is a greater likelihood of the behaviour being carried out. As illustrated in this example, the theory has been used extensively to try to understand health-related behaviours (e.g. McEachan, Conner, Taylor, & Lawton, 2011).

Intentions themselves, however, may not be enough for behaviour to take place; it is self-evidently the case that people sometimes fail to do what they intend to. As philosophers (e.g. McIntyre, 1990) have pointed out, not all failures to follow intended course of action are irrational. People sometimes realize when the time comes that they do not actually want to do what they previously intended, or they realize that they do not want to follow through on their intended course of action as much as they want to do something else that is incompatible with it. In such cases, people rationally accept that their initial intention was misguided and other, new competing intentions take precedence. Other situations are more complicated, where people may have formed an intention towards a goal through controlled rather than autonomous motivation—feeling that they ought to do something without internalizing that motivation to connect to a source of enjoyment or some other value (see Chapter 7). Notwithstanding these instances, weakness of will, or *akrasia*, where someone acts against what they genuinely think is the right course of action for their best interests, is something that most, if not all, people will have experienced. Sheeran and Orbell (2000) point out that although in studies of discrete actions (e.g. health-related behaviours) intention accounts for between 20% and 30% of enacted behaviour, this figure also illustrates that there is often a gap between people's intentions and their behaviour. There is a variety of sources giving rise to not doing something that one intends to do and believes is in one's best interests. One obvious example is simply forgetting, but in other cases people can have difficulties making themselves get started on an activity, they can get distracted and derailed from it, or they can simply run out of energy and give up (Gollwitzer, 2014). Planning has been put forward as a central factor in bridging the gap between motivation (wanting or intending to do something) and volition (choosing to do it). There is good evidence that if intentions can be allied to some sort of specific plan then this increases the chances of someone doing what they intend to. Of course it needs to be acknowledged that many plans will partially depend on the cooperation of other people who may or may not agree with the agent's plans, or even their goals.

Plans and outcomes—correlational studies

Studies on the relationship between plans and outcomes have yielded a large amount of evidence relevant to whether planning facilitates outcomes. The area that has received most attention is health outcomes, especially the question of whether plans help explain health-related outcomes over and above intentions. In the definition of well-being adopted for the present book, health-related outcomes do not themselves constitute well-being, but they are highly relevant given the connection between poor physical health and emotional well-being.

In addition, they provide a useful example of how planning might be important for attaining goals.

Luszczynska and Schwarzer (2003) found that women who reported having had a specific plan about carrying out breast self-examination, including where and when they were going to do it, were more likely to carry out the examination. Van Osch et al. (2008) found that what they called *action planning*—people reporting that they had a plan of when, where and how to implement the relevant behaviour—increased the variance explained in parental sunscreen use over and above intention to use sunscreen, and similar results have been found in predicting engagement in physical activity (Scholz, Schüz, Ziegelmann, Lippke, & Schwarzer, 2008). Van Osch et al. (2010) further distinguished between action planning and what they called *preparatory planning*. This latter type of planning is more concerned with strategic aspects of how the behaviour is going to be performed rather than specifics associated with the time and place of the behaviour occurring. These authors examined fruit eating in a community sample of Dutch adults who were members of a research panel. Measures were taken over an eight-week period, with intention to eat fruit and past fruit eating behaviour measured at baseline, planning measured at four weeks, and fruit consumption at eight weeks. Preparatory planning was measured by questions such as 'Have you made a plan to put a fruit basket on the table?' or 'Have you made a plan to take fruit along with you when you go somewhere?' and action/implemental planning was indicated by the extent to which people reported that they had made a detailed plan about, for example, when and where to eat the fruit. Both types of planning added to the prediction of fruit consumption over and above the known strong predictors of intention and past fruit eating behaviour, with preparatory planning having the stronger path in the model.

Finally, a further distinction has been made between action planning and coping planning. Coping planning refers to the existence of a detailed plan of what to do if something interferes with the plan; it is about how to cope with setbacks and sticking to intentions in difficult situations. For example, someone may have the intention of going running at 7 a.m. three mornings a week, but the coping plan would be to go to the gym instead if it was raining heavily. Scholz et al. (2008) measured in an online sample of volunteers, previous physical activity levels and intention to engage in exercise, as well as action planning and coping planning related to exercise. Two notable findings emerged in addition to the general effect of planning having an incremental effect over intention in predicting behaviour. First, the presence of action planning was only related to actual exercise behaviour in those who had reported high intentions of engaging in exercise: a plan needs an intention[4]. Second, coping planning mediated the intention-behaviour link but only in those with pre-existing high levels of exercise; in other words, it was in those who already engaged in exercise who appeared to benefit from thinking about how to deal with obstacles, presumably because of their prior experience with such obstacles. The second example in Table 8.1 shows that many of the plans the participants generated in relation to the goal of walking more and seeing the countryside are pre-emptive steps to deal with anticipated obstacles, conveying a sense of someone who may well have encountered these sorts of difficulties before.

The distinctions between the different types of planning are quite subtle. Although clear when considered carefully from a distance, these distinctions may not always be quite so clear in the minds of the respondents, particularly when they are measured by the same, or very similar, self-report Likert scales. In fact, the distinction between planning and intention when both are measured in this self-report way may also be very subtle. For example, in a study on parents' use of sunscreen on their children (Van Osch et al., 2008), both preparatory planning, measured by questions such as 'do you plan to bring sunscreen when you are out with your children' and an intention question about how strongly people intended to use sunscreen to protect their children, both rated on similar Likert scales, correlated extremely highly with each other ($r = .71$ in a sample of over 900 participants). This correlation supports the idea that participants might find it difficult to make meaningful discriminations when asked to rate the extent to which they are intending, as opposed to planning, to do something, and similar problems of overlap may be present when asked about different types of planning.

Plans and outcomes—experimental studies

Implementation intentions is the term devised by Gollwitzer (see Gollwitzer, 2014 for a review) to describe a simple but highly specific plan that is added to an intention. In this kind of plan someone identifies an environmental cue that will act as a prompt to their intended behaviour. Such intentions are in the form of 'if then' plans, where upon encountering the cue, the person acts. The environmental cue could be a time or place. In a study with an impressive and practically important outcome, Sheeran and Orbell (2000) recruited a sample of women at a medical practice who were due to attend for a routine cervical smear within the next three months. These women were sent a number of

---

[4] As well as plans needing intentions, it is also an interesting question whether the act of forming plans can have the effect of strengthening intentions.

measures, and half of them were given an extra question in their pack telling them that they were more likely to attend for a smear if they decided when and where they were going to do it, and were then asked to write down details of when and where they were going to attend for the test. Follow-up showed that 92% of those given the extra sentence, compared to 62% of controls not given the extra instruction, attended. Reviews have shown that implementation intention interventions can have impressive effects on a range of behaviours (Gollwitzer & Sheeran, 2006).

In the Sheeran and Orbell (2000) study, participants were not asked to identify a specific environmental cue to trigger the desired behaviour. A more typical manipulation asks respondents to identify a particular cue and specify a behaviour that they will enact when they encounter that cue. For example, in promoting healthy eating, Harris et al. (2014) gave people the start of a sentence (e.g. 'if I eat out during the day'), and participants were asked to complete the stems with what food they would eat (e.g. 'then I will have a banana'). In recognition that, as already described, plans can be derailed, anticipated obstacles can also be built into the implemental plan using the same form. For example, participants in the Harris et al. (2014) study were also presented with stems, such as 'If I start to talk myself out of eating fruit and vegetables', and asked to complete the stems with what their excuses might be and what they would say to themselves to prevent the behaviour being derailed. As indicated by the preceding example, implementation intentions are not always about behaviour; sometimes they are in the form of what someone will say to themselves if they encounter a situational cue. For example, spider phobics might be encouraged to form an if–then sequence of 'if I see a spider then I will remain calm and relaxed', which Schweiger Gallo, Keil, McCulloch, Rockstroh, & Gollwitzer (2009) reported as reducing negative emotional reaction in participants fearful of spiders when presented with pictures of spiders.

Implementation intentions are thought to work through two main mechanisms (Gollwitzer & Sheeran, 2006). First, they provide accessible prompts and reminders for behaviour, thus overcoming forgetting, and improving prospective memory—the simple act of remembering to do something (McDaniel, Howard, & Butler, 2008). A practical example would be remembering to take medication. For example, someone may decide 'when I switch on the kitchen light in the morning I will take my medication'. This kind of example deals with problems of remembering rather than weakness of will. Second, by outsourcing to the environment the stimulus to act, behaviour becomes more automated and therefore less prone to weakness of will. Someone does not engage in the decision about, for example, *whether* they are going to go for that run now or whether to do it later, because the decision has already been made and, in effect, delegated to the occurrence of an environmental cue that triggers it. The most obvious environmental cue is an alarm set for a particular time, but any environmental cue that can act as a trigger can be used. This sort of automaticity, particularly if it is habitual, can be particularly useful when someone's resources of willpower are depleted. Neal, Wood, and Drolet (2013) presented data from a series of studies suggesting that people are more likely to fall back on habitual behaviours, good or bad, when their motivational energy was reduced. In one study, students fell back on their usual eating habits, whether those were healthy or unhealthy, in the run up to exams. Another group of participants, asked to do a simple but resource-depleting task for two days—using one's non-dominant hand for everyday activities (e.g. opening doors, using a phone)—showed increased frequency of behaviours that they had previously reported as being common for them, that is, their usual habits. It did not make any difference whether the behaviours were congruent or incongruent with goals that the participants had described previously—what seemed to matter was their habitualness. Gollwitzer and colleagues argue that implementation intentions do not work by increasing the strength of an intention; rather, they provide a route by which an intention can be realized. It is fair to say, though, that in many of the reported studies, intentions are very high to start with and there is simply little scope to show any increase. In the Sheeran and Orbell (2000) study, for example, levels of intention of the participants to attend for screening averaged 4.6 on a five-point scale.

Although the evidence is clear that, in general, implementation intentions can help people to follow through on actions that they want to perform, the boundary conditions for their usefulness has not yet been fully explored. Some studies have begun to identify circumstances that define some limits of their usefulness. Powers (2005) presented data indicating that implementation intentions might be detrimental for those who are high on socially prescribed perfectionism, which is characterized by self-criticism and sensitivity to living up to the high standards they perceive others to have for them. At the beginning of one January, a sample of students described their most important New Year's resolution and they were followed up at the end of the month to see how they had progressed on those resolutions. There were more academic resolutions than any other, possibly reflecting where the study was carried out. At assessment, all participants were told that focusing on consequences of goals helps to attain those goals, but, in addition, half the students in the sample were asked to think of a specific time (or time sequence) and place to perform actions relevant to their resolution, as well as thinking of if–then procedures to deal with distractions. Socially prescribed perfectionism was unrelated to goal progress for those in the control condition but was significantly negatively correlated with goal progress in those who formed implementation intentions. Implementation intentions appeared to be detrimental to high perfectionists. Powers (2005) suggests that this type of perfectionism combines with implementation intentions to induce a heightened state of self-focus concerned with the possibility of not succeeding that then gets in the way of progress. Preliminary evidence also suggests that implementation intention manipulations appear to work better in situations where there is an absence of pre-existing environmental cues (Chasteen, Park, & Schwarz, 2001), and where people form the plan for one goal at a time rather than many goals simultaneously (Dalton & Spiller, 2012).

One methodological point to note is that typically in implementation intention studies, all participants are given some standard instructions and the implementation intention group is then given additional direction about forming a specific plan. Sometimes this additional direction can be quite extensive. For example, in the Harris et al. (2014) study, those in the implementation intention condition formed five if–then action plans about eating fruit, plus two coping plans. Often there is also a strong suggestion that carrying out this task will make a difference to whether the behaviour is performed or not. It is therefore difficult to disentangle specific effects of 'if–then' thinking from the additional processing that is directed towards completing the targeted behaviour. Effects would be more persuasive in the presence of an active control condition that also asked participants to focus on doing the behaviour to a similar degree but not in an implementational intention sort of way. Finally, it is worth pointing out that even what appear to be very simple plans will also often require wider strategic planning. For example, in order to write down when and where they would attend their screening appointment, the women in Sheeran and Orbell's (2000) study would have had to think about a whole range of factors and other competing demands (e.g. 'how will I get there?', 'who can I get to pick up the kids from school that day if I have to wait', 'will I get back in time to cook the dinner?', and so on), all of which need to be organized as part of the seemingly simple plan.

How are plans linked to well-being?

The most obvious way that plans link to well-being is that they enable goal progress and, as discussed in Chapter 7, goal progress fosters well-being. Plans create a bridge between intention and action, making goal-directed behaviour, and therefore goal progress, more likely. Because plans are so connected with goals, and in fact, describe a level in the goal hierarchy immediately below what is in focus at that point in time as the desired outcome (goal), they are potentially related to well-being in the other ways outlined for goals. Plans provide a sense of engagement, and by providing a path to follow, they offer structure and guide behaviour, all of which will be linked to a sense of well-being. Plans are also associated with a sense of control and agency (Prenda & Lachman, 2001) because they outline a possible path to be taken to achieve goals. This sense of a way forward should give rise to a greater belief in the likelihood of the goal being achieved, something that is known to be lacking in those low in well-being (see Chapter 2). Contrary to this view, Masicampo and Beaumeister (2011) reported in a study of planning for everyday tasks that planning did not increase expectancy of completing the task. However, the outcomes were tasks that participants identified as ones they had to complete in the next few days, which are very different from most life goals. Not surprisingly, these essential small-scale imminent tasks were judged as very likely to happen anyway (6.3 on a seven-point scale), again with very limited scope for showing any increase in expectancy. What is needed are more studies examining effects of planning on the sort of real life goals that people identify as important for themselves, that do not have the inevitability of things that need to be done over the next few days; in other words, the sort of goals described in Table 8.1 at the beginning of this chapter.

Plans also have another interesting quality in that they have the potential to reduce thoughts about the goal. Masicampo and Beaumeister (2011) reported the results of eight studies involving bringing goals to mind, with or without forming plans, and the subsequent effects on goal-directed thought. Not all the results clearly supported the value of planning, but in the most persuasive study (Study 1) people thought of upcoming tasks that needed to be completed in the next few days, with a planning group asked to make plans for doing those tasks, while another group did not form plans. A further control group thought of tasks that had been completed in the previous few days. Participants were subsequently given a reading task during which they were probed about whether their minds were wandering from what they were reading. There was a marginal effect of increased mind wandering (relative to controls) in those who thought of goals without thinking of plans, but not in those whose goal thinking was accompanied by plans. However, the results were clearer on a more objective test of comprehension of the passage: the goals-only group showed worse performance than the other two groups, who did not differ from each other. Masicampo and Beaumeister (2011) interpret the findings as being akin to the Zeigarnik effect (Zeigarnik, 1927). The Zeigarnik effect is named after the work of the Soviet psychologist, Bluma Zeigarnik, who found that people given tasks but interrupted before being able to complete them, showed more frequent recall of the tasks compared to those who were allowed to complete the tasks. The interpretive framework of the time was that goals generate a certain 'energy' within the cognitive system, which is only resolved when the task is completed (see James & Kendell, 1997). Unresolved tasks or goals are manifest as persistent intrusive thoughts, which leads to the possibility that at least some of the intrusive thoughts that are common in clinical groups may partly be accounted for by goals that are unresolved. Most personal goals are ongoing, and therefore necessarily unresolved, so why do they not lead to unwanted intrusions? One possible explanation is that a sense of ongoing satisfactory current progress and likelihood of future success reduces the demand for attention in the form of intrusions or rumination, and that plans are an important constituent of this feeling of progress. Notably, plans for how progress is going to be moved forward in the future enable the existence of future goals to coexist alongside the sort of present-focus that is useful for current tasks that demand attention and is widely seen as beneficial for well-being (Segal, Williams, & Teasdale, 2012). This theme will be returned to in Chapter 11.

There is evidence that planning is linked to well-being and there are plausible mechanisms through which it would exert an influence on well-being, as well as evidence to support some of those mechanisms. There is also direct evidence of a causal relationship from studies that have manipulated planning and observed effects on well-being. The studies conducted by my colleagues and I (e.g. MacLeod, Coates, & Hetherton, 2008) already mentioned in Chapter 7, and described more fully in Chapter 10, speak to this issue. Teaching goal setting and associated planning is a standard practice in life coaching but normally in the context of a package with many other components (e.g. Gaskell, 2000). Isolating just goal setting and planning skills on their own in this way, separated from other intervention components that might enhance well-being, allows for a test of the impact of these particular skills. Goal setting and planning skills training has been shown to increase well-being in a variety of groups (see Chapter 10), supporting a causal relationship between goal setting and planning skills and well-being.

I have argued that planning affects well-being, but there is an equally interesting question of what gives rise to planning. One answer is that as well as benefiting from the exercise of planning, well-being also enables planning. Ashby, Isen, and Turken (1999) and Fredrickson (2001) have shown that positive emotional states broaden attention and increase cognitive flexibility and creativity, which is likely to include planning. To the extent that planning involves thinking flexibly and creatively then it will benefit from positive emotional states. Gable and Harmon-Jones (2011) have argued, however, that this broadening of attention occurs only with low activation positive emotional states, such as feelings of calmness and relaxation, whereas high activation positive states like excitement have the effect of narrowing attention. Gable and Harmon-Jones (2011) suggest that the widely publicized broadening effects of positive mood were based on studies that created particular types of positive mood (amusement or contentment) that are low in activation. These mood states typify post-goal positive mood states, whereas pre-goal positive mood states, which are high activation, function to narrow attention to the goal being pursued. There is even some evidence indicating that negative mood might facilitate prospective memory (Rummel, Hepp, Klein, & Silberleitner, 2012). To the extent that a more detailed, focused type of attention is required, then planning might also benefit from some element of negative mood or low activation positive mood at the planning stage to narrow the focus, after high activation positive mood has facilitated the goal setting stage. Such a two stage model is consistent with the ideas of Oettingen and colleagues, discussed earlier in this chapter (see also Baumeister, Vohs, & Oettingen, 2016). Future work could usefully examine whether different levels of mood activation are implicated at the goal setting and planning stage of the process. As already seen, planning is positively correlated with education and income (Oyserman et al., 2011; Prenda & Lachman, 2001), and is also related to higher levels of social support (Prenda & Lachman, 2001) and more extended social networks (MacLeod & Conway, 2005). With such a cluster of positive psychosocial qualities, it is not easy to separate out causes and effects, but it is plausible that planning is also directly facilitated by these wider factors.

Summary

Plans are the future steps that we think of to reach our goals. A plan can also be a goal to the extent that it, itself, requires planning steps to reach it, reflecting the hierarchical structure within which plans and goals are embedded. Underpinning planning is both an inclination to plan and the ability to formulate steps, both of which appear to be related to well-being. Evidence from both clinical and non-clinical studies supports the link between planning ability and low well-being. Thinking about steps to achieve goals varies in its specificity, from very specific, low-level actions to quite global steps. A substantial body of research has focused on very specific plans that provide a bridge between having an intention and acting on the intention, thus overcoming common impediments to goal attainment, such as forgetting and weakness of will. Such techniques involve setting up simple steps that stimulate action or promote particular thoughts or even pre-emptively deal with obstacles. However, even making apparently quite simple plans will often necessitate more complex strategic planning. Whichever term is used, or within whatever framework the results are situated, the evidence is strong that making specific plans about how to implement behaviour increases its likelihood of occurrence. This increased likelihood of occurrence and the attendant goal progress that accompanies it is an obvious candidate for the mechanism by which plans link to well-being—plans link to well-being by facilitating goal progress, and a sense of goal progress increases well-being (see Chapter 7). Planning also provides direction and structure to life and promotes engagement, all of which may directly foster well-being. In addition, having already formed satisfactory plans may help to reduce intrusive thinking related to goals, which are, after all by definition, unfulfilled and therefore demanding of attention. Reducing intrusive thoughts about goals helps to free up resources for focusing on the present. One way of describing it is that plans help to put goals to bed. But they should not put them to sleep; that is, the plans should not become a substitute for action. Premature imaginal experiencing 'as if' the goal has already been achieved may demotivate real action that would help achieve the goal. There are interesting outstanding questions remaining to be answered about what facilitates planning. Positive mood may operate in a benevolent cycle with planning, benefiting from it and in turn facilitating it. A constellation of psychosocial advantages, involving education, socioeconomic status, social network size, and very likely, cognitive capacity, are some of the factors that may help people to plan.

References

Ajzen, I. (1991). The theory of planned behavior. *Organizational Behavior and Human Decision Processes*, **50**(2), 179–211. http://doi.org/10.1016/0749-5978(91)90020-T

Ashby, F. G., Isen, A. M., & Turken, A. U. (1999). A neuropsychological theory of positive affect and its influence on cognition. *Psychological Review*, **106**(3), 529–550. http://doi.org/10.1037/0033-295X.106.3.529

Baumeister, R. F., Vohs, K. D., & Oettingen, G. (2016). Pragmatic prospection: How and why people think about the future. *Review of General Psychology*, **20**(1), 3 -16. https://doi.org/10.1037/gpr0000060

Carlin, D., Bonerba, J., Phipps, M., Alexander, G., Shapiro, M., & Grafman, J. (2000). Planning impairments in frontal lobe dementia and frontal lobe lesion patients. *Neuropsychologia*, **38**(5), 655–665. http://doi.org/10.1016/S0028-3932(99)00102-5

Chasteen, A. L., Park, D. C., & Schwarz, N. (2001). Implementation intentions and facilitation of prospective memory. *Psychological Science*, **12**(6), 457–461. http://doi.org/10.1111/1467-9280.00385

Cole, M. W., Repovš, G., & Anticevic, A. (2014). The frontoparietal control system a central role in mental health. *The Neuroscientist*, **20**(6), 652–664. http://doi.org/10.1177/1073858414525995

Dalton, A. N. & Spiller, S. A. (2012). Too much of a good thing: The benefits of implementation intentions depend on the number of goals. *Journal of Consumer Research*, **39**(3), 600–614. http://doi.org/10.1086/664500

Fox, M. D., Snyder, A. Z., Vincent, J. L., Corbetta, M., Van Essen, D. C., & Raichle, M. E. (2005). The human brain is intrinsically organized into dynamic, anticorrelated functional networks. *PNAS Proceedings of the National Academy of Sciences of the United States of America*, **102**(27), 9673–9678. http://doi.org/10.1073/pnas.0504136102

Fredrickson, B. L. (2001). The role of positive emotions in positive psychology: The broaden-and-build theory of positive emotions. *American Psychologist*, **56**(3), 218–226. http://doi.org/10.1037/0003-066X.56.3.218

Friedman, S. L. & Scholnick, E. K. (1997). *The developmental psychology of planning: Why, how, and when do we plan?* Mahwah, NJ: Lawrence Erlbaum Associates Publishers.

Gable, P. A. & Harmon-Jones, E. (2011). Attentional consequences of pregoal and postgoal positive affects. *Emotion*, **11**(6), 1358–1367. http://doi.org/10.1037/a0025611

Gaskell, C. (2000). Transform your life: 10 steps to real results. London: Thorsons.

Gerlach, K. D., Spreng, R. N., Madore, K. P., & Schacter, D. L. (2014). Future planning: Default network activity couples with frontoparietal control network and reward-processing regions during process and outcome simulations. *Social Cognitive and Affective Neuroscience*, **9**(12), 1942–1951. http://doi.org/10.1093/scan/nsu001

Gollwitzer, P. M. (2014). Weakness of the will: Is a quick fix possible? *Motivation and Emotion*, **38**(3), 305–322. http://doi.org/10.1007/s11031-014-9416-3

Gollwitzer, P. M., & Sheeran, P. (2006). Implementation intentions and goal achievement: A meta-analysis of effects and processes. In *Advances in Experimental Social Psychology* (Vol. 38, pp. 69–119). San Diego, CA: Elsevier Academic Press.

Harris, P. R., Brearley, I., Sheeran, P., Barker, M., Klein, W. M. P., Creswell, J. D., Levine, J. M., & Bond, R. (2014). Combining self-affirmation with implementation intentions to promote fruit and vegetable consumption. *Health Psychology*, **33**(7), 729–736. http://doi. org/10.1037/hea0000065

James, I. A. & Kendell, K. (1997). Unfinished processing in the emotional disorders: The Zeigarnik effect. *Behavioural and Cognitive Psychotherapy*, **25**(4), 329–337. http://doi. org/10.1017/S1352465800018737

Luszczynska, A. & Schwarzer, R. (2003). Planning and self-efficacy in the adoption and maintenance of breast self-examination: A longitudinal study on self-regulatory cognitions. *Psychology & Health*, **18**(1), 93–108. http://doi.org/10.1080/0887044021000019358

MacLeod, A. K., Coates, E., & Hetherton, J. (2008). Increasing well-being through teaching goal-setting and planning skills: Results of a brief intervention. *Journal of Happiness Studies*, **9**(2), 185–196. http://doi.org/10.1007/s10902-007-9057-2

MacLeod, A. K. & Conway, C. (2005). Well-being and the anticipation of future positive experiences: The role of income, social networks, and planning ability. *Cognition & Emotion*, **19**(3), 357–374. http://doi.org/10.1080/02699930441000247

Marx, E. M., Williams, J. M., & Claridge, G. C. (1992). Depression and social problem solving. *Journal of Abnormal Psychology*, **101**(1), 78–86. http://doi.org/10.1037/0021-843X.101.1.78

Masicampo, E. J. & Baumeister, R. F. (2011). Consider it done! Plan making can eliminate the cognitive effects of unfulfilled goals. *Journal of Personality and Social Psychology*, **101**(4), 667–683. http://doi.org/10.1037/a0024192

McDaniel, M. A., Howard, D. C., & Butler, K. M. (2008). Implementation intentions facilitate prospective memory under high attention demands. *Memory & Cognition*, **36**(4), 716–724. http://doi.org/10.3758/MC.36.4.716

McEachan, R. R. C., Conner, M., Taylor, N. J., & Lawton, R. J. (2011). Prospective prediction of health-related behaviours with the Theory of Planned

Behaviour: A meta-analysis. *Health Psychology Review*, 5(2), 97–144. http://doi.org/10.1080/17437199.2010.521684

McIntyre, A. (1990). Is acratic action always irrational? In O. Flanagan & A. Rorty (Eds.), *Identity, character and morality*. Cambridge, MA: MIT Press.

Neal, D. T., Wood, W., & Drolet, A. (2013). How do people adhere to goals when willpower is low? The profits (and pitfalls) of strong habits. *Journal of Personality and Social Psychology*, 104(6), 959–975. http://doi.org/10.1037/a0032626

Nezlek, J. B. (2001). Daily psychological adjustment and the planfulness of day-to-day behavior. *Journal of Social and Clinical Psychology*, 20(4), 452–475. http://doi.org/10.1521/jscp.20.4.452.22398

Oettingen, G. (2012). Future thought and behaviour change. *European Review of Social Psychology*, 23(1), 1–63. http://doi.org/10.1080/10463283.2011.643698

Oyserman, D., Johnson, E., & James, L. (2011). Seeing the destination but not the path: Effects of socioeconomic disadvantage on school-focused possible self content and linked behavioral strategies. *Self and Identity*, 10(4), 474–492. http://doi.org/10.1080/15298868.2010.487651

Pham, L. B. & Taylor, S. E. (1999). From thought to action: Effects of process- versus outcome-based mental simulations on performance. *Personality and Social Psychology Bulletin*, 25(2), 250–260. http://doi.org/10.1177/0146167299025002010

Platt, J. J. & Spivack, G. (1975). *The Means End Problem Solving Procedure manual*. Philadelphia, PA: Hahnemann University Press.

Powers, T. A. (2005). Implementation intentions, perfectionism, and goal progress: Perhaps the road to hell is paved with good intentions. *Personality and Social Psychology Bulletin*, 31(7), 902–912. http://doi.org/10.1177/0146167204272311

Prenda, K. M. & Lachman, M. E. (2001). Planning for the future: A life management strategy for increasing control and life satisfaction in adulthood. *Psychology and Aging*, 16(2), 206–216. http://doi.org/10.1037//0882-7974.16.2.206

Rummel, J., Hepp, J., Klein, S. A., & Silberleitner, N. (2012). Affective state and event-based prospective memory. *Cognition & Emotion*, 26(2), 351–361. http://doi.org/10.1080/02699931.2011.574873

Scholnick, E. K. & Friedman, S. L. (1993). Planning in context: Developmental and situational considerations. *International Journal of Behavioral Development*, 16(2), 145–167.

Scholz, U., Schüz, B., Ziegelmann, J. P., Lippke, S., & Schwarzer, R. (2008). Beyond behavioural intentions: Planning mediates between intentions and physical activity. *British Journal of Health Psychology*, 13(3), 479–494. http://doi.org/10.1348/135910707X216062

Schweiger Gallo, I., Keil, A., McCulloch, K. C., Rockstroh, B., & Gollwitzer, P. M. (2009). Strategic automation of emotion regulation. *Journal of Personality and Social Psychology*, 96(1), 11–31. http://doi.org/10.1037/a0013460

Segal, Z. V., Williams, J. M. G., & Teasdale, J. D. (2012). *Mindfulness-based cognitive therapy for depression* (2nd edition). New York: Guilford Press.

Sheeran, P. & Orbell, S. (2000). Using implementation intentions to increase attendance for cervical cancer screening. *Health Psychology*, 19(3), 283. http://doi.org/10.1037/0278-6133.19.3.283

Smith, J. (1996). Planning about life: Toward a social-interactive perspective. In P. B. Baltes & U. M. Staudinger, *Interactive minds: Life-span perspectives on the social foundation of cognition* (pp. 242–275). Cambridge: Cambridge University Press.

Spreng, R. N. & Schacter, D. L. (2012). Default network modulation and large-scale network interactivity in healthy young and old adults. *Cerebral Cortex*, **22**(11), 2610–2621. http://doi.org/10.1093/cercor/bhr339

Spreng, R. N., Stevens, W. D., Chamberlain, J. P., Gilmore, A. W., & Schacter, D. L. (2010). Default network activity, coupled with the frontoparietal control network, supports goal-directed cognition. *NeuroImage*, **53**(1), 303–317. http://doi.org/10.1016/j.neuroimage.2010.06.016

Taylor, S. E. (2011). Envisioning the future and self-regulation. In M. Bar (Ed.), *Predictions in the brain: Using our past to generate a future.* (pp. 134–143). New York: Oxford University Press.

Van Osch, L., Reubsaet, A., Lechner, L., Beenackers, M., Candel, M., & Vries, H. (2010). Planning health behaviour change: Comparing the behavioural influence of two types of self-regulatory planning. *British Journal of Health Psychology*, **15**(1), 133–149. http://doi.org/10.1348/135910709X436723

Van Osch, L., Reubsaet, A., Lechner, L., Candel, M., Mercken, L., & De Vries, H. (2008). Predicting parental sunscreen use: Disentangling the role of action planning in the intention-behavior relationship. *Psychology & Health*, **23**(7), 829–847. http://doi.org/10.1080/08870440701596577

Vincent, P. J., Boddana, P., & MacLeod, A. K. (2004). Positive life goals and plans in parasuicide. *Clinical Psychology & Psychotherapy*, **11**(2), 90–99. http://doi.org/DOI: 10.1002/cpp.394

Williams, J. M. G., Barnhofer, T., Crane, C., & Beck, A. T. (2005). Problem solving deteriorates following mood challenge in formerly depressed patients with a history of suicidal ideation. *Journal of Abnormal Psychology*, **114**(3), 421–431. http://doi.org/10.1037/0021-843X.114.3.421

Zeigarnik, B. (1927). Uber das Behalten von erledigten und unerledigten Handlungen [On the retention of completed and uncompleted transactions]. *Psychologische Forschung*, **9**, 1–85.

Chapter 9

Temporal orientation and mindfulness

Introduction

People vary in how much they think about the future, what might be called future-mindedness. Sometimes called temporal orientation or temporal focus, this future-mindedness is quite different from how positively or negatively someone thinks about the future. Two people could be equally future-oriented, but whereas one of them eagerly looks forward to a future which is seen as full of promise, the other is preoccupied with a future that is bleak or threatening. How positively or negatively people think about the future is the main focus of this book, but there are interesting questions about to what extent being future-oriented *in general*, as opposed to being present- or past-focused, is good (or bad) for well-being and mental health. The psychological literature rarely affords answers to such causal questions, but an easier question to address is whether there is a relationship between temporal orientation and well-being. To say that the results are mixed is jumping ahead of ourselves, but it is nevertheless true. Interestingly, as well as mixed findings, different literatures appear to take a different stance on what the answer to the question should be. Some of the temporal orientation literature to be discussed in the present chapter, along with the literature on goals (Chapter 7) and plans (Chapter 8) discussed in other chapters, highlights and promotes the value of being future-minded. In contrast, the growing literature on mindfulness would point to the well-being value of being focused in the present. Although it is true that reminiscence can enhance mood (e.g. Bryant, Smart, & King, 2005), there are few champions for the general value of adopting a past focus.

The present chapter will review some of the findings from these different literatures and attempt to resolve the seemingly conflicting answers, or at least provide some sort of insight into how it is that such different answers can be arrived at. Temporal orientation has been assessed by a number of self-report instruments, and the first half of the chapter will mainly review those measures and the findings arising from them. The second half of the chapter will focus on mindfulness. The mindfulness literature is large in its own right, and growing fast, but its relevance to the present discussion is in its emphasis on a present focus, which would appear, at first glance, to pose a challenge to the importance and value of thinking about the future. The link between mindfulness and well-being, through correlations between self-reported mindfulness and well-being, differences in well-being between meditators and non-meditators, and effects of mindfulness interventions on well-being and psychological distress, will be briefly reviewed. Finally, connected with mindfulness, or, more precisely, lack of mindfulness, some of the key findings on mind wandering and its link to well-being and future-thinking will be described. But before all of that, there is one paradigm—*delay discounting*—to be discussed, the results of which imply that most people are simply too present-focused at the expense of consideration of the future.

Delay discounting

The rather non-intuitively named delay discounting effect is a way of illustrating simply that people place a value on having a reward[1] now as opposed to later. The further into the distance the promised reward is located, the more we begin to value a smaller reward that we can receive straight away. Typically, people are presented with a hypothetical forced choice, for example, 'would you rather have £20 now or £50 in six months' time?' An attempt can be made to make the decision seem more real by conveying to participants that they might actually be able to have the money from some of the choices they make (Kirby, Petry, & Bickel, 1999). How much people prefer the smaller immediate rewards is usually influenced by the size of the difference between the rewards and the length of the delay. Someone might be willing to wait six months for £100, compared to £20 now, but only be willing to wait one week if the delayed reward was only £40. These examples may sound artificial, but something like them does exist in real life, notably, related to saving. For example, the UK government announced in March 2016 a scheme to encourage those on low incomes to save. The incentive was a bonus (up to a maximum of £600) of an additional 50% on money saved over a two-year period. So, someone could save £50 per month (i.e. choose not to receive £50 each month), and after two years receive an extra £600 bonus on the £1,200 that they had saved over that period.

Is the tendency to show delay discounting related to well-being? Lempert and Pizzagalli (2010) measured anhedonia in an unselected student sample using the Snaith-Hamilton Pleasure Scale (SHAPS; Snaith et al., 1995), which asks people how much they agree with statements such as 'I would enjoy being with my family or friends' or 'I would feel pleasure when I receive praise from

---

[1] The term 'reward' is used to describe the hypothetical sums that people are offered, although participants are not asked to do anything to attain it, so it is not a reward in the usual sense of being contingent on their behaviour.

other people'. Higher SHAPS scores were related to lower discounting. That is, people who were more anhedonic appeared to be more future-minded: they were more likely than those low in anhedonia to say, for example, that they would prefer to wait and receive £50 in one month's time rather than £20 now. Lempert and Pizzagalli (2010) suggest that the generally lowered sensitivity to reward that is characteristic of anhedonia reduces delay discounting because of the weaker emotional pull towards an immediate reward. However, Pulcu et al. (2014) failed to find a comparable effect in a group of depressed patients. Currently-depressed, remitted-depressed and never-depressed participants all showed similar rates of discounting. In fact, currently-depressed patients continued to show delay discounting (i.e. preferring smaller current rewards), even when the future reward was high, whereas both control participants and remitted depressed patients showed an increasing preference for delayed rewards as the value of that reward increased. Those meeting criteria for a diagnosis of schizophrenia showed greater delay discounting than a matched group of controls; that is, the value of future rewards tailed away more steeply for the schizophrenia group, an effect that was correlated with performance on a second task assessing how close to the present freely generated significant future events were (Heerey, Matveeva, & Gold, 2011). So, it is not clear whether there is a relationship between well-being and delay discounting. In fact, it is not really clear what the optimal response is to these kinds of situations; it cannot simply be assumed that choosing the larger reward, however long the delay, is the 'right' option. In the real world, things go wrong and the longer the waiting period, the greater chance there is of something going wrong. Even research contexts are not perfect—when it comes time to collect your larger reward six months later, the researcher who carried out the study has left the university and anyone you speak to claims to know nothing about the study!

Self-report measures of temporal orientation

Early research using a variety of methods pointed to lack of future-mindedness as being problematic for mental health. Suicidal individuals were found to be less oriented to the future than their non-suicidal comparison groups in that they provided less elaborate descriptions of the future (Yufit, Benzies, Fonte, & Fawcett, 1970), used fewer future tense verbs (Greaves, 1971), and the prospective thoughts that they did have extended less far into the future (Melges & Weisz, 1971).

The raw, imaginativeness of those early measures has since given way to self-report questionnaires designed to measure temporal orientation. Although there does appear to be quite a number of such measures, some are very specific to a particular concept, context, or group. The Temporal Orientation Scale (TOS; Holman & Silver, 1998) was developed solely with people who had experienced trauma (survivors of incest, Vietnam war veterans, and survivors of firestorms). The TOS is grounded in the idea of those who have experienced trauma needing to free themselves from the past in order to focus on the future and the present. Some items are not tied to that particular conceptual framework (e.g. 'I believe it is important to save for a rainy day') but others arise directly out of the concern for understanding the effects of trauma (e.g. 'I often feel I am reliving experiences from my past'), somewhat limiting the scale's general use. The past subscale appears to be designed specifically to identify problematic ways of thinking about the past in those who have suffered from traumatic experiences, illustrated by the 'Getting "stuck" in the past' part of the title of the original paper (Holman & Silver, 1998, p. 1146).

Also supporting the value of a future time perspective, but this time at the expense of a present-focus, the Consideration of Future Consequences Scale (CFC-14; Joireman, Shaffer, Balliet, & Strathman, 2012) and its longer predecessor (Strathman, Gleicher, Boninger, & Edwards, 1994), were designed to tap stable trait-like individual differences in the extent to which people consider distant as opposed to immediate consequences of their actions. The scale essentially measures a sort of 'sensible' attitude to decision making, where future consequences are considered (e.g. 'when I make a decision I think about how it might affect me in the future', as opposed to 'I only act to satisfy immediate concerns, figuring the future will take care of itself'). Scores on the CFC-14 correlate with a range of health behaviours, such as diet, exercise, and condom use (Joireman et al., 2012). The CFC scale shares a strong similarity to the future subscale of the Zimbardo Time Perspective Inventory (ZTPI; Zimbardo & Boyd, 1999), which is reviewed in detail in a later section in this chapter.

Not only might there be individual differences in time perspective, but it may change as people age. The concept of time perspective has become central to socioemotional selectivity theory (Carstensen, 1993), which suggests that as adults age their perceptions of time change from being more expansive and seeing the world as full of possibilities, to a narrower, more limited time perspective. Along with this shift, people's priorities change from informational goals, which are about looking outwards and learning about the world, to emotional goals and a preference for spending time with a smaller circle of people whom they are close to and who can meet these emotional goals. Driving this change is a shorter time perspective. The Future Time Perspective Scale (see Lang & Carstensen, 2002) was designed to assess time perspective specifically in older adults and contains items such as 'Most of my life still lies ahead of me' and 'I have the sense that time is running out' (reverse scored). Scores on such items are obviously very highly correlated with chronological age (Lang & Carstensen, 2002). The link between future perspective measured in this way and well-being in older adults is not entirely clear (see Kozik, Hoppmann, & Gerstorf, 2015), with some studies showing a negative correlation, whereas Lang and Carstensen (2002) found that those exhibiting limited time perspective adopted more emotionally meaningful and fulfilling goals, which potentially should enhance their well-being.

Zimbardo Time Perspective Inventory

The ZTPI (Zimbardo & Boyd, 1999) is probably the most widely used measure of temporal perspective, including being translated into many different languages and used in a range of cultural contexts (Sircova, van de Vijver, Osin, Milfont, Fieulaine et al., 2014). Like the TOS (Holman & Silver, 1998), the ZTPI has the advantage of measuring past, present, and future orientations as separate constructs. Two subscales measure past orientations (past-negative, past-positive), two measure present focus (present-hedonist; present-fatalistic) and there is one subscale measuring a future orientation (future). The past-negative and past-positive orientations are essentially as labelled: they measure unhappy (e.g. 'Painful past experiences keep being replayed in my mind') and happy (e.g. 'It gives me pleasure to think about my past') ways of thinking about the past. A present-fatalistic orientation measures a sense of lack of control over life (e.g. 'My life path is controlled by forces I cannot influence'), which in western cultures probably does often represent feelings of hopelessness and helplessness as Zimbardo and Boyd (1999) suggest, although it is possible that in some cultures it might not have those same connotations. The meanings of the other two scales are not quite as clear as their labels would suggest. To give an idea of their content, Table 9.1 shows the top three loading items on the principal components analysis reported in the original scale development article (Zimbardo & Boyd, 1999) for both of those two subscales As can be seen from Table 9.1, present-hedonistic essentially measures a risk-taking, excitement seeking in the here-and-now dimension, and it correlates highly with sensation seeking and a measure of ego under control (Zimbardo & Boyd, 1999). The items for the future orientation show that it represents a particular type of future orientation, very similar to the CFC (Strathman et al., 1994) with which it correlates strongly (Zimbardo & Boyd, 1999). Someone scoring highly on the future subscale would be a diligent, responsible, work-focused individual with strong impulse control.

Table 9.1 Sample items for the present-hedonistic and future subscales of the ZTPI

Subscale	Three reported highest loading items (Zimbardo & Boyd, 1999)
Present-hedonistic	◆ It is important to put excitement in my life. ◆ Taking risks keeps my life from becoming boring. ◆ I take risks to put excitement in my life.
Future	◆ Meeting other deadlines and doing other necessary work come before tonight's play. ◆ I am able to resist temptations when I know that there is work to be done. ◆ I complete projects on time by making steady progress.

Journal of Personality and Social Psychology, Putting time in perspective: A valid, reliable individual-differences metric, **77**(6), 1999, 1271, Zimbardo, P. G. & Boyd, J. N., With permission of American Psychological Association.

How do the dimensions relate to well-being? The two past orientations, not surprisingly given how explicitly valenced they are, correlate with measures of well-being in predictable ways. So too does present-fatalistic, again not surprisingly given its strong connotations of hopelessness and helplessness. The other two dimensions are of more interest because of their less overt content overlap with measures of well-being. Typically, although not always, present-hedonistic shows a positive correlation with subjective well-being measures—those who like excitement and take risks to generate it show higher scores on measures of well-being and lower scores on measures of distress (see, for example, Boniwell, Osin, Linley, & Ivanchenko, 2010; Stolarski, Matthews, Postek, Zimbardo, & Bitner, 2014). Moreover, Boniwell et al. (2010) found correlations not only with positive affect, which might be expected but also with life satisfaction and a more eudaimonically-oriented measure of actualization of potential. Future orientation, on the other hand, consistently shows no correlation with measures of subjective well-being. For example, Stolarski et al. (2014), in two studies, and Boniwell et al. (2010), reported correlations close to zero between future orientation and three different aspects of subjective well-being. Boniwell et al. (2010) did report a correlation between future orientation and a purpose in life measure that measures a vigorous, purposeful, engagement with life, and Gruber, Cunningham, Kirkland, and Hay (2012) found symptoms of mania and diagnosis of bipolar disorder to be related to low levels of future orientation, although this latter finding further reinforces the idea of future orientation on the ZTPI as a measure of impulse control.

Zimbardo and Boyd (1999), in their original description of the concept and the scale, introduce the intriguing notion of a balanced time perspective, which they see as the ability to switch flexibly between the different orientations depending on the demands the person is facing in their situation and the personal resources available to them. The idea is most clearly seen in contrasting a future and a present-hedonistic focus. When relaxing with friends or family, for example, a present-hedonistic focus would be the appropriate one (although a quiet family dinner might not obviously benefit from episodes of risk taking and sensation seeking!), whereas failing to shift from that focus to a future focus when there are demands and obligations to meet, most notably work related, would not be adaptive[2]. Similarly, a total future focus (at least as defined by Zimbardo & Boyd, 1999) would be associated with workaholism and weak social connections (Boniwell & Zimbardo, 2004).

Such a subtle and dynamic psychological construct as a balanced time perspective is difficult to operationalize and measure, and, perhaps for that reason, subsequent studies have defined it in a quite different way to its original conceptualization as flexibility. Typically, a balanced time perspective has been operationalized as a particular combination of scores on the different ZTPI dimensions (Boniwell et al., 2010; Drake, Duncan, Sutherland, Abernethy, & Henry, 2008; Zhang, Howell, & Stolarski, 2013). Different techniques have been employed, from simple tertile splits (Drake et al., 2008) to cluster analysis (Boniwell et al., 2010), or different techniques for arriving at the combinations have been compared within the same study (Zhang et al., 2013), but the common underlying assumption is that those scoring high in past-positive, low in past-negative, low in present-fatalistic and high in future orientations will have a balanced time perspective. High scores on present-hedonistic are also sometimes included as part of the definition. Thus, a balanced time perspective appears essentially to have been defined by high scores on subscales that have already been found to correlate positively with measures of subjective well-being (past-positive, present-hedonistic) and low scores on those dimensions found to correlate negatively with well-being variables (present-fatalistic and past-negative). High future scores, even though future does not usually correlate with well-being, are presumably included in a balanced time perspective because having a future orientation is just thought to be inherently valuable (see Zimbardo & Boyd, p. 1272, footnote). It therefore comes as no surprise that a balanced time perspective construed in this way is then found to correlate with subjective well-being measures (e.g. Zhang et al., 2013). A similar

---

[2] It is worth noting that a ZTPI future orientation is not inconsistent with hedonism. A future orientation could derive its value from setting up greater enjoyment in the future through foregoing pleasure now, a calculation that is entirely consistent with hedonism as properly defined (MacLeod, 2015).

sort of circular reasoning using a different measure of time perspective is found in Webster and Ma (2013) who defined a balanced time perspective as scoring highly on both future- and past-thinking. Unfortunately, the scales measuring past- and future-thinking actually represent positivity very strongly, for example, 'Anticipating my later life fills me with hope' (future) and 'I get a renewed sense of optimism when I remember earlier life experiences' (past). It is no surprise, again, that those who score highly on the sum of these items score highly on well-being. Operationalizing, and therefore defining, balanced time perspective in these sorts of ways does not take us any of the way towards understanding the notion of a balanced time perspective as the dynamic ability to switch between, for example, a future focus and a present focus, as originally outlined by Zimbardo and Boyd (1999). It remains for future research to see if such an intriguing and intuitively appealing concept of temporal flexibility can be operationalized, measured and related to well-being outcomes that are logically and conceptually distinct from it.

Separating temporal focus from value

The measures described so far are undoubtedly measuring interesting and useful constructs but unfortunately don't quite answer the question posed at the beginning of this chapter—whether there is a relationship between temporal orientation per se and well-being—either because of being specific to a particular population, or because the way they measure a temporal orientation is very particular to only one way of thinking about it, sometimes imbued with a judgement about its value. As already argued, the sort of future orientation measured by the CFC or future subscale of the ZTPI is one particular aspect of future-mindedness, one that is in opposition (indeed, set up to be in opposition) to a particular type of present focus. There are obviously other aspects of future orientation, such as positively embracing future possibilities and eagerly looking forward to them with anticipation, which paints a quite different picture to the sensible, work-focused, and, frankly, rather dull, future-oriented person who scores highly on the CFC or the ZTPI future subscale. In some sense, a high scorer on the future subscale of the ZTPI need not be especially future-oriented at all, in the sense that it appears to describe someone who is mostly preoccupied with present demands and obligations. In a similar way, the two present-focused possibilities of the ZTPI—resignation and lack of agency, or sensation seeking and risk taking—clearly do not fully cover the spectrum of possible present-focused orientations, something that will become apparent when mindfulness is discussed later in the chapter. Furthermore, and this will be seen in a more frank way when self-report measures of mindfulness are discussed, there is often a pairing of value with orientation. For example, future focus as defined by the CFC and ZTPI is intended to be a valued dimension. Indeed, Zimbardo and Boyd (1999) acknowledge this explicitly:

> At this point, we must acknowledge our theoretical and personal bias toward evaluating decisions from a future orientation. It is only from the perspective of future orientation that the decision to smoke can be seen to have a negative consequence: the future development of lung cancer. If judged solely through the lens of present orientation, smoking is just a pleasurable activity without articulated future consequences. In the context of present orientation, smoking may actually be the 'right' decision because it may lead to pleasure, however short lived.
>
> (Zimbardo and Boyd, p. 1272 footnote)

Shipp, Edwards, and Lambert (2009), in recognizing the problem where temporal orientations are paired with other value qualities, attempted to develop a more neutral measure of orientation, the Temporal Focus Scale (TFS). Twelve items measure past, present, and future focus, and respondents rate how frequently they have the thoughts. The items are shown in full in Table 9.2. These items are quite different from most others reviewed in this chapter in their explicit attempt not to pair a particular orientation with some other quality, often one which is desirable or undesirable. The scale also allows people to score independently on each of the dimensions. Using this measure, Shipp et al. (2009) found differing correlations between the three orientations and measures of well-being. Interestingly, different measures of subjective well-being diverged in how they related to temporal focus, with negative affect (NA) only being related to a past focus, whereas positive affect (PA) only showed any correlation with present and future focus. Low life satisfaction was most clearly related to a focus on the past. Table 9.2 shows the correlations of life satisfaction, PA and NA, with scores on each of the three orientations.

Another way of trying to disentangle orientation (past, present, future) from valence (positive or negative) is to measure both orientation and valence and see how they relate separately or in tandem to well-being. Rush and Grouzet (2012) asked students to keep a daily diary for 14 days. At the end of each day they reported the extent to which their thoughts in the past 24 hours had been past-, present-, or future-focused and rated their levels of PA and NA.[3] In addition, participants described two things from the past and the future that they had thought a lot about in the past 24 hours and rated the pleasantness of their thoughts about each. Interestingly, there was more within-person than between-person variability in focus, that is, people could not easily be

---

[3] For the analyses, NA was subtracted from PA, providing an overall measure of emotional well-being, meaning that it was not possible to compare differential relationships involving the two mood states.

Table 9.2 Temporal Focus Scale items measuring past focus, current focus, and future focus. Each item is rated by participants on a seven-point scale from 'never' to 'constantly'. Correlations of the subscale totals are shown with three measures of subjective well-being

	SWLS	PA	NA
Past focus	−.41**	−.06	.38**
I replay memories of the past in my mind.			
I reflect on what has happened in my life.			
I think about things from my past.			
I think back to my earlier days.			
Current focus	.17	.37**	−.12
I focus on what is currently happening in my life.			
My mind is on the here and now.			
I think about where I am today.			
I live my life in the present.			
Future focus	.24**	.33**	.01
I think about what my future has in store.			
I think about times to come.			
I focus on my future.			
I imagine what tomorrow will bring for me.			

Note: SWLS = Satisfaction with Life Scale; PA = Positive Affect; NA = Negative Affect.

Adapted from *Organizational Behavior and Human Decision Processes*, **110**(1), Shipp, A. J., Edwards, J. R., & Lambert, L. S., Conceptualization and measurement of temporal focus: The subjective experience of the past, present, and future, 1–22, Copyright 2009, with permission from Elsevier.

categorized as one orientation or another; rather, they shifted their focus from day to day. Well-being correlated with present focus and this was not moderated by the valence of the thoughts. Past focus was related negatively to well-being overall, but especially on days when past thoughts were more unpleasant than usual. There was no overall relationship between well-being and future focus, but a relationship did emerge when the valence of the thoughts were taken into account: where future thoughts were positive, well-being was higher, but on days when they were unpleasant, then well-being was lower.

Summary of self-reported temporal orientation and well-being

Early work pointed to suicidality being related to a lack of future orientation, a relationship that is covered in detail in Chapter 2. Subsequent findings on temporal focus and well-being using self-report to measure temporal orientation are somewhat limited either by the measures being designed for a particular population or by them measuring a particular aspect of temporal orientation, often paired with a valued quality. The ZTPI (Zimbardo & Boyd, 1999) is the most widely used measure of temporal orientation. However, the future subscale generally fails to correlate with measures of well-being or shows a low correlation, but it only captures a very particular element of a future orientation, and arguably is actually more about being conscientiously work-focused on current projects. The TFS (Shipp et al. 2009) is an attempt at a more neutral description of temporal orientation, and other more naturalistic measures such as the diary study of Rush and Grouzet (2012) also avoid an a priori pairing of orientation with another valued or disvalued quality. From these studies, it would appear that a tendency to be past-focused is associated with low well-being. Consistent with the earlier work on suicidality, future-focus appears to be linked to higher levels of well-being, although more work needs to be carried out to establish whether different aspects of well-being relate differently to the different orientations. Interestingly, a present focus also shows a relationship to well-being. Over the last two decades, a large body of work has emerged, also emphasizing the importance of a present focus, something that would appear to pose something of a challenge to the idea of future-mindedness as a temporal orientation linked to mental health and well-being. The relationship between mindfulness and mental health and well-being will be the focus of the remainder of this chapter.

Mindfulness

Mindfulness has different definitions (Williams & Kabat-Zinn, 2013), indicating its complexity as a construct, as well as the fact that its origins in Buddhism means that its essence is not always easy to translate into western perspectives. Nevertheless, the way that it is commonly used in relation to well-being and mental health in the psychological literature involves two main elements: a non-judgemental attitude towards one's own thoughts and feelings and, most pertinently for the current discussion, paying non-judgemental attention to present moment experience. It will become apparent as this discussion progresses, that a present moment focus can include thoughts of the past or the future, although it is much more usual for present focus to be interpreted as being about where you are, what you are doing, and the attendant experiences. This quality of mindfulness is illustrated by self-report measures of mindfulness asking about doing things while being unaware of what you are doing, noticing or not noticing sounds, sights smells, and other sensory experiences, and so on. A present focus is seen most clearly in mindfulness meditation practice, the foundation of which is to learn to pay moment-by-moment attention to the sensations in the body, often the sensations of the breath. If attention is drawn away, as it is likely to be, by distractions in the environment, or to thoughts about other things (plans, daydreams, etc.), then this is noted and attention is gently brought back to the breath in a non-critical way. These competing thoughts can be thoughts outside of that moment, such as thoughts of past and future, but they could also be thoughts about what is happening right now. For example, it is not unusual for people to be thinking about how well or badly they are getting on with the practice. The aim of such training is to enable people to be more mindful in everyday life, not just while they are practising meditation.

There has been a huge growth in interest in mindfulness in recent years, with publications rising in an exponential fashion (Williams & Kabat-Zinn, 2013). One large growth area is in trying to understand the impact of mindfulness training on well-being through evaluating the usefulness of such training in helping people suffering from a range of mental and physical health problems. With its emphasis on non-evaluative noticing and acceptance of experience, rather than struggle, mindfulness-based approaches offer a way for people to relate to their psychological disturbance in a different way (Segal, Williams, & Teasdale, 2012). Rather than rationally disputing their negative thoughts and feelings, as traditional cognitive therapy encourages, a mindful outlook emphasizes non-judgemental observation of experiences. By doing so, people are more likely to prevent secondary problems, for example, feeling hopeless-ness about how frequently they feel hopeless, or being critical of oneself for not being able to stop having self-critical thoughts. Such secondary problems can be viewed as being as problematic as the primary problems because they create a vicious spiral, and therefore help to maintain the person's psychological dis-turbance. By gaining insight into one's own moment-to-moment thoughts and feelings, opportunities also arise for change. Two main strands of research exist examining the connection between mindfulness and well-being: self-report measures of mindfulness have been correlated with measures of well-being, and mindfulness-based interventions have been developed to enhance well-being and reduce distress. It is beyond the scope of the present chapter to review these literatures fully, but a brief overview of both will be outlined.

Dispositional mindfulness and well-being

Probably the most widely used and highly cited[4] of the numerous self-report measures of mindfulness is the Mindful Attention Awareness Scale (Brown & Ryan, 2003). The MAAS consists of 15 items, such as 'I break or spill things because of carelessness, not paying attention, or thinking of something else' and 'I forget a person's name almost as soon as I've been told it for the first time'.

---

[4] 1845 citations, retrieved from Scopus, 3 February 2016.

Like these examples, all of the items actually describe the opposite of mindful attention, and not endorsing these items is taken as indicative of mindfulness (subsequently reverse scored so that a high score equals high mindfulness). The MAAS correlates significantly with self-report measures of well-being, including medium to large negative correlations with depression, anxiety, and NA, along-side positive correlations with PA and life satisfaction (Brown & Ryan, 2003).

Despite Brown and Ryan's (2003) title including 'The benefits of being present', the data are clearly correlational rather than causal. However, there are other difficulties with interpreting these findings. As the sample items illustrate, the items contain other elements. These other elements are negative things in themselves—who would like to be the sort of person who goes around breaking things and forgetting people's names? But, in the MAAS these sorts of negative elements are systematically paired with a non-mindful response, leading to a serious conflation of a negative content with a non-mindful response. The scale, in fact, appears to be measuring a state of negatively valued distractedness. It therefore comes as no surprise that it correlates so strongly with low well-being. Furthermore, there is some even more direct construct overlap between the MAAS and well-being. Items asking about forgetfulness or attention problems obviously overlap strongly with some depressive symptoms, rather than being something distinct that can meaningfully be correlated with those symptoms. Again, endorsing these affectively negative items are paired with a non-mindful response. Items such as 'I find it difficult to stay focused on what's happening in the present' or 'I find myself preoccupied with the future or the past' suffer from the same problems. It is self-evident that people low in well-being will endorse items suggesting that they have difficulty with things, and are preoccupied. Pairing that content with low mindful responses will result in those low in well-being scoring low in mindfulness (or to be more precise, high mindlessness). It would be interesting to see what would happen if the items were reconfigured so that the 'good' response was the other way round, for example, 'I am often able to do one thing while thinking about another' or 'I find it difficult to use the time doing routine tasks to think about other more important things' (reverse scored)[5]. A 'non-mindful' response

---

[5] Note, that this is different from the reversal conducted by Brown and Ryan (2003) who did test an alternative positive phrasing. For example, 'I find it difficult to stay focused on what I am doing' became 'I find it easy to stay focused on what I am doing', which is actually what the items should be in the first place for a scale of mindful attention rather than one of mindless attention. However, the 'mindful' response is still being paired with a good quality—finding something easy—which is functionally equivalent to a non-mindful response being paired with a bad quality. The correlations with well-being were slightly attenuated, suggesting that 'difficult' sticks slightly more strongly to low well-being than 'easy' is repelled by it.

in these hypothetical examples is now being paired with a positive element. Such questions are equally biased, of course, but in the opposite direction. Would well-being now correlate positively with these newly configured questions, thereby indicating that well-being is associated with low mindfulness? That remains an empirical question, but my guess is that it would.

The MAAS has also been criticized on the different ground of failing to do justice to the concept of mindfulness, instead, measuring only the single aspect of not having attention focused in the moment (Baer, 2006). In contrast, the other most popular self-report measure, The Five Factor Mindfulness Questionnaire (Baer, 2006) does what its name suggests it might—defines and measures five different facets of mindfulness: (1) observing mental and physical experiences; (2) describing those experiences; (3) awareness of what one is doing; (4) not judging or evaluating inner experiences, and (5) not reacting to inner experiences—simply letting them come and go. Describing and observing have been found to be weakly, or not at all related to measures of psychological distress, both on the full measure (Baer, 2006) and a shortened version (Bohlmeijer, Peter, Fledderus, Veehof, & Baer, 2011). Of the remaining three subscales, acting with awareness, and non-judgement are the most strongly correlated with symptoms of psychological distress, with non-reactivity showing an intermediate level of correlation with distress. Acting with awareness essentially measures the same as the MAAS, drawing on many of the items from the MAAS itself, again, all negatively phrased. The problems already outlined with the MAAS also apply to the acting with awareness subscale. Unfortunately, non-judgement has very similar problems. There is a very strong element of self-criticalness, with six out of the eight items containing negative self-judgement (e.g. 'I tell myself I shouldn't be feeling the way I'm feeling', 'I criticize myself for having irrational or inappropriate thoughts and feelings', 'I believe that some of my thoughts are abnormal and bad and I shouldn't think that way'). Two of the items are more neutral ('I make judgements about whether my thoughts are good or bad', 'When I have distressing thoughts or images, I judge myself as good or bad, depending what the thought/image is about'), and there are no items about judging one's thoughts positively. In other words, non-judgement (which, again, is misnamed as all the items are about *being* judgemental) is about the presence of a particular *type* of judgement, the type of negative judgement that goes along with being psychologically distressed. Finding a correlation with depression and concluding that those who are depressed judge their thoughts more is misleading because what the correlation actually shows is that, not surprisingly, people who are depressed judge their thoughts negatively. What would be of much greater interest would be to demonstrate that self judgement per se, rather than *negative* self-judgement, shows some kind of relationship to well-being. That remains a challenge that has yet to be taken up.

A second way to examine the relationship between well-being and mindfulness is through comparing well-being levels of meditators and non-meditators. The findings are somewhat mixed. Hanley, Warner, and Garland (2015) found that those who reported having a regular contemplative/meditative practice scored higher than non-practitioners on life satisfaction. They also had significantly higher scores, as show in Figure 9.1, on five out of the six subscales of the Psychological Well-being Scale (Ryff, 1989), most markedly on self-acceptance (e.g. 'In general I feel confident and positive about myself') and personal growth (e.g. 'I think it's important to have new experiences that challenge how you think about yourself and the world'). In contrast, Koopmann-Holm, Sze, Ochs, and Tsai (2013) found no difference in positive or negative affect between meditators (who averaged four years of practising meditation), and non-meditators. Clearly, the measures of well-being used in these two studies are really quite different, as are the inclusion criteria, which could account for some of the result variability between these (and other) studies. Koopmann-Holm et al. (2013) also introduced two aspects that were different to most other studies in the area. First, they separated affect into high and low, positive and

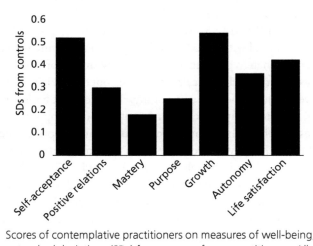

Figure 9.1 Scores of contemplative practitioners on measures of well-being, expressed as standard deviations (SDs) from scores of non-practitioners. All, except environmental mastery, were significantly elevated, although self-acceptance and personal growth are notably elevated—more than half a standard deviation above the comparable scores of the non-practitioners.

Adapted from Hanley, A., Warner, A., & Garland, E. L. (2015). Associations Between Mindfulness, Psychological Well-Being, and Subjective Well-Being with Respect to Contemplative Practice. *Journal of Happiness Studies*, **16**(6), 1423–1436.

negative, affect (enthusiastic, euphoric; calm, peaceful; hostile, worried; dull, sleepy). Second, they measured ideal affect as well as actual affect, that is how much participants would like to experience a particular affective state, as well as how much they reported actually experiencing it. Meditators valued low activation positive affect (calmness) more than non-meditators (although they did not report experiencing it more), and they placed less value on experiencing high activation positive affect (excitement). It is worth pointing out that it is not necessarily clear what well-being effects to expect from meditation practice. Adopting a more complex, multidimensional account of well-being certainly opens up possibilities for finding that different aspects of well-being relate to meditation practice, but as Gowans (2016) points out, there is no simple way to relate contemporary western concepts of well-being to those implicit in traditional Buddhist thinking.

To summarize, the evidence showing a relationship between self-reported well-being and self-reported mindfulness is undermined by problems with the measures of mindfulness, which either have strong and obvious overlap with the constructs that they are attempting to show a relationship to, or they have a clear bias in their questions where an inherently negative quality is paired with a response indicating lack of mindfulness. This is not to say that there is no relationship between mindfulness, or facets of mindfulness, and well-being, simply that the existing self-report measures of mindfulness are incapable of testing this relationship. Studies comparing meditation practitioners with non-practitioners bypass these problems, although of course any results are open to being interpreted as reflecting other self-selection biases in those who practise mindfulness and those who do not. Nevertheless, there are well-being differences between practitioners and non-practitioners, although interestingly, these differences appear to be stronger for the non-affective elements of well-being. All of the findings reviewed in the present section are in essence correlational and do not speak to questions about causality. Studies testing the impact of mindfulness interventions on well-being or distress would be needed to address this issue. A number of such studies have been conducted.

Mindfulness-based interventions

One area where ideas about mindfulness have had a strong impact has been in interventions for psychological distress. A wide array of problems has been subjected to mindfulness-based intervention, starting with mindfulness-based stress reduction (Kabat-Zinn, 1990). Probably the most relevant for the current discussion is mindfulness-based cognitive therapy for depression (MBCT), developed by Zindel Segal, Mark Williams, and John Teasdale (Segal, Williams, & Teasdale, 2002, Second edition 2012). MBCT is a therapeutic approach aimed at preventing relapse in people who have experienced recurrent episodes of depression in the past but are currently remitted. It combines the psychoeducation elements of cognitive therapy (e.g. identifying negative automatic thoughts) with intensive practice of mindfulness meditation. What differentiates it clearly from traditional cognitive therapy is the meditation element, the aim of which is to teach people to be able to focus on their present moment experience in an accepting, non-judgemental way. There is a variety of ways that MBCT might work and attention has turned to uncovering possible mechanisms (Gu, Strauss, Bond, & Cavanagh, 2015; van der Velden, Kuyken, Wattar, Crane, Pallesen et al., 2015). However, essentially, the present moment focus might reduce much of the unhelpful past- (rumination) and future-(hopelessness) thinking characteristic of depression. By adopting an acceptance orientation to ongoing thoughts, the tendency towards continual critical self-evaluation will be minimized, and thoughts (including thoughts about the present) come to be seen as transient mental events rather than necessarily indicators of reality. By practising mindfulness meditation, people learn to be more skilful at experiencing their daily ongoing experience in this way.

Two recent, large-scale randomized controlled trials (Kuyken, Hayes, Barrett, Byng, Dalgleish et al., 2015; Williams, Crane, Barnhofer, Brennan, Duggan et al., 2014) have evaluated MBCT. The studies were very similar in recruiting remitted depressed patients with a history of repeated (three or more) episodes of depression and in comparing MBCT to a defined alternative treatment. Williams et al. (2014) conducted a dismantling trial, comparing MBCT with psychoeducation, which contained the elements of MBCT not linked to meditation, that is, MBCT without the meditation. Kuyken et al. (2015) compared MBCT against continuing treatment with antidepressants. Patients in the MBCT group were encouraged to taper off their antidepressant medication, while those in the continuing medication group were encouraged to persist with it. The results of the studies were also strikingly similar: MBCT performed no better than the alternative treatment either post-treatment or at follow-up. However, additional analyses in both studies showed that a subgroup of patients with a history of abuse showed better outcome if they received MBCT than if they received the alternative treatment. The implications are that while MBCT may not be superior overall to other treatments, there is an identifiable subgroup who may particularly benefit from it. In addition, although strictly speaking, both trials were superiority trials testing whether MBCT produced better results than an alternative treatment, the lack of difference between groups points to the possibility of an equivalently effective alternative treatment that people may choose to follow. A recent meta-analysis of nine randomized controlled trials provides further support for mindfulness as a viable alternative treatment for those with a history of repeated episodes of depression who are currently remitted (Kuyken, Warren, Taylor, Whalley, Crane et al., 2016).

Meditation-based interventions have also been tested in non-clinical contexts. In general, when compared with a control group not receiving a meditation-based intervention, intervention participants show higher levels of well-being following the trial period, although the results are not entirely clear-cut. For example, using a seven-week long loving kindness meditation, Fredrickson, Cohn, Coffey, Pek, and Finkel (2008) found increases in positive emotions but no change to negative emotions. Chambers, Lo, and Allen (2008) compared participants at the end of a ten-day meditation course to those on the waiting list for the course, and found reduction in negative affect and depression, whereas positive affect was unchanged. Koopmann-Holm et al. (2013) found that participants allocated to an eight-week meditation class showed a higher valuing of low activation positive emotions (e.g. calmness) compared to a control group, but did not report experiencing more calmness or show any change in other types of emotions. Interestingly, after a brief 15-minute meditation, Thompson and Waltz's (2007) participants reported *reduced* levels of positive affect as measured by the Positive and Negative Affect Scale (PANAS; Watson, Clark, & Tellegen, 1988), which assesses the presence only of high activation states such as excitement and enthusiasm. Clearly, the types of interventions, the participants, the length of the interventions, and the measures of well-being are all different, rendering it difficult to make comparisons across studies. However, it does appear to be the case that there are well-being benefits to be found in taking part in meditation practice, although questions remain about which particular aspects of well-being are responsive and whether different types of practice are sensitive to different aspects of well-being. Additionally, practice is generally compared with a non-active control, the presence of which would provide a stricter test of effect.

Mind wandering

There is a third strand of findings that appear to speak to the value of a present versus a future or past focus. Data from studies on mind wandering would appear initially to support the value of a present focus, although, again, there are reasons to question that simple conclusion. Mind wandering is the name given to thoughts that have shifted from the task at hand to become focused on something other than that task. The term 'mind wandering' itself has an evaluative quality—the thoughts are *supposed* to be focused on a particular task—but mind wandering during a discrete task is actually a particular example of a broader category of thought which is defined by what it is not: it is thought that is not focused on the immediate sensory input of the moment. To give an everyday example, someone may be walking to work thinking about the meeting that they have later that morning, rather than thinking about putting one foot in front of the other or noticing the sound of the traffic that is going past or the feeling of the wind on their face. This broader category is different from situations where someone is supposed to be paying attention to a particular task, as in experimental tasks, because they may have *intended*, or at least been prepared for, their mind to be on the upcoming meeting. In other words, what really should define something as mind wandering is whether it departs from whatever it is that the person intends, or is happy to be, the focus of their attention. Not paying attention to the immediate environment is, therefore, not necessarily mind wandering. As Baird, Smallwood, and Schooler (2011) point out, being able to engage in mental activity that is about something other than what is happening in the immediate temporal present confers a great deal of mental freedom. Such mental freedom might be of great value. So, rather than mind wandering or daydreaming, or some other term that has a slightly negative tone, a more neutral name for such mental activity is stimulus independent thoughts (SITS; Teasdale, Proctor, Lloyd, & Baddeley, 1993), sometimes also called self-generated thoughts (SGTs; Ruby, Smallwood, Engen, & Singer, 2013) task unrelated thoughts (TUTS; Smallwood, Nind, & O'Connor, 2009) or even stimulus independent and task unrelated thoughts (SITUTS; Stawarczyk, Cassol, & D'Argembeau, 2013), but stimulus independent thoughts, despite its lack of elegance, captures the phenomenon well.

SITs are a common feature of everyday experience. Killingsworth and Gilbert (2010) used a phone app to randomly sample activity, thoughts and feelings during waking hours in over 2,000 US residents. In almost half (47%) of the samples participants answered 'yes' to the question of whether they were thinking about something other than what they were doing. Song and Wang (2012), in an experience-sampling study of Chinese students found 24% of thoughts were described as mind wandering, the lower percentage raising the question of possible cultural differences, although there were also some methodological differences from the Killingsworth and Gilbert study. Particularly interesting for the discussion here is that when the temporal orientation of the mind wandering thoughts in the Song and Wang study were categorized, more of them were about the future, rather than being about the present or the past.

Experimental studies of SITS are able to provide an insight into some of their more detailed aspects. Typically, participants are asked to perform a cognitive task during which they are probed at random points to see whether they are thinking about the task or not. If not, then further questions are asked about the nature of the thoughts they are having. The tasks tend to vary in complexity from simple choice reaction time tasks to more complex working memory tasks. Of course, the assumption is that when people's (usually students') minds are drifting from a tedious laboratory task that they are performing for course credits or a small payment, that this is similar in important ways to what happens when people engage in SIT in everyday life. If we can live with these assumptions, then the results of these studies are informative about SITs.

Most importantly for the present discussion, a lot of SITs reported in experimental tasks are future-oriented. For example, Stawarczyk (2013) found that 43% of off-task thoughts on a simple choice reaction time task were reported by participants as being about the future, compared to 26% about the past. Rather than asking participants directly to say what the temporal focus of their thoughts were, Baird et al. (2011) asked participants to describe their thoughts, which were later coded by independent raters. Just under half of off-task thoughts were coded as future-related whereas only 12% were past focused and 29 % present-focused (the remainder were uncodable).

Traditionally, SITs have been seen as a bad thing because they are related to poorer performance on tasks—not surprisingly, the more people think about things other than the task at the hand, the worse they perform on that task (see Randall, Oswald, & Beier, 2014; Smallwood, 2013). However, rather than being seen simply as a failure of sustained concentration, one view of SITs put forward by Klinger (1971) proposes that SITs have an important role in people's wider personal concerns and goals. In this view, people's minds are drawn to things other than the immediate perceptual input (whether it be a focused task like the experimental tasks already described or broader tasks such as walking to work) when their personal goals or wider concerns are of sufficiently pressing interest to capture their attention. This is most likely to occur when what is happening in the environment is either not very interesting or not very demanding of cognitive resources, or both. It is also likely to happen when concerns or goals are especially pressing.

As well as being intuitively plausible, there are several different sources of evidence to support this view. First, in SITs measured in experimental tasks there is a significant preponderance of self-related and goal-related thoughts concerned with the planning and anticipation of future events (Baird et al., 2011), and this tendency for SITs to be self- and goal-focused is even greater when participants are primed by writing about their goals before the task (Stawarczyk, Majerus, Maj, Van der Linden, & D'Argembeau, 2011). Second, tasks that require executive processes reduce future-directed SITs. For example, as an alternative to describing whether a target is an odd or even number, participants can be asked to describe whether the digit *previous* to the target was odd or even. As Figure 9.2 shows, using this more complex working

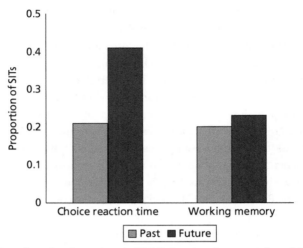

Figure 9.2 Data from Smallwood et al. (2011) showing the proportion of SITs that were past- or future-focused in a simple choice reaction time task or a more demanding working memory task. The working memory task appeared to reduce future- but not past-focused thoughts.

Adapted from Smallwood, J., Schooler, J. W., Turk, D. J., Cunningham, S. J., Burns, P., & Macrae, C. N. (2011). Self-reflection and the temporal focus of the wandering mind. *Consciousness and Cognition*, **20**(4), 1120–1126.

memory version of the task reduces the number of future-directed SITs by almost half but, interestingly, does not affect the number of past-related SITs (Smallwood, et al., 2011). One interpretation is that future-directed SITs are distinct from other SITs in being concerned with autobiographical planning, an activity requiring greater executive resources (Baird et al., 2011; Smallwood, 2013), suggesting that they represent an active constructive process (see Chapter 6). Interestingly, mind wandering during experimental tasks is associated with the activity of the default network (Mason et al., 2007), an interconnected set of neural structures that are associated with goal planning (see Chapter 7). Future SITs are also distinct from past SITs by their standard range of temporal focus: Stawarczyk et al. (2013) found that only 3% of future-focused SITs were about more than one year in the future, in contrast to past-focused thoughts, where 31% were about more than one year in the past.

The preceding discussion has argued that, despite being associated with poorer performance on tasks that demand attention, SITs—and hence the particular type of future-directed thinking that occurs in those situations—can be understood as being something of value. A second challenge to the value of SITs, and one that is particularly salient for the focus of this book, is that they appear to be associated with low mood. Participants in the Killingsworth and Gilbert study (2010) reported lower levels of happiness when they were sampled during episodes where they reported that their minds were on something other than what they were currently doing, compared to times when they responded 'no' to that question. Of course, even from a utilitarian perspective that values feeling good above anything else, episodes of low mood might not necessarily be bad for someone because of their contribution to a greater sum total of positive mood in the long run. Nevertheless, this finding of lower mood in off-task thoughts, which are known to be more future-oriented than anything else, still represents something of a challenge for the link between future focus and well-being. It is often assumed that when lower mood accompanies mind wandering that it must have been caused by the mind wandering. But one plausible alternative is that both mind wandering and negative mood are the result of loss of interest in the perceptual input. For example, it is well established that people's moods are at their lowest at the point of the day when they are commuting (Kahneman, Krueger, Schkade, Schwarz, & Stone, 2004). I am not aware that the study has been carried out but it is not difficult to imagine that rates of SITs would also be found to be very high when people are commuting. Does that mean that the greater frequency of SITs is causing people's moods to be low? Or is it that commuting is such a repetitive and boring activity that it leads to both lower mood and more SITs? This is not to say that there cannot also be causal links between SITs and low mood, but there is an alternative common sense view that both SITs and low mood are part of an overall package of loss of interest in the environmental input.

If this preceding interpretation is correct it should be possible to shift interest from perceptual input (or, in everyday language, for one's mind to wander) and mood not be lowered, if the focus of what a person's mind goes to is sufficiently interesting to them. In fact, that is exactly what has been found. In an experience sampling study where participants had to rate the topic of their off-task thoughts on how interesting they were, off-task thoughts where interest was rated highly had more positive mood associated with them than both off-task thoughts where interest was low and on-task thoughts (Franklin et al., 2013). Killingsworth and Gilbert (2010), in their naturalistic study also found that when people's off-task thoughts were about pleasant topics their moods were equivalent to when they were on-task. In an attempt to look at causality, Ruby et al. (2013) using lag analysis in an experimental task found evidence of negative mood both following and preceding off-task thoughts. Interestingly, within that general pattern, off-task thoughts that were about the past and other people were related to negative mood, consistent with an earlier finding that inducing a negative mood increases the frequency of past-focused SITs (Smallwood & O'Connor, 2011). In contrast, thoughts that were self- and future-related were linked to positive mood, even if those thoughts were not rated as themselves positive. There is clearly a complex relationship between off-task thoughts and mood, much more complex than a simple causal one whereby off-task thoughts produce negative mood.

The present section has covered some of the literature on stimulus independent thought because of the reliable finding that when people are thinking about things other than what is in front of them they are often thinking about the future. Because SITS have often been characterized as mind wandering, with its negative connotations, performance deficits, and low mood states, this seems, again, to present a challenge to the view of future-thinking as being something that might be desirable. Set against this rather negative view of SITs is the idea that spontaneous future-directed thoughts are valuable in relation to a person's goals and concerns. Although SITs may be associated with low mood, that does not appear to be the case when their content is interesting to the person, reinforcing the idea that both low mood and SITs can arise through boredom and loss of interest in the environmental input. Alternative thoughts can also compete for attention if they relate to pressing concerns or interests. It is quite possible that my writing in this chapter would be compromised by my mind wandering, but if in doing so I am reminded that I have to pick up my daughter from school, and so end up not leaving her stranded, then my mind wandering was a good thing. If, however, my writing is impaired by having thoughts that this chapter is not good enough, I will never get it finished and, anyway, no one is going to be interested even if I do, then most people would agree that those SITs are not beneficial for me. What emerges from the naturalistic and experimental work is that there is no simple view of whether SITs are good for a person or not. If current perceptual input and self-generated thoughts compete for attention, what is good for the person will depend on how important each of them is for the person's overall well-being, both short- and long-term, something that is also influenced by the affective tone or content of the thoughts.

In fact, within mindfulness, the mind 'wandering' onto something that is temporally dated as other than the present need not be viewed as a mistake that needs to be rectified by bringing it back to the immediate temporally dated present. Mindfulness training is concerned with training the mind to focus on the immediate sensory present; but if that is conceptualized as simply a way of anchoring the skill of noticing where the mind's attention is and enabling choices about where one would like it to be, then it is perfectly possible at other times to be thinking in a mindful way about the future, or, indeed, the past. The critical point is that, after all, thinking about the future or the past happens *in the experienced present*, and therefore when I am thinking about the future, that *is* my present experience. In other words, the experienced present may involve thinking about the temporal present (e.g. where I am, what I am doing) but the experienced present could equally be filled with remembering something from the past or imagining something in the future, or even with thoughts and emotions that have no particular temporal anchor. It may be good for me, or be my choice, for my subjective awareness in the present moment to be future-focused, and mindfulness can be seen as a way of facilitating the control and awareness of those thoughts, rather than being a dictat to pull thoughts back to my current sensory experience. This understanding of mindfulness being about the experienced present is implicit in some of the writings about mindfulness within the psychological literature, but in the absence of explicit reference to the distinction it is easy to confuse the experienced present, where thinking can quite reasonably be about the future, with the temporally dated present, where thinking about the future can only be seen as a mind wandering error.

General summary and concluding comments

Different literatures appear to have different starting points in relation to whether a future as opposed to a present focus is desirable. Much of the goals and plans literature (see Chapters 7 and 8) emphasizes the value of being future-minded, and some of the literature on temporal orientation reviewed in the present chapter also starts from that point, although data do not always bear it out. In contrast, the concept of mindfulness, with its emphasis on being focused in the present, appears to present a challenge to the value of a future orientation. However, the apparent contrast dissolves if mindfulness is seen as being about the experienced present (which obviously can include thoughts about the future or the past, as well as the present) rather than the temporally dated present. If this is the case, then it is perfectly possible to be mindful about the future, or, indeed, the past. That is, being mindful about the future would essentially mean viewing those thoughts as mental events (like any other) and being able to respond to them in a way that one chooses to. Embracing future-focused thinking is, of course, consistent with the evidence reviewed elsewhere in this book. Obviously, thinking that is about the past can enhance well-being, as in pleasurable shared reminiscence, but a general orientation to the past does tend to be associated with lower well-being.

It remains true that many findings in both the temporal orientation and mindfulness literatures are undermined by self-report measures that do not access their intended constructs without also, in the process, contaminating them by attaching other value elements to those constructs in a systematic way that biases their connection to well-being. Orientation measures that try to avoid such biases indicate there is evidence of both a present- and a future-focus link with well-being, whereas a focus on the past appears to be associated with lower well-being.

There is evidence that people experiencing psychological distress, particularly those currently in remission from repeated depressive episodes, respond to mindfulness-based interventions. The evidence points to meditation practitioners demonstrating higher levels of well-being than non-practitioners. Of course self-selection cannot be ruled out as an explanation for these differences, that is, it might be that those higher in well-being choose to meditate, although there is no obvious reason that presents itself as to why this should be the case. Interestingly, the differences in well-being shown by meditators might be more linked to eudaimonic aspects of well-being and less connected to its affective elements, although no definitive conclusions can be drawn about this based on the existing, limited evidence. In any case, as already covered, if mindfulness proved to be a highly effective way of enhancing well-being this would not have any implications for the value of future-directed thinking because mindfulness and prospective thinking are entirely compatible.

In their development of the ZTPI, Zimbardo and Boyd (1999) raised the intriguing notion of temporal flexibility—being able to shift temporal focus depending on the situation. Asking whether one temporal orientation is better than another might be posing the wrong question. The flexibility to be able to switch temporal focus is the sort of high level skill that might be key to well-being, both short- and long-term. It is possible that mindfulness meditation, by increasing awareness of current experience, develops this skill, rather than simply being about getting people to be more present-focused at the expense of memory and prospection. Clearly, though, in addition to the skill of being flexible, someone would also need to possess the knowledge and wisdom to choose when to think about past, future, and present in a way that functions best for their well-being.

References

Baer, R. A. (2006). Using self-report assessment methods to explore facets of mindfulness. *Assessment*, **13**(1), 27–45. http://doi.org/10.1177/1073191105283504

Baird, B., Smallwood, J., & Schooler, J. W. (2011). Back to the future: Autobiographical planning and the functionality of mind-wandering. *Consciousness and Cognition*, **20**(4), 1604–1611. http://doi.org/10.1016/j.concog.2011.08.007

Bohlmeijer, E., ten Kooster, P.M.. Fledderus, M., Veehof, M., & Baer, R. (2011). Psychometric properties of the five facet mindfulness questionnaire in depressed adults and development of a short form. *Assessment*, **18**(3), 308–320. 10.1177/1073191111408231.

Boniwell, I., Osin, E., Linley, P. A., & Ivanchenko, G. V. (2010). A question of balance: Time perspective and well-being in British and Russian samples. *The Journal of Positive Psychology*, 5(1), 24–40. http://doi.org/10.1080/17439760903271181

Boniwell, I. & Zimbardo, P. G. (2004). Balancing time perspective in pursuit of optimal functioning. In P. A. Linley & S. Joseph (Eds.), *Positive psychology in practice* (pp. 165–180). Hoboken, NJ: Wiley.

Brown, K. W. & Ryan, R. M. (2003). The benefits of being present: Mindfulness and its role in psychological well-being. *Journal of Personality and Social Psychology*, 84(4), 822–848. http://doi.org/10.1037/0022-3514.84.4.822

Bryant, F. B., Smart, C. M., & King, S. P. (2005). Using the past to enhance the present: Boosting happiness through positive reminiscence. *Journal of Happiness Studies*, 6(3), 227–260. http://doi.org/10.1007/s10902-005-3889-4

Carstensen, L. L. (1993). Motivation for social contact across the life span: A theory of socioemotional selectivity. In J. E. Jacobs (Ed.), *Nebraska Symposium on Motivation, 1992: Developmental perspectives on motivation.* (pp. 209–254). Lincoln, NE: University of Nebraska Press.

Chambers, R., Lo, B. C. Y., & Allen, N. B. (2008). The Impact of intensive mindfulness training on attentional control, cognitive style, and affect. *Cognitive Therapy and Research*, 32(3), 303–322. http://doi.org/10.1007/s10608-007-9119-0

Drake, L., Duncan, E., Sutherland, F., Abernethy, C., & Henry, C. (2008). Time perspective and correlates of wellbeing. *Time & Society*, 17(1), 47–61. http://doi.org/10.1177/0961463X07086304

Franklin, M. S., Mrazek, M. D., Anderson, C. L., Smallwood, J., Kingstone, A., & Schooler, J. W. (2013). The silver lining of a mind in the clouds: Interesting musings are associated with positive mood while mind-wandering. *Frontiers in Psychology*, 4. http://doi.org/10.3389/fpsyg.2013.00583

Fredrickson, B. L., Cohn, M. A., Coffey, K. A., Pek, J., & Finkel, S. M. (2008). Open hearts build lives: Positive emotions, induced through loving-kindness meditation, build consequential personal resources. *Journal of Personality and Social Psychology*, 95(5), 1045–1062. http://doi.org/10.1037/a0013262

Gowans, C. W. (2016). Buddhist understandings of well-being. In G. Fletcher (Ed.), *The Routledge handbook of philosophy of well-being* (pp. 70–80). Abingdon: Routledge.

Greaves, G. (1971). Temporal orientation in suicidal patients. *Perceptual and Motor Skills*, 33(3, Pt. 1), 1020–1020. http://doi.org/10.2466/pms.1971.33.3.1020

Gruber, J., Cunningham, W. A., Kirkland, T., & Hay, A. C. (2012). Feeling stuck in the present? Mania proneness and history associated with present-oriented time perspective. *Emotion*, 12(1), 13–17. http://doi.org/10.1037/a0025062

Gu, J., Strauss, C., Bond, R., & Cavanagh, K. (2015). How do mindfulness-based cognitive therapy and mindfulness-based stress reduction improve mental health and wellbeing? A systematic review and meta-analysis of mediation studies. *Clinical Psychology Review*, 37, 1–12. http://doi.org/10.1016/j.cpr.2015.01.006

Hanley, A., Warner, A., & Garland, E. L. (2015). Associations between mindfulness, psychological well-being, and subjective well-being with respect to contemplative practice. *Journal of Happiness Studies*, 16(6), 1423–1436. http://doi.org/10.1007/s10902-014-9569-5

Heerey, E. A., Matveeva, T. M., & Gold, J. M. (2011). Imagining the future: Degraded representations of future rewards and events in schizophrenia. *Journal of Abnormal Psychology*, **120**(2), 483–489. http://doi.org/10.1037/a0021810

Holman, E. A. & Silver, R. C. (1998). Getting 'stuck' in the past: Temporal orientation and coping with trauma. *Journal of Personality and Social Psychology*, **74**(5), 1146. http://doi.org/10.1037/0022-3514.74.5.1146

Joireman, J., Shaffer, M. J., Balliet, D., & Strathman, A. (2012). Promotion orientation explains why future-oriented people exercise and eat healthy evidence from the two-factor consideration of future consequences-14 scale. *Personality and Social Psychology Bulletin*, **38**(10), 1272–1287.

Kabat-Zinn, J. (1990). *Full catastrophe living: Using the wisdom of your body and mind to face stress, pain, and illness*. New York: Delta Trade Paperbacks.

Kahneman, D., Krueger, A. B., Schkade, D. A., Schwarz, N., & Stone, A. A. (2004). A survey method for characterizing daily life experience: The day reconstruction method. *Science*, **306**(5702), 1776–1780. http://doi.org/10.1126/science.1103572

Killingsworth, M. A. & Gilbert, D. T. (2010). A wandering mind is an unhappy mind. *Science*, **330**(6006), 932–932. http://doi.org/10.1126/science.1192439

Kirby, K. N., Petry, N. M., & Bickel, W. K. (1999). Heroin addicts have higher discount rates for delayed rewards than non-drug-using controls. *Journal of Experimental Psychology: General*, **128**(1), 78–87. http://doi.org/10.1037/0096-3445.128.1.78

Klinger, E. (1971). *Structure and functions of fantasy*. London: Wiley-Interscience 1971.

Koopmann-Holm, B., Sze, J., Ochs, C., & Tsai, J. L. (2013). Buddhist-inspired meditation increases the value of calm. *Emotion*, **13**(3), 497–505. http://doi.org/10.1037/a0031070

Kozik, P., Hoppmann, C. A., & Gerstorf, D. (2015). Future time perspective: Opportunities and limitations are differentially associated with subjective well-being and hair cortisol concentration. *Gerontology*, **61**(2), 166–174. http://doi.org/10.1159/000368716

Kuyken, W., Hayes, R., Barrett, B., Byng, R., Dalgleish, T., Kessler, D., Lewis, G., Watkins, E., Brejcha, C., Cardy, J., Causley, J., Cowderoy, S., Evans, A., Gradinger, F., Kaur, S., Lanham, P., Morant, N., Richards, J., Shah, P., Sutton, H., Vicary, R., Weaver, A., Wilks, J., Williams, M., Taylor, R., &Byford, S. (2015). Effectiveness and cost-effectiveness of mindfulness-based cognitive therapy compared with maintenance antidepressant treatment in the prevention of depressive relapse or recurrence (PREVENT): A randomised controlled trial. *The Lancet*, **386**(9988), 63–73.

Kuyken, W., Warren, F., Taylor, R. S., Whalley, B., Crane, C., Bondolfi, G., Hayes, R., Huijbers, M., Ma, H., Schweizer, S., Segal, Z., Speckens, A., Teasdale, J. D., Van Heeringen, K., Williams, m., Byford, S., Byng, R., & Dalgleish, T. (2016). Efficacy and moderators of mindfulness-based cognitive therapy (MBCT) in prevention of depressive relapse: An individual patient data meta-analysis from randomized trials. *JAMA Psychiatry*.

Lang, F. R. & Carstensen, L. L. (2002). Time counts: Future time perspective, goals, and social relationships. *Psychology and Aging*, **17**(1), 125–139. http://doi.org/10.1037//0882-7974.17.1.125

Lempert, K. M. & Pizzagalli, D. A. (2010). Delay discounting and future-directed thinking in anhedonic individuals. *Journal of Behavior Therapy and Experimental Psychiatry*, **41**(3), 258–264. http://doi.org/10.1016/j.jbtep.2010.02.003

MacLeod, A. K. (2015). Well-being: Objectivism, subjectivism or sobjectivism? *Journal of Happiness Studies*, **16**(4), 1073–1089. http://doi.org/10.1007/s10902-014-9561-0

Mason, M. F., Norton, M. I., Van Horn, J. D., Wegner, D. M., Grafton, S. T., & Macrae, C. N. (2007). Wandering minds: the default network and stimulus-independent thought. *Science*, **315**(5810), 393–395.

Melges, F. T. & Weisz, A. E. (1971). The personal future and suicidal ideation. *Journal of Nervous and Mental Disease*, **153**(4), 244–250. http://doi.org/10.1097/00005053-197110000-00003

Pulcu, E., Trotter, P. D., Thomas, E. J., McFarquhar, M., Juhasz, G., Sahakian, B. J., Deakin, J. F., Zahn, R., Anderson, I. M., & Elliott, R. (2014). Temporal discounting in major depressive disorder. *Psychological Medicine*, **44**(9), 1825–1834. http://doi.org/10.1017/S0033291713002584

Randall, J. G., Oswald, F. L., & Beier, M. E. (2014). Mind-wandering, cognition, and performance: A theory-driven meta-analysis of attention regulation. *Psychological Bulletin*. http://doi.org/10.1037/a0037428

Ruby, F. J. M., Smallwood, J., Engen, H., & Singer, T. (2013). How self-generated thought shapes mood: The relation between mind-wandering and mood depends on the socio-temporal content of thoughts. *PLoS ONE*, **8**(10), e77554. http://doi.org/10.1371/journal.pone.0077554

Rush, J. & Grouzet, F. M. E. (2012). It is about time: Daily relationships between temporal perspective and well-being. *The Journal of Positive Psychology*, **7**(5), 427–442. http://doi.org/10.1080/17439760.2012.713504

Ryff, C. D. (1989). Happiness is everything, or is it? Explorations on the meaning of psychological well-being. *Journal of Personality and Social Psychology*, **57**(6), 1069–1081. http://doi.org/10.1037/0022-3514.57.6.1069

Segal, Z. V., Williams, J. M. G., & Teasdale, J. D. (2002). *Mindfulness-based cognitive therapy for depression: A new approach to preventing relapse* (1st edition). The Guilford Press.

Segal, Z. V., Williams, J. M. G., & Teasdale, J. D. (2012). *Mindfulness-based cognitive therapy for depression* (2nd edition). New York: Guilford Press.

Shipp, A. J., Edwards, J. R., & Lambert, L. S. (2009). Conceptualization and measurement of temporal focus: The subjective experience of the past, present, and future. *Organizational Behavior and Human Decision Processes*, **110**(1), 1–22. http://doi.org/10.1016/j.obhdp.2009.05.001

Sircova, A., van de Vijver, F. J. R., Osin, E., Milfont, T. L., Fieulaine, N., Kislali-Erginbilgic, A., … Boyd, J. N. (2014). A global look at time. *SAGE Open*, **4**(1). http://doi.org/10.1177/2158244013515686

Smallwood, J. (2013). Distinguishing how from why the mind wanders: A process–occurrence framework for self-generated mental activity. *Psychological Bulletin*, **139**(3), 519–535. http://doi.org/10.1037/a0030010

Smallwood, J., Nind, L., & O'Connor, R. C. (2009). When is your head at? An exploration of the factors associated with the temporal focus of the wandering mind. *Consciousness and Cognition*, **18**(1), 118–125. http://doi.org/10.1016/j.concog.2008.11.004

Smallwood, J. & O'Connor, R. C. (2011). Imprisoned by the past: Unhappy moods lead to a retrospective bias to mind wandering. *Cognition & Emotion*, **25**(8), 1481–1490. http://doi.org/10.1080/02699931.2010.545263

Smallwood, J., Schooler, J. W., Turk, D. J., Cunningham, S. J., Burns, P., & Macrae, C. N. (2011). Self-reflection and the temporal focus of the wandering mind. *Consciousness and Cognition*, 20(4), 1120–1126. http://doi.org/10.1016/j.concog.2010.12.017

Snaith, R. P., Hamilton, M., Morley, S., Humayan, A., Hargreaves, D., & Trigwell, P. (1995). A scale for the assessment of the hedonic tone: The Snaith-Hamilton Pleasure Scale. *The British Journal of Psychiatry*, 167(1), 99–103. http://doi.org/10.1192/bjp.167.1.99

Song, X. & Wang, X. (2012). Mind wandering in Chinese daily lives–an experience sampling study. *PLoS One*, 7(9), e44423. http://doi.org/10.1371/journal.pone.0044423

Stawarczyk, D., Cassol, H., & D'Argembeau, A. (2013). Phenomenology of future-oriented mind-wandering episodes. *Frontiers in Psychology*, 4. http://doi.org/10.3389/fpsyg.2013.00425

Stawarczyk, D., Majerus, S., Maj, M., Van der Linden, M., & D'Argembeau, A. (2011). Mind-wandering: Phenomenology and function as assessed with a novel experience sampling method. *Acta Psychologica*, 136(3), 370–381. http://doi.org/10.1016/j.actpsy.2011.01.002

Stolarski, M., Matthews, G., Postek, S., Zimbardo, P. G., & Bitner, J. (2014). How we feel is a matter of time: Relationships between time perspectives and mood. *Journal of Happiness Studies*, 15(4), 809–827. http://doi.org/10.1007/s10902-013-9450-y

Strathman, A., Gleicher, F., Boninger, D. S., & Edwards, C. S. (1994). The consideration of future consequences: Weighing immediate and distant outcomes of behavior. *Journal of Personality and Social Psychology*, 66(4), 742.

Teasdale, J. D., Proctor, L., Lloyd, C. A., & Baddeley, A. D. (1993). Working memory and stimulus-independent thought: Effects of memory load and presentation rate. *European Journal of Cognitive Psychology*, 5(4), 417–433. http://doi.org/10.1080/09541449308520128

Thompson, B. L. & Waltz, J. (2007). Everyday mindfulness and mindfulness meditation: Overlapping constructs or not? *Personality and Individual Differences*, 43(7), 1875–1885. http://doi.org/10.1016/j.paid.2007.06.017

van der Velden, A. M., Kuyken, W., Wattar, U., Crane, C., Pallesen, K. J., Dahlgaard, J., … Piet, J. (2015). A systematic review of mechanisms of change in mindfulness-based cognitive therapy in the treatment of recurrent major depressive disorder. *Clinical Psychology Review*, 37, 26–39. http://doi.org/10.1016/j.cpr.2015.02.001

Watson, D., Clark, L. A., & Tellegen, A. (1988). Development and validation of brief measures of positive and negative affect: The PANAS scales. *Journal of Personality and Social Psychology*, 54(6), 1063–1070. http://doi.org/10.1037/0022-3514.54.6.1063

Webster, J. D. & Ma, X. (2013). A balanced time perspective in adulthood: well-being and developmental effects. *Canadian Journal on Aging/La Revue Canadienne Du Vieillissement*, 32(4), 433–442. http://doi.org/10.1017/S0714980813000500

Williams, J. M. G., Crane, C., Barnhofer, T., Brennan, K., Duggan, D. S., Fennell, M. J. V., Hackmann, A., Krusche, A., Muse, K., Von Rohr, I. R., Shah, D.,Crane, R. S., Eames, C., Jones, M., Radford, S., Silverton, S., Sun, Y., Weatherley-Jones, E., Whitaker, C. J., Russell, D., & Russell, I. T. (2014). Mindfulness-based cognitive therapy for preventing relapse in recurrent depression: A randomized dismantling trial. *Journal of Consulting and Clinical Psychology*, 82(2), 275–286. http://doi.org/10.1037/a0035036

Williams, J. M. G. & Kabat-Zinn, J. (Eds.). (2013). *Mindfulness*. London: Routledge.

Yufit, R. I., Benzies, B., Fonte, M. E., & Fawcett, J. A. (1970). Suicide potential and time perspective. *Archives of General Psychiatry*, **23**(2), 158–163. http://doi.org/10.1001/archpsyc.1970.01750020062008

Zhang, J. W., Howell, R. T., & Stolarski, M. (2013). Comparing three methods to measure a balanced time perspective: The relationship between a balanced time perspective and subjective well-being. *Journal of Happiness Studies*, **14**(1), 169–184. http://doi.org/10.1007/s10902-012-9322-x

Zimbardo, P. G. & Boyd, J. N. (1999). Putting time in perspective: A valid, reliable individual-differences metric. *Journal of Personality and Social Psychology*, **77**(6), 1271. http://doi.org/10.1037/0022-3514.77.6.1271.

Chapter 10

Intervention

Introduction

Previous chapters have clearly shown that a variety of ways of thinking about the future are linked to low levels of well-being and to different emotional disorders. Ways of trying to change how people think about the future have been noted along the way, some of which have had more success than others. Chapter 7, for example, discussed efforts aimed at trying to make people less complacent by elevating their beliefs in the likelihood of future health risks. The issues in mental health and emotional well-being, which are the focus of this book, are very different. Here, the questions are about (a) how to help people view their futures in a more positive way, where they anticipate and find ways of bringing about pleasurable and meaningful experiences, and (b) how to help people to stop being preoccupied and worried about threatening and unwanted future possibilities. The current chapter reviews literature on methods that have been developed to these ends.

Interventions can utilize a variety of techniques to help people to view their futures as better ones, some of which might not directly address future-oriented thinking. For example, drug therapy might be used to reduce levels of hopelessness about the future: how someone thinks about the future is the intended outcome, but the process by which that is brought about does not explicitly involve a focus on prospection. In learned optimism (Seligman, 2006), discussed in Chapter 3, people learn to attribute positive events to internal and stable causes, whereas negative events are explained by external, transient causes that are specific to the event. A major goal of the programme is to develop optimism about the future through learning this particular way of explaining events that have already happened. On the other hand, the actual content of the intervention might explicitly be about how someone thinks about the future, with an end point aimed at bringing about a somewhat different outcome. For example, teaching goal-setting and planning skills can be focused on reducing depression.

The present chapter discusses both types of approach, although, of course, sometimes the aim of an intervention and what the intervention consists of will coincide. Discussion will first cover some of the ways that prospection is addressed in clinical practice before moving onto more targeted future-oriented approaches, mainly, but not exclusively, within the non-clinical realm. Finally, one particular kind of future difficulty—lack of specificity—that has been talked about at various points throughout the book (see especially Chapter 6 but also Chapters 7 and 8) will be discussed.

Future-oriented intervention in clinical practice

It is important to make the point that, of course, many existing clinical approaches do include an element of focus on future-oriented thoughts. But it would be equally true to say that this attention to how people see the future does not feature large in many of them. Identifying the clients' goals for treatment is standard in most, if not all, therapies, simply reflecting the fact that people seek therapy because they want something in the future to be different than it is currently. Typically, clients' goals are about relief of troubling experiences, such as wanting to feel less anxious, or less depressed. These desires for symptom relief will often be linked to more positive life goals, like then being able to take one's grandchildren to the park without fear of having a panic attack, or getting back to work, or being able to enjoy going out with friends. The question is whether there is any more of a focus on the future than that within existing, well-established therapies.

Roepke and Seligman (2015) have pointed out that psychoanalysis and behavioural approaches were both, in their own ways, underpinned by a belief in how current experience was shaped by the past (early experiences in the former and learning history in the latter). Beck's cognitive triad (Beck, 1976)—a negative view of the self, the world, and the future—does clearly have an important place for prospection, but it is less clear whether the practice of cognitive behavioural therapy (CBT) has a very strong, explicit emphasis on how someone sees their future. That is not to say that there is none. By eliciting clients' automatic thoughts, CBT therapists will often bring out thoughts about the future, for example, someone's thoughts about being so unattractive that no one will ever want to be with them. As Roepke and Seligman (2015) point out, such thoughts are often in an 'if–then' form, for example, 'if I just try to be myself then people will find me unlovable' or 'if I manage to walk to the local shops by myself I will just freeze and I won't be able to get back home'. Such thoughts can be challenged by testing them out with behavioural experiments (Bennett-Levy et al., 2004), where the client is encouraged to examine the evidence for his or her beliefs by enacting relevant behaviour and seeing what happens (e.g. being oneself or walking to the local shops alone). CBT for depression often starts out with activity scheduling, where clients identify and schedule taking part in future activities that will convey a sense of mastery or provide pleasure. Simulation of future experiences can also be used to elicit thoughts and feelings likely to arise in future situations in order to inoculate the client against them and prevent relapse. For example, in the latter sessions of CBT for suicidal behaviour, someone is encouraged to visualize themselves in a future situation where they begin to feel suicidal, and then to envisage in detail putting into place the coping skills and alternative thoughts and behaviours that they have learned during therapy (Wenzel, Brown, & Beck, 2009).

The role of prospection within a clinical context has been given more prominence in a number of developments intended to give future-directed thinking a more central role. Jennice Vilhauer, in recognizing the centrality of prospection in emotional well-being, developed future-directed therapy (FDT; Vilhauer, 2014) as a treatment for depression. The intervention is built from a broadly CBT foundation, but differs from traditional CBT in the emphasis on clients learning to think about the future in a way that will help them to thrive in life. Sessions include educating participants about the link between thoughts and what happens in the future, identifying valued futures, fostering beliefs in being able to bring about a desired future, goal setting, and dealing with obstacles, as well as mindfulness meditation. The intervention has been evaluated in a non-randomized controlled trial where participants who opted for FDT received 20 group sessions over a ten-week period (Vilhauer et al., 2012). The FDT group was compared with a group who received treatment as usual (TAU), cognitive-based group psychotherapy, for the same period of time. Those taking part in the FDT groups showed significantly reduced depression symptoms and improved self-reported quality of life pre- to post-treatment. The comparison group showed weaker or non-significant effects, not always significantly weaker than the FDT group, although the sample was small and the study power was limited. A second study with a similar design showed no increased benefit of FDT for depression and hopelessness, but those receiving FDT did show significantly greater improvement on quality of life ratings (Vilhauer et al., 2013).

In the Netherlands, Wessel van Beek and colleagues (van Beek, Kerkhof, & Beekman, 2009) developed a future-oriented group treatment specifically targeting hopelessness and suicidality in patients who were experiencing suicidal thoughts. Over the course of ten, 90-minute sessions, those attending the groups learn to identify goals and develop problem solving skills alongside standard CBT components and learning about suicidal thoughts. Initial evaluation against a treatment-as-usual group indicated that those taking part in the future-oriented intervention showed greater reduction in depression, although their scores on self-reported suicidal thoughts after treatment and at follow-up were comparable to those of the treatment-as-usual group (van Beek, 2013). Finally, Roepke and Seligman (2015) have suggested a number of techniques and approaches that could be incorporated into CBT, such as using imagery to visualize steps towards rewarding future outcomes and using a positive version of the downward arrow technique where clients are 'interrogated' to get to the bottom of what it is about a positive future scenario they have described that they find so rewarding. Discovering clients' core purpose and values can help them to identify future valued directions and provide the motivation to pursue specific goals in relation to those directions.

Alongside the clinical tradition there have been a number of attempts at developing methods for helping people to think about their futures in a less negative and more positive way, and the remainder of the chapter will discuss those attempts.

Possible selves

We are able to think about the likelihood of possible future events (Chapter 2) and how we might feel in response to those events (Chapter 4), but we also have the ability to entertain thoughts of what we will be like as persons in the future. Clearly, this idea of future selves is not a new idea discovered by psychologists, but it was brought to prominence by Markus and Nurius (1986) who introduced the term 'possible selves' into the psychological literature, and also developed a way of measuring these imagined future selves. For Markus and Nurius (1986) possible selves were conceptions of ourselves in future states of being, with a strong emphasis on who we would like, and not like, to be. As Erikson (2007) later pointed out, this is not simply an exercise in abstract imagination. The concept of a possible future self is one in which the person contemplates this future self in a personally involved way. To put it another way, it is an autobiographical rather than a script-like or semantic representation.

Of particular interest are desired and undesired possible selves, usually talked about as ideal and feared selves, and these concepts have been examined in relation to well-being. Discrepancies between the actual self, the ideal self, and the feared self are seen as being related to emotional well-being. Within self-discrepancy theory (SDT; Higgins, Bond, Klein, & Strauman, 1986) two types of desired future selves are distinguishable—the ideal self, which is the person someone would really like to be for their own sake, and the ought self, which represent how someone feels they have a duty or obligation to be. Discrepancies between how someone sees themselves now and their ideal self are thought to be linked to depression-related emotions, whereas actual–ought discrepancies are linked to anxiety-related emotions (Higgins et al., 1986; Strauman, 1989). Other studies have, however, not found such clear specificity of depression to actual–ideal discrepancies but still find strong links between future selves and emotional well-being. Both depressive affect (Phillips & Silvia, 2010) and depression symptoms (Vergara-Lopez & Roberts, 2012) have been found to correlate with actual–ought as well as actual–ideal discrepancies.

Best possible self interventions

Possible selves have been used as the basis for trying to enhance well-being. The distinction between ideal and ought selves has not featured in these interventions; rather, each participant is asked to think about their own best possible self, however they define it. In an influential early study, King (2001) divided a sample of students into four groups. Participants were asked to write for 20 minutes each day for four days about a past trauma, their best possible selves (BPS), both of these (two days on trauma, two days on BPS), or their plans for the day. The BPS condition instructed participants to 'Think about your life in the future. Imagine that everything has gone as well as it possibly could. You have worked hard and succeeded at accomplishing all of your life goals. Think of this as the realization of all of your life dreams. Now, write about what you imagined.' (King, 2001, p. 801). Mood was measured before and after each 20-minute writing period and life satisfaction and self-reported optimism measured three weeks later.

Subsequent studies have used similar BPS manipulations based upon this original study by King (2001), with a number of variations. People are normally asked to do the manipulation only on one occasion (e.g. Hanssen, Peters, Vlaeyen, Meevissen, & Vancleef, 2013), but they have also been asked to repeat it once a week over four weeks (Layous, Nelson, & Lyubomirsky, 2013), or encouraged to repeat some of the exercise themselves for a short time each day over the follow-up period of the study (e.g. Meevissen, Peters, & Alberts, 2011). In some studies, specific imagery instructions are added where, at the end of writing, participants spend five minutes visualizing what they have written (e.g. Meevissen et al., 2011).

King (2001) found immediate mood differences following the writing, where those in the trauma group showed less overall mood gain (difference in PA minus NA from pre- and post-intervention) compared to the other three conditions. This comparable mood gain in the 'control' condition to that found in the BPS conditions indicated that perhaps writing about plans for one's day was not a very useful neutral condition, something that would certainly be borne out by the data on planning and well-being reviewed in Chapter 8. Studies following on from King (2001) have, therefore, modified the control condition to writing about a typical day, which is seen as more neutral than having partici- pants write about plans for their current day. Subsequent studies have also usu- ally looked at PA and NA separately, allowing identification of differential mood effects. It is a consistent finding that there are immediate increases in PA follow- ing a BPS manipulation compared to the control intervention, in the absence of any effects on NA (Hanssen et al., 2013; Meevissen et al., 2011; Peters, Flink, Boersma, Linton, 2010; Sheldon & Lyubomirsky, 2006). Interestingly, though, both Odou and Vella-Brodrick (2013) and Meevison et al. (2011) found subse- quent lowered NA when mood was measured at a later point. Odou and Vella- Brodrick (2013) found decreased NA with no significant change in PA one week after the intervention, and Meevison et al. (2011) found increases in PA both immediately and two weeks later, with only reduced NA at the later point of measurement.

As well as immediate and delayed mood, a number of other impacts have been examined. Likelihood of future personal positive events are increased, and negative events decreased following a BPS, compared to a control, intervention (Hanssen et al., 2013; Meevissen et al., 2011; Peters et al., 2010). King (2001) found that a combination of life satisfaction and optimism was higher three weeks later in those who had written about their best possible selves, even when it was combined with writing about trauma. In addition, those who wrote about BPS only or trauma only had fewer visits to the campus health centre in the five months following the study. Hanssen et al. (2013) also reported lower subjective pain ratings when participants were subjected to a cold pressor test, where they had to hold their hands in very cold water for one minute.

A stricter test of the impact of a BPS intervention is where it is compared with another active intervention as well as a control condition. Odou and Vella- Brodrick (2013) included a three good things intervention (TGT; e.g. Seligman, Steen, Park, & Petersen, 2005), where, instead of doing a five-minute BPS imagery exercise each day, people thought about three good things that had happened on that day. The TGT and BPS interventions had equivalent effects on reducing NA one week later. Sheldon and Lyubomirsky (2006) compared BPS with a popular positive psychology intervention—a gratitude exercise— where participants are asked to write about things they are grateful for and found that those in the BPS condition had greater post-intervention PA than those in the gratitude condition.

Goal-based interventions

Not surprisingly, given the extensive literature on goals and their relation- ship to well-being and mental health, there have been attempts to develop goal-based interventions. As already noted in this chapter, existing therapies almost always involve some explicit element of goal-based thinking on the part of the client. What is different about goal-based interventions is that they try to take elements from the goals literature discussed in Chapters 7 and 8, and utilize those findings to design an intervention aimed at enhancing well-being through increasing some aspect of goal-directed thinking and behaviour. In addition, the goals are about positive personal goals rather than related to relief of symptoms. Sometimes these interventions are very brief and sometimes they are lengthy and more resource-intensive, but they all have in common the idea of helping people to identify personally relevant goals and move towards those goals. Interestingly, acceptance and commitment therapy (Hayes, Luoma, Bond, Masuda, & Lillis, 2006) has a component that is similar—people are helped to identify their values and then engage in goal-directed behaviour that is consistent with those values.

Sheldon, Abad, Ferguson, Gunz, Houser-Marko et al. (2010) developed and evaluated a very brief intervention informed by self determination theory (SDT; Deci & Ryan, 2000), which was discussed in Chapter 7. SDT proposes that there are three fundamental, universal human needs–autonomy, competence, and relatedness—and that well-being consists in those needs being met (see Chapter 7). If so, then pursuing goals that meet these needs should enhance well-being to a greater degree than the pursuit of other goals that are unrelated to autonomy, competence, and relatedness. Participants in the study, who were a mix of university staff and students, were asked to identify four goals that they could pursue over the next six months. One group was asked to identify goals that would be about changing their circumstances, for example rearranging their house, changing their hairstyle, or their look, via cosmetic surgery. The other three groups were each asked to identify goals relating to one of the aspects of SDT, autonomy (making their own decisions about something that was meaningful and valuable to them), competence (feeling effective and capable, doing things they were good at), or relatedness (feeling a sense of connection to important others). Subjective well-being was measured at the outset and again after two, four, and six months. Against prediction, at the follow-up assessments there was no overall difference between the four groups in levels of well-being. It is difficult to tell if there were overall differences between time 1 and later time points because analyses focused on comparing degree of change between the different groups, but it would appear not. There was, however, an interaction with progress at the first follow-up, illustrated in Figure 10.1. Participants in the SDT conditions who reported high progress with their goals showed well-being gain and those reporting low progress showed a loss of well-being, compared to those allocated to circumstances goals, where goal progress

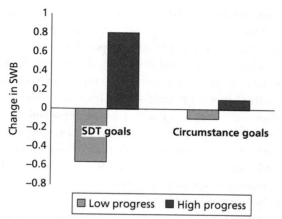

Figure 10.1 Data from Sheldon et al. (2010) showing change in well-being two months after participants had identified goals that they might work on. Self-determination (SDT) goals are compared with circumstances goals for participants who made high and low progress on the goals. Changes in well-being were in opposite directions for SDT goals, depending on progress, whereas circumstance goals showed little relationship to well-being.

Motivation and Emotion, Persistent pursuit of need-satisfying goals leads to increased happiness: A 6-month experimental longitudinal study, **34**(1), 2010, 39–48, Sheldon, K. M., et al. With permission of Springer.

made little difference. However, these effects were not replicated at four months and only weakly at six months.

So, from the Sheldon et al. (2010) study it would appear that (a) simply asking people to identify goals, no matter what they are about, has little overall effect on well-being over time and (b) that there is some, albeit quite weak, evidence for SDT-related goals having more influence on well-being, depending on whether progress is high or low. However, it is also plausible that the goals in the three SDT conditions were just bigger and more important in general than rearranging the house and getting one's hair done, and in ways that are not necessarily tied to SDT. On the other hand, it could also be argued that they were bigger and more important *because* they were related to autonomy, competence, and relatedness. The study by Sheldon did not address this issue, so it remains for future studies to try to disentangle. It is also notable that the study did not take into account any pre-existing differences in the extent to which the different types of goals mattered to people. For example, there are well-established individual differences in sociotropy and autonomy (Clark, Steer, Beck, & Ross, 1995), which reflect the value that individuals place on social connectedness and independent, self-directed activity, factors that would influence how good a fit the different interventions were for different participants.

The Sheldon et al. (2010) study is an example of a minimal intervention— participants were simply asked to identify goals that they could work on. There was no further structured input into either reminders to work on the goals or helping them to think how they would achieve them, and even, it would appear, no strong suggestion to participants that it was important that they should continue to work on their goals. Instructions were unusually relaxed in telling participants that it was up to them whether they followed through with the exercise, and in being very explicit that there was no guarantee of their quality of life being improved. It is possible that people need more structured input in order to derive benefit from goal interventions.

Sergeant and Mongrain (2014) conducted an internet-based study in which they recruited a large sample ($N = 466$) of people who were interested in becoming happier, around half of whom also reported a history of depression. These volunteers were randomly allocated either to the active intervention or a control condition. Of interest to the discussion here is that the active intervention— which they called an optimism intervention—consisted of two elements, one of which was a goals task. Participants were asked to spend 5–10 minutes a day thinking about a goal that they would like to complete in the next few days, along with steps they could take to complete the goal. This goal activity was alternated with a second activity that consisted of listing things that made their life enjoyable or worthwhile and thinking of things that helped them look on the bright side of life. The intervention phase lasted three weeks, during which participants just had to complete an activity every other day, alternating the two tasks on those days (i.e. every four days during the three-week intervention phase someone would do the goals activity). The control conditions were similarly structured, but consisted of participants (a) writing a description of the last 24 hours and (b) writing a description of the next 24 hours, including what they would do, who they would see, and what goals they had. Measures, including depressive symptoms, were taken before the intervention, post-intervention, and at one and two month follow-ups. Like the Sheldon et al. (2010) study, the main results were, on the whole, negative: there was no difference between the groups on depressive symptoms at the end of the three-week active phase or at either of the follow-ups. An effect of the active intervention was found when participants who were high in trait pessimism, who also reported having completed the exercises were examined: relative to similar participants in the control condition, this subgroup of participants in the active intervention group showed lower depression scores compared to similar participants in the control group. Some other effects were found at different time points, including a small follow-up effect on a measure of depressive dysfunctional attitudes and a small immediate effect on a measure of engagement in life, but a number of other measures showed no effects at all.

The approach adopted by Sergeant and Mongrain (2014) provides more demand on participants than that of Sheldon et al. (2010) in expecting them to engage actively in the tasks for a period of three weeks. Consistent with the emphasis on the value of planning outlined in Chapter 8, participants were also asked explicitly to think of steps to be taken towards achieving their goals. On the other hand, the goals element was diluted by having a goal-unrelated aspect in the intervention task, and also through having participants only doing the exercises for 5–10 minutes every other day. This meant that some-one complying fully with what they were asked to do would only spend 5–10 minutes every four days over a three-week period thinking about goals. A final point to note is that half of the control intervention shared some similarities to a goal planning task, where participants were asked to describe their upcom-ing day. It is not possible to say whether this played a part in the findings, but the BPS interventions reviewed earlier in this chapter moved away from that particular control condition because of the possibility of it functioning as prospection manipulation. The relatively weak findings of Sheldon et al. (2010) and Sergeant and Mongrain (2014) might also be due to participants receiving too small a 'dose' of the intervention. It is possible that goal-based interven-tions can be effective in enhancing well-being, but participants need to spend more time on the intervention and need more structured input to enable them to achieve this.

One approach at the opposite end of the intensity spectrum is hope ther-apy (Cheavens, Feldman, Gum, Michael, & Snyder, 2006). Hope therapy was discussed briefly in Chapter 5. It is devised from Snyder and colleagues' con-ceptualization of hope as being constituted of (a) setting goals, (b) develop-ing strategies to achieve those goals, and (c) having the motivation to pursue those strategies (Snyder et al., 1991). The intervention involved taking part in eight, two-hour facilitated group sessions, largely based around helping peo-ple to identify goals, think of strategies, and build and maintain motivation. In a small randomized controlled study with community volunteers, those who participated in hope therapy showed significant benefits on a number of meas-ures (anxiety, self-esteem, purpose in life, and a sense of agency), as well as a non-significant reduction in depression symptoms. Rather like the Mongrain study (Sergeant & Mongrain, 2014), which also recruited community volun-teers, the sample consisted largely of people who currently were experiencing, or previously had experienced, significant levels of psychological distress. The value of the promising results are somewhat offset by the intensity of the input required, both the time demands on participants and the fact that the group was facilitated by two advanced level doctoral clinical psychology students.

Goals and plans training

An approach that falls somewhere between the different level of interventions discussed so far is goals and plans training (GAP; MacLeod, Coates, & Hetherton, 2008). In developing GAP, our intention was to take what was known in the psychological literature about the relationship between well-being and different aspects of goals and planning, and create a package based on that knowledge. Therefore, much of what was reviewed in Chapters 7 and 8 went into GAP. The aim was also to find a balance between, on the one hand, a practically feasible level of participant demand and resource input and, on the other hand, the need to provide support and guidance to people in learning the skills of identifying and pursuing goals. Initially, GAP was devised as a five-session, facilitated group intervention but was subsequently pared down to be able to be delivered in three sessions. The three sessions were spread over a three-week period, each session lasting around 60 minutes, with each group having between five and seven participants. An outline of the sessions is shown in Table 10.1. In addition, a self-help version was also developed.

Table 10.1 Outline of the group sessions for GAP

Session 1
◆ Introductions/welcome/explanation of the sessions and manual.
◆ Explanation of key concepts (well-being, goals).
◆ Selecting and refining goals.
◆ Envisaging goals.
◆ Planning to achieve goals—what constitutes good plans and developing plans of action.
◆ Summary and homework.

Session 2 (one week later)
◆ Review of plan implementation.
◆ Putting goals in perspective.
◆ Obstacles to goal progress—identifying obstacles and solutions.
◆ Pros and cons of implementing plan steps.
◆ Summary and homework.

Session 3 (two weeks later)
◆ Review of plan implementation.
◆ Overview of material covered.
◆ Maintaining progress.
  • pros and cons of using GAP approach
  • dealing with black and white thinking
  • focusing on the path rather than the goal.

Journal of Happiness Studies, Increasing well-being through teaching goal-setting and planning skills: results of a brief intervention, Volume 9, Issue 2, 2008, 194–195, MacLeod, A. K., Coates, E., & Hetherton, J. With permission of Springer.

The initial session includes psychoeducation on goals, well-being, and their connection. Based on the literature showing characteristics of goals that are related to well-being (see Chapter 7), specific approach, rather than avoidance, goals that are self-concordant (chosen for genuine reasons of enjoyment or value) are then selected to work towards from participants' own lists of freely generated goals. Following the work of Oettingen and colleagues, successful outcomes are visualized before detailed discussion of plans and obstacles take place. Oettingen and colleagues (see Oettingen, 2012, for a summary) have shown that mental contrasting, where someone mentally contrasts the desired future with present reality, and thinks about what needs to be done to attain the goal, is associated with greater goal commitment and progress, as long as expectancy for attainment is reasonably high (mental contrasting can be counterproductive if the initial perceived likelihood of achieving the goal is too low). Importantly, for mental contrasting to be effective, the successful outcome needs to be visualized before reflecting on present reality and thinking of necessary steps and pathways. Carrying out the mental contrasting in the reverse order is likely to be demotivating and makes envisioning the future outcome more difficult. On the other hand, simply visualizing outcomes as if they have happened without then contrasting with current reality is argued to be not as effective as mental contrasting. Oettingen (2012) suggests that such pure visualization, which she calls 'indulging', reduces motivation because imagining, in some way, delivers the emotional benefits of the goal outcome being derived without the person actually having to do anything to achieve it. Based on the planning and well-being literature (see Chapter 8), specific plans of action are identified to move towards the goals, then implemented and finally evaluated. Finally, a number of elements are introduced to encourage continued use of the programme. Pros and cons of continuing to use GAP and not use GAP, similar to that used in motivational interviewing (Miller & Rollnick, 2012), help participants to evaluate the benefits of maintaining use of GAP after the programme has finished. Reiterating that progress is often partial rather than being all or nothing (c.f. *black and white thinking*, Beck, 1976) is aimed at avoiding discouragement and demotivation when people have only partial success in their steps. Consistent with the findings that progress is more strongly related than attainment is to well-being (see Chapter 7), there is an emphasis in the final session on the message that 'the path is the goal', thus helping people to focus on engagement with action steps rather than thinking about whether the goal has been attained or not. A self-help version was developed (MacLeod et al, 2008) to test whether any benefits can also be derived from a version with minimal resource input and is therefore easier to access. In both group and self-help versions, participants are given a manual to work from, but the self-help manual is more detailed, supplemented by the material that would occur in the context of group discussions.

In our initial study with a mixed university and community sample of participants (MacLeod et al., 2008), those who took part in the group version of GAP showed an increase in PA and life satisfaction, but no decrease in NA compared to a matched sample, who were not randomized to a control condition but who completed the measures at the same time points. A small community sample randomized to either self-help GAP or wait-list control, showed that GAP participants, relative to controls, showed a significant increase in PA and life satisfaction, as well as a reduction in NA. Three studies have examined the effectiveness of GAP in those with significant levels of psychological disturbance. Ferguson, Conway, Endersby, and MacLeod (2009) used a longer delivery of GAP (six weekly sessions) to accommodate the level of functioning within a group of legally detained psychiatric patients, all of whom had a long history of psychotic illness. In a simple pre-post design, participants showed reduced depression, NA, negative symptoms, and self-reported hopelessness. Levels of positive future-thinking, as assessed by the Future-thinking Task (MacLeod, Rose, & Williams, 1993, see Chapter 2) were also significantly higher post-GAP. All of these variables remained different from pre-intervention levels after a two-month follow-up, with the exception of depression, which was reduced to a trend ($p = .06$). Interestingly, PA showed no difference at any of the time points. The improvement in positive future-thinking reported in this study provides an interesting contrast with findings reported by Andersson, Sarkohi, Karlsson, Bjärehed, and Hesser (2013) using CBT. In comparing two forms of internet-delivered CBT, Andersson et al. (2013) found that after receiving either form of treatment, participants showed significantly reduced negative future-thinking, assessed by the Future-thinking Task, with neither group showing improvement in positive future-thinking. These findings are in line with the idea that CBT targets negative aspects of experience, which would be consistent with its symptom focused rationale, but does not necessarily improve positive aspects of experience, including future-directed thinking.

Testing the self-help version of GAP in those with a lower starting point in levels of well-being, Helen Coote and I (Coote & MacLeod, 2012) recruited members of a depression self-help charity. These participants typically had long histories of depression with multiple episodes, and all were currently experiencing significant levels of depressive symptoms. Participants were allocated initially either to self-help GAP or to a wait-list control condition, with this latter group crossing over to receive GAP after they had acted as controls for the post-gap scores of the group initially allocated to GAP. Compared to the wait-list control group, GAP was associated with significantly reduced NA, and trends towards reduced depression, increased life satisfaction, and increased PA. Both groups provided five-week follow-up data after completing GAP, obviously without a follow-up control because of the crossover design, but the data still indicate the stability of any changes that took place from pre-to post-GAP. As Figure 10.2 shows, gains from pre- to post-intervention were all maintained at five-week follow-up. Finally, Farquharson and MacLeod (2014) used the same randomized, crossover design, this time in a sample of outpatients with long-term mental health issues (main diagnoses being schizophrenia, bipolar disorder, and mood disorder). Those receiving GAP showed very similar positive effects as other studies, with a particularly strong effect on life satisfaction, and, again, effects were maintained at a two-month follow-up in the whole group.

Dubé, Lapierre, Bouffard, and Alain (2007) adopted a very similar approach in developing a goals and planning programme specifically aimed at helping people to adjust to retirement. The intervention was resource demanding, involving participating in at least ten, two-hour weekly group meetings. Each group had

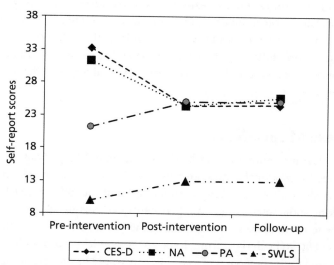

Figure 10.2 Changes in depression (CES-D), negative affect (NA), positive affect (PA) and life satisfaction (SWLS) in depressed participants receiving GAP at pre-intervention, post-intervention and five-week follow-up. Depression and NA reduced significantly and PA and life satisfaction increased significantly from pre to post, and all changes were maintained at follow-up.

Data from Coote, H. M. J., MacLeod, A. K, *Clinical Psychology & Psychotherapy* **4** (1), 15–24. Copyright © 2012 by John Wiley Sons, Inc. with permission of John Wiley & Sons, Inc.

between seven and ten participants. Sessions involved identifying goals, selecting goals to work on, planning, anticipating obstacles and how to deal with them, as well as time spent pursuing goals and evaluating progress. In a volunteer sample of early retirees, a range of measures including happiness and the Ryff Psychological Well-being scale (PWB; Ryff, 1989) were completed before the intervention, post-intervention, and again six months later. A matched group, who were recruited as controls rather than randomized, completed the measures over the same time periods as the intervention group to provide a set of comparison scores. Self-reported happiness was higher and distress lower in the intervention group compared to the control participants at the end of the programme. In addition, purpose in life from the PWB (Ryff, 1989) was higher in the intervention group. At six months' follow-up, happiness and distress continued to show clear differences between the groups. The goal planning group were also higher on most of the PWB dimensions at follow-up, most notably purpose in life, and environmental mastery, two of the dimensions that might have been expected to benefit most from an intervention that was about helping people to identify meaningful goals and to plan how to achieve them.

Lapierre, Dubé, Bouffard, and Alain (2007) further analysed a subset of participants in the study who had expressed suicidal ideation on one of the self-report measures. The numbers were very small (around ten in each group), but those in the intervention group showed significantly higher hope and lower depression scores following the intervention and at follow-up, although there were many more measures taken that were non-significantly different between the groups.

The case of specificity

There is clear indication that a lack of specificity in thinking about the future is implicated in emotional distress and disorder. Those with a range of emotional disorders show lower specificity of thinking about the future (see Chapter 6). In thinking about intervention, two pertinent questions are whether people can be made to think more specifically about the future and, if so, are there well-being benefits to be derived from doing so? A parallel for promoting thinking about feared future outcomes in a specific way would be the sort of exposure to traumatic memories in those experiencing distress from traumatic past events, where people are encouraged to think about the past event in a detailed, specific way, including, sensory and emotional details experienced at the time (e.g. Leahy, Holland, & McGinn, 2011). Many anxiety treatments share this emphasis on imaginal exposure to a specific representation of the feared object or outcome.

In the case of positive events, there may well be mood benefits to enhancing the specificity of positive future-thinking. Quoidbach, Wood, and Hansenne (2009) asked a group of volunteers each day, for 14 consecutive days, to think about positive, negative, or neutral events that they might experience the following day. Instructions emphasized that events thought of had to be specific and, to that end, participants were asked to write down each event, including detailed phenomenal characteristics, such as people, places, emotions experienced, and sensory details. Participants in each of these three groups completed measures of happiness and anxiety at the start and end of the study, which were compared with responses of a control group who simply completed the same measures on two occasions separated by 14 days. Those who were asked to think about positive events the following day for 14 days showed higher levels of happiness at the end of the study, compared to the other three groups who showed no significant change.

From the Quoidbach et al. (2009) study it would appear that it is the valence of what is thought about rather than thinking of specific events per se that is beneficial for well-being. Certainly, it is encouraging to be able to show that happiness can be manipulated in this way. The study, however, does not completely address the issue of specificity because, although specific events were encouraged, there was no check on whether people were actually thinking of specific events. It might be the case that asking people to be specific is not enough; rather, they need to utilize a procedure or technique that enables them to be specific in their thinking. The specificity induction of Madore, Gaesser, and Schacter (2014) discussed in Chapter 6 is a good example of a method that appears reliably to make people more specific in how they think about future events. To recap, participants watch a video of a routine domestic scene, which is followed by guided recall emphasizing retrieval of details of what was watched. Those who take part in the induction, compared to those undergoing a control manipulation, provide more internal details of the future events they describe, that is, they are more specific (Madore et al., 2014). Furthermore, Madore and Schacter (2014) have shown that those who received the specificity induction showed superior performance on problem solving; compared to a group who received a control procedure, participants receiving the specificity induction provided more relevant means that would lead to problems being solved, both on the Means End Problem Solving Task (MEPS; Platt & Spivack, 1975) and on a list of relevant, common problems (e.g. how to exercise more, how to spend more time with family). Madore and Schacter (2014) argue that, consistent with the earlier suggestion of Williams, Ellis, Tyers, Healy, Rose et al. (1996), the sort of episodic knowledge prompted by the induction enhances problem solving because episodic knowledge is utilized in personal problem solving.

To take this argument one step further would be to show that well-being benefits can be obtained from enhancing specific, episodic thinking. Jing, Madore, and Schacter (2016) addressed this exact issue. Participants (students) first generated a list of worrisome events that might happen to them within the next five years and rated them for level of worry, likelihood of good and bad outcomes, and difficulty of coping with a bad outcome. In later sessions, they received the specificity induction or a control task, followed by two tasks: the MEPS where they had to simulate a good outcome (solution) to the worried-about problem, and a reappraisal task where they had to imagine the negative outcome happening and then reinterpret it so that it became less negative to them, describing in detail their thoughts, feelings, and actions. As before, those in the specificity induction condition provided more internal details on the MEPS. They also provided more internal details in the reappraisal task. The effects of the specificity induction on internal details were also accompanied by greater reductions in worry and bad outcome likelihood ratings, and higher confidence in coping with a bad outcome. A second study replicated these effects and additionally showed a greater impact on affect in the specificity induction group.

It would appear that a prior procedure that encourages overall specificity of thinking subsequently produces more specific, detailed description when people are asked to think about steps to solve, or ways to reappraise, worrisome problems. Furthermore, these effects are associated with reduced worry and negative affect, lower pessimism, and higher optimism, as well as greater perceived ability to cope in the event of there being a bad outcome in relation to the worry. Interestingly, there was also some evidence of differential effects on the two tasks, with the impact of the specificity induction on the MEPS being mainly on enhancing belief in the likelihood of a good outcome (problem solved), whereas on the reappraisal task it appeared to exert more of an influence on minimizing the perceived impact of a bad outcome, which is exactly what a problem solving task and a reappraisal task, respectively, might be expected to show.

Summary and conclusion

A variety of methods have been used to change prospection. These methods either identify changes in future-thinking as an outcome, or use an intervention that targets how people think about the future in order to influence some other outcome, such as depression or affect. In some cases, both process and outcome are oriented around prospection. Existing clinical approaches do obviously attend to how people think about the future in what they routinely do, but it is not the main focus of therapy and neither is it particularly informed by the general literature on future-directed thinking. There has been some development of specifically future-focused interventions, but these are at the early stages and will need further evaluation. More attention has been paid in the non-clinical literature to how changing future-directed thinking affects mood. Thinking about one's best possible self has immediate and short-term effects, although whether there are more lasting effects is unknown. Interventions designed to foster goal-directed thinking and action have shown some effects on mood, but where these interventions are very minimal the effects are less than compelling. More time-intensive goal-based interventions have shown promising results, although they could usefully be compared with active control conditions, but the value of these results are rather offset by the resource cost and the demand on participants' commitment and time. There is further work to be done in finding the right balance between cost and effectiveness. Finally, the specificity induction was highlighted as a promising intervention, worthy of further investigation, due to its remedial effects on an underlying deficit (lack of specificity) that has been found in a number of mood and anxiety disorders and some initial, promising findings relating to well-being related outcomes.

References

Andersson, G., Sarkohi, A., Karlsson, J., Bjärehed, J., & Hesser, H. (2013). Effects of two forms of internet-delivered cognitive behaviour therapy for depression on future thinking. *Cognitive Therapy and Research*, 37(1), 29–34. http://doi.org/10.1007/s10608-012-9442-y

Beck, A. T. (1976). *Cognitive therapy and the emotional disorders*. Madison, CT: International Universities Press.

Bennett-Levy, J., Butler, G., Fennell, M., Hackmann, A., Mueller, M., Westbrook, D., & Rouf, K. (2004). *Oxford guide to behavioural experiments in cognitive therapy*. Oxford: Oxford University Press.

Cheavens, J. S., Feldman, D. B., Gum, A., Michael, S. T., & Snyder, C. R. (2006). Hope therapy in a community sample: A pilot investigation. *Social Indicators Research*, 77(1), 61–78. http://doi.org/10.1007/s11205-005-5553-0

Clark, D. A., Steer, R. A., Beck, A. T., & Ross, L. (1995). Psychometric characteristics of revised sociotrophy and autonomy scales in college students. *Behaviour Research and Therapy*, 33(3), 325–334. http://doi.org/10.1016/0005-7967(94)00074-T

Coote, H. M. J. & MacLeod, A. K. (2012). A self-help, positive goal-focused intervention to increase well-being in people with depression. *Clinical Psychology & Psychotherapy*, 19(4), 305–315. http://doi.org/10.1002/cpp.1797

Deci, E. L. & Ryan, R. M. (2000). The 'what' and 'why' of goal pursuits: Human needs and the self-determination of behavior. *Psychological Inquiry*, 11(4), 227–268. http://doi.org/10.1207/S15327965PLI1104_01

Dubé, M., Lapierre, S., Bouffard, L., & Alain, M. (2007). Impact of a personal goals management program on the subjective well-being of young retirees. *Revue Européenne de Psychologie Appliquée/European Review of Applied Psychology*, **57**(3), 183–192. http://doi.org/10.1016/j.erap.2005.04.004

Erikson, M. G. (2007). The meaning of the future: Toward a more specific definition of possible selves. *Review of General Psychology*, **11**(4), 348–358. http://doi.org/10.1037/1089-2680.11.4.348

Farquharson, L. & MacLeod, A. K. (2014). A brief goal-setting and planning intervention to improve well-being for people with psychiatric disorders. *Psychotherapy and Psychosomatics*, **83**(2), 122–124. http://doi.org/10.1159/000356332

Ferguson, G., Conway, C., Endersby, L., & MacLeod, A. (2009). Increasing subjective well-being in long-term forensic rehabilitation: Evaluation of well-being therapy. *Journal of Forensic Psychiatry & Psychology*, **20**(6), 906–918. http://doi.org/10.1080/14789940903174121

Hanssen, M. M., Peters, M. L., Vlaeyen, J. W. S., Meevissen, Y. M. C., & Vancleef, L. M. G. (2013). Optimism lowers pain: Evidence of the causal status and underlying mechanisms: *Pain*, **154**(1), 53–58. http://doi.org/10.1016/j.pain.2012.08.006

Hayes, S. C., Luoma, J. B., Bond, F. W., Masuda, A., & Lillis, J. (2006). Acceptance and commitment therapy: Model, processes and outcomes. *Behaviour Research and Therapy*, **44**(1), 1–25. http://doi.org/10.1016/j.brat.2005.06.006

Higgins, E. T., Bond, R. N., Klein, R., & Strauman, T. (1986). Self-discrepancies and emotional vulnerability: how magnitude, accessibility, and type of discrepancy influence affect. *Journal of Personality and Social Psychology*, **51**(1), 5. http://doi.org/10.1037/0022-3514.51.1.5

Jing, H. G., Madore, K. P., & Schacter, D. L. (2016). Worrying about the future: An episodic specificity induction impacts problem solving, reappraisal, and well-being. *Journal of Experimental Psychology: General*, **145**(4), 402–418. http://doi.org/10.1037/xge0000142

King, L. A. (2001). The health benefits of writing about life goals. *Personality and Social Psychology Bulletin*, **27**(7), 798–807. http://doi.org/10.1177/0146167201277003

Lapierre, S., Dubé, M., Bouffard, L., & Alain, M. (2007). Addressing suicidal ideations through the realization of meaningful personal goals. *Crisis*, **28**(1), 16–25. http://doi.org/10.1027/0227-5910.28.1.16

Layous, K., Nelson, K. S., & Lyubomirsky, S. (2013). What is the optimal way to deliver a positive activity intervention? The case of writing about one's best possible selves. *Journal of Happiness Studies*, **14**(2), 635–654. http://doi.org/10.1007/s10902-012-9346-2

Leahy, R. L., Holland, S. J. F., & McGinn, L. K. (2011). *Treatment plans and interventions for depression and anxiety disorders* (2nd edition). New York: Guilford Press.

MacLeod, A. K., Coates, E., & Hetherton, J. (2008). Increasing well-being through teaching goal-setting and planning skills: Results of a brief intervention. *Journal of Happiness Studies*, **9**(2), 185–196. http://doi.org/10.1007/s10902-007-9057-2

MacLeod, A. K., Rose, G. S., & Williams, J. M. G. (1993). Components of hopelessness about the future in parasuicide. *Cognitive Therapy and Research*, **17**(5), 441–455. http://doi.org/10.1007/BF01173056

Madore, K. P., Gaesser, B., & Schacter, D. L. (2014). Constructive episodic simulation: Dissociable effects of a specificity induction on remembering, imagining, and describing in young and older adults. *Journal of Experimental Psychology: Learning, Memory, and Cognition*, **40**(3), 609–622. http://doi.org/10.1037/a0034885

Madore, K. P. & Schacter, D. L. (2014). An episodic specificity induction enhances means-end problem solving in young and older adults. *Psychology and Aging*, **29**(4), 913–924. http://doi.org/10.1037/a0038209

Markus, H. & Nurius, P. (1986). Possible selves. *American Psychologist*, **41**(9), 954–969. http://doi.org/10.1037/0003-066X.41.9.954

Meevissen, Y. M. C., Peters, M. L., & Alberts, H. J. E. M. (2011). Become more optimistic by imagining a best possible self: Effects of a two week intervention. *Journal of Behavior Therapy and Experimental Psychiatry*, **42**(3), 371–378. http://doi.org/10.1016/j.jbtep.2011.02.012

Miller, W. R. & Rollnick, S. (2012). *Motivational interviewing: Helping people change* (3rd edition). New York: Guilford Press.

Odou, N. & Vella-Brodrick, D. A. (2013). The efficacy of positive psychology interventions to increase well-being and the role of mental imagery ability. *Social Indicators Research*, **110**(1), 111–129. http://doi.org/10.1007/s11205-011-9919-1

Oettingen, G. (2012). Future thought and behaviour change. *European Review of Social Psychology*, **23**(1), 1–63. http://doi.org/10.1080/10463283.2011.643698

Peters, M. L., Flink, I. K., Boersma, K., & Linton, S. J. (2010). Manipulating optimism: Can imagining a best possible self be used to increase positive future expectancies? *The Journal of Positive Psychology*, **5**(3), 204–211. http://doi.org/10.1080/17439761003790963

Phillips, A. G. & Silvia, P. J. (2010). Individual differences in self-discrepancies and emotional experience: Do distinct discrepancies predict distinct emotions? *Personality and Individual Differences*, **49**(2), 148–151. http://doi.org/10.1016/j.paid.2010.03.010

Platt, J. J. & Spivack, G. (1975). *The Means End Problem Solving Procedure manual*. Philadelphia, PA: Hahnemann University Press.

Quoidbach, J., Wood, A. M., & Hansenne, M. (2009). Back to the future: The effect of daily practice of mental time travel into the future on happiness and anxiety. *The Journal of Positive Psychology*, **4**(5), 349–355. http://doi.org/10.1080/17439760902992365

Roepke, A. M. & Seligman, M. E. P. (2015). Depression and prospection. *British Journal of Clinical Psychology*, **55**(1), 23–48. http://doi.org/10.1111/bjc.12087

Ryff, C. D. (1989). Happiness is everything, or is it? Explorations on the meaning of psychological well-being. *Journal of Personality and Social Psychology*, **57**(6), 1069–1081. http://doi.org/10.1037/0022-3514.57.6.1069

Seligman, M. E. P. (2006). *Learned optimism: How to change your mind and your life* (Reprint edition). New York: Vintage Books, USA.

Seligman, M. E. P., Steen, T. A., Park, N., & Peterson, C. (2005). Positive psychology progress: Empirical validation of interventions. *American Psychologist*, **60**(5), 410–421. http://doi.org/10.1037/0003-066X.60.5.410

Sergeant, S. & Mongrain, M. (2014). An online optimism intervention reduces depression in pessimistic individuals. *Journal of Consulting and Clinical Psychology*, **82**(2), 263–274. http://doi.org/10.1037/a0035536

Sheldon, K. M., Abad, N., Ferguson, Y., Gunz, A., Houser-Marko, L., Nichols, C. P., & Lyubomirsky, S. (2010). Persistent pursuit of need-satisfying goals leads to increased happiness: A 6-month experimental longitudinal study. *Motivation and Emotion*, **34**(1), 39–48. http://doi.org/10.1007/s11031-009-9153-1

Sheldon, K. M. & Lyubomirsky, S. (2006). How to increase and sustain positive emotion: The effects of expressing gratitude and visualizing best possible selves. *The Journal of Positive Psychology*, 1(2), 73–82. http://doi.org/10.1080/17439760500510676

Snyder, C. R., Harris, C., Anderson, J. R., Holleran, S. A., Irving, L. M., Sigmon, S. T., Yoshinobu, L., Gibb, J., Langelle, C., & Harney, P. (1991). The will and the ways: development and validation of an individual-differences measure of hope. *Journal of Personality and Social Psychology*, 60(4), 570. http://doi.org/10.1037/0022-3514.60.4.570

Strauman, T. J. (1989). Self-discrepancies in clinical depression and social phobia: Cognitive structures that underlie emotional disorders? *Journal of Abnormal Psychology*, 98(1), 14. http://doi.org/10.1037/0021-843X.98.1.14

van Beek, W. (2013). *Future thinking in suicidal patients: Development and evaluation of a future oriented group training in a randomized controlled trial (Unpublished doctoral dissertation)*. Amsterdam: Vrije Universiteit, Amsterdam, the Netherlands.

van Beek, W., Kerkhof, A., & Beekman, A. (2009). Future oriented group training for suicidal patients: A randomized clinical trial. *BMC Psychiatry*, 9. http://doi.org/10.1186/1471-244X-9-65

Vergara-Lopez, C. & Roberts, J. E. (2012). Self-discrepancies among individuals with a history of depression: The role of feared self-guides. *Cognitive Therapy and Research*, 36(6), 847–853. http://doi.org/10.1007/s10608-011-9433-4

Vilhauer, J. S. (2014). *Think forward to thrive: How to use the mind's power to transcend your past and transform your future*. Novato, CA: New World Library.

Vilhauer, J. S., Cortes, J., Moali, N., Chung, S., Mirocha, J., & Ishak, W. W. (2013). Improving quality of life for patients with major depressive disorder by increasing hope and positive expectations with future directed therapy (FDT). *Innovations in Clinical Neuroscience*, 10(3), 12–22.

Vilhauer, J. S., Young, S., Kealoha, C., Borrmann, J., Ishak, W. W., Rapaport, M. H., Hartoonian, N., & Mirocha, J. (2012). Treating major depression by creating positive expectations for the future: A pilot study for the effectiveness of future-directed therapy (FDT) on symptom severity and quality of life: Treating MDD with Future-directed Therapy. *CNS Neuroscience & Therapeutics*, 18(2), 102–109. http://doi.org/10.1111/j.1755-5949.2011.00235.x

Wenzel, A., Brown, G. K., & Beck, A. T. (2009). *Cognitive therapy for suicidal patients: Scientific and clinical applications*. Washington, DC: American Psychological Association.

Williams, J. M. G., Ellis, N. C., Tyers, C., Healy, H., Rose, G., & MacLeod, A. K. (1996). The specificity of autobiographical memory and imageability of the future. *Memory & Cognition*, 24(1), 116–125. http://doi.org/10.3758/BF03197278

Chapter 11

Prospection, well-being, and mental health

Précis

Human beings are, by nature, forward-looking. We are built to be tuned to the future. Of course, attending to the immediate present is a large part of what we do, but much of our present activity is connected to a trajectory running into the future. The past is obviously important, but the fact that the future is seen as more important, as well as more positive, further points to our generally forward-looking nature. The sophisticated ability that humans possess to think prospectively has been important in our evolutionary progress, just as the, albeit more restricted, future-thinking ability possessed by other species has been important in their adaptation. The theme of this book has been how the way we think about the future connects to our emotional well-being.

I began by suggesting in Chapter 1 two main ways that future-thinking can go wrong for well-being and mental health: a preponderance of negative thoughts and feelings, or an absence of positive thoughts and feelings. Evidence has been presented (Chapter 2) for such a two-system view, with absence of positive future thoughts linked to depression, hopelessness, suicidality, and (low) positive affect, whereas the presence of negative thoughts is linked to anxiety, worry, and negative affect. The two systems are, to a large degree, independent of each other. In other words, it is possible to lack positive future thoughts without having an excess of negative future thoughts, and vice versa. Various cognitive processes, involving memory, simulation, and imagery, underlie the ability to think about positive and negative future events, and these processes are involved in both a preponderance of negative thoughts and absence of positive thoughts.

Optimism and pessimism (Chapter 3) are words that are commonly used to describe ways of thinking about the future. They may be independent rather than opposite ends of a continuum, but they are often used as antonyms. It is hard to draw broad conclusions about optimism and pessimism because even within psychological research they refer to a range of very different kinds of responses which do not always converge on similar results or correlate with each other. There is evidence of a general tendency towards optimism, although this is something of a misnomer because most of the findings refer to low beliefs in the likelihood of negative events. The phenomenon might more accurately be called the *lack-of-pessimism-bias*, although that does not sound like a term that will catch on any time soon! I also argued in Chapter 3 that bias is an overused term and should only be employed where there are comparisons with an objective benchmark. On a range of different measures of future outlook, those who are depressed differ consistently from non-depressed participants. Whether this difference constitutes a negative bias or the absence of a common positive bias is not clear because different measures lead to different conclusions about that question. Bias is also different from accuracy. There is little evidence of greater accuracy in those who are depressed.

Prediction need not only describe future events—we also predict and anticipate how we are going to feel in the future (Chapter 4). Taking account of how we would feel if an event occurred begins to get at the value element of future outcomes, consistent with the longstanding emphasis on both expectancy (event prediction) and value in understanding motivation. It is also worth bearing in mind that the value of future events may not reside only in their associated feeling states, although they do represent an obvious element of what makes future outcomes desirable or undesirable. There is evidence of a general impact bias—thinking that positive events will make us happier, and negative events unhappier than they actually will—although it is equally clear that this has been overstated. Those who are depressed or dysphoric, compared to those who are not, do predict lower positive feelings in response to future positive situations. There is less evidence of expecting to feel worse in future negative situations, but few studies have examined this phenomenon, and anxiety would seem to be a more obvious source of higher prediction of negative feelings. The data on how people with depression do actually respond emotionally to positive and negative events when they do happen is very mixed, with quite different results from experimental and naturalistic studies: experimental studies suggest general dampening of response to positive and negative stimuli whereas naturalistic studies have shown a *greater* emotional response to positive events, especially in reducing negative affect. A small number of studies have tried to measure and compare predicted feeling and actual feeling in relation to mood, the results of which have shown dysphoric participants to be positively biased, negatively biased, and both positively and negatively biased relative to control groups. Clearly, more work is needed!

In addition to predicting how we will feel in situations, we experience feelings in the here-and-now when contemplating future situations (Chapter 5). Indeed, those feelings might constitute an important basis for predicting how we are likely to feel in those situations in the future, and can be used to guide behaviour. Fear and hope are the two main feeling states that arise when contemplating future outcomes, with an excess of fear linked to anxiety and a lack of hope to depression and suicidality. Such anticipatory feelings are distinct not only from predicted feelings but also from feelings experienced when events arise. Both predicting and pre-experiencing negative feelings when thinking about a future outcome easily drives avoidance behaviour, which is fundamental to the maintenance of anxiety and a key target of treatment. Avoidance of the feelings themselves, not just the situations that might provoke them, have increasingly been seen as a key element of anxiety (and other) disorders, although it has proven to be difficult to measure. Lack of positive anticipatory feelings—a failure to experience a positive spark of feeling in the here-and-now when contemplating the future—is fundamental to depression. Anticipatory emotions are elusive and difficult to assess, and perhaps for that reason have been little studied, but it is likely that they play a fundamental role in emotional disorders. More work needs to be carried out in this area, especially in developing more direct measures, such as observation and coding of facial expressions.

We are only able to think about the future because we are able to remember the past (Chapter 6). The connection between memory and prospection is shown by the strong similarities in problems remembering the past and problems thinking about the future. A lack of specificity for both memory and the future characterizes a range of clinical problems, most notably depression and suicidality. Anxiety, with the exception of trauma, does not link to lack of specificity. Memories for specific past episodes are important for future-thinking, not via simple retrieval, but through a constructive process of piecing elements from past episodes together to enable thinking about novel future episodes. Semantic memory is involved, too, in scaffolding the construction of specific future episodes, understandably so, because the future is just much more unknown, and therefore abstract, than the past. There are interesting questions to be explored about the extent to which pre-experiencing future events is like re-experiencing past ones. Episodic detail is important for re-experiencing and so is likely also to be so for pre-experiencing. The lack of future episodic detail in those who are depressed will contribute to their inability to experience feeling in the here-and-now, and reduce motivation to engage in behaviour that might lead to rewarding experiences.

Goals and plans (Chapters 7 and 8) represent fundamental aspects of prospection. Goals represent desired future outcomes that someone thinks are likely, or at least possible, and is prepared to expend effort in reaching. Plans represent the routes by which goals are to be achieved. Being able to imagine positive outcomes such as goals being achieved is mood enhancing (see also Chapter 10), but simulating steps to be taken towards the goal (i.e. planning) is important both for achieving goals and conveying a sense that they will be achieved. Very specific plans linked to environmental cues (implementation intentions) make discrete behaviours more likely to be enacted, which can be part of an overall plan towards achieving a goal. Having goals is important, but progress appears to matter more than actual attainment for well-being, as do goals that are about approaching a new, positive outcome rather than avoiding something that is unwanted. The evidence is somewhat mixed, but points to anxiety primarily being associated with avoidance goals and depression with (low) approach goals, even more so when deeper levels of underlying motivation are considered. Pursuing goals because of value or enjoyment rather than obligation or guilt is important, and goals that are about wider concerns (social connection or welfare of others) appear to be linked to well-being more so than do goals that are about fame and, especially, money, although questions of causality still need to be addressed. Having goals that are about feeling states is, understandably, more common in those who are very low in well-being, but the idea that happiness is a distinctively unhelpful goal to have is better interpreted as indicating that a preoccupation with happiness (as with any goal) is associated with low well-being. If goals are not progressing, being able to disengage from them and connect with other goals is valuable, but imbuing these original goals with a unique power to make life worthwhile and oneself happy interferes with being able to disengage and engage with new goals. Those who are suicidal appear to be particularly stuck in a pattern of valuing goals that are seen as unlikely to come about, but at the same time finding it difficult to disengage from them (painful engagement).

The question of whether it is good to be future-minded, as opposed to present- or past-minded was addressed in Chapter 9. Measures of temporal orientation are sometimes limited by being designed for a specific population, or having a very particular concept of future (or past or present) orientation in mind. Evidence does point to a general propensity to be past- rather than present- or future-oriented as linked to low well-being. Chapter 9 also discussed mindfulness because of the apparent challenge for future-mindedness of advocating a present moment focus. Mindfulness is widely used as a treatment for mental health difficulties, most clearly developed in relation to depression. The challenge of mindfulness to future-orientedness only exists if a present moment focus is interpreted as meaning a focus on the immediate sensory input of the moment (temporal present focus); if, instead, the view is adopted that everything, including thoughts of the future and the past, is experienced in the present moment (experienced present), and that mindfulness is a way of relating to that moment, then it becomes possible to reconcile mindfulness and future-mindedness.

Can problems with future-thinking be changed and can treatments target future-thinking to reduce distress and enhance well-being (Chapter 10)? Existing treatments do obviously address how people think about the future (some more so than others), but, other than setting goals for treatment, it is not a very explicit part of psychological treatment approaches, and is largely uninformed by the wider literature on prospection and well-being. There is some evidence that explicitly goal-setting and planning interventions do have effects, even with a minimally resource-demanding approach, but this area needs more systematic testing, including the use of active control conditions. There are some promising early findings that making people more specific appears to have potential well-being benefits.

The subjective future life trajectory

A key underlying theme running through all the previous chapters is that part of what it is to be alive is to have a subjective sense of oneself as having a future life trajectory. We have an ever-constant sense of ourselves in time, of the present unfolding into the future. This sense is so pervasive that it will often be in the background, but at times does come to the forefront of our minds. Obviously, this future trajectory is importantly connected with, and influenced by, what has happened in the past, but the evidence reviewed throughout this book suggests that someone's well-being is critically linked to how they view their future. This future life trajectory is subjective, in that it represents how someone views their own life; it may be quite different from how their trajectory turns out, or even how the person's objective circumstances would suggest it will turn out. Expectancies, goals, plans, hopes, fears, and so on, which are often easily accessible to conscious awareness, are the most obvious manifestations of how someone experiences this felt sense of their future trajectory Alongside these obvious prospective states are background future representations, expectancies that are more like assumptions, which are often only brought to the forefront of awareness when they are disconfirmed, and are most obviously revealed in emotions such as surprise and anger when these assumptions are violated.

I have talked about thoughts about the future, and their relationship to well-being, mainly as if they were all of a kind. Clearly they are not, and an important task for future research will be to develop ways of discriminating between different types of prospection and how the different kinds might connect with different aspects of well-being and mental health. One obvious way to distinguish between future thoughts is in their time frame. The subjective future life trajectory can be divided into two broad classes of representations—those that are about the immediate future and those that are about the longer-term future.

Several lines of evidence point to quite distinct profiles in these two classes of prospection. Thoughts about the immediate future are more specific, detailed, and idiosyncratic than thoughts about the more distant future (see Chapter 6). They are also more plentiful. Most thoughts that people report for the future are for the short-term future, with a strong tailing off of numbers of thoughts the further into the future they go (see Chapters 1 and 6). The preponderance of short-term thoughts is consistent with the idea that a lot of our future-thinking is devoted to guiding action, what Baumeister and Vohs (2016) have called *prag-matic prospection*. This *imminence effect*, a sort of future-oriented version of the recency effect, is an understandable phenomenon, and shows a broadly similar pattern to the temporal decay of episodic memories (Chapter 6). Conway and colleagues have hypothesised a *Remembering-Imagining System* (RIS; Conway, Loveday, & Cole, 2016), whereby we are most oriented to the immediate present, with a tailing off of both memories and prospective thoughts around a three- or four-day window each side of the present.

Although thoughts about the short-term future are more plentiful, those concerned with the longer-term future are seen as more positive and more important, as well as being more script-like (see Chapter 6). It is likely that both kinds of thoughts are important for our well-being, but in different ways. When I first started looking at positive and negative anticipation for differ-ent future time periods in suicidal patients (see Chapter 2), I thought that this group might show a lack of positive thoughts for the long-term future, as this is where I thought the important future life possibilities resided. It turned out that they showed a positive anticipation deficit for the short-term future as much as for more distant future time periods (see Chapter 2). One possibility for future research to test is that distant future thoughts are important for the more eudai-monic aspects of well-being—a sense of purpose and direction or a sense of meaning—whereas thoughts about the nearer part of our future trajectory play more of a role in hedonic well-being.

Many present or imminent activities, thoughts, and feelings will be con-nected in a coherent way to future points in the trajectory. For example, I am writing this sentence entirely focused on it in the present moment, but it is part of an overall aim to complete this book by a deadline, and ultimately for the book to be published, read, and, hopefully, enjoyed. Carver and Scheier (1990) among others, have pointed out the hierarchical nature of goal-based behaviour, where the most proximal level of behavioural responses is con-nected through levels of the hierarchy to ultimate goals. This goal hierarchy is certainly a central part of the trajectory, but, as argued in Chapter 7, what we normally think of as goals are only part of how we experience the future. Many short-term expectancies, such as looking forward to time off work or spending time with the children, (see Chapter 2, Table 2.3) are not necessarily imminent steps in long-term goals, but are, nevertheless, important elements of how a person thinks of their future. In other words, the sense of the self, moving forwards in time in a valued way certainly includes longer-term, larger-scale ambitions, goals, aspirations, and projects, but also includes ongoing, smaller, sometimes routine and repeated, but nevertheless important, events and experiences. These more imminent anticipated experiences may or may not be related to long-term goals, but irrespective, are a coherent component of someone's future life trajectory; they are an important part of the life story and the overall narrative that underpins the person's overall sense of continuity through different temporal periods.

Some elements of our life trajectories that are fundamental may be in the form of underlying assumptions, and may not even be explicitly thought about very much at all. Someone in their mid-50s, told that they only have around ten years to live because of a medical condition, would likely be devastated. That person may have given very little thought to what their life would be like after they were 65, but their emotional reaction shows that it was a vital part of their conception of their future. The subjective future life trajectory contains many important representations in the form of scripts. These scripts are not specific, but at the same time they are not abstract, semantic representations with no personal investment. Frequency or specificity of thoughts about the future are not necessarily indicators of the elements of the trajectory that matter most.

Of course, our life trajectories also have a past that has given them their current form, and which we draw upon in order to manage the present and think about the future. Although the past has already happened, this part of the life trajectory is also subjective in that people make sense of their past and construct a narrative that describes who they are, and which helps make sense of their life as it is now. The past and the future aspects of trajectory are different in important ways and have different functions. When people are asked to think of the past and the future, they are faster and think of more specific episodes from the past (see Chapter 6). Yet, when spontaneous thoughts are measured, there are many more thoughts about the future, and thoughts about the past are relatively uncommon (Chapter 9). This pattern of findings is consistent with the future (along with the temporal present) being what largely concerns our experienced present. Memories of the past provide a repertoire of accessible knowledge and experience that is there, not to be contemplated or thought about much of the time for its own sake, but to furnish us with the ability to think about the unfolding present and the future, and how they connect.

Chapter 9 discussed the apparent contradiction between the value of being future-focused and the emphasis on being in the present that is prevalent in eastern-influenced approaches such as mindfulness. We saw that the contradiction can be resolved by making the distinction between the temporal present and the experienced present. Because of our capacity for mental time travel, our experienced present can be about the temporal present (i.e. what we are doing and where we are now), but can also be about other past or future points in the trajectory. There is also a dynamic relationship between the future part of the trajectory and being able to be focused on the temporal present, that is, what is immediately in front of us at the time. We are able to focus on the present when the future trajectory is in a settled state, that is, supplies meaningful direction, provides positive anticipation, and does not contain high levels of threat. The analogy of a journey might help. If, on a journey, a route has been worked out and a plan is being followed, and we have a sense that we are heading in the right direction and making appropriate progress, then we are freed up to concentrate on the act of driving. If, on the other hand, either we don't know where the end point we are trying to get to is, or we don't know the route, then we are unable to concentrate on the immediate act of driving because we are constantly thinking about the bigger picture of where we are trying to get to, and whether we are on the right track and on time, or even whether we are going to get there at all! Having goals that are linked to values, having an idea of how the goals are going to be achieved, and having a sense of progress provides a settled feeling that one's trajectory is in good shape. We are then freed up to be able to think about what is immediately in front of us.

Two kinds of disruption to the subjective future life trajectory

Those low in well-being and experiencing emotional distress will have a subjective future life trajectory that is disrupted in some way. This can mean effects on short-term and/or long-term prospection, interruptions to goals and associated short-term activities, and failure to anticipate routine or regular enjoyable activities. Problems with memories arise when they are not supporting the person to move forward in life, either through not providing accessible material that will enable future-thinking, or through exerting a pull back to the past because of past experience that is not resolved, for example, a previous trauma. All of these effects might lead to difficulties in being able to focus on the temporal present because the future is not settled. To continue the analogy of a journey, there are two main types of problem that can arise. In the case of anxiety, there may well be a trajectory, but it is perceived to be fraught with danger. For someone who is highly anxious, the future does have a road ahead but it is mined with hidden explosive devices. Moving forward is a case of constantly being vigilant for any sign of the mines. It is an ongoing state of bracing oneself for an encounter with danger, and in extreme cases can lead to avoidance of the road altogether. In either case, the person's life suffers both from strong, sometimes debilitating negative emotions, and the scope for experiencing rewarding aspects of life is curbed.

In depression and suicidal hopelessness, the picture is different. It is more like the road has petered out, so that there is no real sense of a way forward. Or, alternatively, it might be like reaching a river or a canyon and the bridge is down—someone can see the destination on the other side and they want to get there but have no idea how to. In addition, Chapter 5 talked about the kinds of feelings that arise in the here-and-now when contemplating the future, and the fact that these feelings are a motivational source of behaviour. Thinking about the future is not simply a cognitive activity, and anticipatory feelings are vital in guiding action. People need the spark of feeling, which comes from being able to envisage and pre-experience some of the emotion related to good future outcomes. In those who are depressed, the spark of feeling that comes from contemplating future outcomes is weak or absent, meaning that there is no pull towards the future. Various reasons were suggested for this, including generally dampened responding, but it was also suggested in Chapter 5 that being unable to envisage specific aspects of future events would contribute, a difficulty that appears to be underpinned by difficulties with retrieving specific episodic past information (Chapter 6). In terms of the analogy of the bridge being down, the destination on the other side cannot be seen very clearly and, as a result, doesn't exert the same pull to try to find a way to get to it.

Flexibility

The theme of flexibility has emerged in a number of different discussions throughout this book. Forgeard and Seligman (2012) suggested the value of flexible optimism (Chapter 3), that is, a default ongoing state of optimism that can move to pessimism when appropriate. It is likely that a state of ongoing pessimism does brace someone, in the sense of minimizing their negative feelings if things do turn out badly for them. Seneca may well have been right that starting the day thinking about how badly it can go does protect someone against disappointment and frustration. But Seneca was advisor to the capricious emperor, Nero, lived in very unpredictable times and, in fact, ended up being ordered by Nero to commit suicide. In dangerous times, pessimism might be the most sensible stance to take, but in times or circumstances where there is no clear ongoing danger, there is a substantial emotional cost involved in pessimism, even if it does break a fall, should a fall happen.

Chapter 9 argued that mindfulness training develops the flexibility for people to be able to notice their attention and direct it to where they choose, rather than it being automatically directed. Similarly, psychological flexibility is a fundamental concept in acceptance and commitment therapy (Hayes, Luoma, Bond, Masuda, & Lillis, 2006). Zimbardo and Boyd (1999), also discussed in Chapter 9, proposed the idea of a balanced time perspective being optimal, where individuals were able to be flexible and switch their temporal orientation between past, present, and future focus, depending on the circumstances. Other concepts might not mention flexibility explicitly, but they are nevertheless underpinned by it. For example, being able to disengage with goals that do not appear to have a prospect of success and engage with new, different goals (see Chapter 7) is clearly an example of flexibility.

All of these areas mentioned point to the value of being able to adapt, to change and to bend, depending on the circumstances, rather than prescribing a single path. It is difficult to argue with the value of flexibility and, given the complexity of what humans have to deal with it, is not difficult to see that it is an essential meta-capability. There is, though, a need to go beyond flexibility to understand the wisdom and judgement that guides the application of the skill. In the case of temporal orientation, flexibility is about possessing the skills of being able to think about the future or the present or the past, but there is the further question of when is it wise to think about the one rather than the other? In other words, advocating the value of flexibility is relatively easy; what is more difficult is to start specifying the conditions under which it is good to take one specified course of action rather than another. What constitutes a good choice about whether, and when, to think about the past, present, or future? Future-thinking is good when it provides anticipatory positive affect, helps us to see routes to get to desired ends, and provides direction, purpose, and meaning. It is not beneficial when it does not provide these things, or when it gets in the way of engaging in the present or immediate future. For example, enjoying the thought of a positive future can, on occasion, get in the way of taking the sometimes difficult steps necessary to bring it about, or spending a lot of time thinking about some future event can diminish our ability to fully experience the present. Switching to thinking about a negative future is useful when the reasonable possibility of a threat has been detected, especially when a course of action can be taken to deal with it, either behaviourally or psychologically. Bracing, in those circumstances is beneficial, because it will reduce the impact of a negative outcome, but the cost of bracing should not exceed its benefit. As our knowledge increases about how prospection links to well-being and mental health, it will become possible to specify more clearly the circumstances under which to exercise the skill of flexibly switching temporal orientation.

Methodological points

A number of intriguing concepts have been touched upon throughout this book, for example, dispositional mindfulness, emotional avoidance, future-orientation, and temporal flexibility. These are potentially important constructs, and central to many current ideas in emotional well-being but have proven to be difficult to measure. In a number of places (see especially Chapters 5, 7, 8, and 9), I have been critical of self-report measures, including measures of these constructs. I will not repeat all the details here, but will try to summarize what I see to be the issues for future research. Note that this is not a criticism of self-report measures as a method of investigation per se but more of a plea to try to avoid the kinds of problems that undermine them.

Definition creep

It is tempting to widen a construct under investigation and draw into its definition a number of other constructs. These other constructs may well be related to the main construct but are conceptually distinct. For example, Hayes (2004, p. 15) talks about the concept of psychological flexibility as having six aspects, including psychological acceptance skills, cognitive defusion skills, and distinguishing self-as-context from the conceptualized self, none of which are part of any dictionary definition of flexibility (see Chapter 9). These skills may well *enable* flexibility, but this is not the same as them *being*, or *constituting*, flexibility. The same issue can be seen when hope is defined as pathways towards, and having feelings of efficacy for moving towards, goals (see Chapter 5). These are constructs that might well be related to hope, but they are not hope itself, which is defined in most dictionary definitions simply as a combination of desire and expectation. It is worth noting that the opposite problem can also arise, where concepts are defined in a narrow way that only reflects one particular aspect of them. The future subscale of the Zimbardo Time Perspective Inventory (see Chapter 9) describes one particular way of thinking about the future, and, as argued in Chapter 9, the items that measure it may miss many important aspects of future orientation. Similarly, the non-judgement subscale (Baer, 2006), discussed in Chapter 5, is actually a measure of not judging one's thoughts *negatively*, which is quite different from non-judgement per se.

By defining a construct as consisting of elements wider than it (or narrower than it), empirical research establishing those possible relationships to the construct is effectively curtailed, and tests of the relationships of the true construct to other variables is muddied. In addition, if different researchers define constructs in their own idiosyncratic ways, then different research examining ostensibly the same construct is actually talking about quite different ones, making comparisons across different studies difficult. One way forward would be to stick as closely as possible to standard lay dictionary definitions of constructs, rather than creating idiosyncratic ones. If a construct is to be defined differently from its standard dictionary definition, then this should be explicit and a suitable case made.

The constellation of psychological advantage

Definition creep probably arises, at least partly, because of the interconnectedness of so many constructs in the psychological literature. I remember as an undergraduate discussing some correlations I had uncovered between some variables, and my tutor pointing out that most things that are positive tend to co-occur, just as negative ones do. Meehl (1990) colourfully highlighted this point in his discussion of 'the crud factor'. This clustering is certainly true for many of the positive and negative constructs considered throughout this book. People scoring high on, for example, a self-report measure of hope will also score high in optimism, life satisfaction, happiness, and score low in depression, dysfunctional attitudes, self-esteem, and so on. Such individuals can be thought of as exhibiting a constellation of psychological advantage, with the opposite pattern of scores obviously reflecting a constellation of psychological disadvantage, constellations that probably also extend to varying degrees to social, economic, and biological domains. This interconnectedness means that finding relationships between variables is relatively easy, but separating out unique, rather than multiply overlapping, relationships is more difficult. Optimism predicts mortality (see Chapter 3) but so too does, for example, processing speed (Aichele, Rabbitt, & Ghisletta, 2016). Are these variables independently related to mortality or are they part of the same underlying constellation of psychological advantage? We are, understandably, interested in the unique relationships between variables but tend to ignore the shared variance, which is often much larger and is an indicator of the constellation.

The sheer number of overlapping constructs means the challenge of identifying unique relationships, and especially unique causal relationships, is formidable. But that is not to say that progress cannot be made. Sir Austin Bradford Hill is probably most famous for his studies in the 1950s with Richard Doll, establishing the link between smoking and lung cancer (see le Fanu, 2011). In an influential later lecture discussing how to weigh correlations found between environmental variables and disease, he outlined criteria to be met for accepting that one caused the other (Hill, 1965), a number of which are pertinent to the issue here. As well as (a) the correlation between the variables being strong, (b) it should be found consistently, (c) there should be some specificity of the variables relating to each other and not to other variables, (d) there should be a plausible causal mechanism to link the two variables, and (e) if possible, causality should be tested by an experiment, manipulating the hypothesized cause and observing effects on the outcome variable. Adopting criteria like these would help us to sift the possible causal relationships and establish a foundation for accepting those that were likely.

Expectations of participants

What can we reasonably expect of participants responding to self-report measures? I suggested in Chapter 8 that some distinctions may well be conceptually coherent, represent an important element of a theory, and be clear in the minds of researchers devising the items to measure it, but be entirely lost on the respondents. Chapter 8 discussed this issue in relation to the Acceptance and Action Questionnaire (AAQ; Bond, Hayes, Baer, Carpenter, Guenole et al., 2011), with items such as 'Emotions cause problems in my life' or 'My painful memories prevent me from having a fulfilling life'. My first impression on reading the AAQ items some years ago was that this was simply a measure of psychological distress. Becoming more aware of the theoretical perspective, and going back to the items, it becomes clearer that the intention behind these items is to try to get at how people respond to having painful memories or emotions, not whether, or how much, they have them. Can people manage to live meaningful and fulfilling lives despite the presence of painful memories or emotions, or are their lives derailed by having these experiences? These are intriguing and clinically important questions. But it asks a lot of participants to be able to respond to the items in the intended way. They would first need to understand the distinction between having painful memories/emotions and reacting to them, then bring to mind that distinction, put to one side how much they experience the primary problem (e.g. how painful their memories are), and finally give a rating that reflects only how they respond to the memories or emotions, all in a matter of seconds. Is it more likely that the measure will become effectively an indicator of the primary problem itself? Hawkes and Brown (2015) have pointed out the same issue with the Anxiety Sensitivity Index, which aims to assess how people respond to anxiety rather than how much they experience anxiety. The issue does seem especially tricky for any measures that attempt to address secondary responses to an initial problem. The question is whether quite subtle phenomenon, as secondary processes are, can be accessed and measured separately from the primary constructs through the use of simple self-report measures.

Biased items/pairing

A subtler problem, referred to at various points throughout the book, is where items in a self-report measure are inadvertently, but systematically, paired with another value construct that is not ostensibly what the scale is about. Clark and Watson (1995) pointed out that the introduction of an affect term into any item results in participant responses that are highly coloured by general negative affectivity (see Chapter 9). In Chapter 8 this problem was illustrated by directly contrasting two planning propensity questions, where the item that had 'enjoy' as part of it had a higher correlation with well-being than the one that did not. It is also the case that the overall meaning of the item can be negative, such that the effect can be found without the explicit present of a negative affect term, something that was discussed in detail in Chapter 9 in relation to self-report measures of mindfulness.

A different, and subtler, case discussed in Chapters 8 and 9, is in the use of wording such as 'I find it difficult to', 'I find it easy to', 'I am able to'. Such questions, followed by statements reflecting a particular ability, clearly convey what someone who is able and competent will answer. Note that this is not simply the same as social desirability. A dysphoric participant will endorse 'I find it difficult to …' followed by virtually any ability, just as they will not endorse most things prefaced by 'I find it easy', not because of some reverse social desirability, but because the statement genuinely resonates with their feeling of being useless and finding things difficult.

The key point is that the kinds of issues outlined do not just add noise to self-report measures because the value element is systematically paired with the construct that is purported to being measured. All the 'good' responses are taken as indicative of, or example, mindfulness, psychological flexibility, disengagement, and so on, which are clearly the constructs that the authors value. The 'bad' responses indicate low scores on these constructs. Thus, participants who are dysphoric end up scoring low on those valued constructs because their systematic pairing of responses with dysphoric content makes it inevitable that they will!

Future directions

Each chapter in this book has suggestions for future research in relation to the specific topics covered there. There are also more general directions for future research that cut across the topics covered in the different chapters.

Measurement

Self-report measures can be improved. An important point to make, however, is that some of the methodological issues raised cannot be dealt with by statistical analysis: they are conceptual, rather than empirical, problems. It is only through clear and careful conceptual thinking that such problems can be avoided or

minimized. In fact, psychometrics might even on occasion impede such necessary conceptual thinking, a point made by McGrath (2005, p. 142): 'Without
psychometrics, psychologists would not have been so successful at glossing
over the vagueness inherent to psychosocial constructs, the arbitrary quality
of psychosocial scales, and the tenuous relationship between those constructs
and those scales'. Nicholls, Licht, and Pearl (1982) suggest that researchers try
to approach proposed items in a scale, like an attentive, naive respondent. It is
inevitable that those who develop a scale have a particular view of whether it is
measuring something good (and will correlate inversely with measures of distress) or something bad (and will correlate positively with measures of distress).
Care needs to be exercised in ensuring that the value does not creep into the
content and wording of the items. Researchers and potential respondents who
are outside of the theoretical stance and value frame of the developers of the
scale could provide a check. Having scale items reproduced in published work
also enables readers to evaluate the items.

Self-report measures have their limits, something that might account for
problems with efforts to date, attempting to measure secondary processes of
how people respond to their experience. It may be that such subtle secondary
phenomena just do not lend themselves to being assessed by simple self-report,
in which case other approaches need to be developed. Some examples have
been discussed throughout this book of methods that rely on eliciting richer,
idiographic data and coding these responses (see, for example, Addis, Wong, &
Schacter, 2007, Chapter 6; Bauer & McAdams, 2010, Chapter 2; Edmondson &
MacLeod, 2015, Chapter 4; Sherratt & MacLeod, 2013, Chapter 7). This kind
of approach is certainly more labour-intensive and timeconsuming than self-
report measures, but is likely to provide better access to more complex and
difficult to uncover phenomenon. Such methods can be used to elicit and code
simple short responses to probes (e.g. Sherratt & MacLeod, 2013) all the way
through to what participants say in a semi-structured interview format, where
fuller descriptions are elicited and rated (e.g. Tasker & Golombok, 1997). The
benefit is richer idiographic data that can also reliably be converted to numbers
and analysed statistically.

The kinds of subtle secondary responses to thoughts and feelings, in particular, might well be better served by such methods rather than through
self-report. One example would be the measure developed by Richard Moore
and colleagues—the Measure of Awareness and Coping in Autobiographical
Memory (MACAM; Moore, Hayhurst, & Teasdale, 1995; Teasdale, Moore,
Hayhurst, Pope, Williams et al., 2002)—that assesses the extent to which people
see (negative) thoughts and feelings as passing mental events rather than as
aspects of the self. This sort of distancing, or decentring, is a fundamental feature

of cognitive therapy (Beck, 1976), as well as subsequent third wave therapies like mindfulness based cognitive therapy (Segal, Williams, & Teasdale, 2012). The measure involves four stages: (1) giving participants detailed descriptions of situations; (2) asking them to think of specific autobiographical memories brought to mind by the descriptions; (3) using a semi-structured interview to elicit details of the event and, critically, participants' responses to feelings at the time of the event; (4) rating those responses using a standard coding scheme on the extent to which they show immersion as opposed to distance from the feelings.

Experimental methods could also sometimes benefit from eliciting free responses from participants during tasks, an approach that might help in the interpretation of effects. For example, getting people to think aloud (Ericsson & Simon, 1980) during a tasks like Sharot's probability updating task (see Chapter 3) might help shed light on why people fail to update risk estimates in an upward manner when they readily do so in a downward manner. There is a vast territory between laboratory tasks and self-report questionnaires which remains to be fully explored.

Culture and age

Almost all of the research reviewed in the present book was conducted in the west—western Europe and, especially, North America. That is not a flaw with the research, but should place clear limits around the generalizability of the findings. It should also act as a spur to examine the phenomena in different cultural contexts. There are indications of potentially important cultural effects, for example, evidence that optimism as measured by self-other comparisons is weaker in non-western groups (Chapter 3), and evidence that eastern cultures place greater emphasis on valuing the past (Chapter 1). A bigger problem, and a serious weakness of the body of psychological knowledge, is the sheer amount of research conducted on student samples. The most obvious weakness here is age, something that seems an obvious factor in how people think about the future, although socioeconomic status, ethnicity, and educational levels are clearly also influential factors present in the sampling. Students also do not usually have children or other dependents, factors that are likely to influence one's perceived future trajectory. For example, the optimistic bias in predictions of how satisfied people think they will be with their lives in future shows a linear decline with age, levelling out at about age 70 (Chapter 3), and the relationship between goal progress and well-being is significantly stronger in student samples (Chapter 7). It is therefore possible that the presence of effects subsequently taken to be features of people in general are highly dependent on having young, educated, western participants. Again, this is not to deny their value or importance, but it clearly limits their generalizability. More substantially, there is real knowledge to be gained in helping to understand phenomena by knowing how they vary by age and by culture. It has to be a priority for future research to move beyond the convenience of studying psychology students taking part in studies for course credit to more culturally, socioeconomically, and ethnically diverse samples representing different ages.

Multidimensional models of well-being

Finally, one point that has emerged clearly from the studies reviewed in this book is that well-being is not a unitary concept, but is a broad concept covering a number of different facets. The multifaceted nature of well-being has been illustrated by numerous examples in the book: positive affect (PA) and negative affect (NA) correlate differently with different kinds of expectancies for the future (Chapter 2); PA correlates more strongly than NA with goal progress (Chapter 7); mindfulness practitioners are higher than non-practitioners on eudaimonic but not affective indicators of well-being (Chapter 9); and intervention studies show differential effects on different facets of well-being (Chapter 10). There is much work to be done on examining how different facets of well-being are related to different aspects of prospection.

Final word

A subjective future life trajectory that is working well for our well-being and mental health has a number of qualities. We have things to look forward to in both the short and longer terms, which represent the smaller, more routine, idiosyncratic elements of our futures, as well as those that are more script-like and significant (Chapter 2). We have longer-term approach goals that fit with our values, especially transcendent values, and these are connected to ongoing activities and plans that provide us with a sense of moving towards attainable goals (Chapters 7 and 8). We expect positive outcomes in the future (Chapters 2, 3, and 4) and we experience positive feelings in the moment when we think about those outcomes (Chapter 5). We have a predominantly present and future, as opposed to past, orientation, and have the skill to be able to notice and relate to our feelings in a way that enables us to be flexible in our temporal orientation (Chapter 9). We can access specific episodic memories in a way that helps us to think about the future in a specific way (Chapter 6), enabling us to experience positive anticipatory feelings. Related to these positive qualities, there are many ways in which a subjective future life trajectory can go wrong and not work well for us. Low well-being, anxiety, and depression are associated with trajectories that are disrupted in different ways, with suicidal behaviour perhaps being the ultimate expression of when someone simply does not possess a subjective future life trajectory that will carry them any further forward into the future from where they are now. Hopefully, understanding the links between prospection, well-being, and mental health will ultimately enable more effective help being available, especially for those who need it most.

References

Addis, D. R., Wong, A. T., & Schacter, D. L. (2007). Remembering the past and imagining the future: Common and distinct neural substrates during event construction and elaboration. *Neuropsychologia*, **45**(7), 1363–1377. http://doi.org/10.1016/j.neuropsychologia.2006.10.016

Aichele, S., Rabbitt, P., & Ghisletta, P. (2016). Think fast, feel fine, live long: A 29-year study of cognition, health and survival in middle-aged and older adults. *Psychological Science*, 956797615626906. http://doi.org/10.1177/0956797615626906

Baer, R. A. (2006). Using self-report assessment methods to explore facets of mindfulness. *Assessment*, **13**(1), 27–45. http://doi.org/10.1177/1073191105283504

Bauer, J. J., & McAdams, D. P. (2010). Eudaimonic growth: Narrative growth goals predict increases in ego development and subjective well-being 3 years later. *Developmental Psychology*, **46**(4), 761–772. http://doi.org/10.1037/a0019654

Baumeister, R. F., & Vohs, K. D. (2016). Introduction to the special issue: The science of prospection. *Review of General Psychology*, **20**(1), 1–2. http://doi.org/10.1037/gpr0000072

Beck, A. T. (1976). *Cognitive therapy and the emotional disorders*. Madison, CT: International Universities Press.

Bond, F. W., Hayes, S. C., Baer, R. A., Carpenter, K. M., Guenole, N., Orcutt, H. K., Waltz, T., & Zettle, R. D. (2011). Preliminary psychometric properties of the Acceptance and Action Questionnaire–II: A revised measure of psychological inflexibility and experiential avoidance. *Behavior Therapy*, **42**(4), 676–688. http://doi.org/10.1016/j.beth.2011.03.007

Carver, C. S. & Scheier, M. F. (1990). Origins and functions of positive and negative affect: A control-process view. *Psychological Review*, **97**(1), 19–35. http://doi.org/10.1037/0033-295X.97.1.19

Clark, L. A. & Watson, D. (1995). Constructing validity: Basic issues in objective scale development. *Psychological Assessment*, **7**(3), 309–319. http://doi.org/10.1037/1040-3590.7.3.309

Conway, M. A., Loveday, C., & Cole, S. N. (2016). The remembering–imagining system. *Memory Studies*, **9**(3), 256–265. http://doi.org/10.1177/1750698016645231

Edmondson, O. J. H. & MacLeod, A. K. (2015). Psychological well-being and anticipated positive personal events: Their relationship to depression. *Clinical Psychology & Psychotherapy*, **22**(5), 418–425. http://doi.org/10.1002/cpp.1911

Ericsson, K. A. & Simon, H. A. (1980). Verbal reports as data. *Psychological Review*, **87**(3), 215–251. http://doi.org/10.1037/0033-295X.87.3.215

Forgeard, M. J. C. & Seligman, M. E. P. (2012). Seeing the glass half full: A review of the causes and consequences of optimism. *Pratiques Psychologiques*, **18**(2), 107–120. http://doi.org/10.1016/j.prps.2012.02.002

Hawkes, N. & Brown, G. P. (2015). Toward a validity framework for cognitive-behavioral therapy self-report assessment. In G. P. Brown & D. A. Clark (Eds.), *Assessment in cognitive therapy.* (pp. 243–267). New York: Guilford Press.

Hayes, S. C. (2004). Acceptance and commitment therapy and the new behavior therapies: Mindfulness, acceptance and relationship. In S. C. Hayes, V. M. Follette, & M. M. Linehan (Eds.), *Mindfulness and acceptance: Expanding the cognitive-behavioral tradition.* (pp. 1–29). New York: Guilford Press.

Hayes, S. C., Luoma, J. B., Bond, F. W., Masuda, A., & Lillis, J. (2006). Acceptance and commitment therapy: Model, processes and outcomes. *Behaviour Research and Therapy,* 44(1), 1–25. http://doi.org/10.1016/j.brat.2005.06.006

Hill, A. B. (1965). The environment and disease: Association or causation? *Proceedings of the Royal Society of Medicine,* 58, 295–300.

le Fanu, J. (2011). *The rise and fall of modern medicine.* London: Abacus.

McGrath, R. E. (2005). Rethinking psychosocial constructs: Reply to comments by Barrett, Kagan, and Maraun and Peters. *Journal of Personality Assessment,* 85(2), 141–145. http://doi.org/10.1207/s15327752jpa8502_06

Meehl, P. E. (1990). 'Appraising and amending theories: The strategy of Lakatosian defense and two principles that warrant it': Response. *Psychological Inquiry,* 1(2), 173–180. http://doi.org/10.1207/s15327965pli0102_14

Moore, R. G., Hayhurst, H., & Teasdale, J. D. (1995). Measure of awareness in autobiographical memory: Instructions for administering and coding. Unpublished manuscript, Department of Psychiatry, University of Cambridge.

Nicholls, J. G., Licht, B. G., & Pearl, R. A. (1982). Some dangers of using personality questionnaires to study personality. *Psychological Bulletin,* 92(3), 572–580. http://doi.org/10.1037/0033-2909.92.3.572

Segal, Z. V., Williams, J. M. G., & Teasdale, J. D. (2012). *Mindfulness-based cognitive therapy for depression* (2nd edition). New York: Guilford Press.

Sherratt, K. A. L. & MacLeod, A. K. (2013). Underlying motivation in the approach and avoidance goals of depressed and non-depressed individuals. *Cognition & Emotion,* 27(8), 1432–1440. http://doi.org/10.1080/02699931.2013.786680

Sloan, D. M., Strauss, M. E., & Wisner, K. L. (2001). Diminished response to pleasant stimuli by depressed women. *Journal of Abnormal Psychology,* 110(3), 488. http://doi.org/10.1037/0021-843X.110.3.488

Tasker, F. L. & Golombok, S. (1997). *Growing up in a lesbian family: Effects on child development.* New York: Guilford Press.

Teasdale, J. D., Moore, R. G., Hayhurst, H., Pope, M., Williams, S., & Segal, Z. V. (2002). Metacognitive awareness and prevention of relapse in depression: Empirical evidence. *Journal of Consulting and Clinical Psychology,* 70(2), 275–287. http://doi.org/10.1037//0022-006X.70.2.275

Zimbardo, P. G. & Boyd, J. N. (1999). Putting time in perspective: A valid, reliable individual-differences metric. *Journal of Personality and Social Psychology,* 77(6), 1271. http://doi.org/10.1037/0022-3514.77.6.1271

Name Index

Abad, N. 240
Abbey, S. 52
Abele-Brehm, A. 56
Abramson, L. Y. 57
Addis, D. R. 3, 28, 123, 124, 129, 130, 131, 133–4, 135
Alain, M. 247–8
Alberts, H. J. E. M. 239
Allen, N. B. 221
Alloy, L. B. 6, 57, 160
Andersen, S. M. 62
Anderson, R. J. 128, 135
Andersson, G. 246
Anglin, S. M. 139–40
Aristotle 5
Ashby, F. G. 198
Ashworth, L. 3, 106
Averill, J. R. 104

Bagozzi, R. P. 104
Baird, B. 222, 223
Bardi, A. 158
Bargh, J. A. 62
Barlow, D. H. 102
Barnhofer, T. 31, 38–9
Barrett, L. F. 121
Barsics, C. 105
Bastian, B. 165
Bauer, J. J. 159, 163, 168
Baumeister, R. F. 3, 197, 260
Baumgartner, H. 104–5
Bayard, S. 131
Bechara, A. 100
Beck, A. T. 24, 32, 35, 57, 235
Beekman, A. 236
Bekerian, D. A. 24
Bennett, K. 20
Berntsen, D. 128–9, 139, 140, 152
Berridge, K. C. 101
Besner, C. M. 91
Birnbaum, D. 56
Biswas-Diener, R. 85
Bitner, J. 209
Bjärehed, J. 246
Blackwell, S. E. 51
Boddana, P. 156, 187–8
Boersma, K. 21
Bohn, A. 128–9, 140
Bond, R. 159

Boniwell, I. 209
Borkovec, T. D. 111
Bouffard, L. 247–8
Boulenger, J.-P. 103, 131
Bowler, D. M. 131
Boyd, J. N. 208–10, 211–12, 228, 264
Brandimonte, M. A. 27
Bredemeier, K. 17
Bridges, M. W. 50
Broadbent, K. 118
Brown, A. D. 123, 124
Brown, G. P. 25, 26, 109, 267
Brown, K. W. 216
Bruininks, P. 104
Brunstein, J. C. 157
Buchanan, K. 158
Buechel, E. C. 88
Busseri, M. A. 70
Butler, G. 16, 18, 19
Byford, S. 220
Bylsma, L. M. 80–1
Byrne, A. 20, 37

Cabeleira, C. M. 18
Calam, R. 36
Campbell, L. 27
Candel, M. 24, 63
Cantor, N. 49
Carroll, F. 16
Carstensen, L. L. 208
Carver, C. S. 50–1, 153, 160, 260
Cassidy, C. 35
Chamberlain, J. P. 184
Chambers, R. 221
Chan, A. C. M. 71
Chang, E. C. 51
Chapman, B. P. 85, 91
Cheng, S.-T. 71
Chentsova-Dutton, Y. E. 81
Chon, K. K. 104
Clark, L. A. 20, 268
Coates, E. 198, 244
Cochran, W. 150
Coffey, K. A. 221
Cohn, M. A. 221
Cole, L. J. 64
Cole, S. N. 152, 260
Conaghan, S. 38
Conrad, F. 4
Conway, C. 33, 40, 183, 186, 246

Conway, M. A. 260
Coote, H. M. 246, 247
Corballis, M. C. 3
Corcoran, R. 20, 26–7
Coughlan, K. 171
Crane, C. 29, 38–9
Cropley, M. 18, 27
Cunningham, W. A. 209

Dalgleish, T. 121
Damasio, A. R. 100
Danchin, C. L. 170–1
D'Argembeau, A. 4, 32, 105, 124, 125, 128, 131, 135–6, 137, 170–1
Davidson, K. 38
Dawes, R. M. 86
Deeprose, C. 29
Della Sala, S. 27
De Roover, K. 165
DeRubeis, R. J. 60–1
de Vito, S. 27, 139–40
de Vries, H. 24, 63
Dewhurst, S. A. 128
Dickson, J. M. 155, 157, 167, 168
Diener, E. 165, 169
Dittmar, H. 159
Dolan, R. J. 65, 67, 68
Doll, R. 266
Doyle, A. C. 1
Drogendijk, A. 52
Drolet, A. 195
Dubé, M. 247–8
Duberstein, P. R. 85, 91, 93
Dunne, E. 173–4
Dunning, D. 60, 61, 105–6
Duval, C. 134

Edmondson, O. J. H. 95
Ednersby, L. 246
Edwards, J. R. 212, 213
Eelen, P. 119
Ehlers, A. 123
Elliot, A. J. 156–7, 166
Ellis, N. C. 249
Emery, L. J. 126, 135
Emmons, R. A. 150
Epstein, R. M. 91
Erikson, M. G. 237
Esposito, F. 103

Farquharson, L. 247
Fennell, M. J. V. 29
Ferguson, G. 246
Ferguson, Y. 240
Fernandez, J. K. 64, 65
Fetchenhauer, D. 105–6
Finkel, S. M. 221
Flink, I. K. 21
Ford, B. Q. 165

Forgeard, M. J. C. 72, 263
Fournier, M. 52
Fraser, L. 35
Fredrickson, B. L. 198, 221
Freedman, A. N. 55
Fresco, D. M. 58
Fung, H. H. 71, 72

Gable, P. A. 198–9
Gaesser, B. 131, 132, 249
Gamboz, N. 27
Gámez, W. 110
Gard, D. E. 84, 106–7
Gard, M. G. 84, 106–7
Garland, E. L. 218
Garrett, N. 59, 60, 68
Geleijnse, J. M. 53
Gerlach, K. D. 189, 190
German, R. E. 20, 62, 84
Gersons, B. P. R. 52
Gerstorf, D. 71
Gilbert, D. T. 87, 222, 225
Gilmore, A. W. 184
Giltay, E. J. 52, 53
Goddard, L. 26
Godley, J. 36, 163
Golden, A.-M. J. 121
Gollwitzer, P. M. 193, 194–5
Gosling, S. D. 90
Gotlib, I. H. 81, 160
Gowans, C. W. 219
Grace, J. 64
Grässman, R. 157
Green, M. F. 84
Greer, S. M. 101
Grievink, L. 52
Grouzet, F. M. E. 212, 214
Gruber, J. 165, 209
Grysman, A. 139–40
Gunthert, K. C. 62, 84
Gunz, A. 240

Hach, S. 124
Hadley, S. A. 170
Hanley, A. 218
Hansenne, M. 249
Hanssen, M. M. 239
Harmon-Jones, E. 198–9
Harris, P. R. 194, 196
Hassabis, D. 131
Hawkes, N. 109, 267
Hawks, S. 162–3
Hay, A. C. 209
Hayes, S. C. 265
Hay, J. F. 119
Healy, H. 249
Heekeren, H. R. 68
Helweg-Larsen, M. 55, 56
Hepburn, S. R. 31, 38

Hermer, P. 56
Hervig, L. K. 50
Hesser, H. 246
Hetherton, J. 198, 244
Hevey, D. 54–5
Higgins, E. T. 168
Hill, A. B. 266
Hill, P. F. 126, 135
Hirsch, J. K. 51
Hodges, J. R. 133–4, 135
Hoekstra, T. 53
Hoerger, M. 85, 91, 93
Holmes, E. A. 29
Horan, W. P. 84
Horgan, J. H. 54–5
Houser-Marko, L. 240
Hudson, J. A. 139–40
Hughes, T. 36
Hunter, E. 16, 35
Hurst, M. 159
Hu, S. 111
Hutson, M. 139

Irish, M. 133–4, 135
Irvine, J. 52
Isaacowitz, D. M. 72
Isen, A. M. 198
Ivanchenko, G. V. 209
Ivcevic, Z. 128

Jacobsen, H. 37, 125
James, L. 188
Janssen, E. 24, 63
Jeunehomme, O. 137
Jing, H. G. 250
John, O. P. 106–7
Johnson, E. 188
Johnson-Laird, P. N. 153
Johnson, S. L. 160
Jong-Meyer, R. 38

Kahneman, D. 23, 24, 26, 27, 30, 87
Kaplan, R. L. 89
Karlsson, J. 246
Kashdan, T. 85
Kasser, T. 158, 159, 162–3
Keil, A. 194
Kentish, J. 16, 37, 125
Killingsworth, M. A. 222, 225
Kinderman, P. 155
King, L. A. 238, 239
King, M. J. 123
Kirkland, T. 209
Kleber, R. J. 52
Kleim, B. 123
Klein, C. 55, 64
Klein, S. B. 3, 137, 142
Klein, W. M. P. 55
Klinger, E. 6, 223

Klug, H. J. P. 154
Knutson, B. 101
Koestner, R. 157
Koopmann-Holm, B. 110, 218, 221
Korn, C. W. 68
Kosslyn, S. M. 28
Koster, E. H. W. 6
Kring, A. M. 84, 91, 92, 93, 94, 106–7
Kringelbach, M. L. 101
Kromhout, D. 52
Krueger, A. B. 87
Kuczmera, A. 38
Kumaran, D. 131
Kuppens, P. 165
Kusulas, J. W. 50
Kuwabara, K. J. 128
Kuyken, W. 220

Lachman, M. E. 69–70, 185
Lambert, L. S. 212, 213
Lang, F. R. 71, 208
Lang, T. J. 29
Lapierre, S. 247–8
Lardi, C. 128
Lavender, A. 39
Lechner, L. 24, 63
Lempert, K. M. 205–6
Lench, H. C. 89
Levi, A. S. 29–30
Levine, B. 119–20, 124
Levine, L. J. 89
Licht, B. G. 269
Lind, S. E. 131
Linton, S. J. 21
Little, B. R. 150
Llera, S. J. 112
Lo, B. C. Y. 221
Lopez, H. 60–1
Luszczynska, A. 192
Lyubomirsky, S. 239, 240–2

McAdams, D. P. 119, 159, 163, 168
McBride, C. 157
McCulloch, K. C. 194
McGee, H. M. 54–5
McGrath, R. E. 269
MacHale, S. 35
McKinnon, M. C. 124
MacLeod, A. K. 16, 18, 19, 20, 21, 24, 26, 31–2, 33, 34, 36, 37, 38, 40, 83, 84, 95, 118, 125, 126, 156, 162, 163, 167, 168, 169, 170, 171, 183, 186, 187–8, 198, 244, 246, 247, 249, 251
MacLeod, C. 18, 27
McMakin, D. L. 82–3
McNally, R. J. 119, 123
Macrae, C. N. 224
Madore, K. P. 132–3, 189, 249, 250
Maguire, E. A. 131
Maier, G. W. 154

Malle, B. F. 104
Marchetti, I. 6
Markus, H. 149, 237
Marroquín, B. 19, 20, 84
Marshall, G. N. 50
Masicampo, E. J. 197
Massey, C. 63
Masterton, G. 35, 173, 174
Mathews, A. 16, 18, 19
Mathieu, M. T. 90
Mathy, A. 136, 170–1
Mauss, I. B. 164, 165
Ma, X. 211
Meehl, P. E. 266
Meevissen, Y. M. C. 239
Mellers, B. 78, 80, 91, 92
Mennin, D. S. 19
Miles, H. 37
Miller, G. E. 173–4
Mineka, S. 119
Miranda, R. 19, 20, 84
Moberly, N. J. 155, 157
Mongrain, M. 242–3
Moore, M. T. 58
Moore, R. 269
Morewedge, C. K. 88
Morina, N. 29
Morris, B. H. 80–1
Moser, R. P. 55
Moulds, M. L. 29
Moulton, S. T. 28
Murayama, K. 166

Neal, D. T. 195
Nealis, L. J. 91
Nero 263
Neroni, M. A. 27
Newman, M. G. 112
Nezlek, J. B. 186
Nicholls, J. G. 269
Nolen-Hoeksema, S. 84
Norem, J. K. 49
Nurius, P. 237

Oatley, K. 153
Ochs, C. 218
O'Connor, R. C. 35, 36, 39, 163–4, 173, 174
Odou, N. 239
Oettingen, G. 189, 199, 245
Orbell, S. 191, 193–4, 195, 196
Ouellette, J. A. 64, 65
Oyserman, D. 188

Pearl, R. A. 269
Peck, E. 70
Peel, A. 131
Pek, J. 221
Penningroth, S. L. 166

Peters, M. L. 21
Peterson, C. 71
Pham, L. B. 190
Pieters, R. 104
Piguet, O. 133–4, 135
Pillemer, D. B. 128
Pizzagalli, D. A. 205–6
Pote, H. 37
Powers, T. A. 195–6
Prabhakar, J. 139–40
Prenda, K. M. 185
Pryor, J. B. 29–30
Pulcu, E. 206
Pusowski, C. 29

Quirk, S. W. 85
Quoidbach, J. 249

Raes, F. 119
Raffard, S. 103, 131
Railton, P. 3
Rapee, R. M. 109–10
Renaud, O. 4
Rendell, P. G. 131
Riis, J. 87
Ritov, I. 91
Roberts, J. E. 167
Robinaugh, D. J. 119, 123
Robinson, M. D. 69
Rockstroh, B. 194
Roepke, A. M. 235, 237
Rose, G. 249
Rottenberg, J. 80–1
Rubin, D. C. 139
Ruby, F. J. M. 225
Rush, J. 212, 214
Russell, I. T. 220
Ruvolo, A. 149
Ryan, R. M. 158, 216
Ryff, C. D. 8, 69–70, 96, 152–3

Sacchetti, D. C. 131
Safer, M. A. 89
Salaminiou, E. 40, 83
Salovey, P. 56
Santiago, C. D. 82
Santoro, M. S. 91
Sarkohi, A. 246
Savino, N. S. 164, 165
Schacter, D. L. 2, 3, 25, 28, 123, 129, 130, 131, 132–3, 137, 151–2, 184, 189, 249, 250
Scheier, M. F. 50, 153, 260
Schkade, D. 87
Schlösser, T. 105–6
Schmid, M. 29
Schmidt, U. 36, 163
Scholz, U. 192

Schooler, J. W. 222, 223
Schouten, E. G. 53
Schultheiss, O. C. 157
Schwartz, A. 91
Schwarzer, R. 192
Schwarz, N. 87
Schweiger Gallo, I. 194
Scott, W. D. 166
Segal, Z. S. 38–9
Segal, Z. V. 219
Segerstrom, S. C. 50–1
Seligman, M. E. P. 3, 5, 8, 49, 72, 235, 237, 263
Seneca 2, 64, 263
Sergeant, S. 242–3
Sharot, T. 65, 67, 68
Sheeran, P. 191, 193–4, 195, 196
Sheldon, K. M. 156–7, 161, 239, 240–2, 243
Shepperd, J. A. 56, 64, 65
Sherratt, K. A. L. 169
Shipp, A. J. 212, 213
Shirk, S. R. 82
Shnek, Z. M. 52
Sidley, G. L. 36
Sieff, E. M. 86, 90
Simmons, J. P. 63
Simon, P. 182
Sloan, D. M. 80
Smallwood, J. 222, 224
Smith, J. 183
Smyth, R. 36, 163–4, 173, 174
Snyder, C. R. 104, 243
Söderlund, H. 119, 120
Song, X. 222
Spielman, L. A. 62
Spreng, R. N. 2, 137, 184, 189
Sripada, C. 3
Stange, J. P. 160
Stapinski, L. A. 109–10
Stawarczyk, D. 223
Steele, A. M. 29
Stevens, W. D. 184
Stewart, D. 52
Stöber, J. 28
Stolarski, M. 209
Stone, A. A. 87
Story, A. L. 60, 61
Strauss, M. E. 80
Street, H. 170
Strunk, D. R. 60–1, 62
Suddendorf, T. 3
Sumner, J. A. 119
Svoboda, E. 119
Sze, J. 218
Szpunar, K. K. 2, 25, 137, 151–2

Tamir, M. 169
Tata, P. 16, 27, 37, 125, 170–1
Taylor, S. E. 190

Tchanturia, K. 36, 163
Teasdale, J. D. 219, 269
Tesser, A. 150
Thimm, J. C. 17, 18, 19
Thomas, E. J. 206
Thompson, B. L. 221
Thomsen, D. 128
Thrash, T. M. 166
Tonn, B. 4
Tripp, J. 38
Trotter, P. D. 206
Tsai, J. L. 110, 218, 221
Turken, A. U. 198
Tversky, A. 23, 24, 27, 30
Tyers, C. 249

Vaidya, R. S. 71
Valentine, J. D. 20
Van Beek, W. 236
Van Boven, L. 3, 106
Vancleef, L. 239
Van der Does, A. J. W. 38–9
Van der Linden, M. 4, 32, 103, 105, 125, 128, 131
Van der Velden, P. G. 52
Vann, S. D. 131
van Osch, L. 24, 63, 192
Vella-Brodrick, D. A. 239
Vergara, C. 167
Vickers, R. R. J. 50
Vilhauer, J. S. 236
Vincent, P. J. 156, 187–8
Vohs, K. D. 260

Wagner, G. G. 71
Waldron, W. R. 55
Walter, H. 68
Waltz, J. 221
Wang, C. E. A. 17, 19
Wang, X. 222
Warner, A. 218
Waters, E. A. 556
Watkins, E. 39
Watson, D. 20, 110, 268
Webster, J. D. 211
Weinstein, N. D. 17, 54
Weiss, D. 71
Wells, A. 36
Wenze, S. J. 20, 62, 84, 89, 94
Whelan, D. C. 91
Whitaker, K. 36
Whyte, M.-C. 35
Williams, D. M. 131
Williams, J. M. G. 24, 29, 31–2, 36, 38–9, 118, 120, 121–2, 123, 124, 129, 130, 163–4, 219, 220, 249
Wilson, T. D. 87

Winch, A. 157
Winocur, G. 119
Wisner, K. L. 80
Wittmann, M. 3
Wolgast, M. 109
Wong, A. T. 3, 123
Wood, A. M. 249
Wood, W. 195
Wortman, C. B. 50
Wynn, J. E. 91

You, J. 72
Yuan, J. W. 91, 92, 93, 94
Yu, E. A. 51
Yu, M. 55

Zeigarnik, B. 197
Zelenski, M. M. 91
Zimbardo, P. G. 208–10,
    211–12, 228, 264
Zitman, F. G. 52, 53

Subject Index

abuse, history of 220
acceptance 108, 109, 220
Acceptance and Action Questionnaire
(AAQ) 108–9, 267
Acceptance and Action Questionnaire-Revised
(AAQ-II) 108–9
acceptance and commitment therapy
(ACT) 108–9, 240, 264
accuracy 9
absolute 90–1
and dysphoria 91–4
expectancies 14
optimism and pessimism 55, 57–62, 72–3
and reasonableness distinction 58
relative 90
see also under affective forecasting
achievement 8, 128
goals 153, 154, 161
action 196
see also Acceptance and Action
Questionnaire (AAQ)
action/implemental planning 192–3
activity, independent, self-directed 242
activity scheduling 235–6
actualization of potential 209
adaptation 90
adaptive account 88
adaptive thoughts/adaptiveness 6
addiction 34, 101
affect 7n, 9, 250
actual 80–3, 95, 219
depressive 238
experienced 80
heuristic 24
ideal 219
predicted 83–4, 95
see also anticipated affect; anticipatory
effect; negative affect (NA); positive
affect (PA); Positive and Negative
Affect Scale (PANAS)
Affect Intolerance Scale 109–10
affective forecasting 9, 78–96
accuracy 85–91
impact bias 85–9
impact bias critique 89–91
actual affect 80–3, 95
dysphoria and accuracy 91–4
emotional disturbance and predicted
affect 83–4
memory 87, 130
affective valence 102

affiliation 152, 158
ageing 130, 172
agency 104, 157–8, 197, 211, 243
age of participants 270–1
goals 166
memory 124, 125, 131, 132–3, 140
mindfulness and temporal orientation 207–8
optimism and pessimism 67, 69–71, 72
plans 184, 188
agoraphobia 29
akrasia 191
Alzheimer's disease 124–5, 133–4
ambitions 261
amnesia 133
amusement 199
amygdala 99, 190
anger 105, 259
anhedonia
affective forecasting 84, 94
anticipatory feelings 106
expectancies 18, 20
mindfulness and temporal orientation 205–6
anorexia nervosa 163
anterior insula 102
anticipated affect 9, 78, 81, 83, 85
anticipated emotions/feelings 79, 88, 99, 105,
106, 113
anticipated experience 94
anticipation 3, 256
of exam grades 64–5
gain and loss 102
goals 151
memory 138
negative 36–7, 260
of personal events, active 9
positive 36–7, 260, 262
see also under expectancies
anticipatory affect 9, 101, 107, 174
goals 154, 155
negative 107
anticipatory coping 64
anticipatory emotions/feelings 9, 79,
99–114, 263
emotional avoidance 107–13
worry as avoidance 110–13
hope and fear 102–4
liking versus wanting 101–2
measurement 114
positive 257, 271
psychological measures 104–7
somatic markers 99–101

anticipatory pleasure 106–7
anticipatory positive affect 103, 264
anticipatory well-being 156
antidepressants 220
anxiety 1, 6, 7, 8, 255, 256–7, 258, 271
    affective forecasting 80, 83, 88–9
    anticipatory emotions/feelings 9, 102–3,
        107, 111–12, 113, 114
    chronic 17
    expectancies 9
        anticipation 36–8, 41
        processes and mechanisms 24, 28–9
        subjective probability judgements 15, 16,
            18, 19–20, 21, 22
    goal-based intervention 243
    goals 157, 162, 166–9, 170
    high-trait 17
    intervention 235, 238
    intervention and specificity 248–9
    memory 126, 138
    mindfulness and temporal orientation 216
    Mood and Anxiety Symptoms
        Questionnaire 84
    optimism and pessimism 49, 56, 57, 62, 64
    plans 186
    public speaking 111–12
    social 102
    subjective future life trajectory 262–3
    see also anxiety disorders
anxiety disorders 119, 251
    see also generalized anxiety disorder (GAD)
Anxiety Sensitivity Index 267
anxious apprehension 80, 102
anxious arousal 84
apathy 103
arousal 101, 102
    anxious 84
    autonomic 17, 84
    emotional 80
aspirations 159, 261
associative learning 5
assumptions, underlying and life
        trajectories 261
asymmetric updating effect 67–8
attainment 153, 154–8, 245
    see also educational attainment
attention 198
    problems 216
    recent 5–6
    see also Mindful Attention Awareness
        Scale (MASS)
attitude and planning 185, 190
autistic spectrum disorders 123, 124, 131
autobiographical facts 138
Autobiographical Interview 119–20, 123, 124,
        133, 134, 142
Autobiographical Interview-modified 131
autobiographical memory 131

and emotional disorders 118–21
    retrieval 124
    task 32, 130
    see also Measure of Awareness and Coping
        in Autobiographical Memory
        (MACAM)
Autobiographical Memory Test 119–20, 121,
        122, 128
autobiographical planning 224
    task 184
autobiographical remembering 127
autonomic activation 94
autonomic arousal 17, 84
autonomy 8, 218
    goal-based interventions 240–1
    goals 158, 161, 162
availability heuristic 23, 27
'average' 56–7
aversive things 1
avoidance behaviour 257–8
    affective forecasting 88–9
    anticipatory feelings 114
    emotional 107–13, 265
    expectancies 22
    functional 120
    see also Contrast Avoidance Model of Worry
avoidance/suppression subscale 109–10

background future representations 259
balanced time perspective 209–11, 264
base rate probabilities 66–7
Beck Depression Inventory (BDI) 60, 84
Beck Hopelessness Scale (BHS) 32, 34–5, 51
behaviour
    and goals 153, 159
    health-related 190
    and plans 185, 191
    reward-directed 88, 205–6
    see also avoidance behaviour
behavioural activation system see behavioural
        approach
behavioural approach 22
behavioural experiments
    affective forecasting 79–80, 89
    memory 138
behavioural facilitation see behavioural
        approach
behavioural inhibition system 22
beliefs 63–5, 184, 185
benevolence 158
best possible self (BPS) interventions 238–9,
        243, 251
bias 14, 94
    absolute 95
    cognitive 24
    general impact 256
    impact 85–91, 94
    lack-of-pessimism 256

negative 18, 95, 256
  optimistic 54, 55, 56, 57–62, 65, 66, 69, 72–3, 270
  pessimistic 55, 57–62, 72–3
  positive 18, 61n, 95, 256
  systematic 9, 62
biased items/pairing 267–8
bilateral hippocampal damage 131
bilateral prefrontal brain injury 100
bipolar disorder 8
  expectancies 15
  goal-based interventions 247
  goals 159–60, 164, 165
  memory 123
  mindfulness and temporal orientation 209
black and white thinking 245
boredom 226
bracing 64, 71, 72, 112, 264
brain injury 100, 131
brain, regions of
  amygdala 99, 190
  anterior insula 102
  cingulate cortex 101
  dorsolateral prefrontal cortex 184
  frontoparietal control regions 184, 190
  lateral temporal areas 127
  medial caudate 102
  medial prefrontal cortex 127, 190
  medial temporal area 127
  nucleus accumbens 101, 102
  orbitofrontal cortex 101
  parahippocampal cortex 127
  parietal lobes 127
  posterior cingulate 127
  posterior visual cortex 127
  retrosplenial cortex 127
  ventral tegmental area 101
  ventromedial prefrontal cortex 99
brooding 39
Buddhism 153, 214, 219
buffering hypothesis 53
bulimia nervosa 163

calmness 198
cardiac event 52, 54–5
causal reasoning 25
causal thinking 24–5, 28
China 222
choice performance 100
choice reaction time task 135–6, 223–4
cingulate cortex 101
cluster analysis 210
Cluster B personality disorder 34
cognitive-based group psychotherapy 236
cognitive behavioural therapy (CBT)
  affective forecasting 79–80
  anticipatory feelings 108
  goal-based interventions 246

  intervention 235–7
  third wave 108
cognitive capacity and plans 184, 200
cognitive defusion skills 265
cognitive factors and anticipation 41
cognitive flexibility 198
Cognitive Interview 132
cognitive model of emotional disorders 80, 82
cognitive resources and direct memory retrieval 121
cognitive task 222–3
cognitive therapy 270
  mindfulness and temporal orientation 215, 220
  optimism and pessimism 57
  see also cognitive-behavioural therapy (CBT); mindfulness based cognitive therapy (MBCT)
cognitive triad in depression - negative view of the self, the world and the future (Beck) 51, 235
coherence and quality ratings 139
collectivist cultures 169
communion and goals 157–8
community feeling 158
competence 161, 240–1
  see also achievement
confidence 105, 184–5
confirmatory factor analysis 21
congruent predictions and occurrence 85
connection with others 175, 241, 258
Consideration of Future Consequences Scale (CFC-14) 207, 208, 211–12
constructive episodic simulation hypothesis 28, 129–33
constructive process, active 224
consummatory pleasure 106–7
contentment 91–2, 199
content-well-being link and goals 161–3
Contrast Avoidance Model of Worry 112–13
contrast effect 120
contrasting 189
control 68, 197
coping 269–70
  anticipatory 64, 102
  intervention and specificity 250
  plans 192–3, 196
  self-directed 64
core network 127
core purpose 237
correlational studies 19–21, 191–3
craving 101
'crud factor' 266
cues
  environmental 135, 193–6, 258
  situational 194
cue words see word cues

cultural factors 4, 270–1
  affective forecasting 81
  anticipatory feelings 110
  individualistic cultures versus collectivist
    cultures 169
  mindfulness and temporal
    orientation 208, 222
  optimism and pessimism 72
cultural life scripts 139–41, 143
cultural norms 184
cyclical events 4

daydreaming 222
  see also mind wandering
debiasing methods 63–4
Decision Affect Theory 78, 87
decision making theories 78
default mode network see default network
default network 127, 184, 190, 224
defeat/failure task 39
definition creep 265–6
degenerative neurological conditions 130
  see also Alzheimer's disease
delay discounting 205–6
deliberate overdose 122, 156
deliberate self-harm 122, 171, 187
  expectancies 17, 34, 36
  see also deliberate overdose
depression 6, 7, 235, 255, 256–8, 263,
    266, 271
  affective forecasting 80, 81, 82, 83, 84,
    93, 95, 96
  anticipatory feelings 103, 104, 114
  Beck cognitive triad 51, 235
  expectancies 9
    anticipation 32, 36–8, 40, 41
    processes and mechanisms 24, 28–9
    subjective probability judgements 15, 16,
      17, 18, 19–20, 21, 22
  global optimism 51, 52, 55
  goal-based interventions 242–3, 246–8
  goals 155, 157, 165, 166–9, 170–1, 173
  intervention 234, 235–7, 242, 250
  Leiden Index of Depression Sensitivity
    (LEIDS) 39
  Major Depressive Disorder 8, 80–1, 103,
    123–4, 167
  major depressive episode 103
  memory 118–19, 120–1, 123, 124, 126,
    138, 143
  mild see dysphoria
  mindfulness and temporal orientation 206,
    216, 217, 220–1, 228
  optimism and pessimism 72, 73
    accuracy and bias 57–8, 59–61, 62
    optimism as biased correction 68
    optimism for well-being 70, 71
  plans 185, 186, 187

  see also anhedonia; Beck Depression
    Inventory (BDI)
depressive affect 238
depressive dysfunctional attitudes 242
depressive realism 57–8
desire(s) 5, 101, 265
dialectical behaviour therapy (DBT) 108
direction, sense of 143, 264
direct (single comparative rating)
    method 55–6, 57
disability 71
disappointment 91–2, 185
discrete tasks 183–4
disengagement 268
dismantling trial 220
dissatisfaction 185
distraction task 39
distress 8, 259, 269
  affective forecasting 90
  anticipatory feelings 109, 110
  expectancies 20–1
  goal-based interventions 248
  mindfulness and temporal
    orientation 209, 215
  optimism and pessimism 52–3
  see also emotional distress; psychological
    distress
dopaminergic activity/pathways 67, 69, 101
dorsal attention network 184
dorsolateral prefrontal cortex 184
downward arrow technique 237
drug therapy 220, 234
DSM-5 8
duration prediction and intensity prediction
    distinction 89–90
dysfunctional attitudes 242, 266
dysphoria 8, 256, 268
  and accuracy 91–4
  affective forecasting 82–3, 84, 91–3, 94, 95
  expectancies 17, 18
  memory 126
  optimism and pessimism 56, 57, 58

eastern cultures 270
  see also Buddhism
eating disorders 163
educational attainment 189, 199, 200, 270
efficacy 104, 153, 189, 265
ego control 208
emotional arousal 80
emotional avoidance 107–13, 265
  and predicted affect 83–4
emotional difficulties 143
emotional disorders
  and autobiographical memory 118–21
  cognitive model 80, 82
  expectancies 24
  intervention and specificity 248

optimism and pessimism 57
  specificity of future-thinking 121–4
emotional distress 14, 85, 248, 262
emotional disturbance 2, 7, 10, 83–4
emotional intelligence 91
emotion-related aspect of future-directed
  thinking *see* anticipated affect
emotions/feelings 7n, 221, 258, 260
  actual 25
  anticipated 79, 88, 99, 105, 106, 113
  anticipatory *see* anticipatory emotions/
    feelings
  neutral 25
  predicted 94, 256
  see also negative emotions/feelings; positive
    emotions/feelings
emptiness, feeling of 153
energy and goals 155
engagement in life 8, 243
enjoyment 40, 101, 258
  affective forecasting 78, 80, 83, 85, 95
  progress 174
enthusiasm 221
environmental cues 135, 193–6, 258
environmental mastery 8, 96, 218, 226, 248
episodic detail 257
episodic future representations 143
episodic future-thinking 123, 125, 132, 141
  impaired 133
  replacement 138
episodic information 135, 137
episodic knowledge 137, 139, 141, 249
episodic memory 120, 141, 143, 271
  autonoetic aspect 137n
  constructive episodic simulation
    hypothesis 132
  expectancies 30
  and future-thinking 141
  future thoughts as hybrid
    representations 138–9
  impaired 133
  past- and future-thinking 125, 127
  specificity of thinking and emotional
    disorder 123
  temporal decay 260
episodic thinking 127–9, 250
ethnicity 270
  see also cultural factors
eudaimonic approaches 8
Europe 110, 270
European Social Survey (ESS) 185–6
evaluative hedonism 78n
events
  future *see* future events
  hypothetical 106
  interpretation 82
  prediction *see* expectancies
  repeated 138–9

stressful 164
  unpleasant 81
  see also negative events; positive events
excitement (feeling of) 155, 198, 221
excitement seeking 208–9
executive capacity 136
executive control 121
executive processes tasks 223
expectancies 9, 14–41, 256, 259, 271
  affective forecasting 84, 85
  anticipation 30–41
    changes in 38–40
    depression and anxiety 36–8
    looking forward to and not looking
      forward to 31–3
    mechanisms 40–1
    negative 36–7
    positive 36–7
    suicidality and hopelessness 34–6
  anticipatory aspect 14
  approach 22
  future positive events 155
  goals 151
  negative 18, 21
  optimism and pessimism 48, 64, 71
  of particular outcomes 30
  plans 197
  positive 18, 20, 21
  processes and mechanisms 22–30
    imagery 28–30
    memory 26–8
    simulation 24–6
    summary 30
  short-term 260–1
  subjective probability judgements 15–22
    correlational studies 19–21
    group comparison studies 15–19
    summary of findings 22
expectancy-value models 14
expectations 5, 71, 265, 267
experience
  actual 86, 93–4
  anticipated 94
  predicted 86, 93–4
experience sampling studies 222
  affective forecasting 81, 84, 87
  mindfulness and temporal
    orientation 225
experimental manipulations 38, 106
experimental studies 256, 270
  affective forecasting 95
  anticipatory feelings 100
  mindfulness and temporal orientation 226
  plans and outcomes 193–6
experimental tasks 65–6, 223, 224, 225–6
explanation-based reasoning/thinking 30
explanatory style 71
extraversion 50

facial expressions
  observation and coding 257
  positive and negative 80–1
fame 15
fantasies about future outcomes 151
fear 257, 259
  anticipatory feelings 102–4, 105, 109,
    111, 113–14
feelings *see* emotions/feelings
fictitious scene construction 131
Five Factor Mindfulness Questionnaire 217
flexibility 172, 210, 263–4
  cognitive 198
  psychological 108–9, 264, 265, 268
  temporal 228, 265
fMRI data 126, 183, 190
football team result 87
forecasting error, negative 94
forgetting/forgetfulness 194, 199, 216
frontal injury 100
frontoparietal control regions 184, 190
functional network *see* default network
future
  immediate 4, 259–60
  longer-term 259–60
future-directed therapy (FDT) 236
future-directed thinking 1, 3, 152
  expectancies 14
  intervention 251
  memory 10, 118
  mindfulness and temporal
    orientation 225–6, 227–8
  negative aspects of 67
  positive aspects of 67
future directions 268–71
  age of participants 270–1
  cultural factors 270–1
  measurement 268–70
future events 3
  distant 143
  likelihood judgements 68
  possible 237
  specificity 135
  subjective sense of experiencing 142
  see also future negative events; future
    positive events
Future Events Test *see* Autobiographical
  Memory Test
Future Fluency Task *see* Future-thinking Task
future intrapersonal thinking, positive 36
future life trajectory, subjective 259–63
future likelihood of events 27–8, 30
future negative events 9, 15–16, 27–9, 34
  expectancies 25, 38
  health-related 56
  optimism and pessimism 60–1, 62, 65
future-oriented intervention in clinical
  practice 235–7

future-oriented off-task thoughts 135–6
future outcomes, negative,
  overestimation of 23
future outcomes prevention 166
future positive events 9, 27–9, 34, 103
  expectancies 38
  optimism and pessimism 62
future positive outcomes 15, 41
future scenarios, negative 51
future-tense, specific responses in 128
future-thinking 261, 265, 271
  as hybrid representations 137–41
  memory 10, 125–7, 129
  mindfulness and temporal orientation 208–
    12, 213–14, 220, 221, 223–4
  negative 33, 35, 140, 246
  non-episodic factors 133–7
  self-defining 128
  spontaneous 6, 136
  see also episodic future-thinking; future-
    directed thinking; Future-thinking
    Task; positive future-thinking
Future-thinking Task 37–8, 39, 246
  affective forecasting 83
  expectancies 32–3, 34–6, 37
  memory 118, 125
Future Time Perspective Scale 207–8

gains, potential 101–2
gambling task 91–2, 100, 105–6
gender factors 71, 189
general impact bias 256
general intelligence 91
generalized anxiety disorder (GAD) 102–3, 112
general memories 119–20, 121, 122, 139
generative retrieval 136
generative search 135
Germany 71, 110
global beliefs about the future 9
Goal Adjustment Scale 173
goal(s) 10, 149–75, 257–9, 261, 262, 265
  achievement 189, 197
  adjustment, flexible 172
  approach 157, 166–70, 175, 258
  attainment 153, 154–8, 195, 271
  autonomy 158, 161, 162
  avoidance 157, 166–70, 175, 258
  -based interventions 239–48
    goals and plans training (GAP) 244–8
  and behaviour 153, 159
  circumstances 240–1
  commitment 155, 245
  communion 157–8
  consequences of 195
  content 158–65, 175
    happiness 163–5
    mania 159–61
    and well-being link 161–3

definition 149–52
-directed activities 84
-directed behaviour 196
-directed thinking 251
disengagement 172–4, 264
emotional 207
and energy 155
engagement 172–4
external focus 149
extreme, ambitious 160
extrinsic 158–9, 161, 162–3
financial 162
flexibility 172
gain 166
generation 156, 188
happiness 163–5, 170–2, 174, 175
hierarchy 175, 196, 199, 260
importance 155
informational 207
intact 188
internal focus 149
internal motives 156–7
intrinsic 158–9, 161, 162
leisure 182–3
life 159, 183–4, 235
loss prevention 166
maintenance 166
materialistic 159, 161–2
mindfulness and temporal
    orientation 226, 227
motivation 156–8
number of 187–8
orientation 166–70
overvaluing 170–2
perceived likelihood 156
personal 136–7, 150, 174, 187, 189, 198,
    223, 240
and plans/planning 151, 182–3, 224, 243
    correlational studies 191–3
    experimental studies 193–6
    well-being 187, 189, 196–9
popularity 162
positive 190, 240
progress 154–8, 174, 195–6, 198, 200, 245
    anticipated 156
    culture and age 270
    multidimensional models of
        well-being 271
pursuit, tenacious 172
self-goals 188
-setting 2, 170, 198, 199, 234, 236, 259
socioemotional growth communal 159
specific 172
standard 189
structure 170–2
sub-goals 170
task 242
for treatment 235

types of 157
unresolved 198
and well-being 152–4, 161–3, 187, 189,
    196–9, 271
goals and plans training (GAP) 244–8
'good things' in life 8
gratitude exercise 239
grief, complicated 123
group comparison studies 15–19
growth *see* personal growth
guilt 157, 258
gustatory pleasure *see* liking

habitual behaviours 195
happiness 8, 258, 266
    affective forecasting 85, 91–2, 93
    anticipated 84
    goal-based interventions 248
    goals 163–5, 170–2, 174, 175
    intervention and specificity 249
    mindfulness and temporal
        orientation 208, 225
    optimism and pessimism 56, 68
    prediction 84
    Valuing Happiness Scale (VHS) 164–5
health concerns 63
    cardiac issues 52, 54–5
    eating disorders 163
    HIV results 86–7
    multiple sclerosis 37
health outcomes 51, 54–5, 68, 71, 191–2
health-related behaviours 190
heart rate 111
hedonic approaches 7
hedonic hot spots 101
hedonic well-being 260
hedonism
    evaluative 78n
    psychological 78, 87, 95
helplessness 208–9
    learned 49
here-and-now 263
heuristics 30
HIV test results 86–7
Hong Kong 71, 72
hope 102–4, 257, 259, 265
    anticipatory feelings 9, 105, 113–14
    influential model of 104
    and optimism distinction 104
    optimism and pessimism 51
    self-report measures 266
    therapy 243
hopelessness 1, 255, 263
    affective forecasting 83
    anticipatory feelings 9, 104
    expectancies 18, 21, 22, 31–2, 34–6, 39, 41
    goals 170–2
    intervention 234, 236

hopelessness (*Cont.*)
  memory 118
  mindfulness and temporal
      orientation 208–9, 215
  optimism and pessimism 51
  self-reported and goal-based
      interventions 246
  see also Beck Hopelessness Scale (BHS)
hybrid representations and memory 143
hypomania 15, 159–60, 164
hypothetical events 106
hypothetical forced choice 205

ICD-10 8
Iceland 159
idiographic thoughts 14
'if then' plans 193–6, 235
imagery 2, 28–30, 138, 255
  anticipatory feelings 110–11
  cues 135
  intervention 237, 238
  negative 29
  visual 28
  see also vividness ratings
imagining 245
immediate emotions *see* anticipatory feelings
immediate future 4, 259–60
imminence effect 260
impact bias 85–91, 94
implementation intentions 193–6, 258
inaccuracy 94
  absolute 90–1
independence *see* autonomy
indirect method and likelihood
      judgements 55–6
individualistic cultures 169
indulging 189, 245
information
  episodic 135, 137
  semantic 135, 137, 138
injustice 78
intensity prediction 89
intentions 2, 137
  and plans 190–1, 196, 199
  strengthening 193n
interest, loss of 80, 103
internet-based study 242
interpersonal themes 128
interpersonal therapy 157
interpretation of events 82
intervention 10, 234–51, 259, 271
  best possible self (BPS) 237–9
  future-oriented 235–7
  goal-based 239–48
    goals and plans training (GAP) 244–8
  mindfulness-based 219–21
  minimal 242
  optimism 242

specificity 248–50
task 243
intrapersonal thinking 36, 163–4
intravenous drug users 34
introversion 91
intrusive thoughts 198, 200
in vitro fertilization 52
Iowa Gambling Task 100
irritation 91–2
ischemic heart disease (myocardial infarction
      or unstable angina) 52
item wording 21

joy 105
judgement 58
  automatic 62
  negative 20, 217
  self- 217–18
  single 57
  see also likelihood judgements; subjective
      probability judgements

knowledge
  conscious 100
  episodic 137, 139, 141, 249
  long-term 184
  self- 138
  semantic 135, 137, 138, 139, 142

laboratory tasks 63–4, 91
lack-of-pessimism-bias 256
lag analysis 225
lateral temporal areas 127
L-Dopa 67
learned helplessness 49
Leiden Index of Depression Sensitivity
      (LEIDS) 39
Life Orientation Test (LOT) 50, 52
Life Orientation Test - revised
      (LOT-R) 50–1, 52
life satisfaction 7, 266
  goal-based interventions 246–7
  goals 154–5, 162, 165
  intervention 238–9
  mindfulness and temporal orientation 209,
      212–13, 216, 218
  optimism and pessimism 51, 68, 70–1
  plans 185–6
  progress 174
  self-reports 159
life scripts, cultural 139–41, 143
life trajectories 261
likelihood
  beliefs 155
  estimates 17, 64, 65
  expectancies 15, 24
  of future events 27–8, 30
  indicator 29

of negative events 17
perceived 25–6, 27
of positive events 17
of possible future events 237
see also likelihood judgements
likelihood judgements 25
affective forecasting 84
elevated 26
expectancies 31
future-directed 54
future event 68
future events 68
optimism and pessimism 48, 57–60, 62, 63, 65–6, 68
for self compared to others 53–7
subjective 60
Likert scales 193
liking versus wanting 101–2
linkers and goal structure 170
longitudinal studies 51–2, 60
looked-forward-to items 31–3, 40–1, 138
losses, potential 101–2
loving kindness meditation 221

Major Depressive Disorder 8, 80–1, 103, 123–4, 167
major depressive episode 103
maladaptive thoughts 6
mania 159–61, 209
see also hypomania
mastery 68, 154, 158, 236
see also environmental mastery
meaning, sense of 8, 143, 264
Means End Problem Solving Task (MEPS) 132–3, 186–7, 249–50
Measure of Awareness and Coping in Autobiographical Memory (MACAM) 269–70
medial caudate 102
medial prefrontal cortex 127, 190
medial temporal area 127
meditation 218–19, 220, 221, 228
memory 1, 3, 10, 118–43, 255
affective forecasting 87, 130
amnesia 133
autobiographical see autobiographical memory
constructive episodic simulation hypothesis 129–33
content differences 128
episodic memory see episodic memory
expectancies 26–8
external details 120, 123–4, 131, 134
future thoughts as hybrid representations 137–41
general 27, 119–20, 121, 122, 139
hybrid representations 143
internal details

autobiographical memory and emotional disorders 120
constructive episodic simulation hypothesis 131, 132, 133
future thoughts as hybrid representations 140, 141
non-episodic future-thinking 134
past and future episodic thought 128
specificity of future-thinking and emotional disorder 123–4
specificity of memory and future-thinking 125
latency 135
negative 28, 118, 128
non-episodic factors in future-thinking 133–7
over general 118–19, 123, 124
past and future episodic thought, differences between 127–9
past- and future-thinking 125–7
personal 120, 125
positive 28, 128
and prospection connection 257
prospective 199
retrieval 23, 26–7, 28, 30, 118, 136, 188
self-defining 119, 128
semantic 30, 120, 137, 257
specificity 27, 124–5, 129
specificity of future-thinking and emotional disorders 121–4
temporal difference 128–9
temporal distribution 125
themes 128
working see working memory
mental contrasting 245
mental health 7–8
mental shortcuts 22
mental time travel see prospection
metacognitive experience 23
methodological points 265–8
biased items/pairing 267–8
definition creep 265–6
expectations of participants 267
psychological advantage 266–7
mild depression see dysphoria
Mindful Attention Awareness Scale (MASS) 215–17
mindfulness 10, 204–28, 258, 262, 264
delay discounting 205–6
dispositional 215–19, 265
Five Factor Mindfulness Questionnaire 217
interventions 219–21
meditation 236
mind wandering 221–7
practitioners 271
self-report measures of temporal orientation 206–14, 268

mindfulness (*Cont.*)
  temporal focus: separation from
    value 211–13
  Zimbardo Time Perspective Inventory
    (ZTPI) 208–11
mindfulness-based cognitive therapy
  (MBCT) 108, 219–20, 270
mindfulness-based stress reduction 219
mindlessness, high 216
mind wandering 127, 152, 197, 221–7
mood 1, 24, 29, 56, 87, 92
  congruence effects 24
  induction 56
  low 17, 29, 103
  manipulation 38
  negative 31, 94, 199, 225–6, 246
  see also mood disorders; mood disturbance;
    positive mood
Mood and Anxiety Symptoms
  Questionnaire 84
mood disorders 165, 247, 251
  see also anxiety; bipolar disorder; depression
mood disturbance 9
  affective forecasting 95
  expectancies 15, 18, 19, 22, 30
  optimism and pessimism 54, 68, 72
morbidity 60
mortality 60, 71, 266
  prediction 53
motivation/motivational factors 49, 88, 256
  autonomous 157, 163
  controlled 157, 163, 191
  engagement in life tasks 153
  to engage in particular behaviour 14
  goals 154, 155, 156–8, 163
  lack of 29, 143
  plans 184, 195
motivation theories 152
multidimensional model of well-being 152–3,
    154, 271
multiple sclerosis 37
'myopia for the future' 99

narrative coherence 30
narrative simulation-type thinking 30
naturalistic studies 81, 95, 225–6, 256
naturalistic thought sampling method 105
needs 152
negative affect (NA) 126, 255, 268, 271
  affective forecasting 81, 91, 94
  expectancies 20–1, 22, 38, 41
  goal-based interventions 246–7
  goals 153, 154, 162
  intervention 238–9
  intervention and specificity 250
  mindfulness and temporal orientation 212–
    13, 216, 218, 221
  optimism and pessimism 50, 51

Positive and Negative Affect Scale
  (PANAS) 221
negative anticipation 36–7, 260
negative anticipatory affect 107
negative aspects of future-directed
    thinking 67
negative bias 18, 95, 256
negative emotions/feelings 110, 194, 255,
    263, 269
  affective forecasting 84
  anticipatory feelings 112
  avoidance of 9
  expectancies 25–6
  flexibility 263
  optimism and pessimism 68
  plans 190
  prediction 257
  pre-experiencing 257
negative events 256
  affective forecasting 81, 84, 85, 88, 91
  anticipatory feelings 113
  elevated judgements for 14–17
  expectancies 19, 22, 30
  external, transient causes 49, 234
  intervention 234
  likelihood 17
  optimism and pessimism 49, 54, 59, 61–2,
    66–7, 68, 72
  plans 190
negative experience, absence of *see* negative
    affect (NA)
negative forecasting error 94
negative future events *see* future
    negative events
negative future outcomes,
    overestimation of 23
negative future scenarios 51
negative future-thinking 33, 35, 140, 246
negative items 83
negative judgements 20, 217
negative memories 28, 118, 128
negative mental health 7
negative mood 31, 94, 199, 225–6, 246
negative mood induction condition 38–9
negative thinking 2, 5, 255, 269
  anticipatory feelings 102
  expectancies 41
  optimism and pessimism 48
neglect and recent attention 5–6
neglect of safety 72
Netherlands 52–3, 192, 236
neural activation between episodic memory
    and future-thinking 127
neural correlates of cognitive measures 67
neural systems 113, 126
neuroticism 21, 50, 110
neutral emotion 25
non-acceptance and emotional avoidance 109

non-episodic factors in future-thinking 133–7
non-judgement 217, 220, 265, 314–15
non-meditation practitioners 218–19,
        228, 271
non-randomized controlled trial 236
non-reactivity 217
North America 270
    see also United States
not-looking-forward-to items 31–3
nucleus accumbens 101, 102

objective benchmark and judgements of
        likelihood 57–8
objective probabilities 22
obligation and goal pursuit 258
off-task thoughts 136, 225–6
on-task thoughts 225
optimism 255–6, 266, 270
    anticipatory feelings 105
    dispositional 53
    effect, self-other 56, 68
    expectancies 14
    flexible 72, 263
    global 50–7, 63, 71
    intervention 234, 238–9, 242
    intervention and specificity 250
    learned 234
    mindfulness and temporal
        orientation 211
    relative 55
    self-other optimism effect 56, 68
    trait 67
    unrealistic 17, 54–6, 63, 72
    unwarranted 63
    see also optimism and pessimism;
        over-optimism
optimism and pessimism 9, 48–73
    accuracy and bias 57–62
    beliefs, changing 63–5
    explanatory style view 49
    global optimism 50–7, 63, 71
        likelihood judgements for self compared
            to others 53–7
    internal, stable causes 49
    optimism as biased correction 65–9
    optimism for well-being 69–71
    under-estimation 64, 66–7
    under-prediction 70–1
optimism scale, unrealistic 17
optimistic bias 54, 56, 65, 66, 69, 72, 270
orbitofrontal cortex 101
outcome(s)
    bad 64
    desirable 51
    desired future 257
    expectancies 14, 30
    future aversive 22, 166
    future negative 23

future positive 15, 41
future, prevention of 166
future specific 14
goal-based intervention 245
good 64
health 51, 54–5, 68, 71, 191–2
    measures 95
    negative future 15
    optimism and pessimism 64
    perceived probability 30
    and plans 190
    and plans—correlational studies 191–3
    and plans—experimental studies 193–6
    positive 23, 53, 166, 271
    simulations 189–90
    visualization 245
overdose 34
    deliberate 122, 156
        see also deliberate self-harm
overestimation
    affective forecasting 85, 88, 90, 94
    optimism and pessimism 64, 66–7
overgeneral thinking 122–3
over-optimism 63, 65, 72
over-prediction 70–1, 91

pain 78, 88, 239
painful engagement 172, 258
panic attack 138
panic disorder 79, 102, 126
parahippocampal cortex 127
parietal lobes 127
past experience 235
past-negative and time perspective 210
past-oriented off-task thoughts 136
past-thinking 258, 261
    memory 10, 125–7, 129
    mindfulness and temporal
        orientation 220, 227–8
    mind wandering 221, 223–4, 225–6
    self-report measures 208–9, 211,
        212, 213–14
    spontaneous 136
past, value of 4
pathways and motivational
        construct 104
perceived behavioural control 190
perceived likelihood 25–6, 27
perceived probability of outcome 30
perceptual input 226
perfectionism, socially prescribed 195–6
perseverence 172
personal concerns 223
personal growth 8, 68, 96, 218
personality disorder (Cluster B) 34
personal memory 120, 125
personal projects 150
personal strivings 150

pessimism 50–1, 52, 55, 255–6, 263
  defensive 49
  expectancies 14
  intervention and specificity 250
  relative 55
  trait 242
  see also optimism and pessimism
pessimistic bias 60–1
phenomenological experience self-ratings 142
philosophical beliefs 4
phobias 102
phone app and stimulus-independent
      thoughts 222
physical disorders 60
physiological (autonomic) hyperarousal 20
Planned Behaviour Theory 190
plans/planning 2, 3, 10, 137, 182–200,
      257–8, 259
  ability 41, 184, 186
  action/implemental 192–3
  autobiographical 184, 224
  automaticity 194–5
  and behaviour 185, 191
  cognitive capacity 184, 200
  cooperation 191
  creativity 198
  deficit 41
  definition 182–5
  discrete tasks 183–4
  effectiveness 187
  fallacy 63
  goal-based intervention 243
  and goals 151, 182, 183
  hierarchical 199
  impaired 188
  and intentions 190–1, 193
  intervention 238
  life goals 183–4
  mindfulness and temporal orientation 227
  obstacles to 187–8, 189, 193
  and outcomes—correlational studies 191–3
  and outcomes—experimental studies 193–6
  preparatory 192–3
  propensity 184, 186, 268
  skills training 198, 234
  specific 191, 196, 199
  steps, number of 187–8
  and well-being 185–90, 196–9
  see also goals and plans training (GAP)
plausibility and likelihood 25n
pleasantness 80
pleasure 78, 88, 101, 236
  anticipatory 106–7
  consummatory 106–7
  Snaith-Hamilton Pleasure Scale
      (SHAPS) 205–6
  Temporal Experiences of Pleasure Scale
      (TEPS) 106–7

positive affect (PA) 7, 92, 126, 271
  affective forecasting 81, 94
  anticipated 93
  anticipatory 103, 264
  expectancies 20–1, 22, 38, 41
  goal-based interventions 246–7
  goals 153–5, 162, 171
  high activation 218–19
  intervention 238–9
  low activation 219, 255
  mindfulness and temporal orientation 209,
      212–13, 216, 218, 221
  optimism and pessimism 50, 51, 71
  Positive and Negative Affect Scale
      (PANAS) 221
  pre-goal attainment 154
positive anticipation 36–7, 260, 262
positive anticipatory feelings 257, 271
positive aspects of future-directed thinking 67
positive bias 18, 61n, 95, 256
positive emotions/feelings 8, 198, 271
  affective forecasting 84
  anticipatory feelings 109–10
  expectancies 25–6
  goals 165
  memory 143
  mindfulness and temporal orientation 221
  optimism and pessimism 68
  plans 198–9
positive events 256
  affective forecasting 81, 84, 85, 89, 91
  expectancies 18, 19, 22, 25
  internal and stable causes 234
  intervention 234
  intervention and specificity 249
  likelihood 17
  optimism and pessimism 49, 60–2, 72
positive experience *see* positive affect (PA)
positive future events *see* future positive events
positive future intrapersonal thinking 36
positive future scenarios 51
positive future-thinking 40, 246, 249
  expectancies 33, 35–6, 38, 39
positive items 83–4
positive memories 28, 128
positive mood
  affective forecasting 94
  expectancies 31
  mindfulness and temporal
      orientation 225–6
  optimism and pessimism 56, 72
  plans 199, 200
positive mood induction condition 38
Positive and Negative Affect Scale
      (PANAS) 221
positive outcomes 23, 53, 166, 271
positive psychological well-being 7
positive psychology intervention 239

positive relationships 8, 68, 96, 218
positive thinking 5, 41, 48, 163
  absence of 1–2, 155
  anticipatory feelings 102
  mindfulness and temporal orientation 211
  optimism and pessimism 58
possible future events 237
possible selves 237–9
  desired (ideal) 237–8
  undesired (feared) 237
posterior cingulate 127
posterior visual cortex 127
post-traumatic stress disorder (PTSD) 3, 118–
  19, 121, 123, 124
potential negatives 174
pragmatic prospection 260
predicted affect 95
  and emotional disturbance 83–4
predicted emotions/feelings 94, 256
predicted experience 86, 93–4
prediction 2, 137, 256
  congruent 85
  duration 89–90
  for future events 9
  for future feelings *see* affective forecasting
  goals 151
  intensity 89
  mortality 53
  of negative feelings 257
  question, misinterpretation of 89
  see also over-prediction
pre-experiencing 142, 257, 263
pre-goal attainment positive affect 154
preparation 3
preparatory planning 192–3
present focus *see* present thinking
present-thinking 258, 271
  experienced 227, 258, 261–2
  fatalistic 209–10
  hedonistic 209–10
  mindfulness and temporal orientation 220,
   221, 223, 227–8
  self-report measures of temporal
   orientation 208, 211–12, 213–14
  temporal 227, 258, 261–2
prevention orientation 168
pride 105
priming effects 88
principal components analysis 20–1, 208
probability and monetary value conditions 92
probability updating task (Sharot) 270
probes 132, 269
process and outcome overlap 109
process simulation 189–90
process thinking 190
promotion orientation 168
prompts 194
prospection 1–8

importance 2–5, 6
mental health 7–8
neglect and recent attention 5–6
pragmatic 260
well-being 7–8
see also episodic future-thinking
psychoanalysis 235
psychoeducation 220
psychological acceptance skills 265
psychological advantage 266–7
psychological challenge 51
psychological disorders 6
psychological distress 39, 108, 114, 243
  mindfulness and temporal orientation 205,
   217, 219, 228
psychological disturbance 8
psychological flexibility 108–9, 264, 265, 268
psychological hedonism 78, 87, 95
psychological measures 104–7
psychological stressors 53
psychological variables 52
psychological well-being 7, 8, 68
Psychological Well-being Scale 218, 248
psychotherapy, cognitive based, group 236
psychotic illness 246
  see also mania; schizoaffective disorders;
   schizophrenia
public speaking anxiety 111–12
pure visualization ('indulging') 189, 245
purpose in life 8, 143, 218, 243, 264
  goal-based interventions 248
  goals 158, 171
  measure 209

quality of life ratings 236
quality ratings and memory 139–40
quality of relationships enhancement 162

randomized controlled trials 220–1, 243
realism 48, 72
reappraisal task 250
reasoning, explanation-based 30
recall 197
recency effect 260
re-engagement 173
re-experiencing past events 142, 257
relatedness and Self-Determination Theory
  (SDT) 161, 240–1
relationships
  positive 8, 68, 96, 218
  quality enhancement 162
relaxation 198
  see also meditation
remembering 194
  autobiographical 127
Remembering-Imagining System (RIS) 260
reminders 194
reminiscence 204

reminiscence bump 140
repeated events 138–9
replacement episodic future thought 138
resignation (emotional) 211
retrieval and memory 23, 26–7, 28, 118, 136
retrosplenial cortex 127
reward-directed behaviour 88, 205–6
risk 55
risk judgements about environmental and
    health risks 24
risk-taking 208–9, 211
rumination 120–1, 198
    task 39
    see also past thinking

sadness 57, 105
sample meeting criteria 94
satisfaction *see* life satisfaction
Satisfaction with Life Scale (SWLS) 213
scenarios construction 2, 23, 30
schizoaffective disorder 84, 94, 106
schizophrenia 8
    affective forecasting 84, 94
    anticipatory feelings 103, 106
    goal-based interventions 247
    memory 123, 124, 131
    mindfulness and temporal orientation 206
scripts 261
secondary process model 113
self
    actual 237–8
    best possible self (BPS) interventions 238–
        9, 243, 251
    ought 237–8
    sense of 2, 261
self-acceptance 8, 158, 218
self-as-context and conceptualized self
        distinction 265
self-concordance 157, 163
self-consciousness 91
self-criticism 195, 215, 217
Self-Determination Theory (SDT) 161, 240–1
self-directed coping 64
self-discrepancy theory (SDT) 237
self-enhancement values 158
self-esteem 162, 186, 243, 266
self-focus 196
self-generated thoughts (SGTs) 226
self-harm *see* deliberate self-harm
self-identity statements 134
self-judgement 217–18
self-knowledge 138
self-narrative ability 125
self-other comparisons 270
self-other discrepancy 72
self-other optimism effect 56, 68
self-ratings of phenomenological
        experience 142

self-ratings of vividness and sensory detail 128
self-referential thinking 184
self-regulatory model 153
self-related thoughts 226
self-reported life satisfaction 159
self-report measurements, improvements
        in 268–70
self-report measures 265, 266, 267, 268–9
    anticipatory feelings 108
    memory 137
    plans 186
self-report questions 104–5, 270
self-schemas 121
self-transcendence 158
self-worth 171–2
semantic dementia 133–4
semantic-episodic hybrids 142
semantic information 135, 137, 138
semantic knowledge 135, 137, 138, 139, 142
semantic memory 30, 120, 137, 257
semi-structured interview 269
sensation seeking 208, 211
sensory detail 128, 139
Sentence Completion for Events from the Past
        Test (SCEPT) 119, 128
serotonin agonist 67
shame 105, 157
Sharot's probability updating task 270
simulation 2, 24–6, 137, 151, 255
    constructive episodic simulation
        hypothesis 28, 129–33
    of future experiences 236
    goodness 25
    heuristic 23, 27–8, 130
    narrative simulation-type thinking 30
    process 189–90
situational cue 194
skin conductance responses (SCRs) 100
Snaith-Hamilton Pleasure Scale
        (SHAPS) 205–6
social anxiety 102
social connectedness 175, 241, 258
socially prescribed perfectionism 195–6
social networks 41, 199, 200
social norms 184
social support 199
sociodemographic factors 55, 72
socioeconomic factors 15, 41, 158, 159, 188–9,
        199, 200, 270
socioemotional selectivity theory 207–8
sociotropy 241
Somatic Marker Hypothesis 99–100, 101
somatic markers 99–101
specificity
    affective forecasting 84
    future events 135
    of future-thinking and emotional
        disorders 121–4

goals 167
  induction 132, 133
  intervention 248–50
  lack of 257
  memory 124–5, 128, 133, 135, 142, 143
  plans 187–8, 199
spontaneous thinking 261
  about the future 6, 136
  about the past 136
stimulus independent thoughts (SITS) 222–6
stressful events 164
subjective future life trajectory 259–63
subjective likelihood judgements 60
subjective norms 190
subjective pain ratings 239
subjective probability judgements 14, 20, 25,
      29, 30–1, 60
  see also under expectancies
subjective sense of experiencing a future
      event 142
subjective well-being 7, 51
  goals 158, 159, 166–7, 173
success, future, likelihood of 198
suffering 78, 80
suicidal ideation 32, 35, 248
suicidality 255, 257–8, 260, 263, 271–2
  affective forecasting 83, 84
  anticipatory feelings 104
  expectancies
      anticipation 32, 34–6, 37–8, 39, 40–1
      processes and mechanisms 25, 26, 29
      subjective probability judgements 17, 18
  goals 155, 164, 165, 170–2, 173
  intervention 236–7
  memory 118, 122
  mindfulness and temporal
      orientation 206, 213–14
  plans 187, 189
  progress 174
surprise 259
systematic bias 9, 62
systematic review and meta-analysis 154

task performance 49
tasks, unresolved 198
teleology 5
telic theories 152
Temporal Experiences of Pleasure Scale
      (TEPS) 106–7
temporal flexibility 228, 265
temporal focus see temporal thinking
Temporal Focus Scale (TFS) 212–14
temporal orientation 2, 3, 204, 258, 264, 271
Temporal Orientation Scale (TOS) 207, 208
temporal present-thinking 227, 258, 261–2
temporal thinking 204
  separation from value 211–13
  see also temporal present thinking

tertile splits 210
thinking aloud 136–7, 270
thinking/thoughts 260
  adaptive 6
  automatic 235
  black and white 245
  causal 24–5, 28
  episodic 127–9, 250
  explanation-based 30
  future see future-thinking
  idiographic 14
  intrapersonal 36, 163–4
  intrusive 19, 200
  maladaptive 6
  narrative simulation-type 30
  negative see negative thinking
  off-task 136, 225–6
  on-task 225
  over general 122–3
  past see past-thinking
  positive see positive thinking
  present see present thinking
  present-fatalistic and
        present-hedonistic 209–10
  self-generated 226
  self-referential 184
  self-related 226
  spontaneous see spontaneous thinking
  temporal see temporal thinking
third wave cognitive behavioural
      therapies 108
thoughts see thinking/thoughts
threats
  anticipatory 111
  expectancy subscale 110
  future, possible 102
three good things intervention (TGT) 239
time frames 17, 32–3, 139, 259–60
  see also temporal entries
time perspective, balanced 209–11, 264
Time Perspective Inventory (Zimbardo)
      (ZTPI) 207, 208–12, 214, 228, 265
Tower of London task 183–4
trait optimism 67
trauma 119, 207, 238–9, 248
  see also post-traumatic stress disorder (PTSD)
treatment studies 38

UK Medical Research Council 31
uncertainty 22
uncontrollability, sense of 102
unhappiness 162, 208
United Kingdom 72, 205
United States 55, 70, 72, 159, 185, 222
universalism 158
unpleasant events 81
unrealistic optimism 54–6, 63, 72
  scale 17

valence 5, 102
  affective 102
  memory 128, 139–40
  see also negative thinking; positive thinking
Valentine's Day study 85–6, 93–4
value(s) 256, 258
  adaptive 3, 6
  goal-based interventions 240
  goals 152, 158
  intervention 237
  and orientation pairing 211–12
  plans 184
  progress 174
  self-enhancement 158
  and temporal focus, separation
    from 211–13
  transcendent 271
Valuing Happiness Scale (VHS) 164–5
ventral tegmental area 101
ventromedial prefrontal cortex 99
verbal control task 132
verbal fluency task 33
virtue 78
visualization, pure ('indulging') 189, 245
vividness ratings 28–9, 51, 138, 139
  self-ratings 128
volition 191
vulnerability 24, 39, 84

war veterans 123
  see also post-traumatic stress disorder (PTSD)
wealth and well-being, positive relationship
    between 161–2
welfare of others 258
well-being 7–8
  detriment 138
  and dispositional mindfulness 215–19
  and goals 152–4, 161–3, 187, 189,
    196–9, 271
  hedonic 260

high 8
low 6, 9, 23, 161, 164
multidimensional model 152–3, 154, 271
and optimism 69–71
participatory 156
and plans 185–90, 196–9
positive 1, 6
psychological 7, 8, 68, 218
therapy 83
see also subjective well-being
Willingly Approached Set of Statistically
    Unlikely Pursuits (WASSUP) 160
willpower 195, 199
word cues 140–1, 142
  autobiographical memory and emotional
    disorders 118–19, 121
  constructive episodic simulation
    hypothesis 129–30, 132
  non-episodic factors in future-
    thinking 135, 136, 137
  past- and future-thinking 125
  specificity of future-thinking and emotional
    disorder 121, 122, 123
words, high-activation 21
working memory 135
working memory tasks 136, 223–4
worry 255
  anticipatory feelings 105
  as avoidance 110–13
  chronic 24, 26
  Contrast Avoidance Model of
    Worry 112–13
  expectancies 17, 21, 22, 24
  reduced 250

Y2K problem 105

Zeigarnik effect 197
Zimbardo Time Perspective Inventory
    (ZTPI) 207, 208–12, 214, 228, 265